T0331403

'This book successfully debunks the idea that neo-liberalism and austerity are firmly established in Europe. In fact, austerity is constantly contested by a new, disruptive form of agency at the workplace and across society. This volume is a contribution of utmost importance to understanding exploitation and resistance in Europe, a must-read for everyone interested in progressive ways out of the crisis!'

Prof. Andreas Bieler, Professor of Political Economy,
University of Nottingham

'This book brings a breath of fresh air to the debate about Neoliberal Europe. Prevalent Marxist CPE approaches to European integration fail to connect Critical Political Economy with the disruptive force of labour struggles at the grassroots. To engage with this, the authors offer a disruptive-oriented approach to CPE. They call this approach "minor Marxism" for it focuses on disruption rather than domination. I believe that this minor Marxism is a major contribution to an understanding of the pre-figurative power of old and new working class resistances. The book shows that they can do both: challenge nationalistic and authoritarian tendencies of European integration and organise new anti-austerity radicalisms in defence of the commons, leading to an alternative integration from below.'

Dr Ana Cecilia Dinerstein, University of Bath, UK

Beyond Defeat and Austerity

Much of the critical discussion of the European political economy and the Eurozone crisis has focused upon a sense that solidaristic achievements built up during the post-war period are being continuously unravelled. Whilst there are many reasons to lament the trajectory of change within Europe's political economy, there are also important developments, trends and processes which have acted to obstruct, hinder and present alternatives to this perceived trajectory of declining social solidarity. These alternatives have tended to be obscured from view, in part as a result of the conceptual approaches adopted within the literature.

Drawing from examples across the EU, this book presents an alternative narrative and explanation for the development of Europe's political economy and crisis, emphasizing the agency of what are typically considered subordinate (and passive) actors. By highlighting patterns of resistance, disobedience and disruption, it makes a significant contribution to a literature that has otherwise been more concerned with understanding patterns of heightened domination, exploitation, inequality and neoliberal consolidation. It will be of interest to students and scholars alike.

David J. Bailey is a Senior Lecturer in Politics in the Department of Political Science and International Studies at the University of Birmingham. He is the author of *The Political Economy of European Social Democracy: A Critical Realist Approach* (Routledge) and co-editor of *European Social Democracy During the Global Economic Crisis: Renovation or Resignation?* (Manchester University Press). He recently co-edited a special issue of *Comparative European Politics*, on contention in the age of austerity in Europe.

Mònica Clua-Losada is Associate Professor in Global Political Economy at the Department of Political Science at the University of Texas Rio Grande Valley. She is also an executive board member of the Johns Hopkins University-Universitat Pompeu Fabra Public Policy Centre in Barcelona. Her research focuses on the contestation, subversion and resistance by labour and other social movements of capitalist relations of domination. She has written and researched on the effects of the current financial crisis on the Spanish state, the British labour movement and social movements in Spain. Her work has been published in different languages and outlets.

Nikolai Huke is a Research Assistant and Lecturer in Political Science at Eberhard Karl's University, Tübingen. He is the author of two recent books on social movements in Spain during the Eurozone crisis (*Krisenproteste in Spanien* [2016] and *'Sie repräsentieren uns nicht'. Soziale Bewegungen und Krisen der Demokratie in Spanien* [2017]). His research interests include European integration, democratic theory, critical international political economy, vulnerability and resistance, everyday agency, transformations of welfare states, industrial relations and migration policy.

Olatz Ribera-Almandoz is a PhD candidate at the Department of Political and Social Sciences at Universitat Pompeu Fabra, Barcelona. She is also a visiting PhD student at the University of Manchester and a member of the Johns Hopkins University–Universitat Pompeu Fabra Public Policy Centre. Her doctoral research investigates the interaction between social movements and the state in contexts of multilevel political arrangements, with special focus on the (new) demands for social justice, reproduction and welfare in Spain and the United Kingdom.

Ripe Series in Global Political Economy

Series Editors: James Brassett *(University of Warwick, UK)*, Eleni Tsingou *(Copenhagen Business School, Denmark)* and Susanne Soederberg *(Queen's University, Canada)*

The RIPE Series published by Routledge is an essential forum for cutting-edge scholarship in International Political Economy. The series brings together new and established scholars working in critical, cultural and constructivist political economy. Books in the RIPE Series typically combine an innovative contribution to theoretical debates with rigorous empirical analysis.

The RIPE Series seeks to cultivate:

- Field-defining theoretical advances in International Political Economy
- Novel treatments of key issue areas, both historical and contemporary, such as global finance, trade, and production
- Analyses that explore the political economic dimensions of relatively neglected topics, such as the environment, gender relations, and migration
- Accessible work that will inspire advanced undergraduates and graduate students in International Political Economy.

The *RIPE Series in Global Political Economy* aims to address the needs of students and teachers.

For a full list of titles in this series, please visit www.routledge.com/RIPE-Series-in-Global-Political-Economy/book-series/RIPE

Critical Methods in Political and Cultural Economy
Johnna Montgomerie

Neoliberalism and Climate Policy in the United States
From Market Fetishism to the Developmental State
Robert MacNeil

Beyond Defeat and Austerity
Disrupting (the Critical Political Economy of) Neoliberal Europe
David Bailey, Monica Clua-Losada, Nikolai Huke and Olatz Ribera-Almandoz

Civil Society and Financial Regulation
Consumer Finance Protection and Taxation after the Financial Crisis
Lisa Kastner

Beyond Defeat and Austerity

Disrupting (the Critical Political Economy of) Neoliberal Europe

David J. Bailey, Mònica Clua-Losada,
Nikolai Huke and Olatz Ribera-Almandoz

Routledge
Taylor & Francis Group

LONDON AND NEW YORK

First published 2018 by Routledge

2 Park Square, Milton Park, Abingdon, Oxfordshire OX14 4RN

52 Vanderbilt Avenue, New York, NY 10017

Routledge is an imprint of the Taylor & Francis Group, an informa business

First issued in paperback 2019

British Library Cataloguing-in-Publication Data
A catalogue record for this book is available from the British Library

Library of Congress Cataloging-in-Publication Data
Names: Bailey, David J., author.
Title: Beyond defeat and austerity: disrupting (the critical political economy of) neoliberal Europe / David Bailey, Mònica Clua-Losada, Nikolai Huke and Olatz Ribera-Almandoz.
Description: Abingdon, Oxon; New York, NY: Routledge, 2017. |
Series: RIPE series in global political economy | Includes bibliographical references and index.
Identifiers: LCCN 2017007664| ISBN 9781138890541 (hardback) |
ISBN 9781315712314 (e-book)
Subjects: LCSH: Economic development–Political aspects–European Union countries. | Neoliberalism–European Union countries. | Europe–Economic integration. | European Union countries–Economic policy–21st century. | European Union countries–Economic conditions–21st century.
Classification: LCC HC240 .B246 2017 | DDC 330.94–dc23
LC record available at https://lccn.loc.gov/2017007664

ISBN: 978-1-138-89054-1 (hbk)
ISBN: 978-0-367-87238-0 (pbk)

Typeset in Times New Roman
by Deanta Global Publishing Services, Chennai, India

Contents

Illustrations

Figures

Table

Acknowledgements

This book brings together research into the impressive range of actions, campaigns and sometimes imperceptible forms of rebellion that occur at the level of the everyday. Our biggest acknowledgement must therefore go to those who have sought to challenge, contest and disrupt capitalist domination in all its forms, especially since the onset of crisis in 2008, which is the main focus of our study. We were extremely lucky to have over 65 such activists – some of whom are named, whilst others remain unnamed – agree to participate in the interviews we conducted for the book. We are immeasurably grateful for those individuals for sharing their views and experiences, and we hope that we have helped to disseminate the lessons that they have learned, both accurately and in a way that amplifies the means of disruption. We are also grateful to Kelly Rogers and Saori Shibata, for conducting some of the interviews, and to Deborah Hermanns for helping to arrange a number of the interviews. Stephen Bates played an important part in helping with the initial design of the research project. We are grateful to Maka Suárez for allowing us to use her photograph for the front cover. The book benefited from funding awarded by the University of Birmingham School of Government and Society Research Fund and the project AJOVE12 funded by the Catalan government on 'Social Inequality and Political Participation during the crisis'. We are also grateful for comments and support given by Joan Benach, Jordi Guiu, Albert Jiménez, Pere Jodar, Vicenç Navarro, the members and administrative staff of the Johns Hopkins–Universitat Pompeu Fabra Public Policy Centre, the participants at the ESRC Seminar in Barcelona (July 2016), Clyde Barrow, Ian Bruff, Tobias Haas, Tim Haughton, Laura Horn, Paul Lewis, Phoebe Moore, Magnus Ryner, Vera Weghmann, Angela Wigger, and Shaun McCrory. Itsuki and Masaki wanted to be mentioned for making one of the authors' lives more joyful (done), and also thought that Snoozer and Spark should be noted for the fact they did the opposite of help (also done). Lastly, this book was completed the day after Trump was inaugurated – 'don't mourn, organize!'.

Introduction

Over the past two decades critical political economy (CPE) scholars have made significant advances to our understanding of European integration (for some of the key contributions, see Overbeek, 1993; Bieling *et al.*, 2000; Bieler and Morton, 2001; Cafruny and Ryner, 2003; Apeldoorn *et al.*, 2009; Nousios *et al.*, 2012b; Jäger and Springler, 2015b; Ryner and Cafruny, 2016). This work has highlighted key problems and limitations in the 'mainstream' literature, in particular showing how we need an appreciation of the pressures, tendencies and tensions association with capitalism if we are to understand fully the process of European integration. By 'bringing capitalism back in', the CPE of European integration has made clear the neoliberal underpinnings of European integration. CPE has identified the specific capital fractions that form the social forces driving the process of European integration (Apeldoorn, 2002), highlighted the way that this has constitutionalized austerity and neoliberal competitiveness (Gill, 2001), and illustrated the impact of these processes upon social forces within the nation states (Bieler and Morton, 2001). For CPE scholars, moreover, there is an ever-present need to give due attention to the role of European integration's capitalist elements in understanding the ongoing legitimation crisis facing both the project of European integration and that of European democracy, both inside and outside of the EU institutions (Ryner and Cafruny, 2016: 9).

Building upon, but also seeking to extend this tradition, this book develops what Eugene Holland terms a 'minor' Marxist approach, applying it to the process of European integration (Holland, 2011: 128). That is, we seek to contribute to the existing CPE account of European integration from a position that is both sympathetic to established accounts, but nevertheless also aims to address what we see as a tendency to focus on macro-analyses that depict forebodingly powerful structures of inequality and domination. In contrast, we claim, a minor Marxist account addresses and seeks to expose the gaps, limits and challenges that face those seemingly foreboding structures. 'Macro' (or capital-focused) Marxist accounts, we argue, have successfully highlighted the class character of the European project, but have proved largely unable to address or inform those seeking political strategies that are able to oppose and challenge the devastating effects of neoliberal European integration. This shortcoming, we claim, results from their excessive focus on structures of domination; alongside a concomitant tendency to under-estimate, obscure and sometimes deny moments of disruption (for an article-length exposition of this view, see Huke *et al.*, 2015). As a result, the CPE account of European integration tends to evince what Wendy Brown has termed, 'left melancholy':

> a Left that has become more attached to its impossibility than to its potential fruitfulness, a Left that is most at home dwelling not in hopefulness but in its own marginality and failure, a Left that is thus caught in a structure of melancholic attachment to a certain strain of its own dead past, whose spirit is ghostly, whose structure of desire is backward looking and punishing.
>
> (Brown, 1999: 26)

As Brown argues, the problem with such an approach, in which 'unified movements, social totalities, and class-based politics' each tend to become reified, is the possibility that, 'it literally renders itself a conservative force in history – one that not only misreads the present but installs traditionalism in the very heart of its praxis, in the place where commitment to risk and upheaval belongs' (Brown, 1999: 25).

The left melancholy of the established CPE account of European integration is reflected in more recent accounts of the European crises that erupted in 2008. Whilst some have focused on the apparent inability of the European elite to construct a crisis resolution strategy that is able to steer Europe out of this crisis (Ryner, 2015); others have noted the elite's continued (and insistent) determination to adopt a pro-market, 'neoliberal', programme despite the widelyheld view that it was precisely this neoliberal doctrine that produced the crisis in the first place (Wigger, 2015). This view holds that neoliberalism, along with its commitment to inequality, financialization, competitiveness and the retrenchment of the welfare state, have each become more embedded still at the European level as a result of the crisis that especially hit the Eurozone countries in 2010.

There is, however, much less work within the field of CPE that either identifies or analyses potential avenues of resistance to this seemingly unstoppable consolidation of neoliberalism. Instances of disruption or resistance are routinely disregarded, typically on the grounds that they are too weak to challenge existing power relations. CPE accounts of mass protest in the context of the European crisis have tended therefore to conclude that, regardless of such opposition movements, austerity and wage cuts have nevertheless continued relatively unabated (Becker *et al.*, 2015: 91). In contrast, the present work is grounded in the view that, whilst 'objective' indicators such as recession, monetary crisis, and credit shortage are clearly necessary in order for us to understand the political economy of crisis, we need also to include concern for both subjectivities *and their effects* (Hardt and Negri, 2011). To that end, the present research, which is based on over 65 qualitative interviews conducted with activists from a range of anti-austerity campaigns, industrial conflicts, and housing and education movements in Spain and Britain, provides an account of the post-2008 European crises that contrasts with existing CPE accounts.

This current round of crises, we argue, has not only led to a 'hardening' of European and national state structures, but has also witnessed novel forms of organizing from below, and resistant subjectivities that – albeit sometimes having the appearance of being both fragile and temporary in nature – nevertheless opened potential avenues for radical social change. Rather than the defeat of social movements during the crisis, therefore, we instead witness a process of what Candeias and Völpel have tellingly labelled 'successful failure' (Candeias and Völpel, 2014: 11). Whereas some commentators have witnessed a process characterized by sometimes surprising, but nevertheless ultimately ineffective, instances of social protest (including Occupy, 15-M, and a range of student movements); instead we see a legacy left by such events. Even when these events cease to be publicly visible their legacy nevertheless shapes and disrupts the way in which dominance is executed. As Arditi is at pains to point out, whilst those in authority have a habit of re-acquiring the machinery of government, those who they seek to govern nevertheless themselves acquire a new taste for demanding accountability and in the process shape the terrain of what is considered possible and what those who seek to govern perceive as necessary in their calculations of how to execute that governance, in such a way that pre-empts the reoccurrence of dissent. In this sense, insurgency and rebellion, in manifold forms, has a 'spectral afterlife' that,

> manifests itself in the cognitive shifts insurgencies generate, the learning experience of life in the streets and of discussions in general assemblies, the memories they create, the leaders that are made in the process of occupation, the subsequent campaigns and partnerships they foster and the policy changes they bring about.
>
> (Arditi, 2012: 14–15)

It has become commonplace, therefore, to reduce protests conducted during the European crisis to the notion that 'new social movements largely failed to galvanize long-term support and stop the contested fiscal adjustments' (Genovese *et al.*, 2016: 940). This, we argue, is short-sighted. Indeed, our claim is that the post-2008 context has witnessed the emergence of a new disruptive form of agency – the pragmatically prefigurative worker - who combines (in a somewhat contradictory and surprising way) the radical instinct towards prefiguration with more conventional demands, especially for voice and material resources. We call her a worker, but in doing so we are using the broad definition of the term. That is, her work might be waged and in the formal workplace, but it might also be unwaged and in the home, the school, or the university. Her status as a worker might be defined by her *inability* to find paid work, but also possibly by her *unwillingness* to do so. What defines her as a worker is her inability to join the ranks of those who can afford to live by virtue of their exploitation of others, alongside her vulnerability to being one of those exploited in order for others to afford to live. It is the pragmatically prefigurative worker, we claim, who through the course of the post-2008 crises has acquired the skills, capacity, inclination and on several occasions experience of destabilizing political and economic authority, and who therefore represents both a potential source of social change and a major target for control.

Our argument perhaps boils down to the claim that all is not (ever) lost. Whatever the state of despair that we might feel as capitalism moves through various formations, it nevertheless remains the case that we as workers continue to have a disruptive form of agency. We are able to dissent – even if sometimes only 'imperceptibly'. For those of us who wish to challenge the structures of inequality that constitute capitalism, patriarchy, and racialized hierarchies, it makes sense for our analyses of inequality to focus on both the occurrence, and the causal impact, of the forms of disruptive agency that manifest themselves at particular times. In Linebaugh and Rediker's (2000) terms, the 'many-headed hydra' of resistance, rebellion, refusal and rejection of authority has a tendency, once defeated, to reappear in new forms and new manifestations, creating new problems for those who seek to assert their authority. This does not, we hope, mean that we resort to a voluntarist celebration of all or any (however futile) forms of resistance; instead we seek to show how the agency of labour (broadly defined) *always-already* acts to disrupt *attempts* to secure relations of domination. In this sense, therefore, rather than referring at all to relations of domination, we might instead be better off referring to a process of seeking domination, that is never quite complete; or better still, one of becoming-disruptive, which is always occurring and always ongoing. Domination, we assert, never quite exists and never quite manages to stabilize itself. It always-already faces those who would and do object to it. It is this contestation, and the possibility for agency, resistance, and the opportunities for change that are created by it, that we focus on in the present study.

In developing this disruption-oriented approach to the political economy of the European Union we therefore present an alternative narrative. In our version of events, it is not domination and the consolidation of neoliberalism that are foregrounded. Rather, we present an account that focuses on the forms of agency, resistance, rebellion and refusal that create and cause problems for those striving to secure the smooth reproduction of capitalist social relations. In highlighting the place of workers (broadly defined) within the story of European integration, we emphasize the capacity for, and actuality of, disruption. What problems have workers created for European capitalism over the past thirty years? This replaces the more commonly addressed question: in what way have workers been subordinated since the 1970s? What problems, frustrations and disappointments have the elite suffered? What elite-level responses have been necessitated by the pressure placed upon them by acts of resistance and rebellion? This, we claim, results in a strikingly different analysis of Europe, European integration, and of the European crises.

In contrast to the conventional account of European integration, therefore, our alternative one highlights a process of disruption instead of domination. The established CPE account of European integration highlights the way in which stagflation during the 1970s prompted a move by Europe's political and economic elite to strip away the welfare state, to introduce a stronger dependence upon the market mechanism, to privatize much of the public sector, and to de-democratize the European economy and state. Much of this, the established account spells out, was facilitated and/or consolidated by the process of European integration – especially through the Single European Act of 1985 (which created the single market) and the Maastricht Treaty of 1992 (which created the single currency and the convergence criteria which eventually became the Stability and Growth Pact) (Apeldoorn 2002; Gill 2001). In turn, this process was further consolidated by the Lisbon Agenda of the 2000s, and was echoed in the response to the crises that erupted from 2008 onwards, itself the result of the dominance of German capital (Cafruny 2015; Lapavitsas *et al.* 2012). This is a narrative of defeat for the European working class, and one in which those in power continue to shore up their position of domination.

In adopting a perspective in which the working class is considered continuously disruptive, and in which it is those in power who experience ongoing difficulties, problems and frustrations in their attempts to maintain relations of domination, the narrative we portray looks decidedly different from that which those adopting a domination-oriented perspective tell. In our alternative account the stagflation of the 1970s was itself a product of the heightened inclination for refusal on the part of the European working class that emerged throughout the 1960s and into the 1970s. The increased tendency to engage in militant industrial action that swept many European countries during the 1970s pushed up the European wage share and created a profit squeeze that was at the heart of the economic problems suffered by Europe's political and economic elite. It is in this context that we understand the pursuit of neoliberal reforms during the 1980s, in part through the institutional architecture of European integration, *in response to an earlier wave of militancy.*

Yet this attempt to impose neoliberal reforms on European society went on to encounter *further* difficulties, problems and obstructions. Protest movements emerged across Europe to challenge attacks on the welfare state, to promote the interests of Europe's growing unemployed, and to oppose the most striking forms of European de-democratization. For Europe's political and economic elite, the period was partly one of frustration at their own *inability* to achieve what were routinely referred to as necessary welfare and labour market reforms. Likewise, the attempt to deregulate and/or restructure the workplace was, throughout the 1980s and 1990s, focused upon a drive to increase productivity – especially productivity in comparison with the US. This goal however consistently foundered, witnessing Europe's political and economic elite routinely lament their own *inability* to achieve sufficient improvements in labour productivity. In part, we argue, this resulted from the ongoing capacity of Europe's working class to resist attempts at subordination – through both visible forms of refusal and militancy, and through an obstinate form of everyday indiscipline in both the formal workplace and outside of it. Whilst the Lisbon Agenda of the 2000s has been the subject of much critique by critical political economists for having sought to consolidate the European Union's neoliberal agenda (see for example the volume edited by Apeldoorn *et al.* 2009), we recall that the Lisbon Agenda was also widely recognized by the political elite themselves as having failed to achieve its agenda. It was relaunched in 2005 and following the onset of global economic crisis in 2007 was largely forgotten.

Turning to the global economic crisis, our alternative account of the imbalances that built up during the period prior to the crisis again highlights the capacity for, and actuality of, disruptive activity on the part of European workers; and the disappointment, disruption, obstacles and frustrations experienced by European political and economic elites. The lack of regulation of US and European financial and housing markets had compensated some of the welfare losses experienced by subordinate classes. An expansion of credit availability enabled living standards to be maintained, in part, despite the reduction in the wage share and the declining welfare generosity that occurred across the advanced industrial democracies. Likewise, the influx of low cost imports from developing countries during the pre-2008 period in part offset the disgruntlement felt by many of Europe's working class, as well as enabling growth to continue (although, of course, this also contributed to those same economic imbalances that would eventually produce the 2008 crisis). Frustration amongst Europe's political elite also focused on their inability to achieve the fiscal orthodoxy they had been seeking prior to the creation of the Euro, and have been seeking since its adoption. At the same time, disaffection on the part of the European populace fed into growing antipathy towards the political elite, declining voter turnout, rising Euroscepticism, growing discussion of a 'democratic deficit', the emergence of an anti-globalization movement that included European integration in its sights, and a growing right-wing populist party family.

Following the onset of crisis in 2008–10, the challenge that faced the European political and economic elite was how to *restabilize* European society given the now highly visible consequences of economic 'imbalances', the growth of which the same elite had governed over during the pre-2008 period. In other words, how could spending deficits be reduced, and the productivity of Europe's working class be increased, in a context in which the population had become increasingly disaffected and disloyal to the political elite? Faced with a vibrant anti-austerity movement, as well as extra-institutional protest movements challenging representative democracy, and alternative forms of social reproduction emerging in some of the more heavily indebted populations and regions, Europe's economic and political elite have struggled (and arguably failed) to restabilize European capitalist social relations.

Our central argument, therefore, is that the European crisis is characterized by three interrelated developments: First, an intensification of disciplinary or authoritarian neoliberalism that seeks to further reduce the fiscal capacity of EU member states, combined with a hardening of the European ensemble of state apparatuses due to new forms of authoritarian crisis constitutionalism (Bruff 2014; Oberndorfer 2015; Sandbeck and Schneider 2014); Second, a trend towards disembedding the market that forms part of a move towards the construction of 'descent societies' characterized by increased social polarization and everyday vulnerability (Natchwey 2016); Third, a flaring up of community organizing, a process in which new pragmatically prefigurative subjectivities and spaces of presentist democracy are constituted and which have witnessed non-standard forms of conflict, civil disobedience and a self-enforcement of social rights (Bailey *et al.*, 2016). The effects of these developments on European integration, we show, are a deepened legitimacy crisis, a fragmentation through uneven developments and a partial disintegration. In our conclusion, we discuss four potential futures of European integration in this context: (i) a sustained, but fragile governance without consent; (ii) a fundamental reform of the EU; (iii) a reestablishment of Europe from below; or (iv) dissolution through nationalism and right wing populism. Which of these options prevails, we argue, ultimately depends on the social struggles which we hope here to contribute to with our disruption-oriented CPE approach to European integration and which we seek to develop in the present book.

In what follows, then, we confront what we consider to be the established critique of European integration, with what we hope represents one that focuses more centrally and explicitly on emancipation, and which is therefore more 'disruption-oriented'. Where the established account in CPE highlights and explains the way in which European integration is intrinsic to the consolidation of inequality, competition, and individualization across European society; our 'disruption-oriented' account highlights the way in which European integration is both a response to, but also has been unable to prevent or abolish, the acts of contestation that invariably problematize any attempt to produce relations of domination. This, we hope, is what makes this book worth reading (at least, it is what made it worth writing, for us). There is always contestation; and that contestation ensures an ever-present problem for those who would otherwise seek to oversee, and benefit from, relations of domination and exploitation. It is to this contestation, then, which we need to look in studying Europe, integration, crisis and the current state of European and global capitalism.

1 Beyond left melancholy
Towards a disruption-oriented account

Our starting point is our sense that there exists a need to balance the established critical political economy (CPE) account of European integration – which views the EU as neoliberal, pro-market, anti-welfare and pro-inequality – with a narrative that challenges what otherwise appears as a stable neoliberal project. As we noted in the previous chapter, we aim to develop such an account by drawing on what we refer to as a 'minor Marxist' perspective (Holland, 2011: 128). Whilst we agree that the EU is a market-building project, we also wish to add greater historical context to its market-building purpose. In particular, we seek to show how the pursuit of marketized European integration is itself an attempt to achieve a broader goal: the unattainable, but necessary, pacification of labour. We seek to highlight, therefore, the way in which EU-based attempts to deal with worker insubordination are themselves part of a broader historical attempt to deal with what is ultimately an insurmountable problem, and in doing so, Europe's political and economic elite have produced only a shift in, and adaptation of, a problem which capital is unable to resolve, thereby prompting new forms of insubordination to emerge in the process. From this perspective, we hope to show, Europe's crisis can (and should) be viewed as a product of the tension and problem that sits at the heart of contemporary capitalist society: the unachievable necessity of ordering and disciplining labour. This, we claim, explains the onset of crisis, the adoption of more stringent neoliberal measures in an attempt to resolve that crisis, and the seemingly irresolvable nature of that crisis.

Left melancholy: despair and domination in the critical political economy of European integration

The Eurozone crisis, and especially the Greek chapter of that crisis, led many who were previously sympathetic towards the project of European integration to begin to question its socio-economic implications (Hodson, 2016; Souliotis and Alexandri, 2016). These doubts, however, had already been systematically expressed for several years prior to the crisis by those adopting a CPE perspective (see for example Overbeek, 1993; Bieling *et al.*, 2000; Bieler and Morton, 2001; Cafruny and Ryner, 2003; Apeldoorn *et al.*, 2009). Some viewed the treatment of Greece by the EU, especially under the direction of Merkel and Schäuble (themselves representatives of German Ordo-Liberalism), as a wrong turn for an otherwise progressive and peace-loving project of European integration (on the Ordo-Liberal elements of German policy towards Europe, see: Dullien and Guerot, 2012; Young, 2014). Those who had adopted a CPE analysis of the European Union, in contrast, pointed towards a much longer period of neoliberalism and de-democratization; one which transcended the actions of the particular individuals that oversaw the fiscal compact and the Greek debt crisis. As Magnus Ryner put it, 'Far from being the result of some error or mistake, the Eurozone crisis is the consequence of the over-determined ideology and interests that shaped the monetary union in the first place' (Ryner, 2014: 14). In short, critical political economists could declare the European Union is imposing disciplinary neoliberalism on radical Greek dissidents, not because of an inherent antipathy between 'hardworking Germans' and 'lazy Greeks', but precisely because the European Union has been created as a neoliberal institution and therefore knows no solution to neoliberal problems other than neoliberal ones.

Indeed, whilst mainstream EU studies scholars have been content to discuss whether the European Union is an intergovernmental and/or supranational body; critical political economists have long argued that this misses the point – which is that the EU is not defined (at least not primarily) by the location of political authority (national or supranational), but rather by its neoliberal socio-economic content and consequences (see, for instance, Cafruny and Ryner, 2007). The European Union, in short, has a neoliberal project inscribed into its very core.

On these points, we are in broad agreement. We have no reason to doubt that the leaders of the EU's 28 member states seek to impose neoliberal solutions on European social problems. Nor do we have any reason to question claims regarding the neoliberal predisposition of European Commission officials, or of the neoliberal implications of the European Union's institutional design. We are, however, concerned with the conclusion towards which this analysis appears to lead: which is that neoliberalism has been successfully and smoothly imposed upon European society. This, we argue, reflects the domination-oriented approach adopted by many within CPE (Huke *et al.*, 2015). That is, it reflects the fact that CPE has a tendency to highlight patterns of exploitation and the construction of a (neoliberal) hegemonic bloc (Durand and Keucheyan, 2015), along with the (albeit contradictory) authoritarian apparatus required to uphold it (Sandbeck and Schneider, 2014). Such an approach, we argue, concedes too much. In doing so, moreover, it risks reifying the relations of domination that those who seek to highlight them also wish to challenge. As we argued in the introduction, this has a tendency to obscure those patterns of resistance which do exist, and risks adopting a position that Wendy Brown refers to as 'left melancholy'.

What is CPE?

It is perhaps useful at this stage to set out what we view to be common to both domination and disruption-oriented approaches to CPE. That is, we ask, what is CPE, and therefore what assumptions and goals do we share?

We view CPE in terms that have been signed up to by critical scholars of capitalist social relations of production throughout the modern period. Political economy, therefore, we consider to be the study of the social relations of production, distribution and exchange; and *critical* political economy to be a focus on the unequal nature of those social relations, with an explicit acknowledgement that this inequality is itself both consciously produced and constructed, and that its reproduction is undesirable. In this sense, we share with Marx the view that CPE is an attempt to explore and explicate social relations of production as 'nothing but the definite social relation between men [sic] themselves which assumes here [in capitalism] [...] the fantastic form of a relation between things' (Marx, vol. 1: 165). In seeking to make clear the constructed nature of inequality in social relations of production, therefore, CPE seeks to unmask, unveil, illuminate and demystify structures of domination and repression within society (Agnoli, 1968: 13). As van der Pijl puts it, our aim is to 'identify the social forces and processes that determine the structure of class rule and conflict in the world arena' (van der Pijl, 1989: 10).

This definition of CPE is also in agreement with that given by Horkheimer, that critical theory is conducted by 'a definite individual in his [sic] real relation to other individuals and groups, in his [sic] conflict with a particular class, and, finally, in the resultant web of relationships with the social totality and with nature' (1937: 211). That is, critical theory is conducted by real concrete individuals in a web of (unequal) social relations; and the development of critical theory is driven by an attempt to identify routes to human flourishing, or 'concern for the abolition of social injustice' (1937: 242). Knowledge, as such, is both context- and subject-dependent; and in this sense, we also agree with Cox, for whom, 'theory is always for someone and for some purpose' (1981: 128).

Finally, therefore, CPE shares a commitment to emancipation, in that the focus on unequal social relations of production brings with it an assumption (which we hope in the present work to emphasize) that those unequal relations can be, and to the degree that they are contested are already being replaced with more favourable (less unequal) ones. *Critical* political economy therefore has a concern for emancipation located at its centre (Worth, 2011; Shields *et al.*, 2011). As Jäger and Springler put it, CPE contributes to 'emancipatory struggles and to overcome exploitation and power relations' (Jäger and Springler, 2015a: 3). This requires, moreover, a historicization of social structures, in order that we might understand *both* how they have been constructed, *and* how they might be changed (Apeldoorn, 2004: 145; Cox, 1998). CPE thus searches out structural constraints and potentially emancipatory agency, both of which are historicallyspecific and as a result unable to take the form of directly applicable 'formulas' for social change (Esser *et al.*, 1994: 225). In contrast to 'mainstream' approaches, therefore, CPE represents an acknowledgement, and attempt to incorporate the complexity of concrete social relations (including their potential for change) at the centre of the study of political economy (Negri, 1973: 37).

Before the crisis: CPE and the neoliberal European Union

Having provided an account of CPE, we set out here what we view to be the established CPE account of European integration. For much of the period leading up to 2008, critical political economists considering European integration focused predominantly on the neoliberal reforms that the European Union was adopting, the way in which these reforms limited the scope for progressive public policies (at both national and supranational level), how they consolidated market mechanisms, and therefore how they undermined the possibility for more democratic options to be achieved across Europe. Much of this discussion focused on the impact of the Single European Act (which created the single European market) and especially the Maastricht criteria, which imposed tight fiscal discipline upon European welfare – especially as a result of the convergence criteria (which member states needed to meet in order to join the Euro), and subsequently through the pro-cyclical tendencies of the Stability and Growth Pact which institutionalized the convergence criteria.

The earliest contributions developing a CPE account of European integration can be traced back to some of the early Marxist debates at the beginning of the 20th century (Kautsky, 1911; Lenin, 1915; Luxemburg, 1911; Trotzki, 1923). Given that these contributions predated the first concrete steps towards European integration by up to forty years, however, they were unavoidably speculative in considering how those seeking emancipatory transformational social change should approach the question of European integration. A more thoroughgoing attempt to develop a CPE account of European integration emerged with a series of explicitly Marxist accounts that appeared in the 1960s and 1970s (Beckmann, 2006; Deppe, 1976; Elsner and Haeckel, 1973; Mandel, 1968; Cocks 1980; Holloway and Picciotto, 1980). However, it was in the context of the relaunch of European integration in the mid-1980s, and especially after the signing of the Maastricht Treaty in 1991 that CPE perspectives gained momentum (see for example Overbeek, 1993; Bieling *et al.*, 2000; Bieler and Morton, 2001; Cafruny and Ryner, 2003; Apeldoorn *et al.*, 2009; Nousios *et al.*, 2012b; Jäger and Springler, 2015b). This was characterized by a critique of existing 'mainstream' theories of European integration that, it was claimed, failed to conceptualize properly the power relations that comprised the capitalist market that was central to the project of European integration. Thus, it was argued, 'mainstream theories fail to account for the *structural power* that determines the particular trajectory of European integration', and in which, 'market forces have come to constitute the dominant principle of social organization to which all other principles and media of social organization have become subordinated' (Apeldoorn *et al.*, 2003: 17–8, for similar arguments see also Cafruny and Ryner, 2012: 33; Nousios *et al.*, 2012a: 10).

In addition to the shared assumption that accounts of European integration need to 'bring capitalism back in', a variety of different positions can be observed within CPE approaches on European integration (Jäger and Springler, 2015a: 7; for a summary of a number of these different positions, see Bailey, 2010: 326–33). Neo-Gramscian perspectives highlighted the process through which capitalist hegemony is constructed through European integration (Bieler and Morton, 2001; Gill, 2003). Open Marxist accounts point to the inherently capitalist nature of the capitalist state (and by extension the capitalist European Union) (Bonefeld, 2001, 2002). Structural power accounts consider the international, geopolitical and structural relations of contemporary global capitalism as it affects European integration (Cafruny and Ryner, 2007). The strategic-relational approach seeks to inter-relate capital accumulation and European integration, highlighting especially the crisis-prone nature of the former (Jessop, 2007, chapter 9). The so-called 'Amsterdam Project' (Overbeek, 2004) focuses on processes of transnational, capitalist, class formation, mapping the way in which a transnational capitalist class emerged during the 1980s, through fora such as the European Roundtable of Industrialists (ERT), to dominate the process of European integration, resulting in 'a fundamental restructuring of the prevailing European socio-economic order', which included, 'a tendency towards 'disembedding' the market from the institutions that made up the post-war 'Keynesian welfare state', shifting the balance between the public and the private (that is, of private market forces) in favour of the latter' (Apeldoorn, 2006: 306; see also Holman and van der Pijl, 1996; Holman and van der Pijl, 2003; van der Pijl *et al.*, 2011; van der Pijl and Yurchenko, 2014; Apeldoorn, 2002). There exists, therefore, a central focus on the way in which capitalist domination has been secured through the process of European integration, albeit theorized in slightly different ways by different contributions to the CPE debate.

Certain claims within the CPE literature are, however, of particular importance. First, transnational capitalist class fractions are considered one of the key ways in which the process of European integration has become a tool to put pressure on national social compromises, through deregulation, locational competition and neo-liberal competitiveness discourses (Buch-Hansen and Wigger, 2012; Apeldoorn, 2002, 2009). Apeldoorn focuses specifically on the role of the Maastricht agreement. Thus, he notes, 'Maastricht marked the defeat of the Delorist project that at the end of the 1980s had come to challenge neo-liberalism'. This, moreover, is considered a neoliberal package largely accepted by its potential opponents, in part due to the hope that emerged amongst those same opponents with regard to the possibility that a 'Social Europe' alternative to neoliberalism might emerge. Hence, for van Apeldoorn, despite being significantly 'watered-down', the Social Chapter 'nevertheless succeeded in incorporating European social democracy and the trade union movement into the "New Europe"' (Apeldoorn, 2006: 311). Finally, van Apeldoorn also highlights the impact of European integration upon national welfare models:

> At the national level, while welfare states will not disappear, they will be adapted, and social cohesion is to be achieved by letting the labour market work better. Thus, is social cohesion made compatible with, but at the same time also subordinated to, the goal of neoliberal competitiveness.
>
> (Apeldoorn, 2006: 312)

Similarly, other neo-Gramscian accounts have highlighted the way in which European integration has facilitated a more general process of economic restructuring. For instance, Gill developed the twin concepts of 'disciplinary neo-liberalism' and 'new constitutionalism'. These were used to show how states – under pressure to follow macroeconomic policies based on 'market efficiency, discipline and confidence' (Gill, 1992: 168–169) deriving from capitalist accumulation dynamics (disciplinary neoliberalism) – could use European integration to create political constraints, by which 'government policies, especially those which might influence the rates of return on capital' are closely monitored by international financial institutions (Gill, 1997: 219). In order to insulate themselves from popular democratic pressures that might undermine this focus on the return on capital, European integration witnessed the adoption of 'new constitutionalism' as a 'peculiar combination of austerity and authoritarianism' (Gill, 1997: 205), according to which, 'European Union constitutional provisions in Maastricht mean rules-based constraints that circumscribe the room for manoeuvre of (future) politicians' (Gill, 1997: 215). The very purpose of European integration, therefore, 'entails efforts to politically contain challenges to the disciplinary neoliberalism project through co-optation, domestication, neutralization and depoliticization of opposition' (Gill, 2002: 48). Key elements of this 'new constitutionalism' include independent central banks or macroeconomic rules (e.g. regarding debt) enshrined in agreements such as the Stability and Growth Pact of the European Monetary Union (EMU) (Gill, 1997; Stockhammer and Köhler, 2015: 38).

To sum up the claims made within the CPE literature, therefore, the effect of neoliberal European integration is consistently viewed as one marked by a substantial defeat of labour at the hands of capital. As Stockhammer and Köhler put it, in 'continental Europe the organizational strength of labour was eroded by two decades of high unemployment, welfare state retrenchment and globalization' (2015: 37).

Critical Political Economy, the post-2008 European crises and the consolidation of neoliberal domination

> The situation has not improved since. If at all, it has become worse.
>
> (Bieler, 2015: 36)

With the onset of global economic crisis in 2008, and its more specifically European manifestation from 2010 onwards, we have seen CPE accounts and interpretations of the crisis proliferate. In doing so, however, we also witness a continuation of the focus on many of the themes, claims and arguments observed prior to the crisis. Perhaps most centrally, the onset of crisis in 2008 has been widely viewed as integrally related to the development of neoliberalism, as promoted through the institutions of the European Union prior to the crisis.

Four claims are central to this analysis. First, that it was the excesses of neoliberalism that caused both the post-2008 global economic crisis and the post-2010 Eurozone crisis. The inequalities and economic imbalances associated with financialization, welfare retrenchment and market liberalization were shown between 2008 and 2010 to be unsustainable, producing a crisis of neoliberalism. As Bellofiore argues, the Eurozone crisis was caused by twin neoliberal evils: wage dampening, especially in the (German) core; and financialization. These two factors produced the imbalances that constitute the debt-bubble, and which eventually turned into a debt crisis once the periphery was unable to sustain its model of debt-led growth, combined with a housing price and construction sector bubble, and declining relative competitiveness (Bellofiore, 2013).

Second, in terms of responses to the crisis, the continuation of pre-crisis structural and social forces within the managing institutions of the European Union has ensured that neoliberalism has been largely untarnished as a governing project inscribed within both the process and institutions of European integration. Indeed, rather than being undermined or weakened as a result of the crises, neoliberalism has instead – it is claimed – been consolidated by and through the crisis management process. For Bieling, therefore, European crisis management remains 'restricted to the political executive – national governments, the European Commission, the European Central Bank (ECB) – in close collaboration with market 'experts' and representatives of financial and non-financial (trans-)national capital' (Bieling, 2015). Alternative actors have therefore been either side-lined or co-opted: 'social forces in civil society such as protest movements and trade unions only mattered if their initiatives fitted into the overall drive to stabilize European financial market capitalism' (Bieling, 2015: 102). For Wigger, likewise, EU crisis management 'blatantly reflects the demands of organized transnational capital and its unrestricted access to political decision-makers' (Wigger, 2015: 125).

The position of the neoliberal transnational capitalist class therefore remains firmly entrenched within the institutions of the European Union, unsurprisingly resulting in neoliberal responses to the crisis. As Heinrich (2015: 701) puts it, the dominant role of capital in the integration process has been extended, especially that of German capital: 'Pre-crisis export-driven and finance-dominated accumulation strategies broadly remained in place and continue to shape European governance processes', creating a situation whereby political elites 'revitalized established neo-liberal policy frameworks of competition, thus supported the dominant transnational power bloc in the EU to survive the crisis without any major material and strategic losses'. The forms of new constitutionalism identified by Gill at the European level, such as the SGP of the EMU, therefore became 'binding in the crisis, putting welfare state arrangements in question and proving counterproductive as they impose pro-cyclical austerity policies on the countries in crisis' (Stockhammer and Köhler, 2015: 34). Indeed, Gill explicitly makes this point when considering the crisis responses of the European Union, highlighting the fact that, 'in 2012 the European Union made *efforts to further extend new constitutionalist frameworks* via various measures including the new constitutionalist frameworks via various measures including the new Fiscal Compact as well as the policies of the so-called 'troika' (Gill and Cutler, 2014: 10 [emphasis added]). Indeed, the moves towards a consolidation of disciplinary constitutionalism have been most evident, and most noted, in the drafting of the fiscal compact, the institutional measures to provide loans to the European periphery, such as the European Financial Stability Facility (EFSF) and the European Financial Stabilization Mechanism (EFSM) and then the European Stability Mechanism (ESM), as well as other initiatives such as the European Semester, the legislative 'Six-Pack' and 'Two-Pack', the agreement on a so-called 'Euro-Plus Pact', and the 'Fiscal Compact' – all of which implied strict conditionality oriented towards austerity and neoliberal competitiveness (Bieling, 2015: 104; on the implications of austerity for democracy, see also Hayes, 2017).

The combined effect of these measures, therefore, is to place further obstacles in the way of the adoption of a Keynesian counter-cyclical demand management programme, to create further pressure for welfare retrenchment measures under conditions of economic hardship, and therefore to create a consolidation of Europe's pro-cyclical fiscal regime, including a commitment to fiscal orthodoxy and austerity measures in times of economic crisis (Nedergaard and Snaith, 2015). As Bieler (2015: 36) argues, 'austerity in the form of wage cuts in the public sector, cuts in services, pensions, and social benefits has not only been imposed on countries struggling with sovereign debt, but across the whole EU'.

Third, much of the CPE literature has highlighted the way in which, as a result of the neoliberal crisis prompting a neoliberal form of crisis management, we have witnessed an exacerbation of the inequalities and imbalances that constituted neoliberalism prior to the crisis. Most importantly, observers have noted an exacerbation of unequal relationships, both between the EU's core and periphery, and within each of the member states themselves, witnessing heightened domination by the former over the latter. As Bieling describes, we see a 'vicious cycle of public cutbacks, prolonged economic stagnation or even recession, shrinking fiscal revenues and increasing public debt', all of which has resulted in 'an accelerated dismantling of the European social model and the erosion of social cohesion' (Bieling, 2015: 106). This is most apparent in the case of Greece (on which, see Lapavitsas *et al.*, 2012; Theodoropoulou, 2015). The crisis management policies adopted, therefore, 'have put the burden of the crisis above all on lower and middle classes of peripheral countries and deepened the core-periphery divide within the European Union' (Becker *et al.*, 2015: 81).

Finally, more recent contributions to the CPE literature on European integration and the European crises have noted how the institutional design of the European Union has ensured that those protest or opposition movements that have emerged to challenge the consolidation of neoliberalism as a response to the crisis of neoliberalism have in turn proven to be ineffective. Thus, those forms of social mobilization against austerity that have occurred have largely been depicted as uneven and unable to prevent austerity policies and wage cuts from going ahead (Becker *et al.*, 2015: 91; Bieling, 2015: 110). The new institutional design of the EU characterized by a democratic deficit, constitutionalized neoliberalism, irreversible legislation, and the role played by the Euro as an economic straightjacket, have all acted to insulate the institutions of the European Union from any form of popular pressure. Likewise, the extended role of the European Court of Justice represents an additional barrier for trade unions seeking to challenge the erosion of workers' rights, terms and conditions at the national level (Wahl, 2014). For Bieling, in sum, the Eurozone crisis should be seen as a form of passive revolution, in which 'subaltern social classes or groups become increasingly marginalized' (Bieling, 2015: 102).

Pitfalls of critical political economy's focus on domination

> Stressing historical structures, laws and forces tends to minimize the role of intentional action. Things are what they are. Yet the critical approach becomes meaningless if one does not believe that it can serve to inflect human beings' action, and that this action can itself help to change the course of things in the direction of further 'liberation'.
>
> (Boltanski and Chiapello, 2007: x)

As we have argued, our central critique of the literature surveyed in the preceding section is that it overstates neoliberal Europe as a site of neoliberal domination, with the risk that in doing so it elides moments of disruption (Bieling and Deppe, 1996; Bohle, 2006a; Huke *et al.*, 2015). This is not an entirely novel claim, although to our knowledge it is infrequently voiced. Writing as early as 1994, for instance, Drainville argued that CPE had lost touch with the tactical and strategic questions raised by activists involved in social movements. In consequence, he claimed, it had 'very little to say about political resistance to transnational neo-liberalism' (Drainville, 1994: 10). As a result, it was necessary to 'give way to more active sorties against transnational neoliberalism, and the analysis of concepts of control must beget concepts of resistance' (Drainville, 1994: 12). A similar argument was made by Strange in 2002, who argued that CPE had risked a 'retreat from the theoretical analysis of autonomous agency and thus from the politics of contestability and alternative alliance-building' (Strange, 2002: 361). It is also recognized by some within the established CPE literature. For instance, in 2004 Bieler acknowledged that tactics and strategies of resistances to neoliberalism, needed 'further thought' (Bieler and Morton, 2004: 105). Others have highlighted a similar tendency within current CPE accounts of the post-2008 crisis (Featherstone, 2015: 13; Huke *et al.*, 2015).

Perhaps our main concern, however, regards the political implications associated with telling the story of European integration, and its crises, in the way that CPE has done. Put most abruptly, it remains unclear to us which agents can respond to the process through which European integration has facilitated the consolidation of unequal relations of domination across Europe, and how they might seek to do so. There is a risk, therefore, that the analysis contained with the CPE literature implies that any form of agency is essentially futile. This risks becoming a story of absolute defeat, in which European labour is absolutely defeated. Institutions are at risk of being conceptualized as reified apparatuses of capture, beyond resistance. Social outcomes seem to appear as the effect, and never the cause, of elite actions. In such a reading, the only hope remaining for those who wish to see positive social reform (or social transformation) is that the structural contradictions of European capitalism might wear capitalism down, and result in an endogenous process of auto-generated downfall. The likelihood that (defeated and dominated) subordinate classes might themselves be able to bring about such a destabilization of existing relations of domination (or even mitigate the effects of that domination) appears to tend towards zero. The problem, therefore, is that if we adopt a starting point in which the possibility of resistance is already from the outset considered to be incredibly slim, then likewise this seems to suggest that there is little point in *trying* to resist, and indeed little point in studying what will ultimately be futile attempts at resistance. This pessimism, we might add, is neither reserved for academia, nor difficult to understand when we consider the brutal nature of the moves to consolidate relations of domination that we have witnessed since 2008. As one activist interviewed during the research for this book put it,

> For me the success would have been to shift neoliberalism back to social democracy; but we're not even close to that. In that regard, the overall thing has basically been a complete failure.
>
> (interview with UK Uncut activist, April 2015)

It is, therefore, the somewhat bleak implications of much of the CPE literature that marks the point of departure for the present book. These implications, we believe, stem from an underlying domination-focused approach that underpins much of the literature surveyed in the preceding section.

In addition to the tendency to overlook instances of resistance, moreover, a domination-focused approach to CPE tends also to bring with it a tendency to consider resistance (when it's considered) in terms of the degree to which it is able to fundamentally challenge macro-relations of domination. Much of this focus is placed upon largescale, 'visible' acts of resistance, which purportedly contain the potential to challenge the equally largescale (reified) relations of domination that form the basis for the study of much of CPE. This, we suggest, is because in the view of much of the domination-focused literature it is *only* those acts of contestation that have a counter-hegemonic potential that are of interest – i.e. those that can potentially end, reform or transform relations of domination. In considering resistance in terms of the possibility that it contains for counter-hegemony, however, the focus tends to be limited to those actors of the institutionalized left that are commonly considered capable of mounting such a sufficiently well-coordinated mobilization by subaltern civil society actors – i.e. those with the potential to posit, and institute, a counter-hegemonic bloc, such as parties or trade unions (Georgi and Kannankulam, 2012; Worth, 2013). Importantly, actors and actions outside of this privileged category of potentially counter-hegemonic social actors tend to be considered 'unreal or unrealized and, hence, outside the political as such' (Butler, 2011). It is common, therefore, for evaluations of civil society to lament a 'failing substantial counter-hegemonic mobilization' (Gill, 1992: 191). CPE therefore has a tendency to overlook ongoing struggles occurring at the level of everyday politics or, to put it differently, obstinate practices at the 'micro-level'

(Bayat, 2010; Hobson and Seabrooke, 2007). As Worth (2013: 70–1) claims in noting the 'failure of the left', contemporary attempts at resistance have been 'vague in their arguments', 'considered unrealistic by those in power', 'need greater clarity for a counter-hegemonic project to succeed', and require 'greater cohesion [...] between different parts of society for it to gain popular appeal'. Such an analysis, we argue, oftentimes fails to fully capture the complex impact of different acts of dissent, refusal, and resistance, some of which might sometimes be imperceptible, with subtle effects and with something of a 'spectral afterlife' (Arditi, 2012).

In the present book, therefore, we hope to move beyond what we view as the sometimes excessively domination-oriented approach outlined in the preceding section. This, we claim, characterizes much of the established CPE account of European integration and the post-2008/2010 European crises. Instead, we seek to set out an approach that foregrounds those acts – both perceptible and imperceptible, major events and 'everyday' occurrences – that act continuously and constantly to disrupt the relations of domination with which they always-already unhappily co-exist. It is towards this goal that we turn in the following section.

Towards a disruption-oriented account

In seeking to develop a disruption-oriented approach to CPE we draw upon a range of theoretical positions and debates. This includes feminist critiques of CPE and everyday-centred approaches in political economy, both of which consider micro-level interactions within our political economy to be contested, meaningful and open to exploring new possibilities for social formations and experimentation (see especially Gibson-Graham, 2006). This complements our attempt to build upon the contestation-focused elements of what, following Holland (2011), we refer to as 'minor Marxism'; that is, the attempt to understand capitalism from the (disruptive) perspective of labour. Lebowitz (2003) has done much to highlight the way in which the CPE literature is commonly inspired by a reading of Marx that has been written from the perspective of capital (i.e. how capital secures the reproduction of capitalism). This, claims Lebowitz, is at the expense of an equally important account produced from the perspective of labour. In this spirit, we seek here, in developing a minor Marxist approach, to discuss the different ways in which contemporary European capitalism has been, and remains, contested (and thereby disrupted) through the agency of labour. Further, influenced by poststructuralist approaches, we include dispersed, fragmented and less coherent movements and moments of disruption that appear outside of, or at the margins of, what might be termed the 'state–civil society complex'. The move from a domination-focused towards a disruption-oriented account is therefore not only a shift in focus, but necessarily also implies a number of theoretical and analytical reformulations. A disruption-oriented perspective, we argue (and show empirically in the following chapters), sheds a different light on the processes described by domination-oriented CPE accounts of European integration, allowing us to make more visible (sometimes 'micro') potentials for radical social change. This, we hope, deepens our understanding of how social movements change society and – perhaps most importantly – positions social struggle at the centre of our analysis (where, we argue, it ought to be).

The obstinacy of everyday practice

There is a tendency within much of the work within the broad field of political economy to focus on either macro-structures (states, markets, firms) or the aggregated effect of individuals within those structures (consumers, managers, entrepreneurs). Sometimes consideration is also given to 'civil society' as the mass of human activity that exists outside of those spheres. In considering opportunities, possibilities and actualities of disruptive agency, however, a focus on either states, markets or civil society, or on the mass effect of the actions of individual consumers, managers and entrepreneurs, fails to pay full attention to what is often referred to as the 'everyday' (Hobson and Seabrooke, 2007). Concern for the everyday is of particular importance for a study such as ours, in which we seek out instances of disruptive agency that might not necessarily be 'perceptible', mobilized or visible as a mass movement posing concrete demands to institutions of political authority. Papadopoulos *et al.* (2008) refer to such forms of dissent as 'imperceptible politics', meaning the acts of everyday rebellion, refusal, disobedience and non-compliance that might not necessarily pose an organized opposition to established power relations, but which nevertheless represent day-to-day forms of human behaviour that challenge authority and the social structures through which it is exerted (Papdopoulos *et al.*, 2008).

Indeed, it is our claim that we are unable to understand *either* the structures of inequality, or the individual acts that reproduce those structures, without at the same time both studying and problematizing what we refer to as everyday practice (Sauer, 2003: 171). This goes beyond what Waylen (2006: 145) refers to as an 'over-simplistic' concern for the individual acts that relate to the reproduction of broader structures. Such over-simplistic accounts have a tendency to view action as merely a reflection and bearer of roles that relate to the reproduction of wider structures. Social reality, however, is more complex, including struggle, daily contestation, and behaviour which neither conforms to, nor directly challenges, the requirements of social reproduction, all of which routinely takes place within the so-called 'private' sphere (Bedford and Rai, 2010; Sauer, 2003: 171; Waylen, 2006: 153). Whilst many actions that occur within the private sphere are necessary for the reproduction of broader structures, and indeed for the reproduction of capitalist relations of domination and production; likewise, *many are not*. It is this 'unnecessary' element of everyday life, we claim, that represents an 'excess of sociability' which is both central to the development of what sometimes become more visible forms of resistance and which are oftentimes overlooked (Papadopoulos *et al.*, 2008: 253; for a similar argument regarding the need to incorporate the everyday within CPE approaches, see Candeias and Völpel, 2014: 11).

It is perhaps helpful to consider this everyday form of agency in terms of what Benz and Schwenken term, 'obstinate practice'. This is neither structurally determined, nor a fully autonomous form of agency (neither of which are anyway possible (on which, see Böhm *et al.*, 2010), but instead includes those acts of subversion, resistance, withdrawal or disobedience that occur through the process of reproducing social structures (Demirović, 2012). As such, everyday agency not only reproduces structures, but continuously shapes and influences relations of force, social struggles or historical structures. In consequence, everyday practice is neither determined nor autonomous, but instead is 'obstinate' (Benz and Schwenken, 2005).

It is from obstinate everyday practice, moreover, that sometimes surprising and more 'visible' events spring, and which in doing so have the potential to 'trigger social transformation, trigger shifts which would have appeared impossible if described from the perspective of the existing situation'. It is in this sense that 'the mundane, hard and sometimes painful everyday practices that enable people to craft situations that seem unimaginable when viewed through the lens of the constraints of the present' (Papadopoulos *et al.*, 2008: xiii; see Bayat, 2010 for a similar argument, made with reference to what he terms 'non-movements'). In conceptualizing agency as obstinate, therefore, we hope to avoid both romanticizing resistant subjectivities as autonomous, *as well as* dismissing them as insignificant (Benz and Schwenken, 2005).

The disruptive capacity of labour, or: Capital as a social relation beyond integration and defeat

> Negri questioned the standard determinist interpretation of classical Marxism because of its inability to give the subjective standpoint of the working class a central role in the critical process.
>
> (Burgmann, 2013: 174)

In addition to our attempt to develop an approach to the CPE of European integration that incorporates the obstinate agency present within the 'everyday', we also seek to reconceptualize labour in such a way that chimes with the broad tradition of 'minor Marxism' (Holland, 2011). Lebowitz argues convincingly that Marx meant to construct two (dialectically inter-related) theories of capitalism – one from the perspective of capital (which was largely completed in the three-volume *Capital*), the other from the perspective of labour (which he never got to complete and only really exists in fragments and in note form). Whereas the theory of capitalism from the perspective of capital sought to highlight the processes, problems and challenges faced by capital in its attempt to secure its expanded reproduction and self-valorization; the (absent) theory of capitalism from the perspective of labour *would have* traced the capacity of labour to resist, and the way in which the centrality of labour to capitalism creates an ever-present opportunity for insubordination and disruption.

The minor Marxist tradition might also be considered a form of autonomist Marxism, a term coined by Harry Cleaver to describe a broad position within Marxist thought that highlights the capacity for autonomy, self-activity and self-organization of those who work (Burgmann, 2013: 175). Grouped around a number of the innovative attempts by radical intellectuals, students, feminists and workers to construct political and theoretical alternatives to the then-hegemonic PCI in Italy during the time of significant struggles and rebellions in the 1960s and 1970s (including the so-called Hot Autumn of 1969 and the Movement of 1977), autonomist Marxism is a term used to refer to a range of alternative positions and debates occurring within organizations that initially emerged from a split from the Italian Socialist Party, including *Potere Operaio* (Workers' Power), *Quaderni Rossi* (Red Notebooks), and *Classe Operaio* (Working Class). It is perhaps more accurate, therefore, to refer to autonomist Marxisms, or what are sometimes referred to as Post- or Neo-*Operaisms*. These intellectual traditions grew out of the struggles of workers, students and feminists in 1960s and 1970s Italy (Wright 2002, 2008). Key antagonists within these developments include Mario Tronti, Antonio Negri, Mariarosa Dalla Costa and Silvia Federici.

Central to autonomist Marxist theorizing is the view that the capacity, and actuality, of the working class to construct the world is such that attempts to control and contain that capacity are destined to fail. As Rüddenklau argues,

> living labour is the moment that is able to crack the systematic character of rationalized capitalist societal formations, because it is the *substance* of this whole development process; it can be, as capitalist reality shows, subsumed under the capitalist production process, but never in its whole totality, it is the non-subsumable, that which within the capitalist system can never be included without a rest: the non-identical.
>
> (Rüddenklau, 1982: 335, authors' translation)

From this perspective, the working class is not a predefined entity, but rather a constantly decomposing and recomposing capacity of those who make the world, to revolt against those who seek to live off, exploit and extract the benefits of that act of making. This process of class composition moreover leads to a circulation of struggles which occur 'at multiple points, to threaten the whole intricate equilibrium of the social factory' (Dyer-Witheford, 1999: 76). It is in this sense, therefore, that we understand the working class as 'a continuous possibility of revolt, as a capacity for unceasing and repeated attacks on power' and therefore something to be understood in terms of 'the power of attack against capital, and the ongoing invention of forms of organization and struggle' (Negri, 1971, quoted in Burgmann, 2013, 174–5).

The history of capitalism is marked by an ongoing shift 'from one manifestation of class composition to another [...] through "cycles of struggle"' (Burgmann, 2013: 179). The potential and actuality of resistance to capitalist domination is the product of contemporary modes of organization by the working class, which must in turn be responded to by capital in its attempt to secure control. What is of interest at any one historical time and place in capitalism, therefore, is the particular form that resistance is taking (and able to take). This is the composition of the working class. In turn, capital seeks to 'decompose' these particular forms of rebellion, 'by revolutionizing the means of production, by recurrent restructurings involving organizational changes and technological innovations that divide, deskill, or eliminate dangerous groups of workers' (Burgmann, 2013: 179).

It is perhaps for its 'Copernican turn' that autonomist Marxism is most well-known. This is the claim that - rather than capital - it is in fact labour (and especially its ever-present capacity for refusal) that provides capitalism's driving force and explains its development. From this perspective, labour (and its potential for refusal) comes first in any analysis, and capital is understood as the always-secondary attempt to 'catch-up' with, control and contain, those acts of rebellion. Capitalism was born from acts of refusal (most obviously those of the peasant rebellions; on which, see Federici, 2004), and has subsequently transformed, morphed, developed and expanded in response to the refusal of labour. Embracing the Copernican turn, autonomist Marxists wager, opens up the possibility for an alternative analysis of capitalism – in which rebellion and refusal are central to our understanding, rather than marginalized and obscured from view.

From this perspective, moreover, the mechanisms and institutions of containment, integration and co-optation are inherently secondary, porous and incomplete, and as such exposed to ever-present instances of struggle and contestation. Capitalism is considered an always-already incomplete and constantly disrupted *attempt* to secure domination and exploitation. As autonomist Marxists never tire of pointing out, unless we recognize the primacy of labour, and the disrupting and disturbing effects that it always-already has, we end up with a 'narrative of defeat' that is both politically debilitating and analytically inaccurate (Shukaitis, 2007: 104).

Our aim in adopting an autonomist perspective, therefore, is to understand different forms of rebellion at different points in time, as well as the different ways in which capital has sought to control and contain that capacity for rebellion, and the new opportunities for rebellion that emerge (and have emerged) as a result. As an example, we can consider the transition from the Fordist to the post-Fordist mode of production, which witnessed a move beyond the factory as the key site of production. Thus, whereas Fordism was characterized by mass production, within mass factories, staffed by mass workers capable of carrying out mass rebellions; post-Fordism is a response by capital characterized by the disaggregation of the production process, the sub-contracting and splintering of the supply chain, and the employment of workers whose skills, knowledge and capacity to work is the result of more generalized and shared processes that exist throughout the social sphere. One of the consequences of this development, however, is that the capacity for (and actuality of) disruption has also now been spread across society, rather than located in the traditional factory as the site of production. To quote Burgmann (2013) again,

> The result of capital insinuating itself everywhere is that class struggle is refracted into a multiplicity of points of conflict. The front of struggle snakes through homes, schools, universities, hospitals, and media and takes the form not only of workplace strikes and confrontations, but also of resistance to the

dismantling of the welfare state, demands over pay equity, child care, parenting and health benefits, and opposition to ecological despoliation.

(Burgmann, 2013: 178)

As such, the analysis of the disruptive capacity of labour must be extended beyond the narrow sphere of trade unions and include the struggles of workers more broadly conceived, including non-unionized, those in radical unions, those outside of the workplace, and in the home and institutions of education (Clua-Losada and Horn, 2015). We might anticipate, likewise, that disruption of the neoliberal European Union occurs throughout its polity, economy and society.

We can perhaps sum up the key aims of what we have termed here 'minor Marxism', therefore, in terms of the following. First, a focus on the means by which capitalism and other hierarchies of authority and inequality are destabilized through their contestation. Second, a focus on who is doing the contestation, how, why, and with what effect. This includes consideration for how disruptive subjectivities form, how they are constituted, and the qualities that they have (Pasquinelli, 2014). Finally, the minor Marxist approach declares a faith in the impact of disruption, and its unavoidable presence – and therefore its primary role in producing social outcomes in hierarchically organized societies.

Unruly outskirts and margins: beyond the state–civil society complex, and towards poststructuralism

How does social transformation begin? Addressing this question demands that we cultivate the sensibility to perceive moments when things do not yet have a name.

(Papadopoulos *et al.*, 2008: xiii)

As we have argued, in seeking to understand the potential for social change we need to go beyond the conventional approach to CPE, and instead centre our analysis on social struggle (both perceptible and imperceptible, visible and everyday). Such an account enables us to make clear the way in which those struggles routinely and always-already escape the control of both the state (however strategically selective it might be) and civil society. This, moreover, enables us to conceptualize the provisional, fragile, and limited nature of power. As Papadopoulos *et al.* argue

People's escape, flight, subversion, refusal, desertion, sabotage, or simply acts which take place beyond or independently of existing political structures of power, force sovereignty to respond to the new situation which escaping people create, and thus to reorganise itself. Sovereignty manifests in response to escape. People do not escape their control. People escape.

(Papadopoulos *et al.*, 2008: 43)

To avoid reducing social struggle to its already 'policed' and disciplined forms of appearance within state apparatuses, therefore, it is necessary to extend empirical analysis beyond the analysis of state and established civil society actors. In other words, we need to move beyond a focus on *institutionalized* forms of struggle and look out for the ways in which people escape, crack and scream at the different ways in which capitalism attempts to control and discipline.

As Negri argues, the task is to 'reintegrate the complexity of the concrete into the critique of political economy' (Negri, 1973: 37, authors' translation). One of the ways that we have sought to do this in our present study is by systematically integrating the concrete experience of those involved in social struggles as activists. Activist knowledge is specifically focused on social change and as such exists beyond the narrow confines of the state-civil society complex, making it possible to develop new perspectives on social inequality, oppression and dominance. That is, from the perspective of how to challenge, disturb and transcend them (Sauer, 2003: 153; Peräkylä, 1994; Smith Tuhiwai, 2012; Sott, 2016). In this way, the field is opened for thinking about strategies that might point not only beyond Europe's 'embedded neoliberalism', but also towards 'communist' horizons beyond states, governance and capitalist control (cf. Adamczak, 2007; Negri, 1977b: 64).

In our attempt to access this activist knowledge, particularly as it developed during the post-2008 context, we draw on a range of qualitative sources taken from key moments of disruption during the post-2008 period in the UK and Spain. These are often instances during which disengagement has been transformed into more visible forms of disruptive engagement or re-engagement. This is based predominantly on qualitative, problem-centred interviews with over 65 participants in a range of anti-austerity events taking place from 2008 onwards. The aim of these interviews was to systematically integrate the situated knowledge of activists into our research, to develop analyses that follow the 'perspective of the movement' (Tsianos and Hess, 2010: 245, authors' translation). These sources were also supplemented by a range of mainly online materials, including blogs, websites, political statements and documents, forums, video footage produced by individual and collective actors, and secondary sources (for a discussion of such an approach, see Abels and Behrens, 2005; Flick, 2011: 210ff.; Meuser and Nagel, 1991).

Following Gramsci, we consider activists (or, in Gramsci's terms, 'organic intellectuals') those who have combined practical experience with political knowledge and played an organizing role within disruptive events (Merkens, 2004: 22; Sott, 2016). With Negt and Kluge, we understand the experience of these activists to be a process that includes moments of self-enlightenment, but which remains incomplete, as capitalist and other structural dynamics within society are reflected at the level of the everyday only in a fractured, deferred and dispersed form (Negt and Kluge, 1993: 777ff.). By embedding activist knowledge into a CPE framework, therefore, we aim to contextualize activist agency within its structural limitations and alongside the process of institutional feedback (Esser *et al.*, 1994: 225).

When it comes to studying more 'imperceptible' forms of dissent, however, their very imperceptibility clearly poses something of a problem. At times, we rely on official reports, in which political authorities identify symptoms of dissent and disaffection. At other times we rely on secondary studies that have managed to probe the everyday practices that constitute the instances of refusal that we are interested to observe. And other times we draw upon the frustrations voiced by those in authority themselves, providing first-hand accounts of the *inability* of those in power to achieve their goals in the face of an (imperceptibly) disobedient working class.

Contours of a disruption-oriented CPE

Each of the insights developed so far inform the way in which disruption-oriented accounts approach key social institutions such as the state, civil society and the capitalist economy. Thus, rather than focusing on the manifestation of social forces within the state, disruption-oriented conceptualizations highlight a constitutive excess that exists *beyond* (and thereby acts to disrupt) the state. The state is considered a regime of control, but one which is unable to contain the fluidity that constitutes everyday life. There exists an 'ultimate incompleteness of national sovereignty that creates the possibility for social change and for its potential overcoming' (Papadopoulos *et al.*, 2008: 7–8). As such, the state is considered in terms of *attempts* to secure control, and especially the empirical ways in which it has proven unable to do so. The constituting power of the people continuously challenge the constituted power of the ensemble of state apparatuses, revealing a 'crack' between multitude and empire, and the ever-present disruption of mechanisms of capture (Celikates, 2010; Hardt and Negri, 2000; Papadopoulos *et al.*, 2008; Holloway, 2010; Bailey, 2010). Civil society, similarly, tends to be regarded in terms of *attempts* by formal civil society actors and institutions to shield the constituted power or the ensemble of state apparatuses from the political claims of the 'multitude' (Hardt and Negri, 2005). As such, it is marked by attempts to develop mechanisms of exclusion, to silence a range of everyday practices and sometimes entire subjectivities (Butler, 2011), constituting a social sphere dominated by professional intellectuals, an 'institutional expression of domination by leadership and consensus, and a 'structure in itself [that] is a boundary for democracy' (Esser *et al.*, 1994: 224, authors' translation). Emancipation, in consequence – as with the state – is located not so much in rivalries of political projects within civil society – but *beyond*: in imperceptible politics, escape and struggles from 'below' (on the scope of imperceptible politics, see Papadopoulos *et al.*, 2008).

Finally, in terms of the capitalist economy, class struggle (and primarily the agency of the, broadly defined, worker) is considered by disruption-oriented accounts to be central. Labour, it is argued, must be regarded as an 'independent variable' (Negri, 1972: 11), a creative force that develops obstinate practices with regard to the needs of capital accumulation. In consequence, capitalist dynamics are understood to be driven (primarily) by acts of labour, with capital forced to respond to those activities. As Shukaitis (2007: 100) puts it, 'the working class, which is what it does (i.e. labors), exists for itself before it exists as a class against capital'. Disruption-oriented analyses, as a result, focus on the empirical composition and subjectivities of the workforce as well as concrete strategies of labour *within* the production process. This contrasts with domination-focused approaches' concern with 'objective' logics (or laws) of capitalism, strategies of capital, or the formal representation of labour in civil society. Disruption-oriented accounts highlight the creative capacity of labour, the new forms of activity it undertakes, and its endless ability to adapt to and create new social contexts. Capital is thus considered secondary and reactive; its task is 'to harness these social forces and forms of cooperation into its own working', and it exists 'as a snare, as an apparatus of capture that turns the vibrant flesh of life lived in resistance to the living dead humdrum of everyday banality' (Shukaitis, 2007: 100).

In sum, and as Table 1.1 shows, we present two contrasting approaches to CPE: one focused on the actions of elites reproducing relations of domination, conceptualizing institutions such as the state, civil society and the capitalist economy as reified sites of domination, and evaluating acts of resistance in terms of their (limited) prospect for large-scale counter-hegemony; the other drawing our attention to the creative (and broadly defined) worker, always-already acting to disrupt and escape from porous and incomplete social institutions, and representing an ever-present obstinacy that continually prevents domination from being secured. This, we claim, allows for an analytically more adequate conception of European integration, and is better suited to inform emancipatory strategies for social change in the present.

Our aim in this book, therefore, is not to abandon the valuable insights already developed by CPE, but rather to combine them with an understanding of their relationship with acts of disruption. In this sense, developments that appear as

Table 1.1 Comparing domination- and disruption-focused CPE

	Domination-focused CPE	*Disruption-oriented CPE*
Agents of interest	Political and socio-economic elites	The creative and resisting 'worker' (broadly defined)
Approach to social institutions	Reified sites of domination	Secondary, porous and incomplete *attempts* at domination and capture
State	Reflection and consolidation of capital's domination of labour	Incompleteness of sovereignty and control
Civil society	Site of struggles over hegemony in which consent is secured	Institutionalized attempts to secure domination
Capitalist economy	Exploitation and subordination of labour	Site of labour's creativity and disruption
Resistance	Evaluated in terms of counter-hegemonic potential – largely absent or ineffective; left melancholy	Perceptible and imperceptible. Continuous contestation, cracks, and passageways; obstinate practices in the 'everyday'

Source: Huke *et al.*, 2015.

fostering exclusion, a hardening of the state, a loss of democratic representation or a foreclosure of existing channels of participation may occur at the same time as, or even be intertwined with, a re-emergence of an 'uncontrollable anomaly of politics' (Papadopoulos *et al.*, 2008: 108), with a surge of radical-democratic popular movements and demands directed against the state (Poulantzas, 2002: 277), new forms of community organizing or new radical political subjectivities (Huke and Schlemermeyer, 2012; Huke *et al.*, 2015).

Studying disruption in critical political economy: disruptive subjectivities and action

Having made the case for a disruption-oriented approach to CPE, the question remains: how in practical terms do we go about doing it? So far, we have argued that a disruption-oriented approach to CPE must take seriously the inability of capital to maintain itself as a set of relations of domination, both in class terms but also in terms of other (especially gendered and racial) hierarchies. In particular, this means paying attention to those obstinate everyday practices which form a surplus to the structures of domination with which we are concerned, to the working class and the changing (and necessarily disruptive) ways in which it organizes and associates in order to reproduce itself. It also means addressing those social struggles which problematize and add complexity to the social forms that constitute the political economy, in particular with reference to activist knowledge, which consciously seeks to challenge, disrupt and transcend existing relations of inequality. As we show in Table 1.1, where domination-focused accounts highlight the means, methods and sites of domination across contemporary capitalist society; disruption-oriented approaches illuminate the impossibility and therefore the incompleteness of those attempts to stabilize domination, alongside the potential for (and actuality of) escape routes as they manifest themselves in (and disrupt) contemporary capitalism. This remains, however, at a relatively high level of abstraction. More is needed before we can begin to analyze and assess concretely the process of European integration and the post-2008 crises in Europe from a disruption-oriented perspective.

We need to think more concretely still about what it is that we mean when we talk about disruption (both of the everyday and imperceptible kind, and of the visible, organized and perceptible variety). We need to be more clear about the types of disruptive subjectivities and actions that give rise to the everyday practices, working class formations and social struggles that we seek here to study. We set out below, therefore, a sketch in general terms of some of the key disruptive subjectivities and actions that both have and continue to characterize and problematize the reproduction of European capitalism. This guides our analysis of the concrete development of European integration in later chapters. In doing so, however, we try to avoid foreclosing our analysis before it has begun. The aim is not, therefore, to set out the findings and describe the types of disruption that we subsequently discover (as if by magic) in 'the field'. Instead, we seek to set out a sketch of the types of disruptive subjectivity and actions that have been both commonplace to much of the history of modern European capitalism, but have also taken on specific forms, especially leading up until the period immediately before the onset of crisis in 2008. This, we hope, will provide a framework through which to begin to construct an analysis of how actual disruptive subjects and actions look once we turn to focus more concretely at the development of European integration.

In this sense, we adopt a qualitative approach that seeks to think 'with theory' (Jackson and Mazzei, 2012). We develop four ideal-types of disruptive subjectivity. These are a means through which to consider the ways in which disruptive subjectivities have developed during both the period of neoliberal capitalism and more specifically during the course of the post-2008 crisis era. We use our typology, therefore, more as a means through which to identify attributes – including motives, attitudes, strategies, and identities – that might help us to put together a picture of disruptive subjectivities and agents of the post-crisis context. In this sense, we follow Jackson and Mazzei (2012: 4–5) in 'reading-the-data-while-thinking-the-theory', in such a way that we are able to 'create new ways of thinking about both theory and data' . As such, 'the theoretical concepts that we engage [that is, our four ideal-types of disruptive subjectivity under neoliberalism] evoke different questions and produce different thought' (2012: 13), by informing and underpinning our engagement with the post-crisis context and the forms of disruptive mobilization that it has experienced. Our theoretical starting point, therefore, informs and connects with our observations of concrete instances and moments of disruption, enabling us to produce a new conceptualization of post-2008 crisis-era disruptive subjectivity and agency. In particular, we consciously seek to draw upon our conceptualization of subjectivity under neoliberal capitalism as a framework through which to understand and explain the qualitative material that we have gathered (and through which to understand new and changing forms of disruption and subjectivity as they developed throughout the period of our study).

We identify four forms of disruptive subjectivity that have featured particularly prominently in capitalism, each of which have developed particular features in the period leading up until 2008. We should note, however, that it is not our claim that the characteristics of each of these four types are discrete, fixed or mutually exclusive. Rather, as we argue below, disruptive subjects can and do display these characteristics in combination with each other, and the inability to achieve their demands through a particular type of agency may often bring them to a different strategic choice, leading to new forms of disruptive subjectivity in new socio-economic contexts. The four ideal-types that we posit therefore, are: the disengaged, disaffected and disinterested political (non-)actor; the vocal agent of political representation; the refusal-prone materialist; and the prefigurative radical (see also Bailey *et al.*, 2016 for further discussion).

The *disengaged, disaffected and disinterested political (non-)actor* disrupts structures of domination through a simple lack of engagement or refusal to comply. This includes activity such as the 'infrapolitics' of foot-dragging and 'hidden transcripts' that critique power informally outside of formal public forms of interaction (Scott, 1990), as well as the 'imperceptible' and micro-level politics

(Papadopolous *et al.*, 2008) of non-compliance that includes, for instance, absenteeism, circumvention of welfare benefit rules, and/or disaffection with or disengagement from formal political institutions of representative democracy (Huke *et al.*, 2015; Armingeon and Guthmann, 2014; Ezrow and Hellwig, 2014). This type of subjectivity evinces despondency, disaffection, and/or pessimism towards the prospects for success of more 'visible' or 'perceptible' forms of struggle or resistance, but nevertheless includes a refusal to consent to, or comply with, relations of inequality and domination. This includes political and civic disengagement, but also what we might term 'empty labour', or the new types of 'non-work at work' associated with the rise of the internet in the post-Fordist workplace (Paulsen, 2014; 2015).

For lower skilled/lower education/lower income workers, or those in regions that were unable to adjust to the apparently post-industrial context, disengagement had a greater tendency to include everyday forms of rebellion - petty crime, drug dealing and using, gang activity (oftentimes sparking moral panics amongst an elite concerned about 'anti-social behaviour') (Benz, 2014; Pare and Felson, 2014; Fraser, 2015). This might also include a culture of evasion with regard to public authorities. For one example, Lisa McKenzie (2015) describes mothers trying to navigate the British welfare system, in which women share information amongst themselves relating to how they might answer the questions asked of them by the welfare officials: 'Lesson one of the 'knowledge' is that the people who work in welfare benefits offices are nosey and want to get their noses stuck into your business'. As a result, answers to welfare officials' questions are routinely evasive. In one instance, McKenzie explains, a woman ('Yvette') was forced to describe the father of her child, the name of whom she claimed not to remember as they had only met once:

> When asked to describe her baby's father, she described him as a 'hunchback with one eye' … The thought of the woman in the benefits agency having to write down 'hunchback with one eye' caused fits of uncontrollable laughter. Yvette felt she had won a small battle that day by using humour, and 'taking the piss'.
>
> (McKenzie, 2015: 50)

The *vocal agent of political equality*, in contrast, draws upon contemporary democratic values, discourses and legal rights to espouse their right to a voice, and for that voice to be heard with an equal degree of attention to that of others within the political community. This is a longstanding form of subjectivity within capitalist modernity. Indeed, representative democracy largely came about by excluded groups – especially the working class – demanding, through disruptive acts of protest, dissent and political violence, that their voice be heard (Przeworski, 2008; Roper, 2013). It was also central to many of the demands for decolonization. This demand for a voice, and for it to be heard, remains an important disruptive mechanism within contemporary democracy, albeit one that is often framed differently by different collective actors. In the period immediately prior to the crisis, populist movements had increasingly begun to cause consternation for much of the mainstream political elite in contemporary democracies, drawing largely upon a critique that accuses that elite of being self-serving and unresponsive and therefore failing to listen to 'the people' (Mudde, 2004), who are typically those 'disaffected and disillusioned' workers left behind by the neoliberal phase of capitalism (Werts *et al.*, 2013). Likewise, the much-noted trend over the past three decades, away from 'conventional' forms of political participation towards 'unconventional' (or 'innovative') forms of participation, often rests upon a concern that formal channels of political representation fail to enable a voice to be expressed and/ or heard. In this latter case, participation is more likely to be conducted by women with higher levels of education, suggesting that the growing trend in innovative forms of political participation represents an attempt by vocal middle class agents of political equality to redress non-class based forms of discrimination (such as sex/gender) (Marien *et al.*, 2010). Indeed, for much of the pre-crisis period the unemployed were less likely to engage in these non-institutionalized, innovative forms of political participation (Kern *et al.*, 2015).

The *refusal-prone materialist* is both a subordinate actor within contemporary relations of production, but also empowered by that position of subordination (and the requirement for consent that it creates). This subject is therefore prone to participation in collective acts of refusal – including, most obviously, strikes (both official and unofficial), but also extending to mass demonstrations, occupations of property, and acts of disruptive civil disobedience (such as road-blocking) – as a means by which to impose (potential) sanctions upon dominant actors in pursuit of a material improvement in, or redistribution of, the range of resources available to her. The capacity for the powerless to cooperate with each other in this sense disrupts the experience of domination and enables a material improvement in resources available (Bailey, 2015). The refusal-prone materialist is often a waged worker, and obviously the most common reference is to the organized industrial working class, but might also be a benefit claimant, a woman conducting gendered care work, and those who struggle to resist the privatization of public spaces. The impact of the three neoliberal decades prior to the crisis, however, did much to undermine the capacity for refusal-prone materialists to flourish. The post-industrial working class has tended to be more precarious and less able to organize (albeit at the same time witnessing the emergence of more skilled post-industrial service sector employees with greater access to the skills and tools of creative work and action, facilitating the possibility for alternative forms of cooperation). Further, the renewed commitment by both the capitalist class and the state to confront strike activity has created a situation in which the frequency of strike incidents declined across the advanced industrial democracies (Gumbrell-McCormick and Hyman, 2013).

The *prefigurative radical* is our final ideal-type of disruptive subjectivity of prominence during the period of neoliberal capitalism prior to 2008. She actively attempts to create new, alternative social relations, or what we might term autonomous forms of social reproduction (Federici, 2012). By posing and working towards the creation of alternative and radically egalitarian social relations, the prefigurative radical actively and directly disrupts established relations of domination through her existence and activity (Graeber, 2009; Katsiaficas, 2006). The prefigurative radical rose to prominence within the alter-globalization movement, which focused directly on challenging the key tendencies of neoliberalism, and was arguably a legacy of '1968' and the subsequent new social movements which emerged following the transition from the Keynesian consensus to neo-liberal capitalism. Rather than seeking demands from the state, capital, and/or other hierarchical structures of authority and inequality, the prefigurative radial attempts to secure autonomous forms of social reproduction that disrupt existing hierarchies by virtue of being able to offer alternative means by which humans can co-exist, cooperate and co-produce. She refuses to accept the possibility that formal political institutions of representative democracy, or the operation of the capitalist market, can effectively meet societal requirements, and instead values self-determination and direct action (or a 'do-it-yourself' attitude towards the challenges of social reproduction), eschewing externally imposed forms of hierarchy and domination, and adopting a thoroughgoing politicization of all forms of everyday life (Dinerstein, 2014a). In Dinerstein's terms, the prefigurative radical seeks the, 'creation of alternative relations and arrangements that assert a dignified life beyond capitalism', including through, 'new forms of production, self-management and cooperative work, nonrepresentational politics, anti-oppressive education, the notion of 'living well', communal property, and economic possibilities' (2014b: 369).

Disruptive subjectivities also give rise to a broad variety of different (intentional or unintentional) forms of action. This includes strategies and tactics within the everyday, civil society, the production process and the state. There exists, therefore, a broad variety of forms in which disruption may appear. At the level of the everyday, disruption can articulate itself in fragmented and individualized acts of disengagement, disaffection, obstinate practices or a refusal to comply. If many of these actions are performed at the same time, they potentially act – in the terminology of Bayat – as 'nonmovements' (Bayat, 2010) that are able to reshape relations of force and question existing structures of domination. Furthermore, confronted with and challenged by domination or repression, nonmovements may act as a point of departure for more (self-)conscious social movements within civil society. These kinds of movements politicize issues that previously were dealt with in the private sphere and thereby challenge the boundaries and strategic selectivities of both civil society and the state. Nonmovements can furthermore constitute structures of autonomous social reproduction, in which a self-sustained development takes place that is (at least partially) independent from capitalist logics and state policies or even subverts them.

Within civil society, disruption may appear in the form of events and discourses that challenge hegemonic interpretations and reconstruct meanings from subaltern or non-hegemonic positions. We also witness the formation of contradictory collective organizations within the sphere of civil society, such as trade unions, which both constitute (and therefore act to consolidate) established relations of domination, but also disrupt those relations through their declared (albeit contradictory) commitment to mobilizing or lobbying towards social reform (Hyman, 1979). The capitalist accumulation process is continuously disrupted by strikes – either of the formal, institutionalized and official variety, or when they take on an unofficial wildcat nature – but also by more 'imperceptible' forms of action such as absenteeism, refusal or sabotage. Politically, the expansion of workers' rights, limitations of capitalist control or a (partial) de-commodification and (re-)communalization of production each act as disruptive barriers to accumulation. Within or in confrontation with the state, disruption has a tendency to appear as resistance to the implementation of policies or as political opposition to hegemonic or dominant policies – be it from parties, civil society organizations or at the level of everyday practice. It can also take the form of crime or illegal action, or of civil disobedience that seeks to de-legitimate the state and representative democracy (think, for instance, of the commonly used slogan: 'They don't represent us').

Our aim, therefore, is to study the political economy of European integration through a critical lens that takes seriously disruptive subjectivities and the forms of action to which they give rise. This, we claim, enables us to understand and explain the development of European integration and the post-2008 crisis in Europe in a way that foregrounds the role and development of disruptive agency. In doing so, we discuss developments across the European Union, but also focus in more detail on specific events in the United Kingdom and Spain. These two countries are chosen because, in each case, the global economic crisis (and its European manifestation) occurred in similar political and economic forms (including electoral defeat for the main centre-left party and public policy responses that shifted from direct intervention to deficit reduction), and witnessed a range of new forms of protest, dissent and disruption. At the same time, however, the socio-economic contexts also varied, especially in terms of Eurozone membership (with Spain a Eurozone country, and the United Kingdom not), levels of unemployment that were much higher in Spain than the United Kingdom, a much longer history of representative democracy in the United Kingdom than in more recently democratized Spain, and the overall severity of the crisis (which hit Spain considerably harder than the United Kingdom). In Tarrow's (2010) terms, therefore, a most different system approach to paired comparison is adopted, allowing us to study the forms of disruption that have emerged in the European context during the period of the post-2008 crisis, in order that we might identify both common and different forms of disruptive subjectivity and action as it has developed across these different contexts (for more discussion of this choice of cases, and their similarities and differences, see Bailey *et al.*, 2016: 5–6).

We divide our discussion into what we consider to be four key spheres of contestation in contemporary European capitalism: the workplace, welfare, education, and housing. In each sphere, moreover, we combine a general narrative highlighting the forms of disruptive subjectivity and action that have emerged, and more specific cases of individual conflicts that are able to provide more detailed insights into particularly acute forms of disruption. We hope, therefore, that the study is able to provide key insights into the disruptive subjectivity that we claim has emerged during the European crisis, which we argue has both emerged in part in response to processes of European integration and which now is key to understanding the state of European integration today. We turn first to consider these developments in the sphere of work, in the following chapter as part of a more general history of European integration and its relationship with the workplace. Chapter 3 subsequently turns to consider the contestation of work in the context of the European crises. Chapters 4, 5 and 6 subsequently turn to consider European integration from the perspective of the contestation of welfare reform, the marketization of education, and the residualization of housing, respectively. Our final chapter brings our research findings together, highlighting the forms of disruption that have prevailed throughout the European crises, and their implications for contemporary trajectories of social change.

2 The limits of market-based pacification

Labour unrest and European integration

European integration has from its inception promoted heightened economic competition, through the expansion and intensification of market exchange, as an
attempt to seek social order and to pacify or pre-empt instances of labour dissent.
This strategy has not, however, been universally successful. Instead, the strategy
of competition through European integration has been met by a series of changing forms of struggle, in which the disruptive capacity of labour has continued
to re-occur in different and shifting ways (Burgman, 2013: 179; Negri, 1996).
As we shall see, this chapter highlights three phases. First, we identify an initial
pre-1945 period, marked by a wave of major social and economic unrest that seriously threatened the authority of employers and owners. In an attempt to respond
to this unrest, moreover, we witness the development of a governing strategy
that sought to combine productivism, scientific management and Keynesian economic management, albeit in a somewhat faltering and uneven manner given the
simultaneous development of the authoritarianism that would eventually result in
the Second World War. In post-1945 Europe, we see a second phase emerge, in
which Europe's political and economic elite (under the guidance and influence of
the United States) moved more consistently to adopt the methods of integration
and pacification that had been trialled prior to the war. Productivism, scientific
management and Keynesian economic management were each increasingly relied
upon, but importantly – as we shall see – they each became associated with key
processes of European integration, especially the launch of the European Coal and
Steel Community and the signing of the Treaty of Rome. European integration
offered an opportunity to those advocating a market-based model of social order,
to create a series of depoliticizing external constraints, especially arising from
heightened economic competition, that it was hoped would act as an impediment
to those actors opposing the consolidation of a liberal economic market across
western Europe.

Eventually, however, a third phase can be witnessed in our brief overview of
European capitalism, again witnessing a central role for European integration.
This third phase emerged during the 1980s, in large part as a response to the
increasingly visible militancy of European labour that grew throughout the 1960s
and 1970s. The initial move to adopt the European Monetary System in 1979 was
explicitly linked to an attempt to create a system whereby member states would be

forced, through a form of market discipline created by the threat of currency speculation, to end excessive wage claims and wage inflation. This consolidation of market discipline was subsequently extended, moreover, through the creation of both the single European market and the single currency, and through successive rounds of enlargement. European integration was adopted as a tool through which the transnational capitalist class sought to exert further market discipline, particularly through processes of deregulation, locational competition and neoliberal competitiveness (Buch-Hansen and Wigger, 2012; Apeldoorn, 2002, Apeldoorn, 2009). As we shall see, this however resulted in the emergence of new forms of disruptive activity, which have in turn come to be associated with the crises that dramatically erupted in the post-2008 period.

Pre-1945: the eruption of radical refusal-prone materialism

The immediate pre-1914 period is widely noted for the rapid mobilization of the industrial working class across much of the industrialized core of capitalism at that time. Most countries witnessed a rapid growth in union membership, sharp increases in strike action and increasingly turbulent industrial relations. In most of the core capitalist countries the onset of the First World War in 1914 resulted in an initial subsidence of class conflict – as the call to patriotic conformity was able to produce increased loyalty as well as justifying greater repression for those who continued to dissent – but the extreme hardship experienced during the war quickly brought about a return to dissent and mobilization. Indeed, by the end of the First World War much of Europe was facing a potentially revolutionary situation.This saw the eruption of militant labour uprisings and mass strikes, accompanied by attempts (often informed by radical ideologies, especially Marxism, Bolshevism, anarchism and syndicalism) to produce self-governing forms of association (such as councils, soviets, strike committees, and factory committees) that would directly challenge the authority of both capitalist managers and the capitalist state. This went beyond the control of the officials responsible for governing the trade unions through which much of the militant action was (at least ostensibly) being coordinated (Sirianni, 1980: 31–2; on the influence of syndicalism see Darlington, 2008; on the influence of other radical left ideologies, especially Bolshevism, Marxism and communism, see Hobsbawm, 1993: 72–3; Lindemann, 1974). Whilst the events in Russia clearly witnessed this outbreak of revolutionary fervour in its most extreme and lasting form, similar developments occurred across western Europe. As such, 1910–1920 remains one of the most militant periods in European labour history (Screpanti, 1987).

Some of the most significant instances of disruption caused by this mass movement, which in terms of our different forms of disruptive subjectivity introduced in the previous chapter represented a fusion of refusal-prone materialism and prefigurative radicalism, directly challenged and oftentimes replaced (if only temporarily) the authority of workplace managers and owners. Some of the most significant events included the Clydeside shop steward organizations and the immediate post-war struggles that have come to be associated with the term 'Red

Clydeside', the Turin factory councils and *Biennio Rosso* of 1919–20, the mass strikes of Paris 1919, and the German revolutionary councils (*Räte*) which mobilized as a mass movement for workers' control and socialization of production and witnessed mass strikes in Spring 1919. Each of these events witnessed similar scenes of militant mass refusal and successful attempts to produce autonomous forms of decision-making within the firm and/or the military.

In the case of Red Clydeside, the contestation of the workplace was part of a wider prolonged and militant struggle that was to have significant impact upon much of class and parliamentary politics of the first half of the twentieth century (on the leadership role played by the Clydeside workers for the British labour movement see Rosenberg, 1987). For instance, engineering workers that took part in a strike for two weeks in Clyde in 1915, in protest at food shortages, inflation, and working hours (all resulting from the war effort, and despite official union instructions to the contrary) were subsequently followed by 200,000 miners in south Wales later that year (Geary, 1981: 137–8). This built upon an earlier wave of mobilization in the period leading up to the First World War – the so-called 'Great Labour Unrest' – which had occurred across much of industrial Britain. This consisted of huge national strikes by dockers, seamen, and railway workers in 1911, and by miners in 1912, witnessing trade union membership grow from 2.5 million in 1910 to over four million by 1914 (Darlington, 2008: 78).

The rapid growth in trade union membership and militancy during this period was often explicitly influenced by syndicalism, as well as industrial unionism and socialism (Glasgow Labour History Workshop, 1992: 81–2). For instance, the Cambrian Combine coalfield dispute was directly influenced by the syndicalist publication, *The Miners' Next Step*, which advocated various means through which the miners could render the mines unprofitable (Mates, 2016: 3–5; see also Holton, 1976). Other episodes saw leading syndicalist Tom Mann lead the Liverpool transport strike of 1911, in which mass pickets were witnessed and the strike committee began to exercise control over the running of the city's transport system (Darlington, 2008: 78). Glasgow and the wider West Scotland region saw a fourfold rise in days lost to strike action between 1910 and 1914, reaching a record 38 million days in 1912. This also posed a direct challenge to the authority of the employers and managers, witnessing engineering unions challenge the right of employers to dictate how machinery should be operated. Similarly, in boiler making and mining workers successfully insisted on a labour force made up only of union members. Following the war, industrial conflict resumed, witnessing a return to the demands for workers' control, including a 40-hour strike in 1919 that sought to shorten the working day and address the problem of mass unemployment, with the period of social conflict eventually leading to the General Strike of 1926 (although the General Strike itself is often viewed as having failed) (Pelling, 1966).

In Germany, a revolutionary period is often considered to have begun in 1917, with workers' councils and revolutionary shop stewards organizing a wave of strikes, largely against the demands of the trade union leadership, which was increasingly felt to have been too unwilling to oppose the war effort (and in the process lost the support of much of the union membership). By 1918 this wave of militant opposition had grown into a series of mass anti-war strikes and mutinies by both workers and sailors that made the position of the military leadership increasingly untenable. In turn, the mutiny by German sailors on 30th October 1918, in which they refused to follow a near-suicidal order given to them to attack British fleets, followed by a hoisting of the red flag, marked the beginning of the revolution proper. This quickly spread and became nationwide, witnessing the creation of workers and servicemen councils, which together took responsibility for the running of most of the still-functioning government operations. However, partly as a result of the counter-revolutionary actions of a number of social democratic leaders (most obviously, Friedrich Ebert) and the creation of a right-wing paramilitary organization (*Freikorps*) the revolution was put down (including with the infamous killing of Rosa Luxemburg and Karl Liebknecht). Despite this defeat, however, armed radical workers' movements continued to display resistance, including through the creation of the Red Ruhr Army in 1920, which was formed to block an attempted coup (Kapp-Lüttwitz Putsch), although again the radical workers were eventually outmanoeuvred as they agreed to relinquish their arms in exchange for a set of conditions that were subsequently flouted by the Ebert Government (Zukas, 2009).

In Italy, the so-called *Biennio Rosso* (Two Red Years) between 1919 and 1920 witnessed mass and often spontaneous outbursts of social protest, alongside a rapid growth in membership of both the Socialist Party (PSI) (which grew to around 250,000 members) and the anarchist-led Italian Syndicalist Union (Unione Sindicale Italiana, USI) (which grew to around 400,000 members). The Italian anarchist movement was also thriving at the time, considerably inspired by the presence of Errico Malatesta. The commonplace outbursts of social protest took the form at certain points of outright rioting, including food riots and looting. This, moreover, built upon an earlier wave of militant mobilization, including a two-day general strike which marked Italy's entry into the First World War, and a general strike and spontaneous insurrection in 1917 that erupted in response to the hardships of war (and was inspired by the February Russian Revolution) (Darlington, 2008: 80). Between 1919 and 1920 we also saw the rapid growth of the factory councils – which under Gramsci's leadership acted to transform official 'internal commissions' into worker-led councils, and in Turin successfully challenged the authority of the factory owners and managers (Levy, 1999). In response to a lockout by the employers at the end of March 1920, a general strike was called in Turin, and by the end of September metalworkers across Italy had occupied their factories, largely under the leadership of the USI (and despite opposition from the PSI), as well as being defended by paramilitary troops (Red Guards) in opposition to the threat of further lockouts from employers (Di Paola, 2009).

Other significant threats to capitalist authority within the workplace could also be observed across Europe. The Swedish syndicalist organization, *Sveriges Arbetares Centralorganization* (the Central Organization of Sweden's Workers, SAC), grew rapidly during the 1920s to reach over 30,000 members at a time when Sweden was experiencing one of the highest rates of industrial conflict across all of Europe (Kuhn, 2014). French miners, metalworkers and construction workers all engaged in massive strike waves in 1919 and 1920, often led by the (then) syndicalist trade union, the CGT (Darlington, 2008: 79). Catalonia witnessed a rapid expansion of the syndicalist union, the CNT, growing from 15,000 members to one million between 1914 and 1918 (Geary, 1981: 134–5). The same period also witnessed a series of general strikes across Europe, including in Belgium (1902), Holland (1903) and a city-wide strike in Dublin (1913–14) (Darlington, 2008: 82).

Capitalist authorities were therefore faced during the first three decades of the twentieth century with an urgent need to regain control of the workplace (Maier, 1987: 163–4). The solution that was arrived at across much of western Europe was a combination of productivism (the attempt to achieve class compromise in return for increased economic rewards for both workers and firms), scientific management (Taylorism) imported from the United States, and/or authoritarianism (including the authoritarianism of fascism, most obviously in Germany, Italy and Spain) (Whitston, 1995; Kipping, 1997). As Carew shows, in the inter-war period in the United States the response to a similar wave of radical factory mobilization (as typified perhaps by the Flint sit-down strike) was a move under the New Deal to accept the need for labour representation and social welfare, in an attempt to facilitate class compromise around this specific agenda of productivism, scientific management and economic growth (Carew, 1987: 40–2; on the inter-war mobilization of industrial workers in the United States, see Fox Piven and Cloward, 1977: chapter 3).

The assumption underpinning this move towards productivism and Taylorism was that class compromise could be secured within the workplace and through the wage relation. Thus, economic growth, provided it was associated with rising productivity, could lead to both increased wages and a growth of profits. In this sense, it was hoped, the interests of workers, managers and owners could coalesce around a unified goal. As Taylor himself put it,

> The great revolution that takes place in the mental attitude of the two parties under scientific management is that both sides take their eyes off the division of the surplus as the all-important matter, and together turn their attention toward increasing the size of the surplus until this surplus becomes so large ... that there is ample room for a large increase in wages for the workman and an equally large increase in profits for the manufacturer.
>
> (quoted in Maier, 1987: 26)

Those who were unemployed or for some other reason unable to take advantage of rising wages could also be compensated through an expansionary welfare state (on the emergence of the New Deal as a means by which to achieve stable growth and social compromise, see also Blyth, 2002). With Taylorism and the development of scientific management, moreover, capitalist authorities hoped to be able to achieve a degree of discipline within the workplace that would also bring with it the social order and regulation that was so urgently needed. As Maier notes,

[p]reoccupied with the problem of 'soldiering' or labour slowdowns, Taylor timed basic work actions, developed programmed task instruction cards for employees, recommended factory planning departments, and devised wage scales based on piece work, such that the productive worker shared in the expansion of output, but would fall below a subsistence wage and be forced to quit were he to prove inefficient.

(Maier, 1987: 24)

This Taylorist solution presented the political and economic elite with the tantalizing opportunity to shore up managers' authority within the factory, in particular by dividing up and specifying tasks 'down to the tiniest detail,' as some of the French advocates of the Taylorist methods put it (quoted in Maier, 1987: 165).

In pursuit of these goals, Taylorist techniques were introduced throughout much of Europe during the inter-war period, including by those in both fascist (Germany and Italy) and communist (Russia) regimes (Maier, 1987). The experience in Spain was in some ways indicative of this approach. Thus, the Francoist regime established in 1939 relied primarily on repressive means to both regain control within the factories and modernize an underdeveloped economy by introducing Taylorist production techniques and large-scale industries. Strikes as well as independent workers' associations were illegalized. At the same time, authoritarian corporatist institutions were established to enclose labour (the *sindicato vertical*). Many left activists from the working class, who had previously fought against the Francoist *coup d'état* were imprisoned, executed or fled into exile. Working days were prolonged, while real wages fell continuously. Everyday living conditions were miserable and characterized by hunger and the rapid spread of diseases such as typhus or tuberculosis. As collective forms of organizing were obstructed by repression, large parts of the population were forced into individualized or familiar 'muddling through' survival strategies. For the first years of the Francoist regime it is therefore possible to speak of a 'negative' or 'forced consensus'; although even during this time a number of subversive obstinate practices can be observed (such as black markets and acts of sabotage) (Huke, 2017).

Whilst fascism eventually prompted Europe's descent into the Second World War; after 1945 the United States again took up productivism and scientific management as central goals underpinning its attempt to promote European reconstruction, especially under the guise of the Marshall Plan (Carew, 1987: 40–2).

Post-1945: the Marshall Plan, European integration, and the pursuit of market-based discipline

Following the end of the Second World War, Europe experienced another wave of industrial and social unrest similar to that which had occurred after the First World War. This time, however, the threat to industrial peace was lessened, in part, by the more rapid turn to inclusive methods of industrial relations, and attempts to incorporate (and moderate) labour within the decision-making structure of the post-war polity. Europe's political and economic elite had learned a number of lessons from the inter-war period. As noted in the previous section, moreover, in doing so there was an attempt to use the methods that had been developed during the inter-war period and which had been expanded and consolidated during the wartime period, especially that of productivism and scientific management – both of which would come to be associated with the United States' approach towards European reconstruction, most obviously as pursued through the Marshall Plan (Hogan, 1987; on the expansion of scientific management during the war period, see especially Tiratsoo and Tomlinson, 1993; Weatherburn, 2014). In this sense, the early steps towards European integration were directly linked to attempts to limit industrial unrest and specifically avoid a repeat of the far more turbulent experience of post-World War I.

Some of the most visible signs of industrial unrest to strike western Europe in the immediate post-war context occurred in France, Italy and Belgium (Crouch, 1993: 202). Whilst this marked a return of considerable refusal-prone militancy, it was considerably less associated with the syndicalist forms of prefigurative radicalism that had marked the immediate post-World War I period. For instance, France and Italy both witnessed a considerable growth in support for the communist party (with each growing to become the largest party in their respective countries), although in each case the support of the communists for industrial unrest was tempered by their participation in national unity governments.

In France, strikes in the railways and postal services in the summer of 1946 were initiated by the Socialists and witnessed the Communist Party taking an ambivalent position due to its position in government. The internal tension that this created for the Communists, however, eventually became overwhelming. A major strike at Renault at the end of April 1947 was initially met with opposition from the Communists, but eventually gained their support following concerns that they would be outflanked by the Socialists. This, in turn, resulted in the Communist Party being forced out of office due to their inability to support the Government's wage policy. Once out of office, the Communist Party returned to a more traditional role in which it sought to encourage and coordinate strike action, witnessing major strikes by dockers, and the gas, electricity and railway workers. By the end of 1947 France faced a *de facto* general strike, with 2.5 million workers involved in industrial action, although this was promptly extinguished by draconian anti-strike legislation and the use of national troops (Carew, 1987: 30–5).

Italy also experienced heightened conflict over material resources in the immediate aftermath of the war. Middle class opposition to escalating inflation prompted the government to adopt a bold anti-inflation policy in 1947. However, this in turn resulted in the immediate collapse of prices and a massive rise in unemployment, to well above two million (Esposito, 1995: 81). This led those who were suffering at the hands of the anti-inflationary policies to themselves begin to mobilize. Pressure was already mounting in the immediate aftermath of the war, with the sudden growth within firms of 'councils of administration'. These had been created under Mussolini and their growth represented rank-and-file pressure for workers' control over the running of enterprises after the war ended, similarly to that which had been witnessed in the factory council movement of Turin following the First World War. This development was met with support by the PCI, which sought (unsuccessfully) to grant them legal status, although this support itself was for rather more moderate ends than those underpinning the growth of workers' participation in the councils (Carew, 1987: 27–8).

As had happened in France, however, in 1947 the Italian Communist Party was forced out of office by the Christian Democratic leadership of the Government, prompting the Communist-led trade union, CGIL, to facilitate an already burgeoning strike wave that included local-level general strikes in Milan and Rome, and the convening of a national congress of the councils of administration which was attended by the Garibaldi Brigade in a clear attempt to put pressure on the Government. From 1949 onwards, grassroots pressure and militant mobilization grew. This included an eruption of urban riots and land seizures by peasants (especially in the South), with demands focusing especially on an end to the deflationary policy (which was creating unemployment), increased investment for growth, and fiscal and agrarian reforms (Esposito, 1995: 84; Carew, 1987: 37).

It was in this context of mass industrial action in 1946–7 in both France and Italy that the US administration designed its plan for Marshall Aid. The goal of the US administration was to use Marshall Aid as a means to politically isolate and exclude the Communist Party of each country, and to promote an agenda of industrial compromise through the combination of productivism, scientific management and welfare provisions that had been adopted during the inter-war period under the New Deal. Indeed, by making it clear that receipt of Marshall Aid was conditional upon the exclusion of communist parties from office, the United States ensured that this desired outcome occurred in both France and Italy by 1947. Having secured the political exclusion of the communists, moreover, the US administration sought to ensure that there would be no other significant opposition to the principle of a competitive market economy (upon which the successful promotion of productivism and scientific management rested). For instance, General Lucius Clay, proconsul of the American zone of Germany, effectively vetoed British attempts to nationalize the Ruhr mines, as part of a general effort to ensure that policies or political actors posing alternatives to a market-based political programme were effectively side-lined from the post-war consensus in Germany (Maier, 1987: 144).

This move to consolidate a market-based system of social discipline in order to achieve social order, economic growth and prosperity also included the early attempts to move towards European integration. European post-war reconstruction was thus built in part upon a concerted effort by Europe's political and economic elite (under the tutelage of the United States) to secure a class compromise that would achieve as full an eradication of social unrest as possible. Indeed, this was explicitly recognized by the US elite, for instance witnessing John Hickerson of the State Department European Division write that, 'The trend in Europe is clearly toward the left. I feel that we should try to keep it a non-Communist left and should support Social-Democratic governments' (quoted in Carew, 1987: 45). This promotion of moderate social market-based competition can be seen from the beginning of the period of integration onwards, albeit with the market element of this compromise increasingly emphasized at the expense of the more social part of the compromise (especially, as we shall see, from the late-1970s onwards). The development of capitalism in Europe in the post-war period was in consequence characterized by an attenuation of the conflict between capital and labour. The number of strikes decreased, while militant forms of labour action were redirected towards corporatist institutional arrangements of conflict resolution, while the social situation of parts of the workforce improved due to an expansion of the welfare state (Schmalz *et al.*, 2015: 50). This embedding of class struggle at the institutional level was therefore also made possible by the social confrontations of the preceding period, along with the continued organizational strength of the labour movement. As Bieler argues, 'successful class struggle by labour forced employers into making concessions and ensured the class compromise around the welfare state' (Bieler, 2015: 25).

The importance of the project of European integration to this programme of market-based social order should not be understated. Indeed, as Milward (1992) has shown in rich detail, the first steps of European integration were explicitly linked to elite concerns regarding their inability to control domestic labour without the support of a wider supranational framework. The political elite also explicitly sought to heighten market competition, through European integration, in order to impose external constraints upon potential domestic opponents. Both of these supranational mechanisms of market discipline – an external authority that could be blamed, and the underlying pressure generated by market competition – were made directly available through the creation of the European Coal and Steel Community (ECSC); and it was this which represented a major attraction to those elites in their decision to take the first steps towards European integration. As Milward highlights,

> the Belgian Government always saw the purpose of the supranational authority as a buttress for national policies. It was a source of authority outside the nation which could be appealed to for help, blamed for unpopular policies which were also those of the Government itself, and, when it suited the mood, caricatured as a technocratic dictatorship trampling the rights of Belgians underfoot.
>
> (Milward, 1992: 101–2)

In particular, the aim of the ECSC member states (and especially that of the Belgian Government) was to overcome domestic opposition (including the clear potential for further unrest on the part of organized labour) that would otherwise prevent both a reduction in wages and productivity gains from being achieved through a reorganization and rationalization of the production process (which brought with it the risk of unemployment). Once an international market for coal was constructed it became almost impossible for organized labour to effectively oppose restructuring, faced, as it was, with a choice between either unemployment (as uncompetitive firms went bankrupt), a cut in wages, and/or acquiescence to economic rationalization. The institutional design of the European institutions was also from the very beginning characterized by a democratic deficit. The ECSC was only submitted to juridical control, while parliaments were practically without influence. In this sense, the first initiatives of European integration acted to disable democratic decision-making, representing an attempt to construct a sense of powerlessness and a lack of representation amongst the national populations (Abendroth, 2008: 213).

With the creation of the European Community (EC) and the signing of the Treaty of Rome in 1957, moreover, we can see similar tendencies. That is, member states continued to act in alliance with the Commission to promote market-based growth and heightened (but controlled, or in Ruggie's terms 'embedded') competition as a means through which to seek the disciplining of labour. Turning again to Milward, we see how the notion of market competition and market integration was repeatedly taken up as a means to achieve these goals. Thus,

> Governments whose main desire was to sustain the growth of productivity and incomes were eager for any device which made this seem possible. No matter what rigorous theory suggested, they turned eagerly to the belief that in the circumstances of the 1950s a faster growth of foreign trade would entail a faster growth of national income.
>
> (Milward, 1992: 111)

This was particularly the case in France where planners were keen to view liberalization of trade as a means by which to force industry to modernize in order to be able to compete in a larger (and therefore more competitive) market (Milward, 1992: 115). As such, the construction of a freer market thus created pressure for conformity to wage and productivity norms across the market.

Indeed, these goals of an expanded market, increased trade, heightened competition, and therefore improved productivity, growth, industrial harmony and social order, each appeared to have been achieved (at least in part) during the first two decades of post-war European integration. The creation of the customs union led to a boost in intra-EC trade, from one-third of total trade in 1960 to around 50 per cent in 1972. This also saw the emergence of a relatively new phenomenon – 'intra-industry trade' – which went beyond the expected increase in the international division of labour (in which certain countries would specialize in certain goods), representing a new degree of competition in that domestic firms increasingly became exposed to heightened international competition from foreign firms producing the same type of manufactured good (Egan, 2015: 97). This was also facilitated by the European Payments Union (EPU), which had been created in 1950 to facilitate trade in goods other than coal and steel. As Eichengreen puts it,

> the fact that European countries traded extensively with one another allowed efficiency-enhancing arbitrage to operate, minimizing price distortions. And the fact that Europe, notwithstanding its troubles, possessed a number of efficient industries allowed intra-EPU trade to drive prices down to the levels established by the least-cost producer.
>
> (Eichengreen, 1995: 186)

After the initial stages of European integration, therefore, the 1960s witnessed a moderation of class conflict in Europe as the relationship between labour and capital was increasingly mediated by heightened market integration, in combination with neo-corporatist institutions in most European countries (or in the cases of Italy and France they were at least moving in the direction of neocorporatism). This was facilitated, moreover, as had been hoped for, by an increase in economic growth and low unemployment, both of which were conducive to relatively stable industrial relations (Crouch, 1993: chapter 6).

Whilst this industrial compromise is often viewed in terms of it being associated with wage restraint on the part of Europe's workers (Eichengreen, 2007), there is however little data to support this view (Hatton and Boyer, 2005). Indeed, as Bengtsson shows, it is more likely (and consistent with the data available) that the growing strength of organized labour from 1945 until the late 1970s resulted in a consistent rise in wages above productivity (Bengtsson, 2015). This observation is also compatible with those accounts that stress the role of post-war reconstruction in facilitating the rapid growth of the 1950–65 period, as firms raced to accumulate capital following its widespread destruction during the Second World War (Vonyó, 2008). That is, the growth afforded by the destruction of capital was such, following the Second World War, that wage growth could initially outpace productivity growth. From the late 1960s onwards, however, strong wage growth became gradually less tenable as capital accumulation had 'caught up' (so to speak) following the destruction caused by the war. It is at this point, moreover, that the intractability of the 'labour problem' became increasingly evident and pressing for West European capital. We turn in the next section to consider the effects of this increasing emboldenment of European labour throughout the first two decades of the post-war period.

1968: the end of the post-war pacification and the neoliberal resort to 'more market'

The post-war class compromise (if that is the correct term for it) was increasingly eroded by the above-productivity wage rises mentioned in the previous section. From the late-1960s onwards, however, more visible forms of class conflict made a dramatic return to European society. This witnessed the re-emergence of what we have referred to as the 'refusal-prone materialist', with another high point of worker militancy between 1968 and 1974, similarly to that of the earlier 1910–20 period (Screpanti, 1987). Industrial conflict rose sharply in most West European countries between 1968 and 1970, and inflation after the 1973 oil shock further destabilized wage and price expectations, prompting even further contestation over wages. This took the form of an increasingly militant refusal-prone wage worker exhibiting 'disaggregated, localized shop-floor strength of a tenacious kind', itself the result of the relatively long period of full employment that Western Europe had experienced for much of the 1950s and 1960s (Crouch, 1993: 233–4). In turn, this rising militancy initially prompted wage rises and therefore further exacerbated the inflationary pressures created by the oil price hikes, witnessing a spiral of soaring inflation and heightened contestation over wage claims for much of the 1970s (Crouch, 1993: 259–60).

Whilst the conditions for growth and social pacificity appeared to have been created in the immediate post-war period, therefore, it is probably more accurate to say that new forms of rebellion and disruption were instead being fostered throughout the post-war period of social and industrial 'peace'. As Negri argues, the 'traditional trinity of political economy in the welfare state – Taylorism in production, Fordism in the political sphere, and Keynesianism in economic planning – was no longer able to guarantee law and order and economic development' (Negri, 1977: 96, authors' translation). As we have highlighted, this became increasingly visible from the late-1960s onwards, most obviously with the events of 1968, but also occurring on a more long-term scale. In addition to the effect of relatively long-term full employment upon the confidence and ability of European workers to organize, those workers themselves were also in many cases new to the experience of production line wage labour. Labour shortages and the attempt to reduce the cost of labour witnessed a new group of wage labourers enter the labour market, especially women and migrant labour (migrants from both rural regions to cities, and from colonies to the metropoles). These newer members of the labour market, moreover, oftentimes had little connection to the established post-war ideologies and organizations, such as trade unions and political parties, that were associated with the more established members of the working class (Crouch, 1978: 10–11). This created a potent mix of disengaged or disinterested attitudes towards formal institutions of worker representation, with a strong commitment to refusal in the workplace, resulting in an increasingly autonomous mass movement of militant refusal-prone wage workers across much of western Europe.

In many countries, strike activity rose throughout the 1960s, peaking in the late-1960s or early-1970s (Shalev, 1978; Screpanti, 1987). As Dubois shows, this rise in industrial conflict was largely prompted by increased grievances amongst workers, who faced a new wave of wage repression and/or a productivity drive arising out of the need on the part of firms to be more competitive (particularly in the context of liberalized trade due to heightened European integration). The effect of this heightened conflict, moreover, was in most cases a sharp further rise in wages during the 1970s (Dubois, 1978: 15–6). Indeed, as Soskice (1978) shows, a chain of events can be witnessed across Western Europe during the 1960s. Firms increasingly faced declining profit margins, in part due to the increased ability of the relatively secure European workforce to demand wage increases *above* the rate of productivity growth (Bengtsson, 2015). This was followed by governments responding to the problems associated with these economic trends by increasingly intervening in wage negotiations, in the form of wage and incomes policies. Employers themselves also sought to respond from the mid-1960s onwards, through workplace rationalization, a restructuring of wage negotiations (away from plant-based negotiations) and through lower wage offers. As a result of these measures, the onset of higher levels of US inflation (and therefore world market inflation) in the later 1960s resulted in higher prices in Europe without a corresponding wage rise, thereby prompting a reaction from workers (who were already upset about the other interventions of governments and firms). Finally, this combination of mechanisms witnessed heightened unrest amongst wage labourers, prompting wage explosions during the 1970s as employers sought to quell incidents of militant dissent (Soskice, 1978: 233–4).

In this sense, therefore, the strike activity of the late-1960s was a recomposition of the working class as it reproduced itself within a changing landscape, in which capital was seeking new opportunities for profitability following a profit squeeze that an increasingly secure European working class had produced throughout the 1960s. The subsequent attempt by capital to confront this situation in the late-1960s, however, resulted in a fierce backlash by European labour, witnessing wage levels rise further still as a consequence (Soskice, 1978: 234–5; Glyn and Sutcliffe, 1972).

The period from 1968 to 1973 thus witnessed serious instances of industrial conflict across Western Europe. The strike wave that hit France in May–June 1968 was the largest post-war mobilization to affect Western Europe since 1945. It was followed, moreover, by another extended period of conflict between 1971 and 1973. In both cases this consisted of both factory-level strikes and a broader national movement. In 1968, a resolution to the (workers') conflict was brought about by a significant rise in wages (agreed in the *Protocole d'Accord de Grenelle*); in 1971–73 the demands of the national strikes were more political, including retirement, minimum wage, employment, the cost of living and social security. In Italy, the 'hot autumn' of 1969 witnessed mainly factory-level strikes, but with broader demands including those related to housing and transport policy. The United Kingdom witnessed political strikes against the Industrial Relations Bill (1970 and 1971), the mass protests and near-general strike opposing the initial imprisonment of the Pentonville Five, and a one-day strike against the incomes policy introduced in 1973. In Germany, a wave of unofficial strike action took place in 1972 in support of the SPD Government. In each case, moreover, the experience of highly visible national strikes was in turn followed by a level of industrial conflict that was higher than experienced prior to the onset of conflict – meaning that the post-conflict 'lull' which took place after each of these major flashpoints nevertheless witnessed heightened conflict in comparison with the pre-flashpoint period. In each case, moreover, outbreaks of industrial conflict witnessed heightened levels of self-organization by workers, witnessing a shifting of power away from the formal trade union leadership and officials (Clua-Losada, 2010; Dubois, 1978: 5–8).

In Spain, in contrast, the period between 1939 and 1975 was politically, socially and economically very different to most Western European countries. The Fascist uprising against the democratically elected Spanish Republic in 1936 initiated a dark period for Spanish society. However, the dictatorship was never able to fully subjugate Spanish workers, and rebellions were common. From the early days of the dictatorship, with the organized resistance of the Maquis, who attempted to re-occupy Spain from the Pyrenes and liberate it from Franco, to the increasingly organized, albeit clandestinely, workers' movements around the *Comisiones Obreras* (the workers' commissions, today's largest trade union in Spain). Informal structures of workplace organization developed especially within the 'Fordist' industries in the most industrialized regions in Catalonia and the Basque country. These were strengthened by Francoist 'efforts' of import-substitution and 'catch-up' Fordism. The commissions served as channel of interest articulation *vis-à-vis* the employers; their organizational structures were fragmented and precarious. They focused mainly on everyday needs and problems within the firms. In order to achieve their goals, they pragmatically used windows of opportunity within and outside the *sindicato vertical*. In organizing struggles at the workplace level they were able to put such strong pressure on employers that – in many cases – informal workplace arrangements were reached that exceeded wage guidelines set by the state.

In consequence, the Francoist regime during the 1950s saw itself forced to loosen its grip on labour relations and decree major wage increases in order to prevent major social unrest. Collective bargaining at company level was legalized in order to prevent agreements outside the legal framework. While strikes remained illegal, a certain level of workplace conflict was tolerated. The extension of bargaining possibilities at the workplace level led to a rise in collective agreements as well as industrial actions (Huke, 2017). By the 1960s, similar patterns of workers' struggles to those witnessed in the rest of Western Europe began to emerge in Spain, with the exception that the level of state repression which they met tended to be both harsher and conducted in a more open way. Shared grievances (especially low wages, high inflation, extension of the workdays) in combination with fragile and fugitive elements of a workers' counter culture, led to a surge in informal, self-organized workers' commissions, in which the communist and Christian left played a major role. Perhaps the clearest sign that the control imposed by Franco was beginning to erode came in 1966. This marked the beginning of a new period, witnessing important student strikes and occupations, such as *La Caputxinada*, the siege of the University of Barcelona in April of that year, and on 30 April 1966 when the University was closed down – something that hadn't happened since the 1920s (Georgel 1972: 111). Whilst the Spanish context was different, therefore, it nevertheless experienced similar trends in terms of an increasingly restless working class acting to erode the post-war social order.

In explaining the emergence of this increasingly autonomously acting worker across much of Western Europe we should focus on the productivity of what has been referred to as a 'mass worker'. This was a 'new type of wage labourer who, without skills, with no pride of workmanship, often uprooted from his culture and his native country must be as mobile as international capital itself' (Kirchlechner, 1978: 173). Shared experiences and the scope for everyday communication between mass workers allowed for a transformation of everyday needs into collective demands. The structural power of the mass workers, moreover, provided strengthened their power resource (Bologna, 2009; Castoriadis, 1980). As a result, it is claimed, the mass worker was able to make demands 'autonomously' and without concern for ideology but rather derived from the necessities and experience of everyday life. As Kirchlechner observed at the time,

> These demands are, moreover, not born in the heads of leftist strategists. They are the autonomous reaction of the mass workers to their work and to the lives

they are forced to lead. The unity of life and work is reflected, for example, in the Pierburg women's demand for a paid housewives' day or in their demand that no one should have to forfeit his wages in order to visit a doctor.

(Kirchlechner, 1978: 174)

The autonomous mass worker also showed 'no traditional loyalties to unions or political organizations', which were seen as the instruments of the privileged and skilled 'native' and male workers, in contrast with the typically female and/or migrant workers that commonly took on the characteristics of the autonomous mass worker. Whilst the formal institutions might have been utilized at certain points, to secure improved wages or working conditions, these were nevertheless evaluated 'instrumentally', with longer-term objectives 'not part of the calculus of interest' (Kirchlechner, 1978: 174). Indeed, in many cases the official union would side with the firm *against* the mobilized mass workers.

A variety of forms of strike action were witnessed during this period – many of which utilized the disruptive capacity of the potential for withdrawal in experimental and creative ways. In France 1968, this included 'sit-ins, evicting top management from the plant, [and] strikers taking over plant security duties and continuing some forms of production activity' (Dubois, 1978: 9). One of the most acrimonious disputes, for instance, was the 1973 Lip dispute, which included *grèves perlées* (go-slows), *grèves tournantes* (sector-by-sector stoppages designed to cause disruption without a total loss of earnings for striking workers), appropriation of the products of the factory (watches, in this case) and factory occupations (Dubois, 1978: 8–9). Similarly, Italy witnessed the use of coordinated in-plant stoppages – normally undertaken by migrant workers who had been recruited from the south of the country precisely because they were un-unionized. The effect of this employment strategy, however, was to create a workforce that was less, rather than more, manageable. In the words of labour historian Giuseppe Berta, 'FIAT did not know its workers anymore. They had become an abnormal mass' (Berta, 1998: 153, quoted in Pizzolato, 2004: 426). These coordinated stoppages were referred to as 'checkerboard strikes', whereby action would take place at only one point of the production line but in doing so would prevent production altogether, before moving to a different part of the line once the dispute was resolved in the first part, thereby rotating through different parts of the factory in order to maximize disruption whilst minimizing the number of workers taking part in the industrial action and thereby also minimizing lost pay (Lumley, 1990). Other forms of disruption in Italy's hot autumn and subsequent years of heightened class conflict included blockades in front of the factory gates, marches inside the factory, absenteeism, industrial sabotage and intimidation of non-striking workers and of works supervisors (Dubois, 1978: 9; Negri, 1977: 64).

An exemplary case of the disruptive capacity of the mass worker was also witnessed in Spain, despite the authoritarian nature of its labour relations. For instance, in an effort to reintegrate the increasingly autonomous and interconnected movement of the workers' commissions, the Francoist regime staged elections for roughly 200,000 positions in works councils in 1966. The workers' commissions, however, achieved a landslide victory, after which they declared their willingness to create a unified workers' association (Comisiones Obreras, CCOO). The Francoist regime reacted with fierce repression that included the dismissal of activists and the declaration of a state of emergency for the industrial region of Guipuzcoa. However, the regime proved unable to defeat the workers' commission due to their massive support amongst Fordist mass workers. As a result, the workers' self-confidence grew further still, for instance witnessing wage guidelines increasingly regarded as a minimum, to be transcended by trade union action, rather than a cap. Franco's repression, furthermore, led to a politicization of workplace struggles, as the Francoist regime increasingly became the main point of attack. While industrial action had been limited to conflict-prone sectors in certain regions during the 1960s, it was subsequently extended throughout the 1970s to a variety of sectors, cities and occupations. Between 1964 and 1972 workers consistently achieved wage increases above productivity, thereby further eroding the accumulation strategy of the regime. The state continuously decreed higher wages in an increasingly desperate attempt to prevent an escalation of social unrest. But in doing so it proved unable to regain control of the situation. As such, we might consider the movement by mass workers to have been the spearhead of the successful struggles for democratization in 1970s Spain (Huke, 2017).

In Britain, a growing shop stewards' movement became increasingly influential within the labour movement of the 1960s, rising to challenge the authority of the formal trade union leadership. This was perhaps most clearly evinced by the concern showed for it by both Labour and Conservative Governments at the time. Thus, the Donovan Commission, appointed by the Labour Government under Harold Wilson in 1965, highlighted a rise in unofficial strikes, pointing out that about 95 per cent of stoppages are unofficial, that these are becoming more common, and adding that 'the informal system [especially that orchestrated by shop stewards] [has] come to exert an ever-greater influence on the conduct of industrial relation' (quoted in Banks, 1969; see also *Relations industrielles/Industrial Relations*, 1968). In seeking to respond to this situation, in 1969 the Secretary of State for Employment and Productivity, Barbara Castle, introduced a Government White Paper *In Place of Strife* which sought to limit unofficial strike action. In her own words, the White Paper sought to resolve the problem whereby workers would,

> just down tools – like that. And they were about 1.8m of these unofficial strikes compared with some 600 of the official ones, the great big ones … I and employers used to say we don't mind the major strikes as much as this chaos. Because if you know you're going to have a great showdown with a big union, you can prepare some defences. But, if suddenly, as happened at Girlings' Brakes Works, a dozen key men down tools, without warning, and walk out. They're helpless and so are the rest of the staff.
> (interview with Barbara Castle, 1999, quoted in Davis, 2009: 270)

Likewise, the Industrial Relations Act introduced by the Conservative Government in 1971 (and which eventually led to the Government's downfall in 1974) focused explicitly on, in its own words, an attempt to 'strengthen the unions and their official leadership by providing some deterrent against irresponsible action by unofficial minorities' (Conservative Party manifesto, quoted in Davis, 2009: 275). In addition to mass strikes, more innovative forms of disruption that emerged during the 1970s included flying pickets, overtime bans, work-to-rule and so-called 'secondary boycotts' (in which a supplying or contracting firm is targeted, rather than the firm with whom a dispute is against) (Dubois, 1978: 9–10). This use of flying pickets rose to prominence as a strategy in the miners' strike that began in 1972, with the then unofficial leader of the so-called 'Yorkshire Left' of the National Union of Mineworkers, Arthur Scargill, pioneering the strategy in using it to form the mass pickets seen in the so-called 'Battle of Saltley Gate' in February 1972 (Cohen, 2006: 19–21).

In addition to direct industrial conflict, firms in West European economies also experienced challenges to their internal authority as direct action by workers acted to either displace or occur alongside formal management functions. For instance, in Britain the labour movement consistently referred to the legal provision for 'customs and practice' (whereby established workplace practices were enshrined in the [unwritten] contract of employment) as a point on which to challenge any attempt at interference or change by the company's management. Mass absenteeism was also routinely adopted as a way of imposing rules upon the management of firms. For instance, workers would routinely miss work *en masse* on New Year's Day until it was eventually declared an official public holiday in 1974 (Dubois, 1978: 12). Workers would also sometimes decide to continue production even if the management of the company had decided that production was not viable (or in cases of bankruptcy). This happened, for instance, in the case of the Upper Clyde Shipbuilders who conducted a 'work-in' between July 1971 and October 1972, taking over occupation and management of the shipyard in opposition to its threatened closure, and witnessing a similar strategy of occupations subsequently being adopted by workers across the country, for instance by the Plessey workers, those in the River Don steelworks in Sheffield, Fisher-Bendix in Kirkby, Sexton Shoes at Fakenham, BP Chemicals at Stroud and Bryant Colour Printing in South London (Cohen, 2006: 26).

Similar observations can be made of Italy and France. Thus, in Italy workers autonomously altered hours and job routines, and also created the right to hold workplace meetings by simply holding them. Outside of the workplace, workers sought to challenge the erosion of real wages, for instance by avoiding rent increases and public transport fare rises by paying old rates (sometimes with union backing). Finally, in the case of France workers directly ignored management instructions in order to secure the outcomes that they sought. For instance, the passenger ship *France* was 'kept at sea for nearly a month by the crew in protest against the decision by the shipping company to lay her up'. In order to avoid workplace boredom, moreover, workers autonomously rotated jobs within the factory, and (as in the case of the Upper Clyde Shipbuilders dispute) in the Lip dispute in France the workforce decided to continue production despite the management of the company declaring production to be unviable (Dubois, 1978: 12–4).

Heightened and tense battles over wages continued during the 1970s. Wage negotiations between German public sector workers and the Government in 1973–74 became increasingly heated. The Government had sought to dampen wage expectations through the publication of relatively low inflation predictions, but workers responded with a wave of strikes that forced the Government to offer a massive 15 per cent pay rise. The strikes were impressive, well supported, and highly disruptive in key service areas such as transit and garbage collection. It was in this context that SPD Finance Minister, Karl Schiller and Bundesbank president Karl Klasen first announced their intention that inflation would be kept low regardless of the impact that it would have upon unemployment (McNamara, 1998: 117). Similar events were witnessed in France, where wage gains achieved in the mid-1970s were explicitly tackled by the incoming Prime Minister, Raymond Barre, in his so-called Barre Plan, which had a central goal of securing wage restraint in order to achieve lower inflation – with the need to maintain price competitiveness in international markets (including a stable exchange rate) explicitly cited as the means by which to achieve this goal (McNamara, 1998: 130–1). Likewise, wage pressures associated with high levels of worker mobilization in Italy (and especially the permanence of wage rises created by the *scala mobile*) witnessed the Andreotti Government adopt a reform package in 1976, with the support of PCI leader, Enrico Berlinguer, and the head of the CGIL, the central pillars of which were austerity measures and wage restraint (McNamara, 1998: 133–4).

The ongoing experience of industrial unrest, wage rises, an associated profit squeeze and resulting decline in investment and productivity, therefore, all combined by the end of the 1970s to prompt more dramatic attempts by the governments of the advanced industrial capitalist states (both in western Europe and in North America) to create conditions more conducive to stable economic growth. Perhaps the most infamous instance of this strategy was witnessed with the so-called Volcker shock that was initiated in late-1979 in the United States, and which witnessed the US Federal Reserve push up interest rates to such a degree that it would prompt a recession and (most importantly) a sharp rise in unemployment, thereby using unemployment as a means by which to combat wage rises and bring about a decline in the wage share. This move towards a neoliberal assault on organized and disruptive labour was often complemented by symbolic attacks on organized labour, with the defeat of the Air Traffic Controllers in the industrial dispute of 1981 in the US, and in the UK the defeat of the miners in the Miners' Strike of 1983–84, perhaps being the most commonly referred to examples (Harvey, 2005). Finally, the same period witnessed a concerted attempt to reduce welfare state generosity (Huber and Stephens, 2001). With each of these measures, therefore, advanced industrial democratic states consistently moved to adopt a more punitive approach, in an attempt to secure lower wage rises and thereby confront the ongoing problem of rising wages, low profitability, low investment and low productivity (Glyn, 2006: 1–49; see also Schmalz *et al.*, 2015: 51). This therefore represented the beginning of the neoliberal response of capitalist authorities to the disruptive potential of the increasingly autonomous mass worker subjectivity that had emerged in the context of the post-1945 compromise, itself made up of scientific management, productivist class compromise, and an expansionary welfare state – all of which had been promoted by and through, and embedded within, the institutions of European integration.

The relaunch of European integration as part of the neoliberal response

The relaunch of European integration in the mid-1980s should be considered part of this neoliberal move documented in the preceding section, in which the role of the market was extended in an attempt to achieve social control over Europe's increasingly disruptive working class. Indeed, as we show below, and echoing many of the insights of the critical political economy literature, each of the major attempts to advance European integration following its relaunch with the 1985 White Paper have represented an attempt to construct, consolidate or engender a heightening of the role of the market through the promotion of increased integration between member states (Ziltener, 1999). European integration was viewed by capitalist authorities as a means by which to steer a path towards the marginalization and exclusion of labour, weakening its power resources by streamlining production processes, increasing locational competition and overseeing a fragmentation of the workforce (Bologna, 2009; Negri, 1996). Indeed, what we refer to as the locational competition connected to the European (and global) integration of capitalist markets was specifically designed to erode previously existing institutions of corporatist interest mediation (Schmalz *et al.*, 2015: 51). As Bieler highlights, the

> transnationalization of production and an increasing focus on finance were a response by capital to the declining rate of profits and the deep economic recessions of the 1970s. As part of general policies of neoliberal restructuring, it was a strategy to restore capitalist class power over labour.
>
> (Bieler, 2015: 31)

It is in this sense, therefore, that we view the relaunch of European integration as part of the neoliberal response to the crisis of the 1970s – that is, an attempt to impose heightened market competition on European society in order to achieve greater levels of social control and discipline, and thereby secure the (unobtainable but nevertheless necessary) pacification of labour. As we shall see in our discussion in this and later chapters, however, this pacification has been far from achieved (as, indeed, we might expect, given its unobtainability).

One of the earliest indications that a relaunch of European integration would be used in an attempt to further market discipline was witnessed with the introduction in 1979 of the European Monetary System (EMS). This represented an explicit shift in policy consensus amongst Europe's political elite, away from the notion that wages, prices and (especially) employment levels could be directly controlled through state activity, towards the use of monetary policy to impose sanctions upon recalcitrant economic actors in order to achieve a more indirect form of discipline and (especially) low wage claims, which in turn it was hoped would bring inflation under control (McNamara, 1998: 62). Thus, through the EMS, European member states sought to create a situation in which excessive wage (and therefore price) inflation would result in downward pressure upon a national currency vis-a-vis its partner countries within the EMS. This, in turn, it was expected, would require member states to act in order to ensure that those inflationary pressures were removed. From this perspective, the infamous Mitterrand U-turn of 1983, in which international speculation is commonly viewed as the reason for the U-turn, can instead be interpreted as a direct outcome of the constraints that member states had purposefully placed upon themselves with the adoption of the EMS in 1979, as a means to 'lock in' low inflation and market discipline (McNamara, 1998: 139).

It was on these terms, therefore, that the creation of the EMS was agreed to by the member states – as a means by which to lock in their own renewed commitment to lowering inflation, and especially wage inflation, in an attempt to impose tighter discipline upon their respective national workforces. The commitment by European leaders to such an anti-inflationary strategy was explicitly acknowledged by the governments themselves at the time, as McNamara (1998) documents. Thus, we see Bundesbank official, Helmut Schlesinger, declaring in 1977 that: 'the recognition is widespread – and not only in light of the experience of the last few years – that, except in the very short term, nothing can be gained from more inflation either for economic growth or for employment' (quoted in McNamara, 1998: 148). Likewise, Barre declared in 1979 that, France was 'rejecting the mirages of a 'general expansion' that would certainly reduce unemployment temporarily but would make inflation and the balance of payments deficit and consequently, in the longer term, unemployment, worse' (quoted in McNamara, 1998: 149).

A central purpose of EMS membership was to create a hard external constraint that would subsequently be used by member states to justify attempts to impose austerity measures and wage restraints (themselves necessary in order to avoid financial speculation against the national currency, which had the potential to force the national currency out of its fixed rate). This was witnessed in the well documented case of the 1983 Mitterrand U-turn. But it also could be seen in the case of Spain, where bankers welcomed the opportunity that the EMS held out for a policy of 'squeeze them and blame the Bundesbank' (McNamara, 1998: 139). It was also the case in Belgium where the 'external pressure [of EMS membership] provided a helpful framework for imposing discipline' (McNamara, 1998, p. 142); and similarly in the Netherlands and Denmark (McNamara, 1998: 141–3).

This move towards a further reliance on European integration as a disciplining tool continued into the 1980s. The declared goal of the Single European Act (SEA), and the Single European Market which it legislated to create, was to introduce greater competition into Europe's socio-economy. This benefited from the political and ideological support secured through the coming into office of Thatcher's neoliberal Government, Lubbers' Dutch Government, Kohl's centre-right coalition in Germany, and the Mitterand Presidency in France following the debacle of the 1983 U-turn away from 'Keynesianism in one country' (Armstrong and Bulmer, 1998: 21). Some have argued that instead of promoting market competition there was, rather, a 'second agenda', which was more genuine. This is the view that the aim of the SEA was to create a large 'home market' in which European firms would be able to grow in scale so that they could match their US and Japanese competitors. Indeed, this was especially the case in the area of information technology, in which European companies increasingly felt that they were unable to compete with their Japanese rivals – resulting in a collaboration between 12 major electronic companies and the Commissioner for research and technology, Viscount Davignon (Sandholtz and Zysman, 1989: 114). This was accompanied by the pressure of the European Round Table of Industrialists, who welcomed the market-building project of the Single European Market (SEM), and the pressure for competition that it would induce (Cowles 1995; although, again, divisions existed within the ERT over whether the goal was competition or competitiveness, on which see Apeldoorn, 2002). Thus, whether the move was an attempt to build increased market pressure within the single market, or to improve competitiveness vis-à-vis the US and Japan (and it was probably both), the processes described in either scenario nevertheless represented a form of market disciplining in which 'European integration has been and is part of the worldwide liberalization process' (Ziltener, 2004). Indeed, as Armstrong and Bulmer show, the SEM project sought also to liberalize a range of both public and private sector activity, including public procurement and the air transport industry (Armstrong and Bulmer, 1998).

This move towards market disciplining was itself facilitated by the institutional architecture of the EC, which engendered the adoption of EU-wide legislation that would consolidate market-making mechanisms and make it difficult for 'market-correcting' policies to be adopted even when there was support for them (Scharpf, 1999). On occasions when clashes occurred between those favouring a strategy which viewed the SEM as a means by which to bolster European firms in order that they might be more competitive internationally, and those who sought to increase intra-EC competition, the institutional architecture of the EC was such that it skewed the balance of power in favour of the (more neoliberal) latter group. This can be witnessed, for instance, in the case of the 1989 Merger Control Regulation (MCR). The Regulation was adopted under the terms of the 1985 White Paper and subsequent SEA, in recognition of the increased rate of mergers and acquisitions with an EC-wide scope and due to their increasing impact upon EC competences. In doing so, it exposed a division between the big four governments (France, Italy, United Kingdom, Germany). France and Italy, with their greater *étatist* tradition (especially in the case of France), sought to create a possibility for the promotion of 'European champions' that would benefit from state support. Germany and the United Kingdom, in contrast, were much more focused on ensuring that the criterion according to which merger and acquisition (M&A) decisions would be made was that of ensuring market competition. The eventual outcome of the negotiations, in which France sought (unsuccessfully) to insert a so-called 'public interest clause' in the legislation eventually resulted in its absence, in order that agreement could be reached on the legislation, reflecting the inherently minimalist and pro-market bias intrinsic to supranational institution building. Indeed, the resulting MCR was considered, 'the most competition-orientated mergers policy in Europe' (Armstrong and Bulmer, 1998: 90–105).

Another of the early major developments in market liberalization occurred in the financial sector. This included the June 1988 Capital Movements Directive, which provided for the full liberalization of capital movements as set out in Article 67 of the Treaty establishing European Community (TEC), and the Second Banking Directive of the same year, which created a single market for banking (Jabko, 2006: 64–6). As the Commission itself explicitly recognized in setting out the rationale for financial liberalization, European integration of financial markets was viewed from the early 1980s as a means by which to achieve liberalization and thereby further increase market competition within European society. As the European Commission itself declared

> several Member States considered it necessary to open up and modern-ize their financial structures in order to keep up with these developments (globalization), and believed that the European dimension was vital to national financial institutions *as a means of achieving the necessary competitiveness.*
> (Commission of the European Communities, 1988: 8, emphasis added)

The Commission, moreover, was explicit about the way that financial liberalization would lock in *further* pressure for market competition. Thus, in order to reap the full benefits, the Commission viewed liberalization as needing to be combined with guaranteed 'healthy competition for intermediaries' and the need to ensure the avoidance of 'the maintenance of protectionist measures' at the national level (CEC, 1988: 10). Going into more detail, the Commission went on to highlight the way in which financial integration would consolidate broader pan-European pressures for market competition. Thus:

> The objective goes beyond the establishment of a financial free trade area in Europe; it is the establishment of a Community-wide integrated financial system. The intensification of intra-Community financial relations, favoured by the lifting of restrictions, will naturally derive support from the progress already made and to be continued in commercial integration and the conver-gence of economic and monetary policies. *It will have to be accompanied by parallel progress towards the creation of a common market in financial ser-vices.* The objective is to establish fair conditions of competition which will favour the development of a diversified range of high quality financial instru-ments and to enable users to exercise their activities throughout the territory of the Community without having to fragment their financial relationships.
> (Commission of the European Communities, 1988: 19,
> emphasis added)

The aim, therefore, was the 'full liberalization of capital movements accompanied by an absence of barriers to the free provision of financial services'. This, it was intended, would 'expose all the national finance systems to a very competitive international environment *to which they will have to adapt*' (Commission of the European Communities, 1988: 31, emphasis added). In addition, it was foreseen that the process of financial liberalization would have an indirect impact upon the public sector, which would no longer be able to rely upon protected national savings. Thus:

> Member States will no longer have direct means of tapping residents' savings and will have to accept financial conditions as regards cost and financing the public debt which are competitive with those of the private sector.
>
> (Commission of the European Communities, 1988: 31)

The 1988 Capital Movements Directive therefore sought to enshrine each of these principles in EU law, subsequently acquiring the support of all of the member states and therefore being adopted unanimously. Germany, Britain and France were all especially keen supporters of the move (the former two due to their having already liberalized their capital markets; in the case of France, due to the experience of the Mitterrand Presidency following its 1983 U-turn). Likewise, the Second Banking Directive was adopted smoothly and with little disagreement between the member states the following year (Jabko, 2006: 65).

As Jabko shows, the initial steps towards financial liberalization opened up the possibility for a broader range of financial institutions to offer a broader range of financial products, for instance creating the possibility that banks could compete with insurance companies to sell insurance products. This 'promised to put huge competitive pressures on actors that operated in non-liberalized segments of the financial sector', which in turn prompted a 'domino effect' in that it 'generated further political pressure in favour of liberalizing other segments of the financial services industry' (Jabko, 2006: 81). Indeed, as we shall see in subsequent chapters, one of the consequences of this development was the prevention of national regulations being used to obstruct foreign firms and non-specialized financial institutions from entering domestic mortgage markets, thereby prompting a rise in mortgage lending (and at a lower cost to borrowers) in those countries (such as Italy) which had previously seen relatively low levels of mortgage borrowing. This, in turn, prompted a rise in demand for housing, contributing to the spiral effect through which increased mortgages and rising house prices fuelled each other (Aalbers, 2009: 399; on the virtuous/vicious circle created by rising housing demand and increased credit provision, see Dokko *et al.*, 2011). Indeed, as Buchanan (forthcoming) makes clear, 'Securitization requires not only an expanding market, but also the deregulation and internationalization of domestic financial markets'. In this sense, therefore, European integration represented an important element in the facilitation of financial securitization and the rapid expansion of mortgage-holders and therefore house prices within the European context during the pre-2008 period.

Financial market liberalization also had the additional effect of heightening the disciplining role of the EMS. The greater ease with which financial transactions (and especially foreign currency exchange transactions) could be conducted resulted in an even greater sensitivity of national governments to speculation against their national currencies. Moreover, the creation of a 'false floor' at the bottom of the band of exchange rates created a significant opportunity for speculators to make sizeable amounts of money by betting against the currency being able to maintain itself within the lower limit of that band. This became increasingly clear during the foreign exchange crises of 1992–3, with the British pound and Italian lira both driven out of the scheme and the Spanish peseta, Portuguese escudo, and Irish punt each involuntarily devalued (McNamara, 1998: 167–8).

As has been commonly noted, the Maastricht Treaty, which came into force in 1993 and committed the EU member states to forming the Economic and Monetary Union and therefore the Euro, represented a further round of anti-inflationary policies (Stark, 2001). In doing so, however, this represented a continuation and consolidation of a process that had begun much early, in the context of the late-1970s move towards anti-inflationary policies with the EMS. The so-called 'convergence criteria', which imposed upon governments the requirement that they have low inflation and (especially) low public debt and deficits, therefore represented a further step towards the use of European integration in an attempt to pre-emptively discipline potentially recalcitrant economic actors and thereby seek to ensure the discipline of the market across European society. As we know, this was subsequently enshrined as a lasting policy of the Eurozone with the adoption of the Stability and Growth Pact in 1998 (Pichelmann, 2002; Bibow, 2006; Gill, 2001).

In addition to the moves to construct a single market and single currency, the enlargement process of European integration also acted to consolidate market pressures. Whilst this has been more routinely noted with regard to the eastern enlargements of 2004–7 (Bohle, 2006b), similar effects can be witnessed with regard to the accessions of the 1980s. For instance, in Spain, democratization was intricately connected with the process of European integration. This in turn caused harsh structural adjustments within many of the previously protected sectors of Spanish industry, as domestic firms sought (largely unsuccessfully) to compete with firms from other European countries. The social democratic Partido Socialista Obrero Español (PSOE) Government that was elected in 1982, after the transitional period, pushed forward a programme of industrial restructuring that included closures and layoffs, and prompting fierce defensive strikes by the affected workers in the process.

Whilst Spanish workers could be expected to resist these moves towards marketization through European integration, the political climate had nevertheless substantially changed. While Fordist mass workers had been able to spearhead the movements for Spanish democracy in the 1960s and 1970s, during the 1980s they became increasingly insulated and oftentimes successfully portrayed as acting to defend narrowly defined self-interest. This consolidated a trend whereby the movement of workers' commissions had already in the late 1970s been eroded by the newly established system of industrial relations that shifted collective bargaining form the workplace-level to more institutionalized procedures. This resulted in the newly legalized trade unions (CCOO and UGT) beginning to rely on institutional influence rather than workplace organizing. Furthermore, the Spanish communist party PCE (which had earlier played an important role within the workers' commissions) became increasingly involved in elite negotiations during the transition, which brought with it an attempt to exert moderating pressure on workplace struggles in order not to endanger the process of democratization. The mass workers' struggles against foreclosures and dismissals during the 1980s therefore became increasingly desperate, leading to violent conflicts, occupations, blockades and even kidnappings. As such, the Spanish accession to European integration, which was widely heralded as a key element in the consolidation of Spain's democratization, brought with it in turn heightened market competition, operating as a (somewhat successful, but nevertheless contested) mechanism of social order during 1980s Spain (Huke, 2017).

Disrupting the neoliberal response, causing the European crises: between manufactured disengagement and peripheral refusal

The foregoing account therefore highlights the aims and intentions behind the process of European integration from the late 1970s onwards. As we have seen, the adoption of the EMS marked the beginning of a period during which European integration was increasingly used as a means by which to promote a neoliberal response to the problems facing European capitalism. In particular, market competition was heightened in an attempt to discipline labour and secure a greater degree of social order within European capitalism. On this point, we are in agreement with much of the consensus within the CPE literature on European integration. As we have argued in the previous section, however, it is important to pay due attention to the means by which this attempt to secure social order also continued to be disrupted by the obstinate agency of the working class. In particular, we see two key disruptive trends emerging during this period.

First, we see a move towards heightened disengagement by workers as a result of being subjected to a dismantling of working class and solidaristic institutions, various forms of managerialism, and increasingly flexible labour markets. This, moreover, was a manufactured form of disengagement, facilitated through a range of mechanisms, but a central one of which was the temporary increase in living standards achieved through the process of financialization, and especially the increase in wealth achieved through rising house prices that this financialization produced. Put simply, in exchange for disengaging from organized and visibly disruptive forms of class struggle, important sections of the working class were increasingly compensated through an increase in wealth produced by a finance-led inflation of their personal assets, especially in the form of housing (on the emergence of what is sometimes referred to as 'asset-based welfare', see Montgomerie and Büdenbender, 2015). Indeed, this was explicitly recognized by the EU member states and the Commission as an underlying purpose underpinning the project of capital market liberalization. As Jabko shows, 'financial modernization was increasingly seen as a welfare-enhancing endeavor and no longer as a danger' (Jabko, 2006: 61). Financialization (financial deregulation, increased lending, and rapid growth in the value of financial assets) systematically corresponded with an increase in consumer spending that was bolstered by debt (especially in those countries in which the assault on wages and welfare had been most pressing). As Glyn (somewhat presciently) showed, this also witnessed a dramatic fall in the savings rate, thereby having a pro-cyclical effect:

> By boosting consumption proportionately more than the rise in incomes this has intensified upswings, with the danger of sharp falls in demand if savings rebound sharply when the expansion slackens and pessimism builds up.
>
> (Glyn, 2006: 53)

Thus, household savings ratios fell whilst household borrowing as a proportion of disposable income rose by around 30 per cent in the United States, United Kingdom and Germany. Mortgage borrowing also rose dramatically (Glyn, 2006: 54). Each of these trends, moreover, have subsequently been shown to have offset political opposition to welfare reforms. Debt-financed consumption was also able to offset (to a degree) popular discontent with poverty and inequality (Kus, 2013); and rising house prices offset demand for redistributive public policy (Ansell, 2014). Thus, whilst wages and welfare were being pushed downwards by governments seeking to regain control over the capitalist economy, both opposition movements and the potential for opposition movements to emerge were prompting governments to facilitate alternative (private debt) forms of support for consumption and income (especially through the rapid increase in housing costs). As we know, moreover, it was this increasing reliance on debt-led consumption and debt-fuelled house cost inflation that was eventually to cause such dramatic and visible damage to the global (and European) economy.

In addition to this financialized form of disengagement, a second disruptive trend can be witnessed during this pre-2008 period of neoliberalism. This took the form of wage demands – especially in the so-called 'Southern periphery' – continuing to be made throughout the period, despite the attempt to pursue neoliberal European integration as a means by which to impose tighter control over the European working class. That is, whilst 'objective' economic conditions produced by heightened market competition dictated that wage growth should be suppressed in those regions, the degree of worker militancy and willingness to enter into industrial conflict was such that these economic conditions failed to produce the required or 'necessary' result. The effect of this militancy, as Christian Thimann, Director General and Adviser to the President at the European Central Bank from 2008 to 2013, makes clear, the key problem facing the Eurozone, and which can be held responsible in large part for the Eurozone crisis, is the lack of productivity and competitiveness in those areas where wage growth remained obstinately high. In Thimann's own words

> there is a remarkable correspondence between the eurozone countries that have significant structural impediments to business growth and the countries

that find themselves under economic stress – and hence a correspondence between microeconomic conditions and macroeconomic performance. *The strongest impediments to growth appear again in the labor market*, exactly where the cost competitiveness problems lie.

(Thimann, 2015: 150, emphasis added)

Thimann also sets out the five key reasons for these labour market imperfections: 'difficult labor-employer relations', 'adverse effects of taxation on incentives to work', 'hiring and dismissal practices', 'the country's capacity to retain talent', and 'female participation in the labor force' (p. 152). It is striking, then, that with the exception of female participation in the labour market, the eurozone crisis, according to a key official based until very recently at the centre of the ECB, is due to the *inability* to achieve the necessary level of reforms with the labour market. Indeed, if we were to re-phrase Thimann's argument into the language of the theoretical framework adopted in this book, it would fit almost exactly with the expectations that we identified. That is: the eurozone crisis was caused by an *inability* to sufficiently discipline European workers, to channel their efforts towards that of productivity in a form that is subordinate to the demands of capital, and to reform labour market laws to a sufficient degree that such a disciplining might be possible. This does not, of course, imply that such goals have not been pursued at the European level, nor that they have failed to be achieved, at least in part (as critical political economists have been right to point out). What it does highlight, however, is that the market disciplining sought through European integration has been insufficient for those advocating and proclaiming the necessity of such reforms. Indeed, Thimann is remarkably candid in his description of the expectation amongst many within Europe's political and economic elite, that such an outcome might be hoped for as a result of European integration. As he puts it

In principle, Eurozone participation should facilitate structural reforms because countries have strong economic incentives to engage in them, and because there are multiple formal and informal schemes for devising and coordinating such reforms. The main incentive for structural reforms, especially to increase the flexibility of product and labor markets, comes from the absence of the exchange rate as an adjustment mechanism … Moreover, enhanced competition should make the costs of rigidity higher; the costs of protection for insider firms and workers should become more visible to consumers and voters; firms facing greater cost pressures from competition should exert greater political pressure for deregulation of the market for services, energy, and transport; and countries should have incentives to improve labor market functioning to foster wage adjustements and labor mobility.

(Thimann, 2015: 154)

The problem – at least from the perspective of Europe's political and economic elite – is that these goals have failed to be sufficiently realised. In order to understand this failure, moreover, we can look to the different instances of opposition and resistance conducted by European workers, who have maintained ongoing willingness and capacity to refuse those attempts by capitalist authorities to impose the discipline of the market upon them.

Indeed, it is perhaps no coincidence that a cross-national comparison of strike trends across Western Europe highlights the higher proclivity to undertake significant strikes in the three countries between 1997 and 2008 – Greece, Italy, and Spain – that were subsequently to become central to the crisis of the Southern periphery following the onset of the Eurozone crisis (Gall, 2012: 676). As Gall goes on to show, within western Europe there is a clear distinction between a low strike rate group of countries (Belgium, Germany and the Netherlands), on the one hand, and a group of countries with higher frequencies of strikes (including France, Italy and Spain), on the other hand (Gall, 2012: 673). This corresponds exactly with the division highlighted by Thimann, between the Eurozone's so-called surplus countries (running a cumulated current account surplus since the start of the Euro) and its deficit countries, which in turn corresponds to a much lower average gross operating surplus for those firms in the deficit countries (Thimann, 2015: 147–8). Strike action during this period was consistently focused on the public sector and transport and communications – together making up over 50 per cent of all sectoral (i.e. non-general) significant strikes. Likewise, when we come to consider general/generalized strikes, which tend to be more political and more focused on creating political controversy rather than economic damage for the employer, we again see a distinction between the Netherlands, Germany and Belgium (now also joined by the United Kingdom), which have low numbers of such strikes; and Greece, Italy and (now) Portugal as the countries with the highest frequencies of such strikes (Gall, 2012). We can see an example of these more political strikes in the case of Italy in response to one of the major moves towards restructuring that began in 1985 was the proposal to abolish the so-called *scala mobile*. This was akin to a pay 'escalator', based on an agreement reached in 1975 that ensured that wages kept up with inflation and the cost of living. Whilst the major trade union – CGIL – accepted the Government's proposal to abolish the *scala mobile* in the mid-1980s, disgruntled workers mobilized against the development, ensuring that it made slow progress in the face of nationwide protest and wildcat strikes. Whilst the initiative did ultimately go ahead (finally agreed in 1993), it nevertheless was also accompanied by the formation in 1987 of the *Comitati di Base* (Cobas), which was an autonomous movement of workers organized along broadly syndicalist principles outside of the formal trade union organizations (Manicastri, 2014; see also Gall, 1995).

In Greece, following the election to office of the New Democracy Government in 1990, which was committed to austerity measures, deregulation of the labour market and de-industrialization, trade unions and workers launched a wave of mass protests that included strikes, demonstrations and violent clashes with the police. As a result, most of the measures were successfully blocked, including pension cuts and the privatization of public companies that included the refineries, Telecom Hellas, Skaramangas-Shipyards, and Olympic Airways. A wildcat strike of bus drivers in Athens in 1992 also witnessed an important victory for the Greek workers' movement. This was marked by the so-called 'battle of Votanikos', which was a suburb of Athens, and which witnessed a clash between 500 bus drivers and residents, on the one hand, and riot police on the other. The level of protest witnessed, moreover, was sufficient to prevent the privatization of public transport (Kritidis, 2014: 78).

Likewise, Spain witnessed a wildcat strike in the port of Barcelona in 1986 that displayed many elements of radical and prefigurative practices, including: horizontal assemblies, the absence of support on the part of the mainstream unions, self-organization by the workers (*Coordinadora de Estibadores Portuarios*, Coordination of Port Stevedores), and worker-led management initiatives such as refusing to load weapons that were due to be exported to Chile. This prompted a strike wave that was increasingly militant and which spread to other parts of Spain – in large part focused on the macroeconomic policies of the Spanish Socialist Government, which was focused at the time on ensuring the smooth integration of the Spanish economy within the European Union (Cattaneo and Tudela, 2014: 102).

Of course, this is not to say that a real and successful assault upon wages and living conditions did not occur as a result of the moves from the mid-1980s to impose greater market discipline through European integration, even in those countries (especially in Southern Europe) that experienced a relatively high frequency of strikes. It is, rather, to say that there was a degree to which workers' mobilization was able to hinder the imposition of poverty, 'efficiency' and lower real wages that was at the time being sought. Indeed, the mere occurrence of strikes does not by itself indicate a confrontational approach by labour towards capital. The case of Spain is instructive in this sense, some of the instances highlighted previously notwithstanding. The system of industrial relations established in Spain during the 1970s and 1980s led to a system of collective bargaining in which trade unions were rather weak compared to that in many other EU countries. Their strategies, as a result, became increasingly focused on institutional influence (such as peak-level wage setting arrangements) rather than mobilizations. Strikes were used frequently, but very often as a symbolic and ritualized measure accompanying negotiations. As a result, real wage increases tended to be low, except for during the early 1980s and early 1990s, and labour markets became increasingly flexible, witnessing a rise of so-called precarious labour. As a result, large parts of the Spanish population had also to rely on debt or increased labour market participation (especially by women) in order to secure or raise living standards (Huke, 2017). As we have seen, however, this precarity was insufficient to satisfy Europe's political and economic elite, or to avoid Spain being a deficit country.

Conclusion

As we have sought to show, European integration has been consistently adopted by the European political and economic elite, as a method through which to impose market discipline through heightened economic competition. Whilst most CPE accounts of European integration have tended to highlight the attempts of the European political and economic elite to adopt a pro-integration position as a means by which to heighten market-based discipline over European labour, nevertheless as we have sought to show in this chapter these attempts were not entirely successful and nor were they met without significant opposition and disruption. Market-based discipline, imposed through European integration, has therefore been met with a number of important forms of disruptive action, resulting in outcomes that have been suboptimal and/or unintended for those in political or economic authority. The chapter has highlighted three phases. First, we have seen an initial pre-1945 period marked by a wave of major social and economic unrest, witnessing militant acts of refusal and oftentimes informed by a commitment to prefigurative forms of workplace democracy. The attempt to respond to this unrest witnessed the development of a governing strategy that sought to combine productivism, scientific management and Keynesian economic management, albeit in a somewhat faltering and uneven manner (with this unevenness largely associated with the emergence of an authoritarian alternative strategy in Germany, Italy and Spain, and the subsequent occurrence of the Second World War). Following the Second World War, Europe's elite (under the guidance and influence of the United States) moved more consistently to adopt the same methods of integration and pacification that had been trialled prior to the war. Productivism, scientific management and Keynesian economic management were each increasingly relied upon, and became associated with key processes of European integration, especially the launch of the European Coal and Steel Community and the signing of the Treaty of Rome.

European integration, we have seen, offered those advocating this market-based model of social order the possibility to create a series of external constraints that, it was hoped, would act as impediments to those actors who sought to oppose the consolidation of a liberal economic market across western Europe. Finally, our third phase emerged during the 1980s, in large part due to the increasingly visible militancy of European labour that grew throughout the 1960s and 1970s. The initial move to adopt the European Monetary System in 1979 was explicitly linked to an attempt to create a system whereby member states would be forced, through a form of market discipline created by the threat of currency speculation, to prevent excessive wage claims and wage inflation. The consolidation of market discipline was subsequently extended, moreover, with the creation of both the single European market and the single currency, and through successive rounds of enlargement. This, however, has prompted (at least) two new forms of disruptive activity to emerge – both of which would be associated with the crises that dramatically erupted in the post-2008 period. These were a debt-fuelled disengagement of key sections of Europe's populace; and a lingering (albeit somewhat depleted) working class militancy that would prove sufficient to prevent the degree of subordination to market discipline that was demanded by the 'objective' economic conditions of market competition. The resulting European crises of the post-2008 context, therefore, reflected in many ways the ongoing disruptive capacity of European labour, albeit expressed in new and different forms, and the significant impact it had upon the market-based strategy for pacification associated with the process of European integration. In what follows in the next chapter, moreover, we explore further changes to the forms of disruptive subjectivity and action that have emerged in the workplace, now in the context of neoliberal Europe's post-2008 crisis period.

3 In search of a new radicalism?

Workers and trade unions during
the European crisis

The experience of economic crisis in Europe from 2008 onwards witnessed a concerted effort to further marginalize organized labour, impose greater market discipline and further a neoliberal agenda. Whilst many of these efforts have been aided by the process and institutions of European integration, thereby consolidating the governing strategy discussed in the previous chapter, this has at the same time prompted the emergence of newly disruptive subjectivities, strategies and actions. It is this process of reinvention, therefore, that we seek to explore in the present chapter.

As we have argued, the post-2008 global financial crisis and post-2010 European crisis can be understood, at least in part, in terms of the continued insubordination or disruptive capacity of European labour. Despite the consistent (and partly successful) assault on wage demands that began in the 1970s, living standards have been bolstered in part by workers taking on excessive personal debt throughout much of the post-1980 period. This, we might argue, represents a form of imperceptible or everyday dissent, at least in the sense that people were increasingly willing to take on more debt than they could afford to repay. Of course, we recognize at the same time that the aim of those who increasingly lent to those unable to repay their debt were doing so because they spotted an opportunity to make money from the impoverishment of others. This does not change the fact, however, that banks were substantially destabilized as a result of the global economic crisis. Further, this lending enabled, in part, a lowering of the social wage, as the immediate effects of that lowering were somewhat mitigated as a result of increased access to credit , thereby acting in part to limit dissent and opposition. Given that an excess of borrowing, moreover, was clearly one of the key factors leading to the financial crisis, we can identify a connection between the heightened debt levels of the post-1980 period and the onset of crisis in 2008. In addition, as we have shown, the imbalances between the core and periphery of the Eurozone, which were central to our understanding of the post-2010 Eurozone crisis, can also be understood in terms of the stubborn unwillingness of workers in the periphery to accept (in full) the productivity demands being made of them in the period leading up to 2010. As testified by Thimann (2015), it was this obstinate refusal which contributed to the imbalances that would eventually underpin the experience of crisis in southern Europe.

Having contributed to the cause of the post-2008 crises, however, European workers came under considerable assault in the wake of those crises. Europe's political and economic elite sought to introduce reforms that would re-stabilize European capitalism, and in doing so adopted a series of measures designed to impose greater market discipline still, and especially to reduce the generosity of the welfare state and push down real wages. This assault, moreover, has been the subject of considerable attention within the (domination-focused) CPE literature (see, for instance, Konzelmann, 2014; Ryner, 2015; Bruff, 2014). The European crisis therefore had severe effects on labour and industrial relations, especially in the most crisis-stricken countries of the European south. Banks and financial institutions were saved 'at the expense of ordinary people's living standard, welfare, and jobs' (Wahl, 2014). As a general tendency, the changes during the European crisis sought to shift the relations of force between organized labour and capital, in favour of the latter (Hofmann, 2015: 201). The structural and organizational resources of trade unions were weakened by rising unemployment and an increase in precarious employment (Huke and Tietje, 2014b). This shift in power relations allowed companies trying to increase their competitiveness in the context of economic crisis to adopt a more confrontational and aggressive stance vis-à-vis labour. The mechanisms of European crisis management at the same time put pressure on wages and employment in the public sector by strengthening austerity-based rules for debt/GDP ratios and current account deficits (for instance, with the Euro Plus Pact, the so-called Six Pack and the Fiscal Compact). To restore competitiveness, national governments – partly pressured by the European institutions – attacked workers' and trade union rights (Erne, 2015: 186). Recommendations by the European Commission in the context of the European semester, the *Memoranda of Understanding* of peripheral countries with the Troika, and policy papers of the DG ECOFIN of the European Commission and the ECB each included explicit demands to limit wage increases by decreasing dismissal protection or changing collective bargaining frameworks (Erne, 2015: 194; Keune, 2015: 477; Phillips, 2011). The use of short-term contracts, in particular, was extended at the expense of permanent contracts (La Porte and Heins, 2016b: 3). Attempts to improve competitiveness by reducing wages were reinforced as central frames of reference for both national and European wage policies (Cruces *et al.*, 2015: 93). National and sector level wage setting was further dismantled and replaced by decentralized, company-level bargaining and a reduction in the number of workers covered by sectoral and regional collective agreements (Keune, 2015: 478–479; Ribeiro, 2016: 14; Bieler, 2015; Schulten, 2014). Meanwhile, some countries strengthened the punitive element of their active labour market policies, with the aim of increasing the disciplinary threat of unemployment (Umney *et al.*, 2015: 16). The tax burden also shifted further from capital to labour, as Value Added Tax (VAT) was increased in some countries whilst taxes on capital were held constant or even decreased (Wahl, 2014).

The role of trade unions also came under pressure during this period. Those channels for influence that had existed prior to the crisis were increasingly closed off unless they functioned as a means to secure stability or to legitimate the advance of further austerity (Erne, 2015: 196; Luque Balbona and González Begega, 2015; Oberndorfer, 2015; Huke and Tietje, 2014b; Nowak and Gallas, 2014: 309). This tendency was less pronounced in the countries with a stronger tradition of corporatist decision-making and with current account surpluses (see Bieling and Lux, 2014: 160). As such, the impact of these reforms was unevenly felt, with labour in the European core being far less affected than labour in the European south. In consequence, 'social mobilisation has turned out to be quite uneven in Europe. Europe-wide co-ordination of trade unions and leftist movements is at best very weak, and a Europe-wide solidarity of the working class is often missing' (Becker *et al.*, 2015: 92–93). This meant that national trade unions were in some instances inclined towards concession-bargaining instead of developing transnational strategies, thereby intensifying the pressure for locational competition. Further, trade unions which had prior to the crisis tended to adopt a so-called 'social partnership' (or class compromise) approach to workplace organizing found it difficult to abandon the model, despite the fact that capital seemed uninterested in compromise. Likewise, trade unions found it difficult to distance themselves from social democratic parties pursuing austerity-based strategies, in part due to the fact that historically they were allies (Huke and Tietje, 2014b; Wahl, 2014).

Nonetheless, the attacks on labour during the Eurozone crisis were far from unchallenged. The increasingly authoritarian implementation of policies left little or no room for interest mediation and trade union lobbying. Labour interests, in consequence, were in part articulated outside established systems of interest mediation, radicalized, and adopted a more critical stance towards the institutions of the European Union. Even trade unions that had traditionally adopted a strongly pro-European stance such as the Irish Congress of Trade Unions (ICTU) or the European Trade Union Confederation (ETUC), increasingly distanced themselves from the EU in the context of its austerity-based system of crisis management (Erne, 2015: 185; Wahl, 2014).

Despite the general reluctance to develop a transnational response, some European trade unions did seek to develop several initiatives which aimed to overcome national fragmentation and to develop a common transnational perspective. The most far-reaching of these attempts was a European general strike which took place on November 14, 2012, although the strike action remained limited to peripheral countries of the European south, while in most countries action was limited to a day of symbolic protests. In participating in the organization of this day of protest and other actions at the European level, the ETUC sought to foster processes of communication across countries. In doing so, however, it proved especially difficult to connect transnational actions to the everyday practice of national trade unions (Bieler and Erne, 2014; Hofmann, 2015). A short-term preoccupation with challenges at the national level assumed priority over cross-border solidarity and the timetables proposed by the ETUC proved largely impracticable (Gumbrell-McCormick and Hyman, 2015: 11).

At the national level, the hardening of the state and the shift in power relations between capital and labour have prompted resignation and defensive individual efforts of 'muddling through' in the context of deteriorating everyday living conditions. The austerity policies also spawned a wave of short-term defensive political and somewhat symbolic general strikes across the EU. Whilst these saw a relatively high level of participation they were nevertheless unable to significantly change policy making. As Nowak and Gallas argue, these strikes nonetheless formed an important part of a 'movement for democratic and social rights at the European level, which is based on a loose alliance of unions, activist networks such as the 'Indignados' and 'Occupy' and political parties of the left' (Nowak and Gallas, 2014: 307). The number of workdays lost by economic sectoral strikes in contrast stagnated during the crisis, despite the fact that a number of strike waves at the national level did occur. As a result, strikes have not tended to be viewed as a core element of the repertoire of protest during the Eurozone crisis (Vandaele, 2014); although that it not to deny that there have been individual cases of importance, especially in the European periphery, representing a significant radicalization of company-level strikes in terms of both duration and the types of actions undertaken by workers (Huke and Tietje, 2014b; see also the case studies documented in the next section). As such, new 'non-standard' labour-related strategies appeared (albeit sporadically) across the EU, including for instance incidents of boss-napping in France, workplace occupations and riots that highlighted the inability of official trade unions to represent the voices or demands of workers. The frequency of protest also increased, especially (but not only) in southern Europe (Ancelovici, 2011: 126; Bailey 2014; Gumbrell-McCormick and Hyman, 2015: 10; Schmalz *et al.*, 2015).

During this crisis period, perhaps the most striking example of labour operating as, in Negri's terms, an 'ineluctable movement which continually breaks the limits of domination and pushes forward the configurations of reality' can be witnessed with the new social movements such as 15-M in Spain or the occupation of Syntagma square in Greece (Negri, 2009: 168). These movements are rarely discussed in academic debates in terms of them being part of national *labour* movements, and indeed are more commonly considered to be removed from both trade unions and workplace issues. Yet, the individual experiences of the participants nevertheless routinely informed these forms of public square occupation-style protests, with many participants being precariously employed workers in the context of austerity. In this sense, movements such as that of the 15-M represent a transformation of the individual experience of workplace grievances into collective demands. From this perspective, the new movements developed a radical-democratic repertoire of action that successfully activated and politicized parts of labour employed in precarious conditions (Huke, 2016b). As Kelly puts it, 'declining conflict at work does not entail declining conflict about work' (Kelly, 2015: 726). In addition to activists with a young and academic profile, public sector users and workers also played an important part in the resistance against austerity (see Chapters 5 and 6). Resistance to austerity and its effects on labour were also articulated in the European core, for instance witnessing the Blockupy protests in Germany, which were conducted mainly by left-wing activists and a limited range of trade union sections and individual trade unionists (Mullis *et al.*, 2016). As such, Blockupy highlighted how traditions of autonomous organizing which has shaped place-based left political cultures in cities such as Frankfurt, and related groups such as the FelS collective in Berlin, have shaped the terms of opposition to austerity in generative ways.

(Featherstone, 2015: 26)

The effects of the European crisis on labour therefore, as we shall see in the subsequent section on our case studies in the United Kingdom and Spain, engendered the development of new resistant subjectivities that were able to deepen the legitimacy crisis of the state, develop and reinvent forms of disruptive action and thereby at least temporarily challenge capital within the production process. Rather than a defeat of labour, we argue, the European crisis is characterized by struggles to shift and reinvent labour strategies due to a change in the political and economic context that hampers 'traditional' trade union strategies (Nowak and Gallas, 2014: 314). As the 'official' trade unions reacted in a 'perplexed and partly paralysed' way (Wahl, 2014), new non-standard labour struggles appeared (as indeed our disruption-oriented approach would lead us to expect). To uncover these new forms of struggle, however, a qualitative analysis of labour-related social conflict is necessary; that is, one that goes beyond the narrow confines of both trade union research and domination-oriented accounts of European integration (Hofmann, 2015: 210; Kelly, 2015: 729; Schmalz *et al.*, 2015: 63). This, we seek to do in the following section, through a discussion of work-related contestation in the UK and Spain during the post-2008 period.

The British post-crisis workplace: precarity and anti-precarity

The response to the onset of economic crisis in the UK from 2008 onwards witnessed both firms and governments adopt a position advocating labour market flexibility and the adaptation of the workforce as the means by which to adjust to the new economic conditions that would facilitate economic recovery and produce a lowering of unemployment. This was, therefore, fundamentally a neoliberal position, in that the economic crisis was interpreted as an illustration of the inability to adopt counter-market or market-correcting measures, meaning that the only available solution was perceived to be the pursuit of heightened competitiveness on the part of the British workers. This, we might expect, given the model of political economy that had been dominant within the UK for much of the post-1979 period. This model included a strong consensus around neoliberal norms across the political elite, and a relatively weak trade union movement that had proved largely unable to challenge successive rounds of neoliberal restructuring. This was especially the case since the symbolic defeat of organized labour in the 1984 miners' strike and the adoption of a series of pieces of anti-trade union legislation during the 1980s, each of which remained in place under the Labour Government in office between 1997 and 2010. It is perhaps unsurprising, therefore, that the experience of crisis in the UK would see both firms and (especially since 2010) the Government grasp the opportunity presented by an increasingly competitive market context to seek to consolidate further market discipline.

In terms of headline figures referring to the rate of unemployment, the post-2008 strategy of labour market flexibilization has been relatively successful. That is, in embracing the pressure arising from market competition, the British economy has witnessed both an intensification of exploitation through the labour market, and an improvement in economic indicators (especially that which measures unemployment). Thus, whilst the British economy experienced an initial rise in unemployment following 2008, one of the notable trends observed in the UK (compared with most other advanced industrial democracies) was a relatively rapid plateauing of the unemployment rate, followed by a relatively successful decline in unemployment from 2014 onwards (Figure 3.1). Further, as Figure 3.2 shows, the United Kingdom has consistently been less affected by problems of unemployment resulting from the global economic crisis than the EU member states on average, and indeed since 2014 has seen unemployment return to pre-crisis levels. This, however, was also accompanied by a number of important trends which sought to undermine the strength of labour within the workplace, and in doing so produce heightened levels of precarity and therefore secure a decline in real wages. Indeed, as Figure 3.3 shows, the proportion of the workforce on temporary or part-time employment as a result of their not being able to find a permanent/full-time job remains considerably above pre-crisis levels. The weakening of labour within the UK economy also ensured that real wages failed to keep up with inflation, as Figure 3.4 highlights.

The post-2008 context therefore witnessed an increase in non-standard (involuntary temporary and part-time employment) and a decline in real wages. In addition, the Coalition Conservative and Liberal Democrat Government elected in 2010 sought to contribute to this lowering of the wage share and destabilization of employees' protection in the workplace through a number of key changes to employment law, most notably the introduction of charges for those seeking

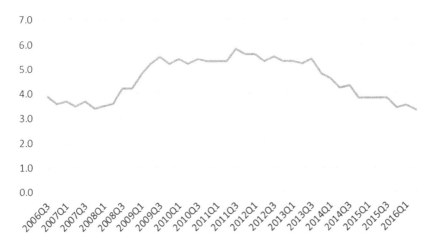

Figure 3.1   UK unemployment rate, 2006–2016.

Source: Eurostat.

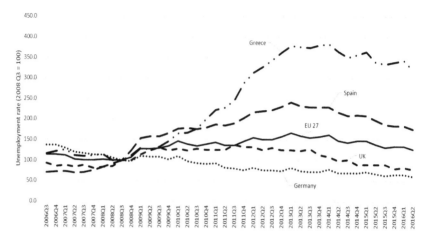

Figure 3.2 Unemployment index (2008 Q3 = 100), 2006–2013.

Source: Eurostat.

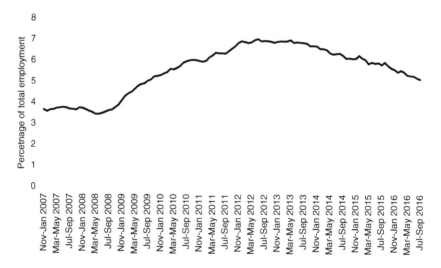

Figure 3.3 Involuntary temporary and part-time employment, as proportion of total employment, UK.

Source: Eurostat.

to make employment tribunal claims, and through an increase in the qualifying period that workers needed to be employed for before they could claim unfair dismissal in an employment tribunal (from one year to two years). In addition, the Conservative Government elected in 2015 further strengthened anti-trade union legislation with the adoption of the Trade Union Act 2016, which (amongst other things) required all strike ballots to reach a minimum 50 per cent turnout. Despite

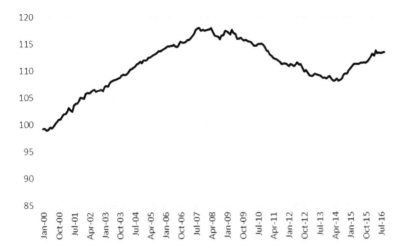

Figure 3.4 Average weekly earnings regular pay: real, seasonally adjusted, 2000 = 100.
Source: Eurostat.

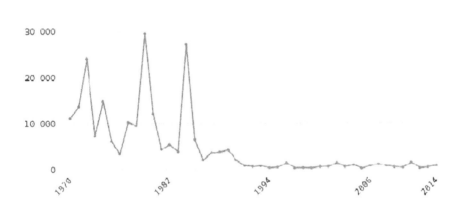

Figure 3.5 Number of working days lost due to industrial disputes (000s), 1970–2014.
Source: Eurostat.

these developments, however, we have also witnessed a range of novel episodes and forms of disruptive worker-led action throughout the post-2008 context.

In the years leading up to 2008, trade union activity had been reduced to a residual level, largely limited to one or two-day routine public-sector strikes, typically around pensions and/or pay (for instance, in 2006 nine unions representing council staff took part in a one-day strike against pension cuts), alongside infrequent flare-ups of discontent at points when industrial relations in specific firms deteriorated in an extraordinary manner (for instance, in August 2005 a dispute over sacked staff in the Gate Gourmet airline food company witnessed 1000 baggage handlers take part in an unofficial strike that lasted over five days and saw Heathrow Airport closed for 48 hours). Thus, as Figure 3.5 shows, since 1984 the number of days lost to strike action had been historically low for a prolonged period of time.

The post-2008 context witnessed a continuation of relatively low levels of official trade union strike action. A number of trends can, however, be observed (see also Bailey 2014). First, the majority of trade union actions during the post-2008 period have been undertaken by public-sector unions attempting to fight battles over redundancies, pay and pensions, oftentimes through one or two-day set-piece strike days and on many occasions without success. Thus, 2010 saw the beginning of a round of such public sector disputes, initially in the civil service over redundancy payments, and throughout 2011 with civil servants, teachers, border staff, local government workers and NHS workers all going on strike in November 2011, and witnessing a repetition of strike action by public sector workers, including by firefighters, care workers, refuse collectors, and librarians in 2012, 2013 and 2014. Trade unions increasingly turned, moreover, to protest events and demonstrations, rather than outright strike activity, in part reflecting the difficulties associated with strike activity as a result of anti-trade union legislation. This could perhaps be most clearly witnessed with the 26 March 2011, March for the Alternative demonstration, which attracted between 250,000 and 500,000 participants and was organized by the Trade Union Congress (on this rising trend of demonstrations, see Bailey, 2016).

More sustained strike actions could also be observed, although these were much less commonplace. For instance, refuse collectors in Edinburgh took action short of strike for 6 weeks in a pay dispute that eventually escalated into an indefinite strike lasting 10 days before a resolution was reached. Leeds also experienced an all-out strike by refuse collectors, this time lasting 11 weeks before a deal was reached. Similarly, the BA Cabin Crew dispute saw three 5-day strikes take place in quick succession during May and June of 2010 over proposals to reduce the number of staff working on flights, before it dragged on into 2011, when an agreement was finally reached with BA agreeing to a pay rise and a reversal of its controversial disciplining of striking cabin crew workers. 2015 also saw a prolonged strike by National Gallery staff that eventually was resolved in October after negotiations led to a deal on pay and conditions, as well as the reinstatement of one of the sacked trade union representatives involved in the dispute.

The initial post-2008 period also witnessed a number of unofficial strikes. Perhaps most prominent of these was the Lindsey Oil Refinery dispute of 2009, which (as we see in more detail in the case study discussed next) saw a wave of wildcat strikes during the year, around the claim that labour migration (facilitated by the single European market) was creating downward pressure upon nationally agreed wages and working conditions. Similarly, an unofficial walkout was staged by prison officers opposed to the privatization of prisons at the end of March 2011.

On a number of occasions, more unconventional means of protest were adopted by disgruntled workers, including workplace occupations. Thus, two key workplace occupations took place in 2009 in two different firms: Visteon and Vestas. In the case of Visteon, which was a company spun off from its parent company, Ford, the announcement that the firm had gone bankrupt and its employees made redundant was made suddenly and without warning in March. This prompted occupations of two of the closing factories, in Belfast and Enfield, eventually resulting in enhanced redundancy payments (which were the main demand of the occupation) and being followed by a lengthy legal dispute over pensions that was only resolved in 2014 (Past Tense, 2009; Unite, 2014). With the Vestas case, the Danish wind turbine manufacturer decided to close one of its factories located in the Isle of Wight. Inspired in part by the actions of Visteon, and witnessing a degree of overlap between those who had participated in solidarity actions in both campaigns, several of the workers in the factory decided to stage an occupation of the Vestas factory (see the case study).

We also witnessed groups of workers or professionals turn to strike (or quasi-strike) action despite historically being reluctant to do so. This, it could be argued, represented an attempt by those actors to seek to exert a voice in a context where more conventional forms of lobbying were increasingly proving unable to prompt a sufficient response from the Government. For instance, in 2012 lawyers, solicitors and barristers began a two-year campaign against the proposed reforms to the funding of legal support for defendants (Legal Aid), including demonstrations outside of courts, and the refusal to take on new cases. Likewise, one of the most high-profile and difficult disputes for the Government was that of the 2015–6 dispute over junior doctors' contracts, which saw the junior doctors stage an increasing number of days and intensity of strike action in opposition to what was viewed as an intransigent approach on the part of the Government to rewriting the junior doctors' contracts. The decision by junior doctors to engage in strike action therefore represented yet another instance whereby staff who were traditionally reluctant to conduct industrial action were moved to the position where they felt no option if they were to be able to express and seek to redress their grievances with the Government.

Finally, with a rise in the number of precarious, temporary/part-time and so-called 'zero hours' jobs we have also a growing trend whereby such workers have managed to organize sustained resistance to their working conditions and wages, despite the notoriously difficult nature of doing so. Thus, care workers working for the firm, Care UK, took part in a 90-day strike over low pay in 2014. Likewise, the Brixton Living Wage campaign of 2014 gained considerable media attention as a result of a combination of a savvy media strategy, eventually resulting in agreement by the employer to a pay rise and climbing down over its attempt to declare the staff 'redundant' following the resolution of the dispute (see the case study). Sports Direct saw a campaign largely led by Unite the Union, which focused on publicizing working conditions within the retail firm and managed as a result to draw attention to the use of zero hour contracts and low pay. This caused a considerable degree of poor publicity for the firm, focusing especially on its founder,

Mike Ashley, and eventually forced the firm to compensate workers who it was found to have systematically paid below the minimum wage. Similarly, 2016 saw a growth in the prominence of small independent trade unions, UVW and IWGB, as they gained considerable media attention for their campaigns around low pay in the so-called gig economy firms, Deliveroo, Uber Eats, and in 2017 in opposition to the retention of tips by restaurants in the major department store, Harrods (Elia and Stone, 2016; Butler, 2017).

As we can see, therefore, the post-2008 context witnessed a combination of both relatively unimaginative (and largely unsuccessful) trade union disputes conducted mainly within the public sector, and a number of more unconventional forms of worker resistance that represented an attempt to reinvent methods of workplace contestation in a national context where official trade union activity has been rendered largely ineffective. This latter process of reinvention, moreover, was particularly conducted by precariously employed workers or by those disgruntled at the heightened effect of market competition. We turn now to consider three of these cases – the Lindsey Oil Refinery dispute, the Vestas occupation, and the Brixton Living Wage campaign. In each case, we see the adoption of more innovative forms of struggle. In turning first to the case of the Lindsey Oil Refinery dispute, moreover, the focus of the action was explicitly targeted at the effects of European integration and the way in which (it was claimed) this undermined the pay and working conditions of those employed within the engineering sector.

Lindsey Oil Refinery: disaffection, populism, refusal

One of the first major signs of workplace rebellion during the post-2008 period came with the Lindsey Oil Refinery dispute. This combined a number of the key forms of disruptive subjectivity that we identified in our earlier discussion: disaffection, vocal demands for equal representation and materialist refusal. These combined, however, in a somewhat contradictory and alarming manner.

The dispute began in January 2009 when 800 engineering construction workers staged an impromptu and unofficial wildcat strike in opposition to what was viewed as an attempt by the East Lindsey Oil Refinery (owned by Total) to employ Italian workers – hired through an Italian contractor, IREM, and in accordance with the European Posted Workers Directive – in a deliberate attempt to undermine the negotiated terms and conditions of existing staff. This initial wildcat strike, moreover, was followed almost immediately by between 3000 and 4000 construction workers staging similar strikes at construction project sites across the country (Ince *et al.*, 2015: 139–40). Around 600 workers gathered outside chemical and steel plants in Teeside, 400 staged a protest outside the former ICI complex at Wilton, and another 200 outside the Corus steel mill near Redcar. The walkouts continued into February, including 700 contractors at the Grangemouth oil refinery and 500 workers at the Longannet power station.

The strike action was unofficial but largely coordinated by members and shop stewards of two unions – Unite and GMB – who joined together to form the Lindsey Strike Committee (Lindsey Strike Committee, n.d.). Thus, although the shop stewards were advised to, and did, resign their posts in order to avoid legal responsibility for the official trade unions – and in doing so formed the Lindsey Strike Committee – they nevertheless clearly retained a number of the trade union contacts that they had already accrued (Ince *et al.*, 2015: 7–8). Using their established skills and contacts, the striking workers were able to mobilize a nationwide protest around what they considered to be a concerted effort to undermine established conditions within the oil refinery industry (interview with strike committee member, May 28, 2014).

In February 2009, a deal was eventually reached, under the facilitation of the government agency ACAS, according to which, 102 new jobs would be made available for 'locally sourced' employees (i.e. 'British workers'). This resolved the dispute, although in June 2009 the issue sparked further industrial unrest as 51 employees were made redundant, apparently as a direct result of their involvement in the February action. This prompted another wave of walkouts, at Lindsey and other plants across the country. Total initially replied by threatening to sack the 647 staff taking place in the unofficial strike action, although eventually a deal was reached in which no member of staff was sacked (including the original 51) and the workforce returned to work (Barnard, 2009: 246–51).

The Lindsey Oil Refinery dispute highlighted the way in which disaffection had emerged and developed both before and after the global economic crisis, particularly as a result of the economic insecurity created by heightened neoliberal market-based competition. In particular, it signalled a move from a passive disgruntlement underpinned by a sense of social injustice to a more active form of disaffection in which both the political elite and establishment institutions of representation (trade unions, parties and the state) were actively opposed and mobilized against. Indeed, the move from disaffection to mobilization could be witnessed in terms of earlier initial steps towards mobilization that had been made around the Staythorpe plant, which had witnessed similar attempts to stage unofficial demonstrations outside the plant, also in opposition to hiring practices (Ince *et al.*, 2015: 146). Two (clearly interconnected) grievances in particular stand out: discontent about the employment of foreign nationals; and the attempt by the employers, Total, to undermine the working conditions and negotiated employment agreements (Ince *et al.*, 2015). As one union activist put it,

> The dispute was about … the threat to jobs. There were hundreds if not thousands of men being summarily dismissed. Cheap labour coming in – European labour we'll call it, for want of a better word. The influx of cheap, European labour, was decimating the construction industry.
> They [the employers] wanted their project finished irrespective of the social damage it caused.
> (interview with LOR strike committee member, 28 May 2014)

Much of the disaffection towards formal institutions, moreover, was rooted in a sense that those institutions were reluctant or unwilling to act representatively. Thus, in the case of trade unions, it was felt that they were unable or unwilling to represent the interests of the workers affected – thereby denying them a voice. For instance, as one of the members of the strike committee declared,

> the unions wouldn't do anything about it … because of the stranglehold of the law … the unions tried to curtail us and say it was nothing to do with them because we were 'mavericks' – but we were elected official representatives.
> (interview with LOR strike committee member, 28 May 2014)

In order to address these issues, therefore, the workforce resorted to mass unofficial strikes. Indeed, it was this willingness to act beyond the established legal framework and especially outside of the institutions of the trade union that highlights the degree to which this might be considered an act reflecting a more widespread sense of disaffection. Indeed, this extended from a sense that trade unions were unresponsive, to include also a similar critique of both parties and the state. In the words of one of the organizers, 'the full-time [trade union] officials and the Labour Government at the time – Mandelson and what-have-you – wouldn't listen to our concerns and complaints' (interview with LOR strike committee member, May 28, 2014).

Alongside this disaffection, the LOR dispute also represented a clear attempt by the oil refinery industry workers to express a voice, and to ensure that it would be heard. In this sense, it marks the emergence of a vocal agent seeking recognition, driven by a view that political elites were not heeding the demands of certain sections of British society. It was also related to a broader concern that British workers' demands were not being represented in the adoption of construction projects that were receiving government support (but that support was not being spent in such a way that it would benefit British employees). For instance, the Staythorpe power station was scheduled to be built, using the contractor Alstom, with Unite claiming that the firm had explicitly stated that it would not hire British employees. In seeking to oppose these moves, moreover, GMB union staged a number of demonstrations, in which it argued that the outright refusal to consider employing British workers represented a form of discrimination (Barnard, 2009: 253). However, in a way that was clearly problematic for the left, and for the minorities it excluded and threatened, this also manifested itself around the slogan that was often repeated within the media – 'British Jobs for British Workers'. Subsequent research found that the use of this slogan was more hotly contested amongst the mobilized workers than was reported at the time. Indeed, the 'British Jobs for British Workers' slogan was not embraced by all the protesting workers, with many subsequently claiming that it represented only one faction within the workforce (see Ince *et al.*, 2015). Nevertheless, the combination of disaffection and demand for recognition clearly underpinned the demands of many of the workforce undertaking strike action, thereby posing a significant challenge to the political elite responsible for overseeing the free movement of labour.

Central to the organization of the Lindsey Oil Refinery dispute was an internet discussion forum, *Bear Facts*, which had been created just a few months earlier in November 2008 by a group of engineering construction workers. This contrasted with the 'official' web forum for the sector, *UK Welder*, which was tightly regulated and monitored by employers. *Bear Facts* therefore represented the use of new technology to produce a worker-run discussion forum that would facilitate discussion amongst employees.

Finally, the militant acts of refusal that were adopted during the course of the dispute were relatively effective in terms of their ability to impose demands upon the employers and the government. Indeed, the 'British Jobs for British Workers' slogan, whilst controversial and having clearly nationalist and potentially racist connotations, was also an effective way of gaining media attention for the protests – although workers themselves eventually began to find the nationalist aspect to the campaign increasingly off-putting (Ince *et al.*, 2009: 149). As we noted, a number of immediate goals were achieved (including the commitment by the employer, Total, to continue to employ local employees and to reinstate those striking workers that had been dismissed), and subsequent attempts by the European Union Commission were made to develop legislation to meet concerns about the impact of posted workers (although these were widely considered to be insufficient).

What is especially noteworthy about the LOR dispute, therefore, is the way in which it prompted a combination of three of our central forms of disruptive subjectivity (disaffection, the search for voice and materialist refusal) to produce a somewhat problematic and troubling series of demands. These considerably problematized, moreover, one of the key elements of the European single market – that is, the free movement of labour. The outcome of the dispute witnessed increased focus at the EU-level on the posted workers issue. Nevertheless, subsequent attempts by the European Union Commission to develop legislation to meet concerns about the impact of posted workers have been largely criticized by trade unions on the grounds that they do not address the substantive problem created by contracting-out and the detrimental impact that this has upon working conditions under conditions of European integration (interview with GMB European Officer, 26 November 2014). The LOR dispute, however, marked an important moment in post-2008 industrial relations and the broader context. In particular, it represented a key moment during which it became apparent that a constituency of British workers harboured growing resentment at what they felt were concerted attempts to undermine their working conditions through the free movement of labour associated with European integration. It also marked perhaps the most visible instance of worker dissatisfaction with the implications of free movement of labour; something which would clearly return to the foreground in 2016 with the Brexit referendum.

Vestas: refusal meets prefiguration

The Vestas occupation also occurred in 2009 and marked a direct response to the disciplining effect of unemployment. The target company, Vestas, a Danish wind turbine manufacturer, announced in July 2009 that it would be closing one of its factories located in the Isle of Wight, selected for closure on the grounds that it was no longer profitable. This was explicitly linked to problems of competitiveness and the need to maximize profit. For instance, the British Wind Energy Association representative, Nick Medic, stated,

> Because of this rapidly rising demand, lots of large corporations are entering the market and *the sector's becoming very, very competitive.* A number of new entrants are coming from India and China, and it could be that the company needs to cut its costs, producing more cheaply and efficiently. […] This is to be expected – they have a clear obligation to shareholders to maximize profits.
>
> (quoted in Phillips, 2009)

In response, and following a series of meetings held by the workers, several employees decided to stage an occupation of the factory, making two key demands: that job losses be avoided by the firm (or redundancy payments improved), and that the government would provide support for the factory (including potentially through nationalization) in recognition that it had environmentalist benefit alongside economic value (Gall, 2011).[1] It is not clear the degree to which the occupation was planned in advance. The political group, the Alliance for Workers Liberty, had seen similar actions work well in the case of the Visteon workers earlier the same year, and sought to encourage the Vestas employees to adopt a similar tactic. However, the employees themselves had also already made moves to organize some form of disruptive action, with one ex-employee claiming 'it was just a spur of the moment kind of thing really', organized by a group of the employees (interview with ex-Vestas employee, 2015; interview with solidarity demonstration organiser, 26 June 2014).

In addition to the occupation, a relatively large solidarity camp was formed outside the factory, and a number of supporting rallies and demonstrations were staged throughout the period of the occupation. Further, as a result of the nature of the campaign it managed to combine support from both the workers' movement and the environmentalist movement. This, combined with significant support from the local community and from those workers who were not taking part in the occupation, meant that the campaign rose to achieve national prominence and considerable support from a broader national labour movement and environmentalist activist community.

As with the Lindsey Oil Refinery dispute, moreover, one of the key grievances expressed by the protesting workers was the apparent refusal of the government to heed any of their complaints or demands. As one ex-employee who took part in solidarity support for the campaign put it,

> We were hoping that the government would do something about it, given that they were going to have to pay benefits to all of us if we couldn't find work. We felt they could have put pressure on Vestas to handle it a bit differently. […] To draw attention to the fact – and I think there was a lot of sympathy as well really. The government could have put conditions on the money that they gave them [Vestas] – they could have made them give jobs to local

people. It just seemed like because they had given them the money they had some responsibility to think about us lot. The general feeling was that we were badly treated because of the fact that they'd got this government grant.
(interview with Vestas ex-employee and participant in the solidarity protests outside the occupation, November 2015)

This combined with a more general concern for the material livelihoods of those who were about to lose their jobs: 'they all had babies and getting mortgages and stuff because they thought they had a secure job for at least ten years [which they had all been told only six months earlier]. [...] Employment on the island is really hard to come by, especially when there's 600 of you looking for jobs at the same time' (interview with Vestas ex-employee and participant in the solidarity protests outside the occupation, November 2015).

The strategy of the campaign focused specifically on the use of a disruptive occupation as a means by which to sanction the firm. As one of the solidarity campaigners put it, 'We reckoned that our chance of success lay in creating a media storm but also in losing Vestas loads and loads of money' (interview with Ed Maltby, solidarity demonstration organizer, June 26, 2014). This was echoed in a number of the speeches given at demonstrations outside the occupation. For instance, one of the demonstrating workers stated, 'we are hitting the company where it hurts – and that is in the pockets. Since we have started out protest the value of the company shares have fallen 6.5 per cent'.[2] The use of a combined strategy of occupations, a solidarity camp outside of the occupation, and a high-profile media strategy resulted in considerable impact – both in terms of generating public support for the campaign and in terms of placing considerable pressure upon Vestas as a result of the adverse publicity that they were experiencing.

As with the Lindsey Oil Refinery dispute of the same year, the Vestas occupation also highlighted the way in which different forms of disruptive subjectivity combined to produce a novel outcome in the post-2008 context. In particular, and in contrast to the LOR dispute, one of the marked novelties of the Vestas protest was the way in which it saw those with a commitment to more radical and prefigurative tactics and methods of dissent – especially those with a background in the radical environmentalist movement – combine with a more conventionally 'materialist' goals of fighting redundancies and seeking improved redundancy compensation in the workplace, as well as mobilizing around the notion of community interests for the Isle of Wight.

In much the same way as had been witnessed in the dispute over the Lindsey Oil Refinery, moreover, those involved in the Vestas protest showed considerable disaffection and disinterest towards a range of political institutions. As such, the protest represented a welcome opportunity to express a voice, and in a way that might have a better chance of being heard: 'it was good at the time just to vent our feelings and show that we weren't just going to disappear. [...] We were angry at the company basically' (interview with Vestas ex-employee and participant in the solidarity protests outside the occupation, November 2015). In addition, the government was widely criticized by the protesting workers on the grounds that it refused to show any sign of accepting their demands for the nationalization of the factory or indeed of offering any other form of support to avoid the job losses or factory closure. For instance, one of the participating workers complained,

> We keep being told by the Government that there are green jobs in the future; that they are going to invest in them; that we are going to have loads of them; but they can't even keep one factory open.[3]

One of the trade unionists involved in the dispute also describes how, at one point during the campaign, Ed Miliband (Environment Minister at the time) addressed the TUC, where he received considerable heckling and opposition on the basis of the Government's refusal to support the Vestas campaign. Similarly, an RMT official criticized Miliband for the failure to substantiate pro-green jobs rhetoric. As the official reports, in dialogue with Miliband, he stated,

> you've just been up on the rostrum and saying you're going to create 50,000 jobs for protection of the environment but you've just arrested two people for doing what you want them to do – fight against climate change …
>
> (interview with RMT trade union official, 25 June 2014)

In terms of attitudes towards formal trade unions, however, there was a somewhat ambivalent attitude amongst the protesting Vestas workers. Most of the workers were un-unionized prior to the occupation. After the protest and occupation began, however, the RMT union actively (and relatively successfully) sought to recruit members. However, at this point there was little that the union could do to support the newly recruited members, other than seek to negotiate improved redundancy payments. Despite this, the solidarity support that was shown by a number of the trade unions and trade union representatives was largely well received – as evinced by the relatively successful recruitment campaign it conducted. As one demonstrator put it, the RMT took the view that,

> we need to get the best deal for the workers in the factory. I tend to think that … they [the RMT] regarded the closure of the plant as much more of a done deal than we [solidarity demonstrators] did. I think that overall the RMT played the best role out of any of the players in the British trade union movement
>
> (interview with Ed Maltby, solidarity demonstration organizer, 26 June 2014)

The views of the employees themselves, however, was more nuanced. Whilst many of them joined RMT at the time, and were therefore largely welcoming of the supportive role that the organization offered, in hindsight, it was not clear the degree to which trade union involvement had been welcomed. As one ex-employee put it, 'I think the unions let us down really, in the end. They promised a lot but I don't think they could have delivered really; it was just wishful thinking' (interview with Vestas ex-employee and participant in the solidarity protests out-side the occupation, November 2015).

To a certain extent, the occupation was unsuccessful. The demand for enhanced redundancy pay was not met, and indeed those who staged the occupation had their initial offer of redundancy pay revoked as they were instead dismissed on the grounds of gross misconduct (rather than redundancy) meaning that they received less compensation than they would otherwise have done. Similarly, the 'demon-stration effect' of the action was minimal, in that no significant additional occupa-tions took place as acts of workplace contention in Britain following the Vestas dispute. This was despite the repeated attempts of a number of left-wing groups to prompt such actions (Gall, 2011). What the Vestas occupation did achieve, however, was a lesson in how to gain the attention of national media and therefore national politicians. This, it was hoped, would have a symbolic effect in terms of the message that it sent to other companies. As one of the interviewees put it,

> I think it's been a success in a way, in terms of other firms thinking, 'we wouldn't want to do that; we wouldn't want that kind of publicity and upset'. So, in a way it's kind of showing that you can push people but when they get pushed too far they respond and fight back a bit. […] I don't know if it achieved much […] but I'm hoping it had that positive effect anyway.
> (interview with Vestas ex-employee and participant in the solidarity protests outside the occupation, November 2015)

Through the innovative use of occupation as a strategy, and an alliance of employ-ees, environmentalists, labour activists and community groups, the issue of redun-dancies and government intervention was put firmly on the political agenda. This was sometimes an uneasy coalition of constituents, with reports of clashes between environmentalist activists more used to an alternative scene clashing with those of a more workerist bent seeking to avoid alienating the local community and workforce. Likewise, for some of the ex-employees there was a sense that their own protest had been 'hijacked' by the arriving full-time activists. Nevertheless, it cannot be denied that the sometimes-strained coalition of actors was effective in putting the issue on the national agenda, witnessing considerable media reports of the protest.

Further, the strategy of occupying buildings – whilst rarely (if at all) used in subsequent workplace struggles within the UK – did nevertheless go on to become an important element in subsequent campaigns around austerity meas-ures, especially with regard to university tuition fees, welfare cuts (UK Uncut), the attempt to highlight inequality (Occupy movement), and housing struggles. In this sense, the Vestas occupation – and especially those forming the solidarity camp in support of the occupation (many of whom would go on to participate in subsequent anti-austerity struggles) – represented an important opportunity for both lesson-learning and the formation and consolidation of networks of anti-austerity campaigners. This does, however, raise the question of why the strategy was relatively unsuccessful in the case of Vestas. In particular, it highlights the difficulty faced by workers mobilizing in the workplace in a context character-ized by a high number of redundancies, low political support for state interven-tion, unwillingness on the part of the firm to continue production, and (perhaps most importantly) a lack of vulnerability by firms that are anyway closing their plants to campaigns that are largely focused on reputation damage. Indeed, in a number of subsequent cases, it was this susceptibility to high-profile campaigns focused on reputational damage which would lead to more significant successes. We turn now to the Brixton Ritzy Living Wage Campaign to consider this strat-egy in more detail.

Brixton Ritzy Living Wage Campaign: from precarity to publicity

At the beginning of 2014 cinema workers employed by Brixton Ritzy Cinema (a branch of Picturehouse) announced that following negotiations between their union (BECTU) and the employer, in which they had been seeking a rise in pay from their then rate of £7.24 to the London Living Wage, which had at that time recently been increased to £8.80, they would be entering into a campaign for a wage rise that would match the Living Wage. The Living Wage is an attempt to calculate the minimum hourly rate that an employee would need to earn in order to live above the poverty threshold (plus 15 per cent to cover unforeseen events). It is set by the Living Wage Foundation, and in London is calculated by the Greater London Authority. Having failed to negotiate a pay rise to the liv-ing wage rate, BECTU and Picturehouse announced that they would be entering mediation through the mediating organization, ACAS.

In seeking to place pressure on Picturehouse, the campaigning cinema staff sought immediately to draw attention to the reputation of the firm, and particu-larly its image as an arthouse and independent cinema, which the workers believed should be matched by a commitment to guard against the low pay and poverty of its employees. As one of the campaign leaflets put it,

> Recently bought out by Cineworld, the Ritzy is one of the highest grossing Picturehouse cinemas. Pitching themselves as an ethical enterprise, they host the Human Rights Film Festival, sell fair-trade chocolate and support chari-ties, whilst not currently paying a living wage to their staff.
>
> (quoted in Brixton Blog, 2014a)

Having failed to reach an agreement in the ACAS negotiations, however, BECTU announced in March 2014 that it would be balloting its members with a recom-mendation that they vote to take industrial action (Brixton Blog, 2014b). In doing so, moreover, they promoted what would become a highly successful social media campaign in support of the living wage. This revolved around both a Twitter and Facebook page which rapidly gathered widespread support and a large number of followers (the Twitter page currently [January 2017] has over 2,900 followers, and the Facebook page has over 6000 'likes'). The ballot result saw overwhelm-ing support amongst the BECTU members for strike action, receiving an 85 per cent yes vote, following which the workers staged their first strike day on 11 April 2014, closing down the cinema for the day (Brixton Blog, 2014c). This was followed by a subsequent 2-day strike set to coincide with the Easter weekend, and another day of strike action the following week, and another strike day in early June which was set to be the sixth day of strike action (Brixton Blog, 2014e).

Throughout the dispute, the location of the cinema and the background of many of its staff both went in the workers' favour. The Ritzy is central to Brixton, and opens out onto a large square (Windrush Square), making it possible for the striking workers to gain the attention of passing customers and residents. Indeed, the striking workers were themselves aware of this benefit (interview with striking worker, May 2016).

The staff, moreover, were predominantly young and many were recent graduates, fitting closely with what is commonly depicted as the demographic of the 'precariat'. The energy of the protesting workers, combined with the location, therefore created an opportunity for highly visible carnivalesque scenes that enabled the dispute to gain considerable attention (see, for instance, Brixton Blog, 2014d). This, combined with the reputation that the cinema had sought to cultivate, of being independent of corporate media and in support of human rights and social justice, compounded the pressure that the living wage dispute was able to place upon the firm.

In addition, the profile of the dispute was such that it increasingly gained the attention and support of media celebrities, adding further to the leverage that the striking workers could place upon Picturehouse. Support was forthcoming from Monty Python's Terry Jones (who supported the workers' call for a boycott of the cinema when it hosted a televised screening of the Monty Python's O2 Arena performance), Eric Cantona, Ken Loach, and Russell Brand.

At the end of July, BECTU announced that it had brokered a deal with Picturehouse. Whilst this did not secure a living wage, it did include a backdated pay rise to £8 per hour and a commitment on behalf of the employer to re-open negotiations around a move towards a living wage, scheduled to take place two years later (June 2016). BECTU recommended that the staff accept the newly negotiated deal, and put it to a staff vote. The staff, however, narrowly rejected the offer on the grounds that it was insufficiently close to the London living wage – with those who voted to accept the offer doing so largely on practical grounds and because both stamina and financial resources were running low (Brixton Blog, 2014f; interview with striking worker, May 2016).

This prompted a second vote on a renewed offer the following month, this time including a commitment from Picturehouse not to victimize any of the staff or trade unionists who had participated in the action (interview with ex-trade union representative, September 2016). This final offer was eventually successful and the campaign was ended. By this point the workers had taken part in 13 strike days in total, normally chosen to maximize disruption – for instance, by choosing weekends or key dates when live events were taking place and being screened by the cinema, such as was the case with the Monty Python event.

They decided times that would impact on the cinema, and also one time when there was a demonstration or march in town so we could join that. ...if you went on strike on Tuesday morning it obviously wouldn't have as much effect as a Saturday daytime because the cinema's got loads of people.

(interview with strike participant, May 2016)

In a twist to the dispute, however, the same month that the living wage campaign was ended and a new wage agreed for staff (October 2014), Picturehouse announced that it intended to make 20 of its 93 members of staff at the cinema redundant. Staff were told that as a result they would need to re-interview for their jobs (creating a risk that more than 20 staff would lose their jobs, as there was no guarantee even that a fixed number of existing staff would be re-hired). This was explicitly connected by Picturehouse to its need to bring down costs due to the increase in pay it had agreed to, despite the fact that it had earlier committed itself not to change working practices (Brixton Blog, 2014g). In response, BECTU again opened up a ballot for industrial action; and again, received widespread support across social media and amongst celebrities who had heard about the campaign due to its visibility. In particular, journalist and author Will Self took up the cause in London's Evening Standard newspaper, writing that people should join in a boycott of the Ritzy. The scale of opposition was such, however, that within three days the CEO of the group which owned Picturehouse, Cineworld, had announced a climbdown and that there would be no redundancies at the Ritzy (Tobin and Spanier, 2014).

Overall, the campaign was considered a success. Whilst the final goal of a living wage was not achieved, the campaign did lead to a significant pay rise, and there was a successful defence of the workforce once the firm sought to impose a punishment following the resolution of the dispute. The campaign also raised considerable attention for the London living wage, raising the prominence of the demand in general (see, for instance, recent demands by Deliveroo workers and by Uber-Eats, in 2016, both of whom had the London Living Wage as their explicit demand, and who were also workers with a 'precariat' profile, working on piece work or faced with highly flexible working conditions). Indeed, one of the central goals for many of the participants in the strike was to highlight the capacity to challenge the experience of precarity. In the words of one striking worker,

We were striking for the principle of the living wage, but also to show that people in low paid jobs don't just need to accept low pay and can campaign for better conditions.

(interview with strike participant, 23 September 2016)

This sentiment could also be witnessed with the return to strike activity in a subsequent living wage campaign launched in 2016. This latter campaign (which at the time of writing is ongoing) saw a considerable escalation of the dispute, this time to include workers at Crouch End Picturehouse, Picturehouse Hackney and

Picturehouse Central (all in London), and with the ballot votes securing a huge yes vote of over 95 per cent in Picturehouse cinemas in Hackney and Central.

Perhaps the most important element contributing to the success of the 2014 action was the strong degree of unity that was achieved. This was largely due to the high commitment amongst the workforce to debating and discussing collectively the strategy, and a strong commitment to acting collectively. As one interviewee put it,

> Everyone, pretty much the entire workforce, didn't cross the picket line and therefore most people were on the picket line so most of the staff were really involved; on strike days there was a lot of involvement; and people would bring different stuff to the picket line (that was nice). [...] We had a quite regular meeting at work during the strike period, not usually to organize strikes; mainly to discuss what was going on with negotiations and stuff, but also planning [...].
>
> (interview with strike participant, May 2016)

In addition, the ability to raise considerable publicity against the Cinema, in a context where its reputation was based on an 'ethical', 'independent' and 'non-corporate' image, represented a considerable advantage for the campaign. Indeed, the inability of the cinema to control the message and image that it was associated with in the media was one of the most impressive achievements of the campaign. This was significantly boosted by a successful social media campaign, as well as high-profile support amongst a number of journalists and in the national press. In addition, the customer base for the cinema were also highly supportive, of both the campaign and of the idea that the cinema should live up to its ethical reputation. This support was most evident in that the boycott was widely supported by a good range of local customers – to the point that even after the boycott had finished staff were still being asked by customers whether it was acceptable for them to attend the cinema, or whether in doing so they would be breaking the boycott.

In terms of the relationship between the workers and the trade unions, one of the key elements of the campaign was the willingness of the official union to encourage worker participation and for the union members to guide the actions themselves rather than rely on trade union officials to dictate strategy to them (interview with ex-trade union representative, September 2016; interview with strike participant, May 2016). Indeed, the only point at which there emerged a tension between the formal union apparatus and the striking workers who it was representing was over the first BECTU recommendation to accept the deal, which was rejected by a vote of the workforce. Whereas BECTU sought to secure agreement for the deal, many of the workers were inclined to continue the dispute until they achieved the living wage. This created a degree of ambivalence, therefore, as BECTU had been consistently supportive of the cinema staff's mobilization, and indeed many of the interviewed workers highlighted the autonomy granted to the striking workers themselves by the official union apparatus, as one of the key features that contributed to the success of the industrial action. As one worker put it,

You always hear about how unions are really bureaucratic and they never let you do anything but I'd never had that experience and then suddenly I kind of saw a tiny bit of that because they were saying 'I think you should take this offer' and I was thinking 'but surely? Why are you imposing that on us because we should just be able to vote and you shouldn't be influencing us' [...] But obviously, they have more of a knowledge and experience of how negotiations work and what happens, so I suppose I was being just a bit naïve.

(interview with strike participant, May 2016)

Summary

The post-2008 UK workplace struggles, therefore, highlight a number of important lessons in terms of the capacity for, and possibility of, disruptive action. Workers faced increased disciplinary pressure emanating from heightened market integration. At the same time, however, contestation of these pressures, and especially their contestation through new and innovative means became increasingly apparent. This was witnessed both in terms of the increased use of non-conventional means of disruption, for instance in the factory occupations of 2009, the increased use of public demonstrations, and the tendency to focus on reputation damage. It was also evinced by the move by traditionally refusal-reluctant actors, such as barristers and doctors, to take part in industrial action or quasi-industrial action. In the case of the Lindsey Oil Refinery, moreover, the focus was explicitly targeted towards the direct effect of European integration upon working conditions, in many ways pre-empting the Brexit vote which was to take place seven years later. In this sense, we have seen what have been at times more 'imperceptible' forms of dissent becoming visible in unpredictable and contradictory ways.

Workplace restructuring and the reinvention of workplace struggle in Spain: 'They want to get rid of everything'

'They want to get rid of everything.'

(Slogan of trade union protests in Spain)

As with the United Kingdom, but with considerably more intensity and visibility, industrial relations in Spain changed significantly during the European crisis. Key elements to this included dramatic increases in unemployment, the urgent need to find an alternative growth model following the collapse of the real estate-led model of growth, a drastic erosion of workers' and trade union rights, and a decline in trade unions' ability to achieve influence within the Spanish economy (Huke and Tietje, 2014b). The European institutions, and especially the mechanisms of crisis management adopted during the crisis, have each functioned as key driving forces during this process. In response to these developments, however, we have also seen a move by both organized and less organized workers to reinvent forms of struggle, including through a combination of (symbolic) general strikes, militant unlimited strikes and forms of social movement unionism and community organizing. In what follows we summarize these trends, highlighting the degree of the assaults upon workers within the Spanish economy, and the responses witnessed within that context.

As has been widely observed, therefore, the effects of austerity policies on industrial relations in Spain were among the harshest throughout the EU. In 2007, the real estate-led growth model collapsed due to a shortage in credit in the aftermath of the subprime crisis in the USA and over-indebted Spanish households (especially in the form of mortgages). At the same time, the car industry suffered cutbacks in production as demand decreased. Mass dismissals – facilitated by the precarious nature of employment in the pre-crisis period – as well as business closures and the destruction of jobs in the construction sector each contributed to a massive increase in unemployment. Under pressure from foreign investors and the instructions of the EU, the Spanish governments of both the social democratic PSOE (until 2011) and the subsequent right-wing Popular Party (from 2011 onwards) introduced a series of far reaching austerity measures. Austerity programmes, combined with the effect of the economic crisis, in turn resulted in intensified everyday precarity across the country (Haas and Huke, 2015; Navarro and Clua-Losada, 2012). The industrial relations of Spain, which prior to the crisis had been characterized by institutionalized cooperation with strong elements of ritualized yet largely symbolic forms of confrontation, transformed into a system of fragmented symbolic cooperation with elements of (spontaneous, but genuine) confrontation (Huke and Tietje, 2014b). Unemployment escalated rapidly, from 7.9 per cent in June 2007 to 24.5 per cent in June 2014. In addition, 9.2 per cent of employees (57.4 per cent of part-time employees) were underemployed (that is, working less number of hours than desired) and precarious employment rapidly substituted formerly secure contracts. Indeed, one of the more commonly noted trends in Spain's post-crisis labour market is the chronic lack of stable employment that emerged in the wake of the crisis. As a result, '[s]ince 2007, one of Spain's greatest structural problems has been its inability to create stable, productive, and qualified jobs' (Carrasco Carpio, 2016).

One of the consequences of these detrimental trends in the Spanish labour market was for foreign and domestic workers to begin to leave Spain in search of work elsewhere, highlighting the degree to which disaffection and disengagement began to set in amongst the workforce of Spain (Carrasco Carpio, 2016). At the same time, the trade unions were unable to overcome their organizational weaknesses in informal, precarious and restructured fields of work, which were precisely those areas of work that were becoming increasingly prevalent as a result of the crisis (Köhler and Calleja Jiménez, 2013: 4–6). Insolvencies and the increased fragility of companies during the crisis both acted to weaken the potential for trade unions to pursue offensive strategies (Huke and Tietje, 2014b). It is in this sense, therefore, that we consider the balance of forces between labour and capital to have shifted significantly towards the latter as a result of the crisis (Haas and Huke, 2015).

This relative weakening of labour could be witnessed in two stages. Under the PSOE Government trade unions were weakened by a wide range of structural reforms adopted specifically to alter the nation's industrial relations (as witnessed with the adoption of Royal Decree-Law (RDL) 10/2010 and Ley 35/2010); and subsequently under Mariano Rajoy's PP Government we witnessed the adoption of a series of measures that would produce a decline in formal influence (such as RDL 3/2012 and Ley 3/2012). These measures each led to a reduction in legal rights against individual and collective dismissals, whilst increasing the possibility for employers to introduce flexible and fixed-term contracts.

As a result of each of these measures, Spain's system of collective bargaining was changed fundamentally. Before the crisis, Spanish industrial relations were characterized by high rates of collective bargaining coverage. This had been sustained largely by an automatic extension of collective agreements (*erga omnes*) and the legal requirement that collective agreements must remain in force until they are superseded by an additional newly adopted agreement. It was also supplemented by a commitment to national-level social dialogue (Cruces *et al.*, 2015). Following the onset of crisis in 2008, and especially from 2010 onwards, however, collective bargaining became increasingly decentralized, particularly being associated with a rise in firm-level agreements. In addition, the terms under which collective bargaining agreements were to be reached was itself reformed so that these would now expire if they had not been renewed within one year of their agreed term (thereby ending the system of automatic renewal), thereby ensuring that employers had increased opportunities to suspend collective bargaining agreements.

Trade unions therefore experienced a prolonged assault from both firms and the government. Previously established forms of social dialogue broke down, as state apparatuses and employers adopted an increasingly confrontational stance vis à vis the trade unions (Campos Lima and Artiles, 2011; Huke, 2013b). As one trade union activist put it,

> We [...] are the dam in defence of social and working right, no? And exactly because the governments and the markets know we are that wall [...] they are trying to tear down the dam and [...] if you read the papers there are daily attempts to discredit [us].
>
> (interview with CCOO trade unionist, 11 November 2013, authors' translation)

This included more explicit forms of repression, including legislation to restrict and criminalise the activities of both social movements and trade unions, as well as media propaganda campaigns designed to delegitimate trade unions (Köhler and Calleja Jiménez, 2014: 376).

Overall, the changes introduced during the crisis tended to be successful in their effort to 'eliminate the system that we had consolidated in matters of labour relations in this country' (interview with CCOO trade unionist, 11 November 2013, authors' translation). As such, the institutional and structural power resources of trade unions were systematically weakened, their ability to influence either public policy or decisions at the level of the firm were both significantly reduced, and each of these measures contributed towards an overall lowering of both wages and social cohesion (Cruces *et al.*, 2015: 92).

Trade unions in Spain found it difficult to react to this range of attacks on what had been an established system of industrial relations. Whilst 2010 saw the two largest trade union federations – CCOO and UGT – each distance themselves from the pro-austerity social democratic PSOE Government, this was done with considerable reluctance on the part of the trade union leadership, not least because of the close links with PSOE that both unions had enjoyed prior to the crisis (Huke and Tietje, 2014b). In the view of one of the trade unionists that we interviewed, 'until that moment, the Government had not legislated anything against the workers' (interview with UGT trade unionist, March 6, 2014, authors' translation). As another interviewee added, the trade unions

> had not prepared or maintained workers for mobilization and nor had they encouraged the development of critical consciousness. […] It was thought that these reforms would not be introduced by a socialist Government. Once the socialist Government did attack the established system of industrial relations, they caught us wrong-footed […], there was no preparedness for confrontation.
> (interview with CCOO trade unionist, 17 July 2012,
> authors' translation)

This inability to pose effective opposition could also be witnessed with the announcement by the PSOE Government in February 2010 that it intended to increase the pension age. This was met with fiercely hostile declarations and rhetoric on the part of the trade union leadership, but more concrete mobilization was limited to sporadic action days with limited participation. This, again, was perceived to reflect a lack of preparedness on the part of the trade union movement:

> We got used to a period of prosperity and there was not the organization and the whole of the workers did not have the view […] or attitude that we were passing from a period of prosperity to a period of cuts and that it was necessary to mobilize against them.
> (interview with CCOO trade unionist, 17 July 2012,
> authors' translation)

The relatively low capacity of the two major Spanish trade unions to engage in effective opposition to the assault upon this established system of industrial relations was also in part due to the patterns of mobilization that they had engaged in prior to the crisis. This was largely characterized by frequent, yet largely symbolic, forms of protest in the pre-crisis years, as well as a growing gap between members of the workforce and the trade unions claiming to represent them. As one CCOO trade unionist noted, "there was no social mobilization on the street strong enough to say, 'let's not make a pact, let's go to the street'" (interview with CCOO trade unionist, 17 July 2012, authors' translation). In consequence, both CCOO and UGT opted for a gradual approach to mobilizing (which proved largely unable to meet the challenges being faced in the post-2008 context) (Montoya, 2012).

The two major trade unions also remained committed to largely cooperative strategies. This led them to agree to social pacts on both pensions and wages, as well as collective bargaining, which were widely perceived as having been too much of a compromise, thereby contributing to a further reduction in their legitimacy in the eyes of many within Spanish society (Gago, 2013). In a spiral-like manner, this decline in legitimacy on the part of trade unions further consolidated their inability to garner popular support for more oppositional or confrontational strategies, therefore contributing to a further decline still in terms of the capacity of the trade unions to offer effective opposition to the reforms with which they were faced (Luque Balbona and González Begega, 2015: 289–290).

As the legal obligations upon firms to enter into collective bargaining agreements were removed, so at the same time the willingness of firms to enter into negotiations with trade unions over such agreements also declined (Fernández Rodriguez *et al.*, 2016: 6). Whilst it remained possible in many instances to retain a commitment to sectoral-level bargaining (largely as a result of both protests and a considerable willingness to 'compromise' on the part of the trade unions), the effect of these agreements was to create a tendency for the further decentralization of the collective bargaining system as the activities of the trade unions increasingly needed to be focused upon firm-level negotiations in order to ensure that sectoral agreements were adhered to. As a result, and as one trade union official put it, 'it is now the company level where the conflicts are' (interview with UGT trade unionist, March 6, 2014, authors' translation). Firms (and especially small and medium sized ones) increasingly attempted,

> to opt out of higher level agreements, or to downgrade negotiated conditions of employment, and are beginning to test the resolve and capacity of a union and its local representatives to counter this. Unions see a significant change in attitude, but there are some sectors where dialogue and informal relations remain strong.
>
> (Fernández Rodriguez *et al.*, 2016: 7)

It was in this context that both employees and trade union officials adopted a somewhat defeatist and individualist response, witnessing disaffection with existing institutions of labour representation continue to rise. As one trade union official described, members of the workforce began to adopt what he referred to as,

> a very 'corporate' position [...]: I try to solve my problem. I do know it is a general problem, but I isolate myself and try to talk to my employer to protect me. It is difficult for them to understand, that they cannot maintain autarkic islands, closed, isolated [...] And in exchange I allow that my own employer create precarious labour all around me, especially with young people. New precarious employment that co-exists with my high level of protection. [...] The trade union tries to avoid it, but sometimes it cannot avoid it. Let's be honest. [...] It's like that [...]. And in the end [...] they throw them out or close them down. Because they are not competitive.
>
> (interview with CCOO trade unionist, 6 March 2014,
> authors' translation)

Unemployment, precarity and impoverishment during the height of the European crisis in Spain each increased the need on the part of workers to accept any form of employment offered to them, thereby creating further pressure to undermine and subvert existing collective agreements (Fernández Rodriguez *et al.*, 2016: 2). Again, in the words of a trade union activist,

> It is now very difficult to even reach a thousand Euros. Because you have a continuous battle [over collective bargaining and the fulfilment of collective agreements] in the companies and what they offer you are part-time contracts, contracts [...] where you have to work more hours than you are really paid and with salaries very inferior to the agreement.
> (interview with CCOO trade unionist, 11 November 2013, authors' translation)

As trade union activists sought to respond to these developments, moreover, they faced a number of serious obstacles relating to declining membership (as the numbers of unemployed rose, therefore witnessing a decline in membership, with increased personal hardship also leading on occasion to an inability to keep up with union membership dues) (interview with CCOO trade unionist, 11 November 2013, authors' translation). This was accompanied by an additional problem associated with the rapidity with which austerity measures were being introduced, creating a sense that unions were overwhelmed and that however much union energy was directed to fending off those measures the level of activity could never be sufficient. As two different trade unionists highlighted,

> If you enter the loop of the crisis [...] it absorbs you. Absolutely, right? All these processes of conflict absorb you, right? [...] Since May 2010 we have not stopped. I am going to a minimum of two demonstrations a week.
> (interview with UGT trade unionist, 6 March 2014, authors' translation)

> Since the crisis started it goes non-stop [...]. There is not a single moment of calm [...]. You hardly gather material because it is always going forward.
> (interview with UGT trade unionist, 19 July 2012, authors' translation)

In such a context, therefore, labour activists were faced with both the necessity of reinventing strategies of disruption, but also significant obstacles to doing so (as we have sought to highlight). One measure that was adopted was the tactic of a general strike. However, this was used in a somewhat faltering manner. Despite the PSOE Government announcing further austerity measures in May 2010 (including a 5 per cent cut in salary for all public-sector workers), the trade unions argued against the need for a general strike. Instead, a strike of public-sector workers was called for 8 June 2010. The same month, the PSOE Government also unilaterally imposed a number of measures designed to increase the degree of flexibilization of the labour market, including through a reform that would significantly reduce dismissal protection (Clua-Losada and Ribera-Almandoz, 2017). CCOO and UGT did now move to call a general strike, which took place on 29 September 2010. But in doing so, trade union leaders explicitly stressed that the strike was not designed to be in opposition to the *Zapatero* Government, but was rather intended to be a 'wakeup call' for the PSOE to change its course (Huke, 2014: 88). It also proved 'very difficult to get the strike going' (interview with CCOO trade unionist, July 17, 2012, authors' translation).

Following the general strike of September 2010, it took the CCOO and UGT more than one year to call the next general strike. This was in response to the PP Government, elected in 2011, following its unresponsiveness to demands that it reverse the labour market reforms that it introduced in February 2012. In response, therefore, the trade unions eventually called for a second general strike to take place on 29 March 2012. This was followed on 14th November 2012 by a further general strike, this time as part of a wider European day of action called by the European Trade Union Confederation (ETUC). What was interesting about the general strikes of 2012, however, was that these were the first strike movements for a large number of years where trade unions, social movements and neighbourhood organizations managed to cooperate in a stable and continuous manner, thereby furthering both the ability to stage the general strikes and to ensure their (partial) success (cf. Montoya, 2012: 156).

In addition to the staging of general strikes, trade unions and workers also tried to increase their capacity for struggle through attempts to engage with broader community-based campaigns, including especially by working with social movements or neighbourhood assemblies (Huke and Tietje, 2014a). One key element of this strategy was the use of the public arena as a means by which to draw attention to grievances and instances of resistance. Workers threatened by closures (for instance, of both shipyards and mines) or massive reductions in employment (such as witnessed in the financial sector) participated actively in public protests (Köhler and Calleja Jiménez, 2014: 374). Apart from in the areas of education and healthcare (see Chapter 5 and 6) the most vivid instances of this tendency were seen with the protests of the striking Asturian miners in 2012, who staged their strike in opposition to cuts in subsidies which in turn threatened their employment (Vega García, 2013). The nature of Spain's austerity phase was such that, whereas strikes have at different times been unpopular due to associated inconveniences for the public, these strikes now came to receive considerable and widespread public support. This could be seen, for instance, in the case of the strike held by the public cleaning service in Madrid in November 2013. Even struggles in private enterprises were able to achieve public recognition and support. Perhaps most clearly illustrating this trend, workers striking against collective dismissals and plant closures by *Coca-Cola* called for a boycott of its products (under the slogan, 'If Madrid doesn't produce, Madrid doesn't consume'), which received widespread attention and which it was claimed resulted in the reduction of sales of *Coca-Cola* in favour of its competitor, *Pepsi* (ECD, 2014).

Unconventional and innovative forms of struggle were also adopted and developed by more radical and smaller trade unions (Roca and Diaz-Parra, 2016). Perhaps the clearest example of this trend could be seen with the actions of the regional federation (SAT) from Andalusia. This trade union, traditionally focused on organizing rural agrarian workers, operated in cooperation with social movement activists in order to produce a combined and innovative response to the austerity measures experienced during the period. This included occupations of abandoned property and farms by rural workers. Furthermore, it witnessed publicly looted products of basic necessity from supermarkets, conducted as acts of civil disobedience to highlight the effects of the crisis as it was being felt by large parts of the local population. While support within the population for these actions tended to be high, the activists of the SAT nevertheless faced considerable police repression, drastic fines and even in some cases prison sentences (Huke and Tietje, 2014a; Roca Martínez and Díaz Parra, 2013).

Perhaps the most vivid means by which labour strategies were reinvented during the European crisis in Spain, however, was that seen with the eruption of the 15-M movement. The occupations of public squares in 2011 and the subsequent rise of neighbourhood assemblies and the 15-M as a social movement represented a break in the protest cycle between the old and the new. The 15-M assemblies served as nodal points for ongoing protests. The movement produced a rupture with the permissiveness and passiveness that had characterized large parts of Spanish society in the first years of the crisis (Huke, 2016). The movement – despite its variety – mainly consisted of young Spaniards with academic training, whose future prospects had rapidly deteriorated during the crisis. Although work and unemployment were key issues of the movement, 15-M did not 'mobilize people as workers but rather as those who are proletarianized and exploited in every aspect of their lives – at risk of foreclosure and unemployment, diminishing futures, increasing debts, and accelerated dependence on a system that is rapidly failing [...]' (Dean, 2012: 57).

15-M also represented a somewhat contradictory mix of both pragmatism and prefiguration. In one sense, 15-M expressed concrete political demands that were social democratic in nature; seeking equality, political inclusion and material concessions. At the same time, however, the empty signifiers it used (such as 'real democracy'), the fundamental rejection of traditional forms of representation (parties and trade unions, but also 'identitarian' leftist collectives) and its adoption of particular social forms (assemblies, politics in the first person, consensus-based decisions and the collectivization of individual social crises) all paved the way for an unprecedented extension of prefigurative radical politics (Morell, 2012). The occupations of the squares sparked an intensive process of grassroots community organizing in Spain and contributed significantly to the creation or revitalization of neighbourhood assemblies as well as thematic working groups and collectives (for instance, in health, education and especially housing). Its 'destituent' moments – the delegitimation of the existing forms of institutionalized representation as well as the activation and inclusion of formerly disengaged, disaffected or disinterested parts of the population – acted as a breeding ground for subsequent alternative movements to emerge, including the movement against the privatization of hospitals and health centres in Madrid (*marea blanca*), protests in the education sector (*marea verde*), and unconventional forms of radical strike action from below (e.g. Panrico, Coca-Cola, Movistar technicians, teachers strike on the Balearic Islands).

We also see during this period the attempt to incorporate new methods adopted by prefigurative radicals. Initially, the trade unions were reluctant to adopt new methods. For instance, CCOO and UGT both showed considerable scepticism towards 15-M at its initiation. As one official put it,

> 15M [...] claimed 'I also represent the citizens and the workers. I am also a legitimate social interlocutor.' [...] It is like the chair game, where you have four persons and three chairs; that is to say that no one wants someone else, another organisation, another association, or another collective, to occupy the space that you already represent.
>
> (interview with CCOO trade unionist, 17 July 2012,
> authors' translation)

In addition to caution on the part of the trade union movement, parts of 15-M itself were equally at times mutually wary of trade unions, which tended to be viewed as too willing to play the part of institutional 'insiders'. As austerity politics continued, however, both 15M and the trade unions gradually overcame their mutual distrust (Roca and Diaz-Parra, 2016). This witnessed, for instance, the major trade unions, CCOO and UGT each adopting more grassroots-based and prefigurative forms into their political repertoire (Huke and Tietje, 2014a), albeit with a degree of pragmatism characterized by 'cautious and partially diverging efforts to revise and modify the prevailing strategies' (Bieling and Lux, 2014: 158).

In summary, many of the general tendencies identified by industrial relations and trade unions scholars during the European crisis can be observed exemplarily in Spain. This includes: a closure of established forms of social dialogue and an exclusion of trade unions from policy making, fundamental changes in the system of industrial relations that shift the balance of power between labour and capital in favour of the latter, and an increase in the importance of symbolic general strikes for trade union strategies. It also includes a divergence of labour strategies between, on the one hand, and concession bargaining and radical, non-standard forms of trade union action, on the other. In this sense, developments in Spain reflect a more general trend witnessed during the crisis, in which we see *both*, 'radical or conflictual responses, and [...] a reinforcement of cooperation and partnership; and often the two types of response have been paradoxically interconnected' (Gumbrell-McCormick and Hyman, 2015: 10).

Panrico: multi-targeted strategy, uniting different struggles

The Panrico workers' strike is the longest lasting strike to have been carried out in Spain since the restoration of democracy after Franco's dictatorship. Panrico is a Spanish company that specializes in the production of packaged sliced bread and pastries, particularly known for its leading product, *Donuts*. It was founded in 1962 by the families Rivera and Costafreda, but was acquired in 2005 by the

UK-based private equity and venture capital firm, Apax Partners. The purchase, which cost €900 million, generated a large debt for Apax that was eventually transferred to Panrico. After decapitalizing the company and selling its property assets in order to repay the debt, and in the midst of the financial crisis, in 2011 it was sold to the private equity firm Oaktree Capital Management, which specializes in 'distressed' assets and high-risk investments in struggling companies. For this purchase, Oaktree spent €11 million and received a debt reduction of 80 per cent, which means it bought the company for about 1 per cent of the price Apax Partners paid five years before (Benítez and Rosetti, 2016).

In September 2013, Oaktree designated Carlos Gila as Panrico's new chief executive officer with the specific goal of restructuring the company – Gila was also involved in other firms' restructuring plans, such as La Seda, Ebro Puleva, Aceites Coosur or Sintel. The latter, one of Telefónica's network installer sub-contractors, was bought by Gila for €1 in 2001, while its workers were on strike, and declared bankruptcy three months after the transaction – as such, we can see clear parallels with the Movistar case (see the next section). A few days after being appointed, Gila announced a delay of an unspecified duration in the payment of wages to employees, and a collective redundancy plan that would reduce Panrico's workforce by 1,900 employees and would affect the remaining staff with salary cuts of 35–45 per cent.

The two main Spanish trade unions – CCOO (which had higher membership levels among Panrico's production workers) and UGT (largely representing office and white collar workers) – called a strike in the ten Spanish manufacturing plants. In order to increase the pressure against Panrico, the workers in Santa Perpètua de la Mogoda, Barcelona, also decided at an assembly meeting to initiate a parallel indefinite strike, which was called by the plant's works committee. The day before the start of the strike CCOO and UGT reached an agreement with Panrico to suspend the strike in exchange for reducing the number of redundancies to 745, with the agreement also including a cut in wages by 18 per cent for the remaining workers. This deal was rejected by the workers in Santa Perpètua, however, witnessing them continue with the action and in addition settling a protest camp outside the manufacturing plant.

The uniqueness of this dispute lies not only in its long duration – it lasted eight months – but also in the fact that it developed a complex and multi-targeted strategy. Whilst the strikers sought to put pressure on Panrico in order to stop the redundancy plan and salary cuts; they also explicitly confronted the Catalan Government, which instead of adopting a mediating role, rather tried to convince workers to accept Gila's plan in exchange for preventing the plant's closure. The campaigning workers also called attention to the fact that one of the members of Panrico's board of directors, Joan Mas, was the brother of the then President of the Catalan Government, Artur Mas. In addition, the protesting workers targeted the leadership of the main trade union in the factory, CCOO, on the grounds that it had accepted the company's redundancy plan against the will of the workers' assembly. In that sense, there was a clear confrontation between the works committee and rank-and-file CCOO members, on the one hand, and the leaders of their trade union on the other hand. After the strike, some of the participants described this triple confrontation in the following way:

> I feel very angry and very hurt, because we didn't have the support of those who should have supported us: the trade union [Comisiones Obreras], the Catalan Government, anyone. And now I see a lot of colleagues that have been fired and I'm very angry. [...] I've been in the company for 42 years. I consider myself as a hardworking, trustworthy and responsible person. I am like this when I work, and I am like this when I fight. We have to fight; we workers have the right to defend ourselves, to fight for our rights, to fight so they can't keep stealing from us. Two years ago, they presented a restructuring plan and they took from us everything that we had achieved in 42 years, every right, and the money from our salaries. And who signed it? The trade unions!
>
> (Documentary Panrico, Panpobre, October 2014,
> authors' translation)

> Comisiones Obreras followed the same dynamics as in other negotiations about redundancy plans: it would have reached an agreement with the company and signed the plan. But at a certain point the process was interrupted by the announcement by Santa Perpètua workers that they would start an indefinite strike. [...] On the one hand, the majority of workers in Santa Perpètua are members of Comisiones Obreras, but on the other hand, they want to sign the agreement with the company. As for the Catalan Government, in theory they should mediate between the two parts, making sure that no one violates legality. However, Panrico used strike-breaking strategies: they substituted the strikers with workers from other plants, and they brought to Catalonia products from other plants to guarantee the supply. This is reported and Inspecció de Treball [organism of the Catalan Government] considered it a violation of the right to strike. But they kept doing it.
>
> (Documentary Panrico, Panpobre, October 2014,
> authors' translation)

The strategies of the strikers consisted of multiple combined actions, including both traditional labour movement tactics – such as picket lines, demonstrations and strike funds – and more innovative forms of mobilization and coordination, such as the use of workers' assemblies, agitprop and the diffusion of strategies beyond the workplace, and the construction of an external support network. In order to make their struggle known and also to distribute calls for action, the striking workers launched an online social media campaign mainly through Facebook ('Panrico SOMOS TODOS') and Twitter (with the accounts @Panricobcn, now closed, and @Panricoenlucha, as well as the hashtag #vagapanrico). In addition, they used other media platforms, such as Youtube, to produce testimony of police brutality, with the latter including attempts to repress the picket lines that the strikers formed at the factory's entrance[4] and to publicize a documentary developed together with the Lacolumna.cat and titled 'Panrico, Panpobre'.[5]

The Panrico strike also witnessed the sustained use of workers' assemblies. This was largely in response to what was perceived to be a failure on the part of both public institutions and trade union officials to represent the workers' interests. As such, the striking workers held weekly assemblies to enable themselves to decide directly and collectively on the future of their struggle. Thus, the assemblies were typically considered by the striking workers to be spaces for self-organization, deliberation and collective decision making, and were essential for creating a sense of unity among the workers. Furthermore, the strikers had a Support Committee formed by a politically diverse but stable group of associations, and social and political movements that included *Iai@flautas*, the *Plataforma de Afectados por la Hipoteca* (PAH) (in English, Platform for People Affected by Mortgages), and students' movements. This external support network helped both to organize the picket lines, and to gather food, supplies and money for the strike fund. It also organized a range of events and demonstrations staged in solidarity with the workers on strike, as well as a boycott of Panrico's products and participated in the expropriation of doughnuts from different supermarkets.

Another important aspect of the protest developed by Panrico's workers was the attempt to unite different strikes and campaigns within a single struggle. One clear example of this was their collaboration with the workers of Coca-Cola's manufacturing plant in Fuenlabrada, who were also on strike to protest against a redundancy plan and the company's intention of closing several factories in Spain. Under the slogan '*Panrico y Coca-Cola, la lucha es una sola*' ('Panrico and Coca-Cola, we are in the same fight'), the striking workers of both companies joined forces and demonstrated together multiple times, both in Barcelona and Madrid. The workers also participated in the Labour Coordinator and Mutual Support 15-M, a platform for the coordination of struggles originated during the eruption of the 15-M movement (Benítez and Rosetti, 2016). As the participants in the protest themselves acknowledge, these collaborations with other movements and workers' struggles were fundamental not only for this specific dispute, but also for the construction of a critical consciousness and a political subjectivity among the workers. One of the workers participating in the strike describes the experience as an internal process of awakening:

> Above us, there is a super mafia. They can do whatever they want with us, with the students, with the pensioners, with all the civil society. We are too calm, too quiet. As a society, we don't know how to respond. This strike is awakening our consciousness. We are now in contact with other social movements, we have been trying to stop evictions with the PAH, we have received food from the neighbours' associations … Because what's happening in Panrico is an example, an example of what they're planning to do to all of us.
> (Interview with striking worker, April 2014, authors' translation)

Another relevant aspect of the protest is the central role of female workers during the strike. They not only organized the strike fund and collected money by selling DIY products in street markets and stalls, but also gave speeches at universities and appeared in different media to disseminate their demands. In addition, they participated in a variety of demonstrations in defence of women's rights, such as the march against men's violence against women or the demonstration against the abortion law reform that the Spanish Government – with a conservative absolute majority – was trying to pass in 2014. A year after the end of the strike, a group of female strikers continued both to provide support and solidarity to other labour struggles (including the Telefónica/Movistar technicians), and to participate in a variety of events to describe their experiences and the lessons they acquired as a result of their participation in the dispute. In addition, the strikers received the support of the women's organization *Pan y Rosas* (Bread and Roses), a platform born in Argentina in 2003 which seeks to make visible the sexual division of labour and the double exploitation of women in the productive and reproductive spheres – a sexual division of labour and a double exploitation which are frequently reproduced during strikes and other disruptive actions – and to integrate a feminist perspective to class struggle.

These solidarity support networks were fundamental in sustaining the eight-month strike, which required enormous amounts of both emotional and physical energy, placing a considerable burden upon the workers' everyday lives. As one of the strikers put it,

> After 8 months of struggle and without receiving a salary, we are exhausted. It's been very difficult to pay the bills – water, electricity, gas, the mortgage … It has completely paralysed our lives. The only thing that keeps us fighting is our unity. We are a family, all Panrico's workers. We are resisting and we can eat thanks to people's solidarity and the strike fund.
>
> (Interview with striking worker, April 2014,
> authors' translation)

This unity was maintained, moreover, despite intensive attempts by the company management to erode it. On the one hand, the firm tried to confront workers from different plants by announcing during the strike that they would concentrate the majority of the planned redundancies in the Santa Perpètua factory, which they would increase by 60per cent, and reduce the dismissals in the remaining plants by 80 per cent. In addition to this attempt to reward passive and non-resistant workers and to punish those actively struggling to oppose attempts to undermine working conditions, the company also purportedly sought to divide the striking workers at Santa Perpètua (between the rank-and-file and the key 'ringleaders') by offering to reduce the number of redundancies if the workers accepted the dismissal of the whole works committee and of other key workers arbitrarily selected by the management (interview with striking worker, April 2014; this was something later denied by Panrico).

In addition to more direct forms of protest and strike activity, the Panrico workers also sought to bring a number of legal challenges against the firm. One such action included a legal claim against Panrico on the grounds that it had violated the right to strike by bringing products from other plants and subcontracting services to replace the striking workers. This violation was confirmed by the relevant agency of the Catalan Government, *Inspecció de Treball*, resulting in Panrico being penalized. Another legal claim saw the workers take action against the company's collective redundancy plan, calling for its cancellation on the grounds that the number of dismissals were disproportionate and unfairly distributed among Panrico's manufacturing plants. In this case, the Audiencia Nacional (National Court) endorsed the redundancy plan by accepting the 589 dismissals planned for 2013 and 2014, whilst forbidding the 154 dismissals planned for 2015 and 2016.

Towards the end of the strike, the Catalan Government offered to resume its role as mediator between the works committee and the company management, advocating a temporary collective redundancy plan that would end the strike and reopen the factory progressively. However, in June 2014, eight months after the strike began, the workers decided in an assembly to reject the offers made by both the firm and the government, and instead to end the strike. In this sense, therefore, the strike was unsuccessful. The company continued with the implementation of its initial collective redundancy plan, including the specific dismissal of the 23 members of the Strikes Committee in March 2015.

In terms of the degree to which the Santa Perpètua Panrico workers had managed to disrupt and obstruct the plans of the company, however, the action had been a significant success. The campaign gained national prominence and represented the significant development of new forms of disruptive agency. In refusing to return to work under worsened terms and conditions, or to abandon the members of the strike committee, moreover, the striking workers highlighted the possibility and potential for obstinate action to disrupt and dislodge attempts by capitalist firms and political authorities to produce the smooth disciplining of workers in the context of the European context. In this sense, therefore, the Panrico dispute highlights the capacity for workers organizing outside of the formal structures of trade unions to mobilize dissent, supported by broad solidarity networks that arose in the context of the crisis, and through the pursuit of a multi-target strategy. In addition, whilst the strike might have ended in 2015, both the struggle of Panrico workers, and the diffusion of the strategies it adopted continue to be ongoing, with the subjectivities and capacity for cooperative action continuing to exist.

Telefónica/Movistar: 'We were the news, they couldn't conceal it anymore'

The case of Telefónica represents one of the main examples of autonomous labour struggles during the crisis in Spain. This telecommunication company, which was created in 1924 under the name CTNE (*Compañía Telefónica Nacional de España*) (Spanish National Telephone Company), was owned mainly by the Spanish Government during Franco's dictatorship, and enjoyed a government-granted monopoly until 1998 (Calvo, 2010). In the 1990s, the telephone services provider experienced a process of gradual privatization that started under successive

PSOE governments (1982–1996) and culminated under the PP Government of 1996–2004 (*Sociedad Estatal de Participaciones Industriales,* 2014). The state's close ties with the company, however, continued after privatization. In 1996, Juan Villalonga, childhood friend of the then Prime Minister of Spain José María Aznar, was appointed its CEO (Aznar, 2012). In addition, several prominent political figures have held important positions in different international branches of the company or have been elected to its board of directors. The most striking 'revolving doors' cases include members of PP (Rodrigo Rato, Elvira Fernández Balboa, Andrea Fabra, José Ivan Rosa, Eduardo Zaplana), PSOE (Narcís Serra, Javier de Paz, Trinidad Jiménez, Paloma Villa), and even the Head of the Royal Household of Spain in the period 1993–2002, José Fernando Almansa and the brother-in-law of the current King of Spain, Iñaki Urdangarín.

In 1994, Telefónica was one of the most profitable public companies in Spain – with a net income of €551 million – as well as one of the largest employers in the country, with 72,207 employees (Telefónica, 1994). After the privatization, however, the company launched several dismissal programmes (EREs) and outsourced key sales maintenance and customer services to hundreds of contractors, subcontractors and self-employed workers. Between 1994 and 2014, Telefónica España's labour force was reduced by 60 per cent – to 30,020 employees – which not only reduced the company's labour costs but also left an important share of the workforce outside existing collective bargaining agreements (Telefónica, 2014). As one of the remaining Telefónica workers and union activist explains,

> [Telefónica] was a state company; the state was its main shareholder, the same as happened with France Télécom or Deutsche Telekom. Then in 1996 Aznar privatized the whole company, 100 per cent. Telefónica was the only telecommunications company in the country, and it had a fair collective agreement: we received 3 extra pay checks per year, network installers worked 37.5 hours per week, telephone operators worked 35 hours per week because they were under more stress, we received 100 per cent of our salary when we were on a medical leave, we had free doctors, dentists … After the privatization and liberalization, a lot of people were left outside this collective agreement, and all that was left for them was either the minimum salary or the general metal industry collective agreement, the conditions of which were far below what we had achieved in Telefónica after many workers' struggles.
>
> (interview with Telefónica worker, CoBas member and activist,
> 3 November 2015, authors' translation)

The replacement *en masse* of Telefónica employees by subcontracted workers increased their precariousness and lack of security, and undermined trade unions' bargaining power (Rodríguez-Ruiz, 2014). However, rather than reducing workers' disputes as expected, it transferred the disputes to the outsourced companies. The *Campamento de la Esperanza* (The Camp of Hope) case illustrates this process of displacement of workplace rebellions. In January 2001, around 1,500 workers of Sintel, one of the largest of Telefónica's network installers, built a campsite in Paseo de la Castellana, in Madrid. The firm had declared bankruptcy, and its workers were facing the threat of the first large-scale ERE executed in the country. The dispute represented an active form of opposition against Sintel's and Telefónica's owners and the conservative Government at that time. It was also a creative way workers used to show their technical skills to potential new clients (Martínez Lucio, 2011), since the initial tents were gradually replaced by hand-made cabins, bathrooms, kitchens, a library, a museum, a meeting hall and even portable swimming pools (Tremlett, 2011). What is more, this unprecedented protest with important prefigurative aspects showed that the occupation of public space was a means through which workers could solve coordination problems derived from the lack of a fixed workspace.

The *Campamento de la Esperanza* was disassembled in August 2001, when Sintel's works council and the Spanish Government reached an agreement to reimburse unpaid salaries, to relocate former Sintel workers in similar telecommunications companies, and to offer early retirement with generous compensation to older workers. According to multiple union delegates and workers involved in the protest, the experience of Sintel did not contribute to the dissipation of Telefónica's outsourcing framework, but rather reinforced it. Currently, Telefónica receives direct or indirect services from ten different contractors and more than 600 subcontractors and self-employed workers (Clua-Losada and Ribera-Almandoz, 2017). As one of the activists puts it,

> Movistar [the brand name under which Telefónica also trades] is not the only company that uses outsourcing to foster the precarization of working conditions. It is a practice that occurs in a large number of firms, which serves not only to divide the workforce ('divide and conquer'), but also as a way to adjust the social achievements of workers. The neoliberal offensive initiated in the 1980s continues nowadays through temporary work agencies, outsourcing, subcontracting, undeclared work, and segregated collective agreements. Unfortunately, this has been endorsed by trade union leaders. [...] We have had to hear them say 'indefinite strikes are crazy', 'if laws allow outsourcing, we can't do anything to prevent it', and the idea of the 'lesser evil', which ends up naturalizing precarious workers and making them pay the consequences.
>
> (Javier, trade union delegate in Cotronic workers' committee in
> Zaragoza, quoted in Ubico, 2016, authors' translation)

Indeed, the atomization and geographic dispersion of the labour force, which has frequently lead to salary reductions, precarization of working conditions and even reductions in health and safety standards, has not faced strong political resistance from the main trade unions. CCOO and UGT both perceived each wave of redundancies and dismissal programmes as unavoidable outcomes in a context of heightened global competition. Thus, they prioritized pragmatic strategies aimed maintaining a certain level of stability for the remaining workers and procuring early retirements to older workers, who were perceived as more susceptible to long-term unemployment (Rodríguez-Ruiz, 2014).

In 2015, moreover, shortly after the application of a dismissal programme that caused around 6,500 dismissals between 2011 and 2013, Telefónica announced the signature of a new contract with the outsourced companies that would produce severe salary cuts for more than 20,000 contracted, subcontracted and self-employed workers.[6] This prompted the Telefónica workers to seek a way in which to respond to this further undermining of their position within the labour market. After a series of assembly meetings, the workers decided to start an indefinite strike in Madrid, and rallied around slogans such as 'They took so much from us that even fear was taken away' ['*Nos quitaron tanto, tanto, que nos quitaron el miedo*']. This inspired Telefónica workers in other cities to respond in a similar way, and as a result the action was soon replicated in Barcelona, Bilbao, Seville and other Spanish cities. This indefinite strike, the first of its kind organized by self-employed workers in Spanish history, was coordinated by the radical grassroots trade unions CoBas (*Sindicato de Comisiones de Base*), AST (*Alternativa Sindical de Trabajadores*) and CGT (*Confederación General del Trabajo*). The established trade unions, on the other hand, planned a parallel two-day strike action without the support of the workers' assemblies. This generated among workers a sense of frustration and discomfort with these unions, who were perceived as unable to represent workers' interests. As a result, slogans such as 'We fight, we negotiate' and 'No, no, no, they don't represent us'– one of the key mottos of the 15M movement – were directed at CCOO and UGT leaders in different demonstrations performed by the striking workers.

The campaign, known as 'The Ladders Revolution' ['*Revolución de las escaleras*'], mobilized a large number of workers. Before the European crisis, a high turnover of employees had enabled workers to find the contractors and subcontractors that offered better working conditions. In doing so, these workers built strong networks (often unconsciously) that were ultimately to be used to coordinate the actions during the protest. After two months of strikes, however, an assembly of subcontracted technicians concerned by the lack of media coverage of the campaign and by the growing fatigue of the strikers decided to combine this conventional strike action with other forms of disruptive action and prefigurative practices. With the support of CoBas, AST and CGT, they decided on direct action and occupied the Telefónica building that houses the headquarters of the Mobile World Centre, a key landmark in the heart of Barcelona. As different workers participating in the occupation explained,

> Our strike started like any other strike action: we thought that if workers from all the contracts stopped working at the same time we would harm the company. But Telefónica is one of the main companies of the Ibex 35 [cc], and they didn't care! So, two months passed, and 5,000 people were on strike, and nothing happened. We tried to gain media attention, but we couldn't. Of course, Telefónica spends millions of Euros on advertising […] So we decided to get into the shop. And not any shop, but the Mobile World Centre,

the apple of their eye. [...] And that's when we broke the barrier with the media. We were the news, they couldn't conceal it anymore. We were everywhere, even in international newspapers.

> (interview with a worker of one of Telefónica's contractors,
> CoBas member and activist, November 5, 2015,
> authors' translation)

During the occupation, workers distributed informative leaflets to passers-by, organized demonstrations and press conferences inside the occupied building, promoted a strike fund and coordinated different fundraising activities, such as street markets, a communal *paella* and a music festival. This time, the campaigners were successful in gaining great public and media recognition. The occupation had thus two main objectives. First, it was a means through which workers made their conflict visible, attracted the attention of the media and launched a campaign focused on damaging the reputation of the company's executives. Their organizational strength, as well as the prefigurative aspects of the protest, were at that time relatively rare within Spanish labour struggles. And, second, taking advantage of the break that the 15M cycle represented, they established an alliance with other social movements, which was also opened up to all those leftist political parties that wanted to participate:

> We learned our lesson during the Sintel struggle. [...] We established links with Iai@flautas, with the health sector workers of the *marea blanca*, the PAH, the IAC [*Intersindical Alternativa de Catalunya*], the pro-Catalan independence radical left movements, etc. They all helped us; we were starting the strike of the century. This unity we showed, with social movements struggling with us inside the Telefónica building, is crucial when you're trying to open negotiations with such a powerful multinational company.

> (interview with a worker of one of Telefónica's contractors,
> CoBas member and activist, 5 November 2015,
> authors' translation)

Furthermore, a week before local elections were held in Spain, the campaigning workers entered into an agreement with some of the candidates for the mayor of Barcelona, including Ada Colau from *Barcelona en Comú*, Alfred Bosch from *Esquerra Republicana de Catalunya* (ERC) and Maria José Lecha from *Candidatura d'Unitat Popular* (CUP). This agreement, known as 'The Ladders Pact' ['*Compromís de les escales*'], saw the potential leaders each commit themselves to only contract services from companies that guaranteed fair working conditions, including a maximum of 40 working hours per week, two weekly rest days and fair wages. The degree to which this agreement could be honoured in practice was however open to question, and indeed the actual effects of the agreement are still to be seen. As one of the strikers puts it,

The problem we're currently facing is that the working conditions are also precarious in all other telecommunications companies, such as Vodafone, Orange or Jazztel. So, if a City Council stops receiving services from Telefónica and hires another company, we will be back at square one. And it's not easy to find an alternative mechanism to enforce The Ladders Pact, because the European Union treaties limit the use of social clauses in the contracts signed by municipalities. The Lisbon Treaty always favours free market and competition over anything else: the right to strike, social clauses, environmental protection ... So, our situation is a bit like Syriza's, isn't it? Even if the Mayor is with us, we don't have that many options.

> (interview with a worker of one of Telefónica's contractors,
> CoBas member and activist, 3 November 2015,
> authors' translation)

What is clear is that, thanks to this coordination with other social movements and political actors, a direct negotiation was forced between the company's executives and the workers, which for the first time was performed without the mediation of the established trade unions. Telefónica is an example of the direct implications of the 15-M cycle on Spanish workers regarding how resistance and struggle are perceived and coordinated. The 15-M meant a rupture not just with the management of the crisis, but also more importantly with the established channels of political and social representation. Both trade unions as well as Left parties were the focus of vociferous criticism for having failed to provide an adequate response to the crisis. Furthermore, these formal institutions were identified as also being part of the problem. The perceived lack of union opposition to the 2010 labour reform (approved by the Socialist Government), as explained earlier in the chapter, despite a general strike, was seen as further evidence of the inability of the established organizations to provide a channel for resistance. The outcome has been an increased level of contention outside and within existing organizations. It could be argued that this was a positive outcome in workplaces where unionization was made difficult by structural conditions (such as the Telefonica subcontracting system), as the accumulated experience since the 15-M in community organizations and square occupations had been a great school of prefigurative action for many people, including some of the Movistar strike organizers.

Conclusion

As we saw in the previous chapter, the period prior to 2008, leading up to the European crisis, witnessed heightened attempts by Europe's political and economic elite to harness the disciplining role of market competition, in order to counter the capacity (and actuality) of labour to disrupt Europe's capitalist social order. This, it was intended, would ensure that disruptive agency would be limited and the market could operate successfully and without the expression of the kind of dissent that had proved so visibly problematic during the late-1960s and through the 1970s. Whilst this was in part successful, nevertheless a number of alternative forms of disruptive action by workers across Europe ensured that important imbalances remained within the European economy, which in turn contributed to the crisis that erupted from 2008 (and especially in 2010). In response, as we have sought to show, the European crisis prompted a heightened attempt to harness the disciplining role of market competition.

In the case of both the UK and Spain this response by political and economic elites has taken the form of a heightened attempt to impose the liberalization of the labour market and conformity to the diktat of market competition, with a further jettisoning of workers' rights and further attempts to undermine the organizational capacity of national trade unions. This, indeed, is the logical corollary of the role sought for European integration; having constructed a competitive European market, the only option available to the political and economic elite in the face of problems or hardship is an attempt to further enforce that same market logic in order that firms and workers can be rendered more 'competitive' still. As we saw, free movement of labour was used by employers in the Lindsey Oil Refinery dispute to seek to undermine existing terms and conditions. The commitment to being competitive in the global economy also underpinned the dispute at Vestas. Likewise, the Telefónica dispute highlighted the prohibition place by the EU upon municipal authorities seeking to introduce so-called 'social clauses' (on the grounds that this would distort a single European market).

As we have sought to show, however, the onset of the European crisis and the associated imposition of further market discipline were not met with a uniform pattern of passivity or helplessness on the part of European labour. Instead, we have witnessed a range of strategies emerge, in an attempt (with varying degrees of success) to produce alternative means of disruption. This has included the attempt to go beyond formal institutions of trade unions, to find innovative forms of solidarity with groups outside of the workplace, to use the media to highlight and politicize struggles that would otherwise beyond the scope of typical forms of trade union organizing, and to use direct action when more conventional means of disruption have proven insufficient. Workers threatened by layoffs and foreclosures have on several occasions outpaced the more formal institutions of trade union in terms of their militancy, developed grassroots structures to pursue their conflicts beyond the strategic confines of the unions, or otherwise (as in the case of the Ritzy workers' campaign for a living wage) seen trade unions cede a much greater degree of autonomy to the union membership than is typically the case.

These observations therefore chime with the argument developed by Schmalz *et al.* (2015), who claim that the disembedding of labour relations by the dismantling of workers' rights has a tendency to lead to the appearance of new nonstandard forms of labour conflict. While in the United Kingdom these conflicts appeared rather disconnected from broader social movements, in Spain they formed an integral part of a dense network of social movements and were discursively, but also in their organizational structure, embedded in broader social struggles against the devastating effects of the economic crisis and the austerity measures implemented.

The work-related conflicts that we have witnessed in both the UK and in Spain have therefore included efforts to create new social alliances, develop creative and unconventional tactics, and establish alternative social infrastructures, all in reaction to the exhaustion of 'traditional' trade union strategies. Whilst the activists participating in these conflicts were typically motivated primarily by the direct material improvements being sought, nevertheless they also tended to see their activities as a part of a larger struggle against the marginalization and political exclusion of the working class. In the British Lindsey Oil Refinery case these feelings of solidarity remained (at least partially) limited to British workers, thereby threatening transnational solidarities between differently positioned workers. As the claim of 'British jobs for British workers' shows, in its everyday capacity for disruption, labour is not necessarily connected to emancipatory demands, but may also be connected to a reassertion of the nation as the primary locus through which grievances are articulated and envisioned (Featherstone, 2015: 21).

Moreover, the instances of opposition that we have seen did not tend to result in broader European-wide solidarity movements (Nowak and Gallas, 2014: 319). On occasion, there was also no expectation that the workplace struggles would be successful; instead the aim has oftentimes been to reduce the severity of proposals for redundancies, rather than to avoid them altogether (for a similar observation, see Gumbrell-McCormick and Hyman, 2015: 10). Nonetheless, these episodes of contention contributed to the politicization of the social effects of the economic crisis and an activation of the workforce that made visible – at least temporarily – the fact that radical struggles at the company-level are possible. As such, they highlight the way in which, as 'the crisis unfolds, the need for a new and radical political course is actually growing day by day' (Wahl, 2014). Market-based pacification therefore – despite the attacks on labour both leading up to, and during the European crisis, and the devastating effects these have had upon the scope for trade union action – has continued to prove unable to contain the disruptive effects of labour.

The combination of these radical forms of action with concrete, proximate demands, have in turn pointed towards a new form of subjectivity, which elsewhere we have labelled *pragmatically prefigurative* (Bailey *et al.*, 2016). At the same time, the crisis seems to have prompted new dividing lines to emerge within the working class, and which became visible as forms of *exclusive solidarity* (Dörre, 2011), especially with parts of the working class perceiving themselves as 'natives', against racialized, foreign or migrant workers (a trend made most apparent by LOR dispute slogan, 'British jobs for British workers'). As the subsequent Brexit vote has shown, moreover, and as we shall discuss in more detail in the following chapters, it is this move amongst sections of Europe's more disaffected working class, towards a nativist discourse, that has posed considerable threat to the project of European integration and its underlying project of disciplinary marketization.

Notes

1 For more details of the demands, see for instance those set out by one of the protesting employees, speaking here: https://www.youtube.com/watch?v=8KC1stnYQdo.
2 See https://www.youtube.com/watch?v=l2t3VR1CmB8.
3 See https://www.youtube.com/watch?v=CKnYTqcASuU.
4 See https://www.youtube.com/watch?v=7FsEWzPUnjI&feature=youtube_gdata_pla.
5 This is a play on words using the company's name that means 'Rich bread, poor bread', see https://www.youtube.com/watch?v=a9Klmyix8oQ.
6 In 2014, Telefónica had one of the biggest pay gaps between executives and median workers in the country. César Alierta, the then CEO of the firm, received a monthly salary of €550,000, a permanent Telefónica employee received an average monthly salary of €2,000–2,200, contract workers received a maximum salary of €1,480 per month, subcontracted workers had monthly salaries of around 800€, and self-employed received a maximum retribution of €700–800 per month (Comisión Nacional del Mercado de Valores 2014). The latter also have to deduct self-employed taxes, social security contributions, and vehicle and equipment expenses from their earnings.

4 Resisting neoliberal Europe, responding to the dismantling of welfare states

As has been widely observed, the struggle over European integration has routinely extended beyond the sphere of work (the subject of the previous chapter), to that of welfare (the subject of the present chapter). Indeed, welfare has been central to the broader contestation of Europe's socio-economic model (Scharpf, 2010; Crespy, 2016). In this chapter, therefore, we discuss the way in which Europe's political and economic elite have addressed the issue of welfare provision and welfare reform through the institutions of the European Union. In doing so, however, we focus more than is typically the case on the way in which these attempts at welfare reform have been obstructed and impeded by the different forms of disruptive agency that have arisen in response. Thus, whereas it has become commonplace to view the process of European integration as disciplining and therefore limiting the scope for welfare provision, we seek to show how a similar (less often noted) process of opposition and disruption has also acted to limit this attempt at welfare retrenchment. As a result, and as we shall see, the onset of crisis in 2008 has witnessed something of a 'double movement', in which increased disciplinary pressures from global markets and European institutions, and an attempt to further de-politicize budgetary discipline through a series of measures largely associated with the European response to the crisis, have in turn been met by increased everyday vulnerability and social inequality, a deepening legitimacy crisis for national and European institutions, but also mass protests that have (at times successfully) pushed for a re-politicization of welfare reforms and seen the emergence of new forms of pragmatically prefigurative disruptive agency.

The European Welfare Model and the (partial) mollification of the working class under Fordism

As we saw in Chapter 2, part of the strategy adopted by Europe's political elite, in its attempt to avoid the kind of disruptive militancy that marked the inter-war period included an extension of the welfare state. While on the one hand the welfare state offered increased security for labour and in many cases significantly increased living standards, it also served as a means to contain labour unrest (Hardt and Negri, 1994). In this sense, we agree with Papadopoulos *et al.* when they claim that the 'grand apparatus of the welfare state came to replace, or better domesticate, the uncontrollable anomaly of the politics which had been intimately connected with life in the period before the Second World War' (Papadopoulos *et al.*, 2008: 108). Social inclusion tended to be accompanied by an erosion of more autonomous forms of labour organizing, and was associated with an (albeit fragile) class compromise underpinned by productivism, scientific management and economic growth (Carew, 1987: 40–42). The inclusive elements of the welfare state, however, were never fully guaranteed, but instead depended upon the ability of labour to successfully exert pressure on capital and the state (Bieler, 2015: 25). Further, the extension of welfare was made possible, in part, by productivity growth generated within the 'Fordist' production processes (although as we noted in Chapter 2, this productivity growth tended to be below that of average wage rises). Finally, exit options were limited for capital as a result of the control of capital enshrined by national governments operating under the Bretton Woods System (Scharpf, 1996: 16; 2000: 24).

Conceptualized in this way, welfare states must be regarded *both* as a victory for labour and as a pre-emptive measure to control it. As Papadopoulos *et al.* put it, the inclusive move of state welfare remained 'always partial, its outcome, the national social compromise, is continually open to being contested and transformed' (Papadopoulos *et al.*, 2008: 6). Inclusion within the welfare state was restricted to the national space and even within the nation states certain groups were excluded. The welfare state, in consequence, did not result in an end to social conflict (regardless of the degree to which that was the intention). Instead, it represented an attempt to regulate conflict by providing channels through which social demands could be steered and contained. However, such an approach unavoidably leaves 'open spaces, excesses to processes of subject production and inclusion', within which 'strategies of subversion' emerge (Papadopoulos *et al.*, 2008: 12–13).

The form and generosity of the post-war welfare state also varied across national contexts, in part as a result of the strength of the labour movement in each country, as well as resulting from the structural position of the particular national context within the wider global accumulation process (Esping-Andersen, 1990; Leibfried, 1993: 128–129; Rodríguez Martínez, 2012: 248). Indeed, it was the dependence of the welfarist strategy upon the capacity to maintain the sustained and expanding reproduction of capital accumulation, and that this latter goal was ultimately shown to be unachievable, that eventually prompted the switch in strategy by Europe's political and economic elite during the 1970s, witnessing the move away from the welfare state.

Further, as the case of Spain shows, the extension of welfare during the 'Fordist' period was far from universal. During the Francoist regime, access to healthcare was never universal. Health insurance coverage was limited to a certain time span and was largely aimed at ensuring that workers returned to work as soon as possible. Social security was fragmented as a number of different regimes existed for different groups of workers. In consequence, social security and redistribution was to a large extent provided by familial solidarity networks. Job security, moreover, was relatively high (as workers enjoyed significant protection against dismissal) but this could nevertheless be easily discontinued in the case of political 'misconduct'. The degree of redistribution achieved by Francoist 'welfare' was therefore extremely low (Huke, 2017).

Under pressure: welfare states, neoliberal European integration and its coming crisis

With the crisis of Fordism in the 1970s, the national welfare state became increasingly politicized. As we saw in Chapter 2, productivity growth stalled and the system of fixed exchange rates broke down, Keynesian welfare strategies became more difficult, and distributional conflicts between capital and labour intensified. Labour and other social movements developed 'excessive' demands for wage increases, as well as demands for a redistribution of wealth and better living conditions that pointed beyond the established forms of the national social compromise (Hardt and Negri, 2011: 143; Papadopoulos *et al.*, 2008: 109; on the notion of excessive demands, see Bailey and Shibata 2014). Capital, in contrast, sought ways to undermine the national social compromises that had strengthened the position of labour within these struggles (Streeck, 1996: 89–90). Employers' organizations (amongst others) pressured governments to decrease social welfare in order to restore profitability and international competitiveness, especially *vis à vis* the United States of America and Japan. The reactions of national governments to both the problems and pressures that they experienced initially displayed striking differences – for instance, witnessing France and Ireland pursuing strategies of demand stimulation, whilst Britain relied instead upon a strategy of austerity (Ziltener, 1999: 125).

Spain during the 1980s differed from these trends, as the period following the democratization process saw an extension of welfare spending and its capacity for redistribution – albeit from the low levels of the Francoist regime. While unemployment benefits and pensions were reduced, access to healthcare and education was universalized. A key driving force of this process were neighbourhood assemblies that had spawned around local everyday social problems during the 1960s and 1970s (see Chapter 7). At the beginning of the 1990s, moreover, a system of regional supplementary benefits (*Renta Mínima de Inserción*) was established and pensions were granted to those who had not contributed sufficiently to social security. However, most of these supplementary forms of social security nevertheless resulted in incomes below the poverty line (Huke, 2017).

During the 1990s, European states increasingly converged around a neoliberal strategy. EU member states increasingly favoured fiscal austerity and competition over Keynesian strategies, with the latter increasingly associated with rising levels of public debt, inflation and unemployment (Scharpf, 2000: 51; Smith, 2005: 22). Public and political support for egalitarian policies and centralized provision declined (Rhodes, 1995: 388). Part of this neoliberal strategy also included the attempt to limit and restructure social welfare provisions, thereby limiting access to public institutions and privatizing social security (Deppe, 2008: 29). This neoliberal strategy was, moreover, also supported by parts of the workforce who hoped it would generate jobs and welfare gains – the so-called 'social partnership model' (Bieling and Steinhilber, 2000; Gill, 1997: 211). In Spain, likewise, the universal system of healthcare and education was reorganized along neoliberal lines (Huke, 2017).

As with the sphere of work, as we saw in Chapter 2, in the sphere of welfare, European integration also played a key role in this process of neoliberal disciplining. Institutions such as the EMS and later the EMU created hard external constraints that were used by member states to justify attempts to impose austerity measures. The Stability and Growth Pact (SGP) of the EMU was designed to ensure that Member States pursue sound public finances, especially through the EU limits for public debt (maximum 60 per cent of GDP) and budget deficits (maximum 3 per cent of GDP), but without direct intervention in social policy (La Porte and Heins, 2016a: 16). The strongest effects of these limitations on welfare could be witnessed during the accession processes in Southern and Eastern Europe in order to fulfil the Maastricht or Copenhagen criteria (Bohle, 2006b; Pavolini *et al.*, 2016: 152).

As has been widely noted, the impact of European integration is best considered in terms of its tendency towards 'negative integration', whereby measures increasing market integration by eliminating national constraints on trade and distortions of competition have predominated over positive moves towards the integration of common European policies at the supranational level (Leibfried, 1993: 121; Scharpf, 1996: 15; Crespy, 2016). This was in part due to an inherent inability for divergent welfare systems to agree on a common EU-level welfare model (Rhodes, 1995: 386–387; Scharpf, 2000; Deppe, 1993: 19; Streeck, 1996: 69; 72). This, in turn, has created a tendency for European integration to be 'anti-welfare', in that market competition is increased, without any corresponding increase in supranational measures to provide for forms of social protection or redistribution (Crespy, 2016; Bailey, 2017).

The Single European Market and other measures to liberalize capital flows each therefore served as powerful tools to extend and intensify what we might consider to be processes of locational competition and competitive deregulation. Both of these processes also acted to undermine the fiscal capacity of the member states and to intensify the exposure of national welfare states to the disciplinary effects of neoliberalism, as well as providing those same states with an 'external' site of decision making upon which to heap the blame in seeking to impose otherwise unpopular 'anti-welfare' decisions. Further, social cohesion was not built into the structure of the EU. Measures such as the European Employment Strategy (EES) and the Open Method of Coordination (OMC) remained limited to voluntary policy coordination (La Porte and Heins, 2016a: 17). Welfare state institutions at the national level, in turn, became increasingly constricted both by the European institutional architecture and the increased structural dynamics of competition under capitalism. The sovereignty and autonomy of member states to pursue national welfare strategies was therefore eroded, a trend that was supported by an increasingly neoliberal, competition-oriented jurisdiction of the European Court of Justice, with major decisions such as the *Laval* and *Viking* rulings highlighting this trend (Buckel and Oberndorfer, 2009; Deppe, 1993: 18; Leibfried, 2000: 45).

The negative form taken by European integration therefore privileged the interests of capital over labour (Beckmann *et al.*, 2006: 313; Streeck, 1996: 91). Labour was no longer able to rely on protective barriers that facilitated the achievement of their policy goals in the post-war decades, but had instead to pursue its welfare demands within tightened constraints of international capitalism (Scharpf, 2000: 71). Subsequently, European welfare states were reorganized in the direction of competition states, with lower standards of social protection (Schmidt, 2013: 37, Clua-Losada, 2015). As Rhodes highlighted, broader social and demographic trends, associated with the transition from Fordism to post-Fordism, were being compounded by regional economic integration, creating what was referred to as a form of 'subversive liberalism', which acted to erode principles of solidarity and welfare, subordinating them to the pressures of economic competition (Rhodes, 1995: 385).

Whilst the foregoing paints a picture echoing that developed within the CPE literature – of welfare states being eroded and neoliberalism imposed across European society – we should add that these processes were disrupted in two important ways. Firstly, they led to an erosion of the legitimation of the European project, creating a 'constraining dissensus' that acted to limit any further reforms (Hooghe and Marks, 2009). Secondly, they met the open resistance of significant sections of labour, hindering their full implementation.

A 'constraining dissensus': the post-Maastricht crisis of the European Union

The neoliberal turn of European integration and its negative effects on welfare in turn resulted in an erosion of the legitimacy of both the EU and – to a lesser extent – national governments (Deppe, 2001; Ferrera, 2009: 222–223). As such, we have witnessed the growth, throughout much of the 1990s, of popular disaffection towards the European project, which itself became increasingly visible (and was expressed through a more active political voice) when asked to vote on the question of European integration. Transnational capital and the European institutions it has promoted have increasingly come to be identified as causes of the dismantling of welfare states (Schmidt, 2013: 37). The discontent of the European population with regard to neoliberal integration became clear in a series of 'no' votes in referendums on the question of European integration (as witnessed in Ireland, France and the Netherlands), thereby articulating a deep and apparently irresolvable legitimacy crisis of the EU institutions (Bailey 2008; Beckmann *et al.*, 2006; Deppe, 2001; Gill, 1992: 190; Richter, 2015: 216–217). European responses to the legitimacy crisis, moreover, such as an extension of European citizenship discourses, remained firmly situated within established neoliberal discourse and as a result were unable to successfully overcome the roots of the crisis (Kaindl, 2013: 27).

The erosion of the national Keynesian welfare state, which had served as a key pillar of legitimacy for national governments and supranational integration, increasingly resulted in the intensification of processes of social disintegration across key sections of the European workforce. The selective system of trust and solidarity enshrined within the welfare state was therefore systematically eroded (Offe, 2000: 5). From the 1980s onwards, it became clear that neoliberalism undermined the living conditions even of the privileged strata of workers, while levels of popular support for social security and decommodification remained high within the EU (Gill, 1997: 213). This was a process, therefore, whereby the elements of a permissive consensus that had characterized European populations' attitudes towards European integration in the pre-neoliberal decades came increasingly to be eroded (Deppe, 2001: 213). This constraining dissensus, however, was only partly connected to leftist social demands, as the distrust expressed towards the EU increasingly articulated itself in racist and nationalist forms (Deppe, 1993: 45; Werts *et al.*, 2013). As a result, a chasm between the projects of European integration pursued by elites and the willingness of national populations to accept them grew increasingly wide (Deppe, 2001: 208). The effect, argue Hooghe and Marks (albeit failing to account for the social roots of the development), was a *'constraining dissensus'*. This replaced what, it had been argued, was an earlier 'permissive consensus', now supplanted by an underlying popular opposition to further European integration. As Hooghe and Marks warned, 'Elites, that is, party leaders in positions of authority, must look over their shoulders when negotiating European issues. What they see does not reassure them' (Hooghe and Marks, 2009: 5).

This erosion of popular support for supranational integration, in turn, partly acted to undermine the potential to pursue radical neoliberal politics at the European level (for instance, as we saw with the Services Directive), whilst also further hindering attempts to develop more substantive forms of social policy (or 'Social Europe'). As a result of this stalemate, in which the disruptive effect of popular disaffection appeared unable to be assuaged, the European project seemed destined to both an economic crisis (on the grounds that it was proving unable to complete its neoliberal market-building/market-liberalizing mission) and legitimation crisis (due to both the increased likelihood of economic stagnation *and* the inability to re-integrate labour through a supranational project of social policy-making (or, Social Europe)). This failure of the European elite to organize public support for their political project was perhaps most clearly highlighted during the pre-2008 period by the anti-European results of referendums in Ireland, France and the Netherlands. This, however, did not lead to a reversal of a neoliberal strategy that seemed unable to secure the conditions of its own legitimation, requiring yet further recourse to a technocratic solution, and thereby creating a vicious cycle of de-legitimation and de-democratization (Huke and Schlemermeyer, 2012; Oberndorfer, 2015).

Refusing welfare reforms, frustrating neoliberalism

Europe's political and economic elite have therefore consistently sought to advance a neoliberal agenda in the field of welfare spending. This was, nevertheless, routinely marked by a sense of frustration (on the part of that elite) at their *inability* to achieve the goals that they had set themselves, due largely to the weight of the obstacles standing in the way of those reforms. Whereas CPE accounts have been right to highlight the agenda and ambitions of Europe's elite, as outlined in the previous section, we need also to be careful to avoid overstating the degree to which that same elite have been successful in the execution of their plans. Indeed, from the perspective of those advocating neoliberalism, this is an agenda that has in part been thwarted.

In addition to the problem of declining legitimation, therefore, we also witness a process whereby more visible forms of disruptive agency have obstructed the attempt to secure a retrenchment of welfare provision through the institutions of the European Union. It is this partial thwarting of neoliberal goals through disruptive action, moreover, that we claim should be understood in terms of the refusal-prone tendencies of European labour, as we seek to illustrate in the next section. Whilst we should note that it would clearly be impossible to trace the development of every proposal for welfare reform that has been made across Europe during the neoliberal period, we can nevertheless highlight some of the more important proposals witnessed, in order to assess the degree to which they experienced opposition, and in what form. We will now consider, therefore, a number of key attempts at welfare reform as they occurred across a selection of the member states of the European Union during the 1990s and early 2000s.

Turning first to the case of Germany, one of the most important set of reforms proposed during the 1990s were those which would have affected pensions and sickness pay, proposed by the Kohl Government in 1996 and 1997. These sought to raise the retirement age, reduce the replacement rate of the pension scheme and reduce sick pay (Hinrichs, 2003). The proposals sparked widespread opposition, especially from the German trade union movement. This included a demonstration in Bonn ahead of the vote in the Bundestag which was attended by 300,000 trade union members. It also included more disruptive activities, including brief work stoppages, and blockades created by human chains and processions of cars (Cowell, 1996). This allowed the opposition party, the SPD, to consolidate trade union opposition by promising to repeal the more austere elements of the reforms, in the process improving its own electoral support, and eventually winning election to office in 1998 as a senior coalition partner with the German Green Party. Once in office, moreover, the new Schröder Government kept its promise to undo the Kohl pension reforms – albeit shortly afterwards signalling its commitment to implementing its own set of pension reforms (this time with significant concessions to key sectors of the electorate in an attempt to ameliorate their effect and pre-empt opposition) (Rürup, 2002: 150; Hinrichs, 2010: 58–60).

Perhaps most infamously, however, it was the Agenda 2010 reforms introduced under Schröder's Government in 2003 that experienced the most high-profile and visibly disruptive forms of opposition. 'Agenda 2010' consisted of a set of reforms to unemployment benefit which included a commitment to lower benefits for the long-term unemployed. In targeting the long-term unemployed, however, the proposed reforms proved to be politically disastrous. Protest events included a demonstration of 100,000 people in November 2003, a series of ongoing 'Monday demonstrations' (staged to resonate with those who remembered the demonstrations that took place at the end of the GDR), sustained trade union opposition, the appearance of IG Metall representatives at the European Social Forum, and a European day of action against welfare cuts. Opposition also resulted in a formal split in the SPD (which contributed considerably to its subsequent 2005 general election defeat) and the subsequent formation of *Die Linke*, which has systematically secured the votes of many of those disaffected with the SPD. In turn, this prompted the SPD to promote worker-friendly reforms to the national minimum wage and a partial reversal of the Agenda 2010 reforms (in terms of their impact upon older workers) (Bruff, 2010: 420–1).

In the case of Germany, therefore, which itself is commonly seen as one of the most *successful* countries in terms of securing welfare retrenchment measures and a lowering of the social wage during the early 2000s (allowing it to out-compete a number of peripheral economies during the post-2008 period), the route to welfare reform was far from smooth and unproblematic. The German case, therefore, as we shall see, is in some sense indicative of a more general problem faced by EU member states prior to 2008, in that attempts by the political elite to meet the spending and borrowing targets they had set themselves through initiatives such as the Stability and Growth Pact proved unable to avoid a range of obstacles to retrenchment placed in their way by different forms of disruptive agency associated with workers across Europe. In this sense, it is also telling that Germany was one of the member states on the Commission's 2005 list of 11 countries with an excessive deficit.[1] Rather than European integration producing the smooth imposition of neoliberal welfare reforms, therefore, we see instead a considerably more contested and problematic process.

Indeed, similar developments can be witnessed across Europe. In France, for instance, fear of social unrest (especially that which might be prompted by ongoing rounds of firm-level restructuring) ensured that social spending actively grew throughout the 1980s. Welfare reforms, moreover, had also been limited for much of the early 1990s (Palier, 2010: 79). It was only when the new Juppé Government sought to impose a substantial round of pension reforms – targeted at the public sector – that a significant attempt to impose neoliberal measures upon the French welfare system was initiated. This move by the Juppé Government, however, prompted massive public dissent, and especially trade union opposition, which erupted at the end of 1995. Indeed, the scale of this public opposition was such that the Government was forced to stage a high-profile U-turn. The debacle, moreover, was the major contributory factor explaining a sharp decline in Juppé's unpopularity and the subsequent general election defeat suffered by his government two years later (Goldhammer, 2013: 139).

The mobilization of opposition to Juppé's reforms itself took on such a form that it posed a significant problem for the Government in terms of its ability to maintain social order. Indeed, the 1995 protests were hugely disruptive. As Bonoli (1997) details, the various acts taken against the Government included a rail strike that halted most of the French railway system for three weeks, and daily demonstrations attended by up to two million people in Paris and other major cities.

These demonstrations had a sizeable impact upon the French economy, especially due to the immobility caused by the public transport strikes, ensuring that commuting from the outskirts of Paris to the city centre would take at least four hours (Bonoli, 1997: 111).

A similar chain of events could be witnessed in the case of the second major attempt to reform France's pension system, this time by the centre-right (UMP) Raffarin Government elected in 2002. Thus, one year after its election to office, the Government proposed another round of pension reforms. As with the Juppé Government's attempts in 1995, these reforms were again met with widescale trade union opposition. This prompted the Government to offer concessions in the form of a pension with a guaranteed 85 per cent replacement rate for those on the lowest incomes, as well as the possibility of early retirement for those currently employed (Palier, 2010: 91). The scale of the opposition that prompted these concessions, moreover, was such that parallels were readily drawn with the 1995 reforms, resulting in significant disruption to the functioning of the French socio-economy. This included strikes and demonstrations over a series of days between April and June 2003. The strikes by transport workers created major disruption. Air France was forced to cancel 55 per cent of its flights, half of domestic high-speed trains were cancelled, a majority of public transport services were disrupted across the country, and huge congestion was caused throughout Paris. Similar strike action in other sectors led to electricity output being reduced by 10 per cent, and public sector institutions, including schools, universities, and hospitals all being affected. Most of the newspaper distribution and mail delivery systems were also significantly disrupted as those taking part in the strikes included postal workers, state bank employees, telecommunications operators, teachers, nurses and police officers. The protests also included public demonstrations outside the National Assembly in Paris, in which tens of thousands of protesters massed outside, vowing to bring the country to a standstill if the bill proposing the reforms became law. This was accompanied by demonstrations in Marseille, Rouen and Nantes. Whilst much of the protest was lawful, moreover, some of the opposition also took the form of violent actions, including stones and bottles thrown at the National Assembly building, shop windows being smashed, rubbish set fire to and left by striking refuse workers, and a performance at the Paris's opera house being disrupted (Smith, 2003; Sciolino, 2003; Tagliabue, 2003).

It was in this high-tension, high-conflict context, then, that the Raffarin Government was ultimately forced to offer considerable concessions to its opponents, in order to at least secure a degree of pension reform. We should also bear in mind, of course, that the risk of such a response had a clear deterrent effect upon any French Government considering *further* reforms (on which, see Bailey, 2015). Again, therefore, the French experience confirms the difficulties that European member states faced in seeking to meet the targets on reduced welfare spending provisions that had been agreed through measures such as the Maastricht convergence criteria.

In addition to pension reforms, a wave of opposition erupted in response to plans to reform unemployed benefits across Europe in the late-1990s. For instance, in Belgium in 1998 we witness demonstrations staged by unemployed workers in response to tighter checks on the unemployed, leading to the mobilization of groups such as 'Active Unemployed' and 'Unemployed, Not Dogs' against checks on unemployed workers' private lives, and including demonstrations outside benefit offices and episodes of street theatre (Krzeslo, 1998). Likewise, Germany during 1998 saw more than 10,000 participants in 100 cities stage demonstrations calling for Chancellor Helmut Kohl's resignation following the announcement of another rise in unemployment (Zageimeyer, 1998).

Perhaps one of the most impressive rounds of mobilization by unemployed workers, however, was that witnessed in France during the winter of 1997–8. This was staged by a growing grassroots unemployed workers' movement that focused on criticisms of both the Government and the trade unions (who played a role in the management of unemployment insurance). The movement was initially launched by the unemployed committee of the French trade union, the CGT, around demands for a Christmas bonus (which had recently been ended). Forms of protest included sit-ins in the insurance fund's offices and other benefit offices, an occupation of the Louvre pyramid and the staging of a debate on exclusion. This eventually developed into a broader call for increased unemployment benefits, including marches that took place across the country, and the further occupation of insurance fund offices. The movement was also sustained by high levels of public support for the actions, with around 60 per cent expressing support or sympathy in opinion polls, and eventually prompting government concessions, including a commitment to increase the benefits for long-term unemployed by 3 per cent, a public transport subsidy for unemployed people resident in the Paris region, and emergency funds for the unemployed (Daniel, 1998). Similar events were witnessed the following year, when Jospin announced a 3 per cent increase in unemployment benefits (on top of an 8 per cent increase which had already been granted following the mobilization of winter 1997–8), this time in response to signs of another round of mobilization by the group 'Act Against Unemployment!', which sought a repeat of the demand for a winter bonus (Bilous, 1998).

In Italy, attempts to reduce the scale of the welfare state also began in the early 1990s, and were largely prompted by (or justified in terms of) the need to meet the Maastricht convergence criteria. Thus, in order that Italy could join the single currency (and also rejoin the EMS, which it was forced out of by financial speculation in 1992) a reduction in the size of the government deficit (to be achieved through reduced welfare spending) was explicitly required by the European Union. One of the first attempts to achieve this goal was witnessed in 1994 when the Berlusconi Government introduced reforms seeking a significant reduction in pension replacement rates. This prompted a massive national demonstration and general strike. In response, the proposal was drastically downscaled and eventually witnessed the resignation of the Government later that year (Jessoula and Alti, 2010: 168). In what appeared to be a case of 'second time farce', in 2003 Berlusconi's second government (2001–6) launched another attempt at pension reforms with similar goals, sparking another round of trade union mobilization and strike action which saw public transport halted, and well attended public demonstrations across the country. This again prompted a series of concessions from the Government, seeing it significantly water down the most regressive elements of its proposals (Jessoula and Alti, 2010: 174; Bruni, 2003). The Italian case, therefore, displays similar trends to those witnessed in Germany and France. That is, an inability of the national government to achieve the spending reductions sought, due to the impact of social mobilization on those occasions when substantial reforms were proposed.

In the case of Spain, a successful general strike took place in 1988. This represented the culmination of tensions which had grown between the Spanish Socialist Government under the leadership of Felipe González and the two main trade union confederations – UGT and CCOO – with the latter becoming increasingly unhappy about the reforms that had been introduced (especially to the Spanish labour market) since the election of González in 1982. The 1988 General Strike represented a flexing of the muscles of Spanish organized labour. Indeed, to a degree it had the desired effect in that it enabled the trade unions to push the Government into adopting a new (non-contributory) pension system which amounted to an important expansion of welfare provision (Guillén, 2010: 190–1).

Efforts at retrenchment in Spain did not begin in earnest, however, until the early 1990s, especially following the adoption of the Maastricht Treaty. Thus, it was the Maastricht Treaty which provided the means by which Spanish Socialists could justify welfare reforms in pursuit of a necessary contraction of public spending (Clua-Losada, 2015), in order to reap the benefits of full participation in European integration (on the disciplinary role of EU membership in underscoring the need to meet spending targets, see Bailey, 2009: 122–5). These reforms included proposals to implement drastic cuts to unemployment protection, a rationalization of the pension scheme and the introduction of efficiency drives within the health system. With regard to pension reforms, a nominal commitment on the part of the Spanish Government, to include trade unions within the decision-making process, resulted in a tripartite agreement (the 1995 Toledo Pact) that compensated the most vulnerable (widows and those with temporary contracts).

Nevertheless, the scale of the reforms introduced under González were such that they had significant political consequences for the PSOE. Most obviously, this included declining popularity and electoral defeat in the 1996 general election. This electoral damage also explains, in part, the turn towards a more (albeit still mild) pro-welfare agenda during its period out of office. Thus, on its re-election to government in 2004 the new Zapatero Government introduced expansionary welfare measures that included paternity leave and the adoption of the tripartite Agreement on Protection of Dependent People in 2005, which provided social protection for around one million people, especially the elderly (Guillén, 2010). The attempts at welfare retrenchment in Spain during the 1990s and early 2000s were therefore fitful in that expansionary welfare measures were often used as an attempt to offset opposition to other elements of the González Government's economic policies. On those occasions where welfare reforms were adopted, moreover, the electoral consequences were such that counter-measures were subsequently adopted in an attempt to win back the electoral support that had been lost in the pre-1996 period. Again, therefore, it is with such a process in mind that we should understand what we shall see has been the ongoing expression of frustration on the part of the European political and economic elite with regard to their inability to achieve the necessary welfare reforms that would have been required in order to achieve a more thoroughgoing reduction in welfare spending.

Many of the East European accession countries experienced similar developments during the 1990s, despite the fact that neoliberalism was pursued much more aggressively than in Western Europe (Bohle, 2006b). As Kaufman (2007) summarizes, whilst the governments of the East European candidate countries for European accession during the 1990s systematically pursued market liberalization programmes, these were nevertheless accompanied by a series of concessions designed to either counter or prevent opposition from key opponents to the pro-market reforms. Thus, we witness relatively enduring social provisions in the cases of Poland, Hungary and the Czech Republic. In Kaufman's words, during the 1990s, these three countries experienced

> continuing pressure to accommodate blue-collar unions, public employees, pensioners, and larger electoral constituencies whose entitlements and protections had been placed at risk by the economic reforms. *Protest, or the threat of protest, from such groups imposed a political cost on adjustment.* Consequently, notwithstanding cutbacks, social spending has remained high relative to other regions and post-socialist countries, even at the cost of recurring fiscal deficits.
>
> (Kaufman, 2007: 116, emphasis added)

A case in point, perhaps, is that of Hungary, where in 1995 the recently elected Socialist Government that was led by Gyula Horn proposed the so-called *Bokros package* of austerity measures. These measures included the means-testing of benefits and a reduction in childcare assistance (Cerami, 2010: 243). The reforms were met, however, with a range of protests that included demonstrations and petitions coordinated by the national teachers' unions and a May Day demonstration attended by 10,000 people (MTI Econews, 1995b; 1995c). In seeking to quell dissent, and to ensure that the measures would be adopted, the Government made a number of concessions to key beneficiaries of the outgoing system. Nevertheless, having seen the measures adopted, the political consequences of the reforms were substantial, witnessing the Orbán Government replace the Horn Government after the 1998 elections. Upon its election to office, moreover, the Orbán Government reversed the family allowance reforms that had been introduced by its predecessor, and the Socialists (now in opposition) promised to increase benefits if they were re-elected to office (Kaufman, 2007: 119–20). The so-called *Bokros package* therefore experienced a fate similar to many of the welfare reforms introduced across Europe – that is, the inability to realize the intended reduction in welfare provision in full; and the effect of subsequent political pressure in leading to the undoing, reversal or amelioration of the impact of those reforms that were adopted.

In sum, the foregoing highlights the importance of dissent and resistance in understanding the retrenchment and reform-focused agenda of the European Union and the governments of its member states. Whilst it is no doubt the case that a neoliberal agenda was associated with the Maastricht Treaty, Stability and Growth Pact, and eastern enlargement, therefore, popular opposition to welfare reforms nevertheless consistently resulted in proposals being opposed, obstructed, reversed, or requiring significant concessions to be made in order for them to be adopted; and in those cases where this was not the case, advocates of neoliberal reform routinely suffered substantial political consequences which would act as a deterrent upon other political actors considering austerity measures and/or incentivize them to shift towards a more pro-welfare position. It is with this in mind, perhaps, that we might consider this a period of *hindered* welfare reform.

Indeed, in contrast to what one might expect on the basis of the CPE literature on European integration, rather than satisfaction at the successful imposition of neoliberal reforms, Europe's political elite have consistently shown signs of frustration at their *inability* to complete their project. Examining the views of pro-neoliberal reformers expressed during the late-1990s and early-2000s, from the vantage point of today, we see a considerable degree of frustration. One telling example is that of Guillermo de la Dehesa, Vice Chairman of Goldman Sachs Europe. Writing in 2006 in his book *Europe at the Crossroads: Will the EU Ever Be Able to Compete with the United States as an Economic Power?*, de la Dehesa complained that the 'main obstacle to introducing structural reforms in the EU is that Europe prides itself on a political system that rests solidly on an institutionalized cooperation between governments and social partners'. De la Dehesa lamented this commitment to social cooperation on the grounds that it had consistently hindered attempts to reform the European welfare model. Thus, whilst recognizing that, 'the social partners' dialogue is an excellent and democratic idea', nevertheless for de la Dehesa, 'it has become a stumbling block that makes it more difficult for governments to undertake structural reforms', and as a result, 'excessive product and labor market regulations continue to impede growth and employment' (de la Dehesa, 2006: 139–40). The obstacle to welfare reform that de la Dehesa found most troubling, moreover, was the obstinate attitude of Europe's population: '[u]nfortunately, most Europeans seem not to understand these issues' (de la Dehesa, 2006: 148).

The view that Europe as a whole had been too resistant to welfare reform was widely shared across Europe's political and economic elite. This is perhaps most evident in the language used by the European Commission during the period leading up to the global economic crisis. This paints a similar picture of elite dissatisfaction to that expressed by de la Dehesa. For instance, in its 1999 Annual Economic Report, the European Commission considered the EU to have failed to achieve adequate levels of economic growth, directly as a result of it having 'failed to make sufficient progress in improving the functioning of its product, service, capital and labour markets' (CEC, 1999: 6). This failure to achieve necessary market reforms, moreover, was intimately linked to the inability to reform the welfare state; a failure which it was claimed had resulted in higher taxes and real interest rates (and thereby crowded out the possibility of private sector invest-ment), distorted markets, and prevented more growth-oriented policies from being adopted. In short, the neoliberal reforms that were sought by the Commission, and signed up to by its member states, had been insufficiently realized, thereby hinder-ing growth and competitiveness. In the Commission's own words

> During the 1990s reforms were implemented throughout the EU. But pro-gress was initially slow and member countries did not adopt a sufficiently comprehensive approach. As a result, sub-optimal functioning product and labour markets, high tax pressures and *inefficient welfare systems* bore down on the EU's growth and employment performance.
>
> (CEC, 1999: 51, emphasis added)

Likewise, when we come to view the Report from the High Level Group chaired by Wim Kok (the so-called Kok Report), published in 2004, and which was initi-ated to review what was at the time widely viewed to be a failing Lisbon Agenda, we see a similar depiction of lagging growth and insufficient reform in a con-text of a Europe that is overly resistant to change (HLG, 2004). Again, therefore, Europe's political elite lamented its 'disappointing delivery' in implementing the reform targets it had set itself (HLG, 2004: 6). And again the inability of the EU's member states to adequately tackle their own excessive public spending was identified as a key factor explaining these poor outcomes. In particular, 'the weak budgetary positions with which some European Member States entered the economic downturn,' was identified as problematic, and was a result of member states, 'insufficiently consolidating their finances during the previous economic upturn' (HLG, 2004: 10). This insufficient consolidation of public finances, we should add, was itself oftentimes a direct result of mobilized opposition, as we have seen. Indeed, this inability to achieve sought-after levels of welfare retrench-ment was tacitly recognized by the Commission in 2005 in noting that 11 of the (then) 25 member states had failed to meet their 3 per cent GDP deficit ceiling target (CEC, 2005: 2). In the language of the Commission: 'slippages between budgetary plans and outcomes have been frequent and sizeable in some years, even controlling for growth surprises. Such slippages seem mainly associated with *differences between planned and realised expenditure/GDP ratios*' (CEC, 2005: 5, emphasis added).

Welfare during the European crisis: the age of impeded austerity?

As we have seen, the period prior to 2008 was characterized by growing constraints upon the welfare state, and increasing pressure for retrenchment, each caused by both heightened economic competition and associated locational competition arising from membership of the single European market, as well as institutional constraints arising from the process of European integration (most obviously, the Maastricht convergence criteria and subsequent Stability and Growth Pact).

These processes were limited, however, by both a growing legitimacy problem for the European Union, and a series of protest movements that sought (successfully at times) to obstruct the process of welfare retrenchment. As we shall see, however, the post-2008 period witnessed a heightened attempt still to reform, restructure and reduce the generosity of Europe's welfare states. The increased capacity of investors to scrutinize national governments further limited welfare spending. This, moreover, was combined with a renewed commitment on the part of Europe's supranational elite to adopt institutional rules that would lock-in a commitment to fiscal orthodoxy and major attempts at welfare retrenchment.

This austerity agenda, however, prompted the development of new anti-austerity social movements, expressing deep-rooted hostility to the established political and economic elites. As a result, rather than a smooth process of neoliberal restructuring post-2008 (and especially post-2010 when the European manifestation of the crisis became most intense), we witness instead a dramatic heightening of the politicization of welfare. Governments' attempts to dismantle the provisions for social security faced massive opposition. These protests were at least partly able to hinder austerity-based attacks on welfare, whilst at the same time contributing to a political crisis by successfully questioning governments in their attempts to claim, 'There is no alternative'. As we have seen, however, whilst this crisis of legitimacy was in some ways a source of hope for those seeking to develop more radical and prefigurative forms of disruptive agency, at the same time the depth of disaffection and disengagement that it reflected of wider society was also a phenomenon that could be fostered and built upon by political actors propagating right-wing populist welfare chauvinism. These developments are each charted in the next section.

Welfare under pressure: European integration and the intensification of disciplinary neoliberalism

As an effect of financial instability in the aftermath of the US financial crisis and during the European crisis the disciplinary effects of global capitalist accumulation intensified (Roos, 2016). As investors became more sceptical with regard to the sustainability of economic development (especially in peripheral countries within the EU), there was an increased structural necessity for elected governments to generate an image of, in Gill's terms, 'market efficiency, discipline and confidence' (Gill, 1992: 168–169). A central role in this transmission of capitalist discipline was played by rating agencies. As Altvater highlights, these agencies would

> autocratically decide on a country's standing on financial markets and hence on the debt-service levels to be paid out of the budget. Rating agencies are a key determinant of the necessary surplus of the primary budget to meet interest payments, and thus implicitly the amount of revenues which remain to finance all other state expenditures – from social services to infrastructure.
>
> (Altvater, 2011: 278)

As a result, the European countries that had high debt/GDP-ratios (exacerbated by either the economic downturn and rising debt levels associated with automatic stabilisers, or by state interventions in the financial sector at the peak of the crisis) were exposed to tremendous pressures from financial markets and increased difficulties in refinancing their economic activities. The European crisis therefore represented a context in which a growing need for social protection measures faced highly indebted states and declining government revenues (van Kersbergen *et al.*, 2014: 884). The institutional deficiencies of the Eurozone – that is, a missing *lender of last resort* and a deflationary bias – further reinforced these pressures upon those member states that had adopted the Euro (Stockhammer, 2012). Further, as countries could not indebt themselves directly with the ECB, private banks instead took cheap money from the ECB in order to lend it to governments at the market rate, thereby increasing the vulnerability of states to financial markets (Altvater, 2011: 280). The effect was a deepening of the earlier noted trend of 'subversive liberalism' (Rhodes, 1995: 385), placing existing welfare models under further stress and further eroding the principles of universalism and solidarity in welfare provision.

Whilst the financial crisis of 2008 had a significant effect upon the scale of welfare spending, therefore, this was compounded by the system of European crisis management that saw the incremental introduction of a range of different measures (such as the 'Six Pack', the 'Two Pack', the European Semester, the Memoranda of Understanding (MoU) or the EFSF and the ESM). These acted to 'lock in' competitiveness in a step-by-step manner, leading to austerity being the only viable political solution to the crisis (Huke and Schlemermeyer, 2012; La Porte and Heins, 2016a; Oberndorfer, 2015). This new form of economic governance created political pressure through constant surveillance, combined with a 'mix between conditionality and 'backroom' diplomacy' (Pavolini *et al.*, 2016: 134). As a result, welfare state arrangements were destabilized and pro-cyclical austerity policies were imposed, each of which threatened to dismantle the European social model and erode social cohesion (Bieling, 2015; Stockhammer and Köhler, 2015: 34). As Ladi and Graziano argue, the consequences of this locking in of austerity

> are intuitive: since 28.2 per cent of GDP was spent on social protection in 2010 [...], it emerges quite clearly that [measures such as] the fiscal compact treaty would trigger welfare state policy cuts – especially in the most exposed sectors (such as pensions and health care), and in countries where the public debt/GDP ratio was particularly high (such as in Greece and Italy).
>
> (Ladi and Graziano, 2014: 115)

The role of the European institutions in this process are particularly important to note, and especially that of the European Commission. Thus, as the debt problems facing Europe – and especially the peripheral European economies – became apparent in 2010, the European Commission began to focus in earnest on the issue of fiscal consolidation, as did the financial markets. With the task of managing Europe's public debt beginning to look increasingly difficult, the

Commission consistently voiced concern that public debt could rise to over 100 per cent (European Commission, 2010). As we noted previously, this problem of Europe's excessive public debt was rooted in the long-term inability of member states to bring public spending under control in the face of routine bouts of visible and disruptive opposition to welfare reform initiatives that had occurred prior to the crisis. As the Commission itself highlighted,

> the deterioration in underlying fiscal positions dates back to well before the crisis. In many countries, credit and asset price booms had led to improvements in fiscal positions in the years preceding the crisis, and this partly obscured the deterioration in underlying positions. The failure to fully account for the direct and indirect effects of strong asset prices on fiscal positions led to a distorted and overly optimistic assessment of the true fiscal stance in these 'good' years. When the bubble burst and the crisis unfolded, tax revenues fell sharply and the dramatic increase in budget deficits became apparent.
>
> (Commission, 2010: 31–2)

The prescription advised by the Commission, therefore, was a sharp contraction of public spending: 'Very sizeable budgetary consolidation will be necessary in many Member States to bring public finances back on a sustainable path' (p. 33). This necessary reduction in net public spending, the Commission estimated, would amount to around 5 per cent of GDP.

It is with these concerns in mind that we can understand the attempts by the Commission to consistently push for fiscal contraction during the 2010–15 period. Out of the 27 member states, 23 were subject to the SGP Excessive Deficit Procedure during this period. In addition, the case was consistently made for the possibility of what economists have termed 'expansionary contraction' (for a well-cited example of this argument, although without direct use of the term, see Alesina and Ardagna, 2010; for a critical discussion of the soundness of 'expansionary fiscal contraction', or 'expansionary austerity', see Guajardo *et al.*, 2011, and Jordà and Taylor, 2016). Expansionary contraction, it was claimed, was a process whereby 'confidence gains' that it was hoped would be achieved as a result of reduced public debt would ultimately result in a 'recovery of investor and consumer confidence' which has 'positive implications for output in the medium and longer term', as well as acting to 'reduce future tax liabilities which also strengthens private demand'. From this perspective, postponing consolidation only acts to increase the overall cost of debt servicing over time (and should therefore be avoided). As a result, the Commission recommended a 1 per cent GDP reduction in debt per year, double that which was constitutionally required by the terms of the SGP (European Commission, 2011: 5–4).

There was, therefore, clearly downward pressure upon public spending, and especially welfare provision, throughout the post-2010 period, as a direct result of the process and institutions of European integration. It is important to note, however, that this political pressure produced only a small reduction in average government deficits, which fell from an average of 3.9 per cent of GDP between

2007–11, to 2.2 per cent in 2015 in the Eurozone countries (and from 4.2 per cent to 2.5 per cent in the EU member states), whilst government debt rose from 76.5 per cent to 93.5 per cent for the Eurozone states (and from 70.4 per cent to 87.2 per cent in the EU). The reduction in government deficits that was achieved moreover, was done largely through an increase in revenue rather than through the successful reduction in public expenditure, with the latter actually rising from 48.4 per cent of GDP to 48.7 per cent in the Eurozone states between 2007–11 (average) and 2015, in large part due to increases generated by automatic stabilisers (European Commission, 2016: statistical annexe). Much of the CPE literature has focused on the pressure emerging from the European Union and its impact upon national welfare states and welfare retrenchment during the European crisis period. We need also to consider, however, the new forms of disruptive agency that have emerged in this context of heightened pressure for retrenchment, which we might argue acted to restrict the degree to which welfare retrenchment could be carried out as intended by Europe's political and economic elites.

Frontal attacks on the welfare state: austerity-based reforms during the European crisis, and an emerging defence

> Today we are witnessing a frontal attack – and there is no other word to describe what is happening – on the welfare states of the countries of the Eurozone, which is accentuated in the periphery of this monetary union.
>
> (Navarro, 2013: 189)

As a result of the global and European crises, member states across the European Union undertook measures that sought to reduce the cost and generosity of their welfare provisions. This therefore represented a continuation of developments which, as we have seen, were initiated before the crisis (La Porte and Heins, 2016b: 3). In general terms, the reforms were characterized by welfare retrenchment, activation policies that sought to make welfare provision conditional upon (and therefore designed to produce) a willingness to return to paid work, and a reduction in universal risk prevention programmes (Borosch *et al.*, 2016: 770).

The following five tendencies were especially prevalent. First, public sector employment witnessed large cuts or freezes of wages as well as dismissals or the freezing of hiring new members of staff, in turn reducing the quality of the public services provided and witnessing a turn towards greater privatization of welfare provision as those who could afford to do so turned towards private services because of the poor quality of public services (Bernal Agudo and Lorenzo Lacruz, 2012). Second, welfare retrenchment systematically focused on pensions, as early retirement was restricted or abolished, the retirement age was raised, and the level of pension provision was reduced. This was especially marked in the case of Greece, where basic pensions were reduced by 20 per cent for those pensions that exceeded €1200 (Borosch *et al.*, 2016: 776; Heins and La Porte, 2016: 213; Pavolini *et al.*, 2016: 143–144).

Third, health systems witnessed general budget reductions, cost containment measures, selective privatizations (such as increases in co-payments or the outsourcing of staff) and – in some cases – the exclusion of previously included groups, such as illegalized migrants in Spain (Borosch *et al.*, 2016: 775; Ruiz-Giménez, 2014). Fiscal austerity measures also led to an increase in the degree to which the public sector was overloaded in terms of its capacity to deliver services. For instance, access to health care became increasingly difficult, resulting in an increase in the rate of outbreaks of infectious diseases (Karanikolos *et al.*, 2013). Fourth, unemployment benefits were reduced, whilst employment rights were hollowed out (Borosch *et al.*, 2016: 777; Haas and Huke, 2015; Ladi and Graziano, 2014: 118). Finally, access to universal social protection measures such as minimum income schemes was restricted and the amount of money invested in social exclusion programmes was reduced (Borosch *et al.*, 2016: 785; Navarro and Clua-Losada 2012; Pavolini *et al.*, 2016: 151).

European integration played an important role in both pushing for, and consolidating, this round of welfare reforms, witnessing the creation of 'more constraints in terms of policy, politics and governance' (La Porte and Heins, 2016b). This included more direct forms of intervention, such as the conditions imposed by the ECB upon member states seeking to make purchases on the secondary market; and the strict conditionality contained in the Memorandums of Understanding, which significantly strengthened what had up until that point been a relatively weak capacity on the part of the European institutions to have direct influence in the field of welfare policies (Pavolini *et al.*, 2016: 145–46). Party politics, public and parliamentary debates, and organized interests all saw their influence decline, while the European Commission (EC), the International Monetary Fund (IMF) and the ECB played a heightened role in decision-making processes (Dukelow, 2016; Pavolini *et al.*, 2016: 131–132; della Porta and Parks 2016).

Whilst some would argue that the recommendations of the European Union represented only a soft form of discipline (in that member states could ultimately decide to ignore those recommendations, albeit with associated fines for those countries that signed up to the Fiscal Compact), this ignores the fact that EU-level recommendations also had an important market signalling effect. As Sacchi has shown, even monitoring processes and recommendations with implicit conditionality represent significant EU-level effects when coupled with the external disciplinary power of market forces (Sacchi, 2016: 159). The chasm between the institutions of the European Union and popular demands, which had already become visible as part of the legitimacy crisis that the EU had faced from the adoption of the Maastricht Treaty onwards, thus widened further still. The requirements of capitalist accumulation were, therefore, 'insulate[d] [...] from contradictory democratic demands for social justice' as an explicit result of the process of European integration (La Porte and Heins, 2016b: 3). Indeed, this, as we have seen, was exactly the intention that underlay the agreements that the member states themselves had reached in creating the disciplinary mechanisms that constituted European integration, as far back (at least) as the European Monetary System of the late 1970s.

Rather than proceeding uncontested, however, this austerity agenda also fostered its own instances of disruption (Ancelovici, 2015: 197). The attempt by the institutions of the European Union to shield the requirements of capital accumulation from the contradictory democratic demands for social justice therefore remained fragile, and their success was only limited and partial. In the two country cases that follow we show how the various attempts to heighten market discipline in the UK and Spain met with a number of obstacles that limited their degree of success. Pressure for welfare reform grew as a result of the combined pressures of debt, market integration and the institutions of the European Union. Yet this pressure, and associated attempts at welfare retrenchment and austerity, at the same time prompted a multiplication of different forms of disruptive agency. This includes growing disaffection and despondency. The rate of depression, anxiety disorder and suicides grew significantly in some member states (Karanikolos *et al.*, 2013). But it also includes disaffection in the form of Euroscepticism and 'Euro-criticism', witnessing a growing sentiment that 'the EU not only fails to deliver prosperity to its citizens, but does so through opaque and unaccountable decision-making procedures' (Dokos *et al.*, 2013: 2). Disruptive protest and the demand for a voice has been consistently made, sometimes in the form of anti-austerity protests, other times witnessing demands for the voices of women and minorities to be heard above the din of public service withdrawals and cutbacks. Finally, what we have termed the 'prefigurative radical' emerged at points in the crisis, as the most effective agent able to insist upon a voice, to combine this with material demands *and* at the same time to pose a radical alternative to the dystopian and undemocratic 'logic of no alternative' offered by European capitalism and its institutions of European integration.

Further, as we have seen, whilst the crisis of legitimation suffered by the European Union has at times been associated with emancipatory demands and movements, it has also provided the potential for the emergence and growth of right-wing populism. As the rise of UKIP perhaps shows exemplarily, different forms of welfare chauvinism have also emerged in response. In the words of Keskinen *et al.*, this uses the welfare state to draw distinctions 'between 'us' and 'them' – the natives that are perceived to deserve the benefits and the racialized 'others' who are portrayed as undeserving and even exploiting the welfare system at the cost of the 'rightful' citizens' (Keskinen *et al.*, 2016: 2; Komp *et al.*, 2013; Chalari, 2014: 131). We turn now to consider each of these trends in the specific settings of the UK and Spain.

UK welfare reforms and disruptive subjectivity

One of the first major protest events that took place after the 2008 crisis, and which arguably initiated the UK's anti-austerity movement, was the two-day series of demonstrations against the G20 meeting which took place in London on 28 March and 1 April 2009. These witnessed a combination of moderate (28 March) and radical (1 April) protests, designed to allow a plurality of different protesters to highlight their displeasure at the crisis and to demand a social justice focus in response. This was also the first major set of summit protests after the global economic crisis struck in September 2008, witnessing the more militant of the two days (1 April) focus on a range of grievances and causes, with four starting points each led by one of the 'Four Horsemen of the Apocalypse', and converging on the Bank of England. The symbols used for the demonstration were: a red horse against war, a green horse against climate chaos, a silver horse against financial crimes, and a black horse against land enclosures and borders. In bringing together peace movements and anti-environmentalism, within a demonstration that was explicitly focused on anti-austerity and the global economic crisis, this demonstration represented an important opportunity to build alliances between different groups and activists with different backgrounds and attitudes. Indeed, some of the experiences gained by both the peace movements (especially in opposition to Israel's Operation Cast Lead, and to the perceived lack of an appropriate response by the British Government) and the environmentalist movement (especially through the Camp for Climate Action), as well as the tradition of summit-based protests that were associated with the anti-globalization movement, would all subsequently contribute to the development of the anti-austerity movement, especially from 2010 onwards following the election of the Coalition Government (and its immediate declaration of heightened austerity).

The moderate G20 march, *Put People First*, initially gained more media attention, and received more friendly media reporting in comparison with the more radical event (*G20 Meltdown*) (Bennett and Segerberg, 2011: 786). This, however, was subsequently reversed following the controversial policing methods employed at the latter event, including kettling that was eventually declared unlawful by the High Court, and perhaps most notoriously the death of the newspaper seller, Ian Tomlinson, who was uninvolved in the protest.

In seeking to express a voice in opposition to what were perceived as a range of injustices associated with the crisis, demonstrators used a variety of symbols, slogans and methods to call on governments to respond to the crisis in a way that was mindful towards concerns about social justice. This included an effigy of a banker carrying a board with the words, 'Eat the Bankers', highlighting the public anger that was directed towards the financial industry as the cause of the global economic crisis. Slogans on protesters' banners and placards also made similar reference to the financial sector and to the perceived greed of bankers personally, including 'Bankers are Evil', 'Bankers and Coppers Revolt! Resist Your Own Oppression', 'Capitalism, Epic Fail', and 'Greed is Good Bad' (Liao, T.F., 2010). In addition to contributing towards the building of alliances between different groups of activists, therefore, the 2009 demonstrations also made an important contribution in terms of building awareness of the political economy of the crisis, a focus on the financial sector, and generating a narrative that focused on the role of the financial industry, unregulated greed and the role of contemporary capitalism in explaining the crisis, each of which would become increasingly important themes for the anti-austerity movement from 2010 onwards.

Indeed, as already noted, upon its election to office in 2010, the incoming Conservative-Liberal Democrat Coalition Government embraced a programme of thoroughgoing welfare reform. This was underpinned and justified in terms of an analysis which portrayed public debt as excessive and almost out of control (Stanley, 2014). Given its status as a non-Eurozone member, the UK was clearly not subjected to the same degree of EU-level control as other member states. The UK was also one of only two countries that chose not to sign the so-called 'fiscal compact' in 2012, thereby further releasing the Government (at least in principle) from the need to cohere with EU-level demands for fiscal orthodoxy. That said, the Stability and Growth Pact does apply to the UK and as a result it was subjected to the EU's system of annual 'convergence reports', according to which budget deficits were required to be within a target of 3 per cent of GDP. Moreover, the Coalition Government consistently pointed to the impact of high levels of public debt in the Eurozone peripheries, and the subsequent sovereign debt crises experienced there, as an indication of the need for national debt to remain low. This approach was evident immediately after entering office. For instance, speaking in June 2010 Prime Minister David Cameron was quick to highlight the risk of 'becoming-Greece' and the urgency with which austerity therefore needed to be adopted:

> even more worrying is the example of Greece – a sudden loss of confidence and a sharp increase in interest rates. Now, let me be clear: our debts are not as bad as Greece's; our underlying economic position is much stronger than Greece's; and crucially we now have a government that I would argue has already demonstrated its willingness and its ability to deal with the problem. But Greece stands as a warning of what happens to countries that lose their credibility, or whose governments pretend that difficult decisions can somehow be avoided. [...] That's why we have already launched and completed an in-year Spending Review to save £6 billion of public spending.
> (David Cameron, Prime Minister's speech on the economy,
> 7 June 2010)

In this sense, therefore, the UK experienced many of the same 'peer pressures' that come with EU membership – both in the sense of experiencing pressure from the Commission to conform to fiscal orthodoxy, but also with regard to the impact that came with market integration and the pressure to be 'competitive' (as well as assisting members of the national political and economic elite in justifying a national obedience to that pressure). Indeed, it is this latter pressure that was most relevant in the case of Cameron's Coalition Government, for whom the pressure to conform with fiscal orthodoxy was openly embraced, and the 'basket case' status of those European countries that refused to accept it was enthusiastically condemned, along with a heralding of the detrimental consequences for those who adopted the 'basket case' option. As we noted above, moreover, these 'softer' pressures to comply with EU-level recommendations also had coercive effects as a result of the market signals that they created and which financial integration had increased the effect of (Sacchi, 2016; see also Roos, 2016).

In addition to providing an external constraint that Britain's political elite could call upon to justify austerity measures, Britain's position on European integration under the Coalition Government also acted to ensure that these constraints would remain in place. Britain's half-in/half-out status within the European Union enabled its domestic political elite to *both* proclaim the need for fiscal orthodoxy, on the grounds that liberalized financial markets (in part achieved through European integration) necessitated fiscal orthodoxy, *and* ensure that more substantively political and interventionist (Keynesian) alternatives to this fiscal orthodox response would not be developed at the EU level, as such measures would be vetoed on the grounds of infringing on national sovereignty. That is, the United Kingdom remained under Cameron both committed to being too 'out' of European integration to be able to endorse an EU-level programme of fiscal stimulus, and too 'in' to be able to withstand the pressure to conform with the demands for fiscal conservatism emanating from economic competition within the single market. Whilst the United Kingdom's non-membership of the Eurozone suggests that its domestic elites are free from the need to conform to the demands of the Troika, therefore, it would be erroneous to suggest that European integration played no role in the domestic elite's attempt to impose tightened market discipline upon British society, including when it comes to considering its attempt to secure welfare retrenchment.

In seeking to consolidate the national budget, the Coalition Government proposed a number of welfare reforms, including reductions in social security and benefits, expenditure for local government services, a new system of workfare, and a contractionary recalculation of state pension provision. This represented a major reform agenda that was widely viewed as a substantial restructuring of the state-society relations in the United Kingdom – systematically accompanied by a declared need to conform to the market pressures emanating from broad market integration, of which European integration was a part, and with consistent reference to the plight of countries such as Spain and Greece as an indication of what happens to those countries which fail to 'obey'. It is within this context, moreover, that we also witness the emergence of an anti-austerity movement that sought to challenge the austerity agenda of the Cameron Government. We map out here those elements of the movement that related specifically to welfare (with discussions of movements specifically focused on education and housing reserved to Chapters 5 and 6).

Perhaps the most significant and sustained form of visible campaigning against welfare austerity was that witnessed with the UK Uncut campaign. This began in October 2010, in direct response to the Comprehensive Spending Review published in the same month, and lasted for nearly a year before its activity (which remains ongoing) was seriously curtailed following the arrest and conviction of a number of UK Uncut activists during the Fortnum and Mason protest in March 2011. The main aim of the protest movement – which typically focused on the occupation of retail stores, or disruptive direct action protests directly outside the stores – was to both highlight the unfair way in which the budget deficit was being addressed, and to advocate an alternative means of doing so, through measures to end tax avoidance (see the next section for a fuller discussion).

This use of occupations and direct action tactics was also invoked by other anti-austerity protest initiatives. For instance, the February 2011 *Save Our*

Libraries campaign used a combination of both 'mock' occupations (in which library users staged 'read ins' to highlight the popularity of the libraries) and 'real' occupations (for instance in the case of Barnet library, the closure of which was avoided as a result of an occupation and taking control of the library by local residents and activists). Similarly, the Occupy movement, which began in October 2011, focused explicitly on anti-austerity goals. For instance, the Occupy London Economics Statement, agreed at the General Assembly by St Paul's Cathedral on 6 December 2011, included a clear attack on the Government's austerity agenda:

> Cuts to public services are having a disastrous impact on education, employment, business, health, social care and law and order. We oppose the unfair cuts and regressive taxes, currently inflicted on those vulnerable groups least able to bear the burden. Women especially pick up the pieces, often through unwaged work. Deep and painful cuts, coupled with increased taxation, have been put in place based on political motives and flawed beliefs. The strategy is misguided, damaging and not working.
>
> (Occupy London, 2011)

More standard public demonstrations were also routinely conducted throughout the austerity period. This includes the March 2011 demonstration staged by the TUC, and annual demonstrations by the People's Assembly Against Austerity that began in 2013, as well as the protests staged by the group Anonymous every November since 2014 (although the grievances underpinning the Anonymous protests are less clearly defined). In addition to demonstrations, the public sector unions have staged a number of industrial disputes, part of the purpose of which has been to draw attention to – and to oppose – the Government's austerity programme (in the form of either a freeze or a reduction in public sector pay and pensions) (as we saw in Chapter 3).

The UK anti-austerity movement therefore witnessed a series of protest events that sought to contest the imposition of austerity upon British society. This included both more confrontational events, including the occupations associated with UK Uncut, and those more focused on demonstrating opposition to government policy through more 'set-piece' rallies and protests, such as the TUC demonstration of 2011. In seeking to explore the methods of anti-austerity mobilizations in the UK, however, and to evaluate their effectiveness, we turn here to consider what were perhaps two of the most prominent campaigns (UK Uncut and Boycott Workfare), in order both to consider how they became so prominent, and the impact that they had upon government policy.

UK Uncut: 'Open up actions to everyone'

The emergence of UK Uncut in the second half of 2010 represented a concerted attack on the austerity and welfare retrenchment agenda of the newly formed Coalition Government. The strategy that UK Uncut adopted was one of direct action. This involved performing stunts in or outside of shops accused of tax avoidance, in such a way that would maximize disruption and the publicity and attention that the shop in question would experience. The purpose of the campaign was to force the shop in question to do more to pay taxes owed, and to bring attention to the issue of tax evasion around which UK Uncut were campaigning, as well as demanding that the Government do more to collect these taxes (Street, 2015: 131). These were tactics that had been developed over time by a number of the campaign participants, with many having links to more recent environmentalist groups, especially the annual Camp for Climate Change which was a high-profile direct action environmentalist event on the activist calendar prior to 2008, and the campaign group People and Planet, as well as being connected to the student movement happening concurrently alongside the UK Uncut movement (see the following chapter for more on the student movement). Others had gained their first taste of political activity earlier in the anti-Iraq demonstrations (interviews with UK Uncut activists, January 2015, April 2015, August 2016; Street, 2015: 132).

One of the aims of the campaign was to insist that austerity measures were neither necessary nor unopposable. As one UK Uncut activist put it,

> Part of the campaign was to say that the cuts weren't necessary. I suppose, for me, tax dodging was one way of saying that – as a way of opening the door to saying that.
>
> (interview with UK Uncut participant, 22 September 2015)

The initial target taken up by UK Uncut was Vodafone, chosen due to the allegations circulating that it had benefited from an alleged £6 billion tax write-off deal with the Government. Protests took place both online and in physical space, with 1000 people signing UK Uncut's online petition in October 2010. This was a move accompanied by the first action of the group, in which activists gathered at the Oxford Street London branch of Vodafone to stage an occupation of the store in protest at its alleged tax avoidance. At the time of its initiation, moreover, the group of activists set out explicitly to 'kick-start' an anti-austerity social movement (Street, 2015: 132, 135). In many ways they were successful in this sense. As one interviewee put it,

> Twitter was still was quite new. And so the fact that me and my friends who had been doing our anti-cuts thing [...] and organising people here – being able to see, live, as it was happening, a protest taking place, was new.
>
> (interview with UK Uncut participant, 22 September 2015)

This first event was subsequently followed during November and December by staged occupations and protests outside the premises of Vodafone in stores across the country, including Brighton, Glasgow, Birmingham, Liverpool, Edinburgh, Leicester, York, Bristol, Portsmouth, Southampton, and Cambridge. December also saw UK Uncut prompt another Twitter attack on Vodafone, this time in response to the company's Christmas-focused PR stunt. At this point, Vodafone had been seeking to improve its reputation through a PR stunt that promised to reward Twitter users who tweeted things they liked about Vodafone using the hashtag #MadeMeSmile. This gave UK Uncut a perfect opportunity to encourage twitter users to invent their own, more critical, responses – witnessing a wave of tweets, estimated at around 3000, highlighting the company's alleged tax dodging behaviour. Moreover, the company had set up its own website to repeat the tweets, meaning that the negative publicity was being amplified by its own website.

The nature of the UK Uncut strategy was such that it could be readily replicated across the country. This created an open, fluid and creative element to the organization and the actions it put on. As one participant put it

> My own interest in working with Uncut came from a desire to give expression to my political ideals more freely, away from the – at times – constraining world of non-governmental organizations (NGOs), with their established modes of working and tightly defined mission statements.
>
> (Street, 2015: 135)

The practice of opting to target high street stores also ensured that the actions were amenable to open participation. In the words of another activist:

> […] because you've got a Vodaphone and a Top Shop and whatever else on every high street in the country, it means that you can open up actions to everyone – we don't need to go to the headquarters of the company because there's one that you can simply get a bus to […]
>
> (interview with UK Uncut activist, April 2015)

As another participant in the UK Uncut protests highlighted, UK Uncut represented for many an attempt to participate in direct action forms of protest for the first time; whereas in the past participation in such events had been largely reserved for more hardened activists.

> It created a friendly, fluffy, populist kind of illegal action. Before then the idea of taking part in illegal action was usually framed for me as at the hardcore end of political involvement, the kind of thing that you do if you've been involved for a while, kind of showing off your battle scars, the sort of thing you did to demonstrate your commitment. This isn't quite true but it [UK Uncut] sort of felt like the first time that you had silly, fun, irreverent potentially illegal action which would be the first political thing that people might do. Because it was framed through silliness and joy rather than through confrontation.
>
> (interview with Adam Ramsay, 22 April 2015)

Many of the UK Uncut protests staged in or outside of shops were highly disruptive, forcing the shops to close whilst protesters were forcibly removed by police. Thus, during December 2010 the strategy moved to focus especially on shops owned by Philip Green, who was also accused of tax dodging, witnessing protests that were moved on from one shop immediately proceeding to a different Green-owned shop in order to cause a similar level of disruption. Moreover, given that the protests were taking place on Saturdays during December there was a clear attempt to maximize disruption in a context of the Christmas shopping peak for the year. Indeed, the extent of the protests was such that they began to prompt fears that hundreds of shops would be closed during the Christmas shopping period. On some occasions, moreover, the impact of the protests was considerably amplified simply by the fact that the shop in question was known to be one targeted by UK Uncut (that is, especially those owned by Philip Green, including Topshop, Dorothy Perkins, Burton and Miss Selfridge) (Lewis *et al.*, 2010). This meant that in many instances the shops known to be targets would close themselves in advance – removing the need for any protest actually to take place. On one occasion, shops along a planned route for a trade union-led anti-cuts march, which UK Uncut had announced it would participate in, closed ahead of the march due to fear that they would be targeted by the UK Uncut activities (interview with UK Uncut activist, April 2015).

An additional element to the UK Uncut strategy was the attempt to gain media attention. This, the group found, was particularly well-suited to their strategy of high-street shop occupations, used in combination with an effective social media campaign. As UK Uncut activist, Tim Street, puts it

> Occupations of high-profile shops were also a very effective means of getting a platform from where to promote Uncut's ideas – simply because the act was so novel and difficult to ignore. Indeed, given the enthusiastic media response to such actions it soon became clear for Uncut's members that if occupations almost guaranteed coverage, then that was a clear opportunity to draw attention to the damage caused by the cuts and discuss alternative policies that might not otherwise be heard. In this sense direct action was a blunt instrument – people sat down in tax dodgers and banks to point their finger at the real cause of the economic crisis and the real gap in public finances. This was done purposefully to counter the Government's propaganda campaign for austerity, which had misdirected public anger towards blaming both the previous Labour Government for overspending and the people receiving welfare benefits … Crucially, Uncut activists therefore invested significant time and energy before, during and after protests in engaging with mainstream media (such as traditional print and broadcast outlets) and social media (for example, Twitter, Facebook) in order to amplify the impact of their actions.
>
> (Street, 2015: 140)

The UK Uncut protests continued into 2011, targeting Boots in a day of action during January. In February, UK Uncut moved to target over 40 high street banks across the country, staging short occupations in which the banks would be symbolically turned into socially useful locations serving the community, such as libraries, creches, health services or job centres (Street, 2015: 142). This was a deliberate attempt to highlight the negative social impact that the financial industry's focus on profit had caused, and instead to highlight that through direct action bank buildings could be put to more socially useful purposes. Other actions included support events for the Occupy movement, and stunts targeting key agents of austerity, such as a protest outside Nick Clegg's house in May 2012 and mock evictions of the houses of Welfare Minister, Lord Freud, and Work and Pensions Minister, Iain Duncan Smith, in April 2013 (Street, 2015: 144).

Perhaps the most notorious act of UK Uncut, however, was the occupation of Fortnum and Mason. This was timed to coincide with, and (at least informally) form part of the TUC march against austerity that took place on 26 March 2011. Whilst the TUC march convened at Hyde Park, more radical protesters targeted Piccadilly, an upmarket street in central London that hosted a number of high-end stores and hotels. This resulted in the Ritz being targeted with paint bombs and having its windows smashed. It also saw UK Uncut stage a non-violent occupation of the expensive department store, Fortnum and Mason. This was the culmination of a day of occupations, in which other stores, including Boots, were also targeted for disruptive actions (interview with UK Uncut activist, January 2015). Whilst the occupation was eventually surrounded by police, protesters were given the promise that they would be allowed to leave freely, provided that they did so promptly. Upon leaving the occupation, however, the protesters were immediately arrested and several of them were subsequently charged and convicted for aggravated trespass and issued with a six-month conditional discharge and £1,000 fine for prosecution costs (Malik, 2011). This was considered by many to be a deliberate attempt to end the UK Uncut actions, by arresting and charging the participants of a high-profile protest (interview with UK Uncut activist, January 2016). It was also relatively effective in doing so, witnessing a significant tailing off of UK Uncut protests after the Fortnum and Mason action. As one activist recalled

> [...] It seemed like UK Uncut came across quite an effective tactic whereby it was causing a lot of disruption with sit-ins and so on, without breaking any laws. It seemed like it was going to be very effective; but then the police were willing to arrest 100-odd people on no real basis. [...] that really took the sails out of the movement and made it very difficult to organise actions as well because it's one thing using Facebook and getting people to go and do one of these sit-ins or occupations if they're unlikely to be arrested but you can't do that if there's a high chance that people are going to be arrested because people need to know what they're getting themselves in for.
>
> (Interview with UK Uncut activist, January 2015)

Following the Fortnum and Mason event the frequency of UK Uncut events fell quite dramatically. A number of subsequent events that did take place included a joint event with NHS campaigners – Block the Bridge, Block the Bill, which saw an occupation of Westminster Bridge by over 2000 people in opposition to proposed reforms to the NHS – and another protest in January and then September 2012, when UK Uncut and Disabled People Against the Cuts (DPAC) joined together to protest against the Welfare Reform Bill, blocking roads in central London by chaining together wheelchairs (Walker, 2012), and then in September demonstrating outside the Department for Work and Pensions in opposition to the decision to allow ATOS to sponsor the Paralympics. In addition, a series of actions took place in December 2012 against Starbucks as it was discovered that the firm paid no corporation tax (and even though the firm 'volunteered' to pay £20 million tax in an attempt to stem the public outcry) (Neville and Treanor, 2012). In July 2013, a UK Uncut action forced the closure of HSBC branches as it targeted the bank in 13 locations across the country in July 2013 (Press Association, 2013), and also saw a return to the targeting of Vodafone in June 2014.

In addition to high profile protest events, UK Uncut also entered into legal proceedings against the Government's tax collection office – Revenue and Customs (HMRC) – alleging that the Government had purposefully been lenient towards Goldman Sachs and let it get away with £20 million in unpaid tax. Whilst the legal case was unsuccessful for UK Uncut, the ruling did lead to HMRC being exposed and criticized for having taken into consideration the potential embarrassment that would have been felt by the Chancellor, George Osborne, in making its decision (Syal, 2013).

In terms of the impact of the protests, the two central goals were to highlight and politicize tax avoidance as an issue that was undermining public funding, and therefore move away from a discourse that blamed excessive welfare spending for poor government finances. In addition, the movement sought to question the discourse of the Government – that austerity measures were both unavoidable and that the burden of addressing the shortfall in public finances was being shared across the population. As one of the activists involved in the protests argues, whilst the broader goal of preventing austerity measures from taking place was not in large part achieved, these more immediate aims were broadly met:

> What UK Uncut haven't achieved is an end to tax dodging. In no way has that happened. But what they did achieve is they put it right at the top of the agenda, which is a massive achievement. And there have been campaigns around tax avoidance before particularly around the Daily Mail and they did not get anywhere at all. They [UK Uncut] killed two of the big slogans which the Tories had, which (and it depends how important you think this is), is 'there is no alternative' and 'we're all in it together'. As soon as they said that we could say, 'well of course there is an alternative – you've got to stop people dodging tax'; and with 'we're all in it together', we could say 'well of course we're not because Philip Green doesn't pay any tax'.
>
> (interview with UK Uncut activist, April 2015)

Indeed, it is difficult to deny that the UK Uncut activity had a significant impact upon government policy. Chancellor of the Exchequer, George Osborne, announced to Parliament on the 20th of March 2013 an overhaul of the taxation system. This, he claimed, would produce, 'one of the largest ever packages of tax avoidance and evasion measures presented at a Budget'.[2] Further, in 2015, the

Chancellor announced a significant additional investment of £800 million over the next five years for HM Revenue & Customs, to boost its work on non-compliance and tax evasion (Dudman, 2015). Finally, the fierce row that broke out following the Panama Papers leak in April 2016, again exposing the Government over tax avoidance/evasion, further highlighted the degree to which tax and tax avoidance had been politicized. The role of UK Uncut in setting this agenda in the early stages of the crisis cannot be denied.

In addition, UK Uncut inspired other groups to take similar actions. For instance, in March 2011 a group calling itself NHS Direct Action targeted the firm, Care UK, on the grounds that it stood to benefit from the Government's reforms to the NHS. Toby Simmons, speaking on behalf of the campaign, was explicit in highlighting how the strategy that the group was set to deploy – i.e. protesting outside the company's UK offices – was directly inspired by the actions of UK Uncut. In his own words,

> We're taking UK Uncut's idea of a simple message linked with a viable alternative. UK Uncut changed the rules by showing that spaces – even inside shops – are perfectly legitimate places to protest. It's harder to use the same methods with the private health firms that are circling the NHS – they don't have the same high-profile public image as Topshop or Vodafone – but we're attempting to show that the NHS is for everyone rather than for the elite few to make a profit from.
>
> (quoted in Paige, 2011)

Likewise, in 2011 the incoming NUS President, Liam Burns, called for actions similar to those staged by UK Uncut to be done by students: 'UK Uncut has identified legitimate targets for occupation, bringing attention and support to its cause' (Shepherd, 2011). 2015 and 2016 also saw the emergence of the group, Sisters Uncut, staging similar protests, including another 'block the bridge' style protest in November 2016 that sought to highlight opposition to government cuts to domestic violence services.

In sum, therefore, UK Uncut managed to use an innovative strategy of direct action protest, coordinated in an open and loose manner that was easily replicable. It caused significant media attention and politicized both the decisions of the Coalition Government to focus on welfare cuts as the means by which to balance the budget, and the unequal way in which it was doing so. The method of protest, moreover, produced direct disruption to the operation of a number of key firms that were alleged to be benefiting from the Government's leniency towards them. As such, this represented a significant problem for the Government, particularly in terms of the impact that it had upon (a) their claims to have their hands tied by the budget deficit, and (b) their claim that 'we are all in it together'. Indeed, it is perhaps noteworthy that almost all of the austerity measures imposed by the Coalition Government were announced in its first 2010 emergency budget; that is, before the significant politicization of the issue of austerity, which UK Uncut contributed considerably towards. Moreover, attempts to reduce the scale of the deficit turned out to be much less successful than it was earlier claimed that they would. Whilst the Government's commitment to austerity, and the severity with which austerity measures were imposed, should clearly not be under-empha-sized, what we might at the same time take away from this narrative is that with a more amenable political environment – i.e. one in which the Conservative-led coalition were not being successfully tarnished as the pro-business and anti-poor party – these austerity measures might have been more austere still. As a result, ministers were reluctant to call for specific welfare cuts, with the concern that they would be tarnished as a result. Indeed, journalist Matthew D'Ancona, who had considerable insider access to the Government, notes how Ian Duncan Smith 'often found that Tory colleagues who called for tough measures in general were the most squeamish about specific savings' (D'Ancona, 2013: 334). Further, the Coalition Government failed to reach its public sector spending savings and balanced budget during its 2010–15 term, in part due to the adverse publicity it had attracted as a result of its attempt to do so (Bailey and Shibata, 2017; cf. Stanley, 2016).

Workfare and anti-workfare: 'If you exploit us, we will shut you down'

One of the Coalition Government's most draconian set of welfare reforms was in the area of 'workfare'. This represented an extension of what was commonly referred to as the 'employability' agenda of the preceding government and sought to tackle unemployment through the use of a range of work experience schemes. It also represented both a privatization of the scheme, as private sector providers – e.g. A4e, Serco, G4S, and Avanta – were increasingly used to find work place-ments. Further, it was an intensification of the preceding workfare scheme in that sanctions were increasingly used to enforce participation (Rees *et al.*, 2014: 224). The Coalition's workfare programme therefore represented an attempt to reduce welfare provision by increasing the degree to which unemployed benefit claim-ants were coerced into alternative forms of work (many of which would have otherwise been resisted), through a combination of sanctions for benefit claimants and financial incentives for private sector placement providers (who were also therefore incentivized to impose sanctions as a means by which to discourage unemployment benefit claimants from taking up benefit entitlements) (Ball 2012; Mason and Perraudin, 2015). Throughout its implementation workfare became increasingly notorious and unpopular as a government scheme. A range of forms of contention – both visible and more 'everyday' – emerged in response to the programme, consistently causing problems and hurdles for the Government in its attempts to impose the draconian policies.

In terms of everyday forms of dissent, perhaps one of the most marked was that highlighted in the work of Rees *et al.* (2014). They showed how unemployed workers who proved most difficult to place in the scheme often found themselves 'parked' by private firms that were paid according to their performance in terms of achieving long-term employment. This payment system therefore incentivized firms to concentrate their efforts on those most likely to achieve long-term employment. As a result, benefit claimants were able to 'game' the system due to private placement firms' much greater focus on those unemployed workers who the firms felt were most likely to be employable and therefore likely to find a longer-term placement (as this would result in the private firms being financially rewarded).

Alongside these imperceptible forms of everyday dissent, a prominent and at times highly successful campaign organization – Boycott Workfare – emerged to promote the interests of those being subjected to workfare provisions, and to seek to find ways to oppose the reforms. The group was formed in 2010 following the announcement of the new Conservative Government, that it would be introducing a number of new workfare policies. by a collection of people affected by workfare, and largely with a background in campaigning against government welfare cuts (interview with Boycott Workfare participant, June 2016). The group has no ideological or partisan connections, although many of the listed anti-workfare groups displayed on its website adopt a broadly non-hierarchical position, including the IWW (syndicalist trade union), Solfed (anarcho-syndicalist organization), and Haringey Solidarity Group (non-hierarchical community grassroots group), and many of the organizing meetings for the group were held at the anarchist Freedom Bookshop. That said, the group is explicit in its non-partisan or non-ideological position, rather seeking to bring together those who are angry about the sense in which workfare represented a move to wards forced labour and punishment for unemployment. As one activist put it

> The idea is that basically we're sort of apolitical. Now obviously the actual cause itself is obviously a very left wing cause – right-wingers think that people working for nothing is 'market forces' – but we don't tend to ... we try to be apolitical – so we don't ... if you look at our website you won't get ... we won't criticise the Tory party because they're right-wingers, we criticise them because they're just awful; exactly the same thing with the Labour Party if they get in and they start doing workfare.
>
> (interview with Boycott Workfare activist, August 2016)

Many of those involved from the outset had experience with direct action groups, such as UK Uncut, and were also themselves benefit claimants, unemployed and/or disabled (interviews with Boycott Workfare activists, April 2015; August 2016). The strategies adopted by the organization were largely of a direct action nature, with a prevailing sentiment that this was necessary in order for the voice of the unemployed and other benefits claimants to be heard. In the words of one activist

> When it comes down to it there's no point in saying, 'please stop doing this', and being all nice about it; because they just don't listen, what we've found is that direct action is the way that they actually suddenly take notice of you. Even just attacking them from the PR front, as it were, that tends to work really rather well.
>
> (interview with Boycott Workfare activist, August 2016)

From its outset this focused especially on targeting retail stores (interview with Boycott Workfare participant, April 2015). At the early stage in the development of the campaign, links were also being formed between activists who had involvement in Boycott Workfare, UK Uncut and the journalists covering the report (especially Shiv Malik, who did much of the most high-profile reporting in the Guardian) (interview with UK Uncut/Boycott Workfare participant, April 2015).

The campaign used a combination of tactics, including: publishing online material that spelled out the implications of the government's workfare scheme and seeking to build opposition to it; publicizing the names of the companies that were participating in the scheme, in an attempt to associate the reputation of the company with what was portrayed as an unfair and immoral scheme that undermined the voluntary nature of volunteering; publicizing the experiences of individual participants in the scheme; direct action demonstrations outside of and sometimes inside the premises of participating companies and charities; support for legal challenges against the scheme (although this was normally moral support rather than financial); disrupting public meetings at which government ministers were speaking (Boycott Workfare, 2013e) and a series of freedom of information requests (and making public how others could submit FoI requests) that sought to highlight and publicize those companies that were involved in the scheme.

Much of the campaign work undertaken by Boycott Workfare, therefore, relied upon reputation damage – using the slogan, 'If you exploit us, we will shut you down!' – and highlighting and publicizing the companies involved. In doing so, moreover, it was successful in securing the withdrawal of participation of a sizeable number of organizations – to the extent that the Government increasingly found it difficult to operate the scheme.

An early sense of the likelihood that the Boycott Workfare strategy of disruptive direct action might be successful, and the risk for participating organizations that they would experience damage to their reputation as a result of their participation in the scheme, could be witnessed in 2011. Inside Government, a firm organizing public sector conferences, was forced to move a conference it was seeking to hold, called 'Making Work Pay'. This sought to bring together organizations interested in participating in the Government's welfare reforms and workfare scheme. The conference was set to be disrupted by Boycott Workfare who had chosen this as an opportunity to launch their campaign, at the time to be named Welfare Uncut (although most subsequent actions simply went under the name, Boycott Workfare). In response, Inside Government was forced to move the conference to a secret location, highlighting the sensitivity of the scheme, and its susceptibility to being disrupted through tactics that focused on reputation damage (Boycott Workfare, 2011a).

Further evidence of the potential for reputation damage came when another high-profile protest, conducted by a different group that was also formed to protest austerity and workfare, Right to Work, took place in February 2012. In this protest, a Tesco Express next to the Parliament was occupied to highlight the use by the company of unpaid labour, apparently (so it was claimed) as a form of 'voluntary' work experience, and following the revelation that anyone leaving the scheme would have their benefits sanctioned (Watt *et al.*, 2012). As a result of the public outcry associated with the non-voluntary nature of this apparently voluntary work experience scheme, the Government was forced to announce that the sanctions would be postponed.

In March 2012, and building on the publicity gained as a result of the Tesco Express protest, Boycott Workfare coordinated a series of nationwide actions. These were timed to coincide with the action of Liverpool Uncut, to take place at over 35 locations across the country. This was aimed at highlighting and publicizing those firms taking part in the scheme (Boycott Workfare, 2012b). Whilst many of the protests had fewer than fifty participants at them (Boycott Workfare, 2012c), nevertheless the nationwide nature of the coordinated actions, and the readiness of the national press to report on them, gave rise to considerable adverse publicity for participating firms and charities – many of whom jealously guarded their public reputation due to the importance of their status as high street brands. In the context of this ongoing negative publicity, participating companies and charities increasingly moved to withdraw from the scheme – claiming that they did not want to participate in a scheme which was not voluntary – this included Sainsbury's, Waterstones, HMV, Marie Curie, Shelter, Matalan, 99p Stores, Maplin, and Burger King. The number of withdrawing companies and charities also continued to rise throughout the following years. Indeed, the Government itself acknowledged the impact of the protests in its ongoing attempt to avoid releasing the names of participating organizations. This followed a ruling made by the Information Commissioner in 2013 that the Government must release the names of participating firms in the workfare scheme. It was not until July 2016, however, after a four-year legal battle led by Boycott Workfare member, Frank Zola, that the Government was eventually forced to release the information stating which organizations had been involved in workfare (with over 500 organizations named) (Boycott Workfare, 2016b). In challenging the freedom of information request, the Government claimed that 'if the public knew exactly where people were being sent on placements political protests would increase, which was likely to lead to the collapse of several employment schemes and undermine the Government's economic interests'. Likewise, in another statement, the Government said:

> Previous targeted campaigns had resulted in the withdrawal of providers from MWA [Mandatory Work Activity scheme] and WE [work experience] … Put simply, disclosure [of names] would have been likely to have led to the collapse of the MWA scheme.
>
> (Quoted in Boycott Workfare, 2013a)

Moreover, at the tribunal, the Department of Work and Pensions (DWP) confirmed that some of the UK's biggest charities, 'including the British Heart Foundation, Scope, Banardo's, Sue Ryder, and Marie Curie' had all withdrawn from the scheme, causing a significant loss of placements (Malik, 2014a). And similarly in appealing the decision of the Information Commission the Government went on to state that

> a great many placement organisations' had ceased to offer placements. That in turn reduced the numbers of opportunities available across both programmes with a loss of many placements and prospective new placements being at risk. [...] charitable organisations were particularly susceptible to adverse publicity and pressure.
>
> (DWP and the Information Commissioner vs. Frank Zola,
> Appeal Nos. EA/2012/0207, 0232 & 0233, 3 May 2013)

At the same tribunal, the Government highlighted the 'possible commercial detriment suffered to third parties if details of WP placement hosts were to be disclosed' (DWP and the Information Commissioner vs. Frank Zola, 2013). Further still, in its own evaluation of the workfare scheme, the Government announced that, 'The high-profile withdrawal of placements from a number of larger charities meant a sharp reduction in placements' (DWP, *Evaluation of Mandatory Work Activity*, 2012, quoted in Boycott Workfare, 2013g). There is, therefore, substantial evidence, provided by the Government itself, that the actions of Boycott Workfare had a significant impact upon the attempts to implement its Workfare scheme.

Along with participating firms and charities withdrawing from the scheme, adverse publicity also led on occasion to the Government itself cancelling some of the workfare contracts. For instance, in May 2012 the Government announced that it would be ending the workfare contract it had with A4e for the South East, citing 'a background of public commentary on A4E' as the factor which prompted the investigation that led to the ending of the contract (DWP, 2012). Similarly, in December 2013 Boycott Workfare was able to report that UK councils had benefited from half a million hours of unpaid work as a result of the scheme, a story that was taken up by both the Guardian and the Mirror (Boycott Workfare, 2013i; Malik, 2014b; Beattie, 2013). This adverse publicity was sufficient to prompt one council – Scarborough Borough Council – to move almost immediately to end their participation in the scheme (Boycott Workfare, 2014a).

Adverse publicity was therefore both a central and a successful element in the campaign against workfare. In response to several rounds of protest, including so-called 'twitter storms', many firms continued to pull out of the scheme. Holland and Barrett was one of the largest profile companies to pull out of the scheme, after initially employing 1000 unpaid workers between 2011 and 2012 – eventually citing 'bad press and in-store protests' as its reason for withdrawal. A number of charities that initially participated in the scheme also chose to publicly announce that they would be leaving the scheme on the grounds that it forced the unemployed and/or disabled to do unpaid work. Others were forced into making embarrassing admissions of their use of the scheme – for instance the retail firm, Homebase, was publicly exposed for having internally advertised the work experience scheme as a good way to secure free labour.

Buoyed by the success of its first nationwide action in March 2012, and by the attention in the press and the large numbers of firms pulling out of the scheme, Boycott Workfare scheduled another day of action for 31 March 2012, again in July 2012 (prompting retail store Holland and Barrett to pull out of the scheme ahead of the July protests), and again in March 2013 (this time prompting Superdrug to withdraw ahead of the planned actions). Further, in September 2012, and again in December 2012, Boycott Workfare moved to focus specifically on charities involved in the workfare scheme. Due to this pressure a number of charities also moved to withdraw from the scheme, with one of the most obvious signs of success coming in February 2013 with the withdrawal of the charity, *Sue Ryder*, just hours after the launch of an online rolling picket of the firm via twitter that had been coordinated by Boycott Workfare (Boycott Workfare 2013c, 2013d).

In 2014 the Government introduced a new scheme – Community Work Placements – which threatened to impose six-month unpaid work placements upon unemployed people. The scheme, however, suffered from the same adverse publicity that surrounded other government workfare schemes. The most significant sign of this was the creation in April of a campaign, *Keep Volunteering Voluntary*, which was initially set up with input from Boycott Workfare and signed up to by over 25 groups, including Oxfam and the National Association for Voluntary and Community Action (Boycott Workfare, 2014b). Since its creation the initiative has secured the support of a huge number of charities, with 150 groups signing up by the time of the launch of the scheme, and by 2016 boasting over 600 signatory organizations, including Child Poverty Action Group, Friends of the Earth, the Scottish Council for Voluntary Organisations, Shelter, Sue Ryder, Unison and scores of volunteering groups.[3] The organizations that signed up to the scheme pledged not to participate – creating considerable problems for the Government in terms of finding participants and thereby delaying its full implementation. Trade unions were also opposed, with Unite's assistant general secretary, Steve Turner, condemning the scheme on the grounds that it was, 'nothing more than forced unpaid labour and there is no evidence that these workfare programmes get people into paid work in the long term' (quoted in Press Association, 2014).

In 2014, another week of action resulted in the withdrawal from the Community Work Placements scheme of Scope, Barnados, the British Heart Foundation, and Traid (Boycott Workfare, 2014d). Indeed, the lack of participating organizations in the Community Work Placement scheme was such that by 2015 it became clear that around half of those claimants who had been referred to the scheme had been unable to be found a placement. For instance, in January 2016 Manchester homeless charity, Mustard Tree, announced that it was pulling out of the MWA scheme due to a long-running campaign by Boycott Workfare; this mirrored a similar series of events at North London Hospice, which had been subjected to a campaign of public disruptive protests by Boycott Workfare and Haringey Solidarity Group (Boycott Workfare, 2016a).

One of the effects of the lack of participating organizations in the workfare scheme was the need on the part of the Government to rescind on some of its workfare plans. The Government announced in 2011 that it intended to place claimants on a six-month work placement if they reached the end of the two-year Work Programme scheme and still had not got a job. However, by the time of 2013 when the details of the scheme were released, there was no mention of this element of the post-Work Programme plan, suggesting that the scheme had become unworkable over the period due to the declining number of participating organizations (Boycott Workfare, 2013f). Likewise, in announcing in November 2015 that the Government would be ending both the Community Work Placements scheme and the Mandatory Work Activity scheme there was a clear suggestion that this was in part due to the problems associated with finding organizations willing to participate (Boycott Workfare, 2015).

By publishing exposés based on first-hand reports written by participants in the workfare scheme, Boycott Workfare were also able to inform some of the organizations that were themselves, sometimes unwittingly, participating in the scheme. For instance, in September 2013 Boycott Workfare published an article highlighting the experience of a claimant that had been forced to apply to volunteer at the Brisfest community festival. As a result of this article, it became clear that Brisfest itself had not agreed to participate in the scheme, and had only managed to become involved because it had happened to advertise for volunteers in the local Job Centre. As a response of the Boycott Workfare campaign, Brisfest pledged both to make sure that none of its volunteers were being forced to 'volunteer' under the Government's workfare scheme, and that it would cease to advertise for volunteers at the Job Centre (Boycott Workfare, 2013h).

As a result of the adverse publicity it had received, the workfare scheme also received considerable scrutiny in parliament. The Work and Pensions Committee published a Report on Tuesday 24 March 2015 in which it called for a full independent review to be established in the new Parliament, to investigate whether benefit sanctions were being applied appropriately, fairly and proportionately, across the Jobcentre Plus (JCP) network. This followed the earlier Oakley Review, an independent review set up by the Government to examine the implementation of the Jobseekers (Back to Work) Act 2013, which was critical of a number of the features of the sanctions scheme. Indeed, the degree to which sanctions have even improved employment rates has been consistently questioned and shown to have no beneficial effects (and indeed appear to have negative effects upon the likelihood of gaining employment) – this, despite an ongoing long-term rise in their use.

Alongside attempts to expose the participation of organizations and firms in the workfare scheme, Boycott Workfare were also able to provide information to participants in the scheme, spelling out their rights and elements of the scheme that they had the right to refuse to participate in. For instance, in 2011 the organization made it clear that participants were under no obligation to provide confidential personal information, which A4e (one of the scheme providers) was requesting from participants (see, Boycott Workfare, 2011b). Likewise, in 2012 it was able to advise claimants of the voluntary nature of a new Jobmatch scheme, a new computer system set up to facilitate job searching (and which had a number of problematic issues surrounding the accessibility of personal data) (Boycott

Workfare, 2012d). Similarly, the group were able to offer advice on the implications of the High Court ruling which stipulated that the workfare scheme (except for Mandatory Work Activity) were unlawful (Boycott Workfare, 2013b).

The work placement scheme also prompted some high-profile individual acts of refusal. For instance, John McArthur, 59, refused to attend his work placement in 2014 on the grounds that it was a job he had previously been paid to do. In protest, he paraded outside the company for two hours a day for three months, with signs saying 'Say no to slavery' (Malik, 2014a). In July 2012, the scheme gained considerable attention in the media, including the publication of an open letter by a number of charities, trade unions and campaign organizations, criticizing the scheme on the grounds that it, 'does not create a single job', punishes the unemployed and calling for 'all organisations to challenge forced unpaid work by boycotting workfare'.

Finally, one of the most high-profile forms of opposition to the Government's Workfare programme was the legal challenge brought against it by two benefit claimants who had been forced to do unpaid work in order to continue to receive their benefits. In one case, the claimant (Cait Reilly) was forced to give up her voluntary work in order to work in Poundland. In the other case, Jamie Wilson was required to do unpaid cleaning and renovation work. In bringing their challenge against the Government the two claimants built their case upon a number of key claims, including: that the Regulations upon which the scheme was based were legally insufficient (i.e. the Secretary of State had acted beyond the powers granted by Parliament); had not been properly followed; and that the scheme amounted to a Human Rights violation on the grounds that it constituted forced/compulsory labour (Adkins, 2015: 3–4). Despite losing their initial claim, upon appeal (in 2013) it was decided that the Government had acted outside of the terms set by Parliament, and so the scheme was deemed unlawful (although the claim of forced/compulsory labour was not upheld by any of the courts). This subsequently led the Government to pass emergency legislation – the Jobseekers (Back to Work Schemes) Act 2013 – which *retrospectively* ensured that the scheme was lawful and that therefore no claim to recover benefit sanctions could be made (Adkins, 2015: 5).

In sum, therefore, the Government's workfare scheme – a particularly draconian attempt to impose tight conditions upon the unemployed and to significantly scale back the generosity of unemployment benefits, to the point that many claimed it had moved to the imposition of forced labour – met with fierce public opposition, using a range of oppositional tactics. These especially sought to build upon a broad public opposition to the scheme, publicizing the most obnoxious forms that it took, and seeking (oftentimes successfully) to disrupt the implementation of it through a name-and-shame approach that combined physical protests in high street stores and online adverse publicity. This was a strategy that was consciously adopted by the group. Thus, in the words of one participant

I think the strategy was a good one – of scaring off participants. And if you look at the review of the scheme produced by the Government themselves – they have actually explicitly recognized that getting charities to agree to be part of the scheme and to offer placements was one of the key problems that they faced.

(interview with Johnny Void, Welfare Rights Blogger and
Campaigner, 17 June 2016)

As we have seen, the welfare reforms imposed by the Coalition Government experienced considerable contestation and on many occasions the strategies of those opposing the reforms were successful in creating important limits and obstacles to welfare retrenchment, as well as consequences for those advocating such measures during the so-called 'age of austerity'. It is through our focus on these forms of disruption, we claim, that we are able to highlight these different forms of opposition. In the following section, we now turn to the Spanish context, where both the austerity agenda and the pressure to resist austerity were even greater in scale.

Spanish welfare retrenchment and protest movements: 'For a society that puts people first'[4]

For a society that puts people first. […] Let us save people, not banks.

(iaioflautas, 2016, authors' translation)

The Spanish welfare state prior to the crisis was characterized by a number of the characteristics typically associated with the 'Latin rim' or 'Southern model' of European welfare states. These include its clientelistic design and undeveloped nature of its family and labour market policies (Busch *et al.*, 2013: 15). Historically, this development can be traced back to the underdevelopment of welfare and the variety of selective welfare measures introduced under the Francoist dictatorship. Despite the fact that the PSOE Government extended welfare provisions and made them more universal during the 1980s, nevertheless the Spanish welfare state continued to be markedly less generous in comparison with other European countries (Navarro, 2004). The European accession process, as well as Spain's fragile and dependent form of economic development, which was based largely on niche sectors with limited international competition (such as tourism and real estate), served as powerful dynamics to limit the further extension of welfare provision (Haas and Huke, 2015; Huke, 2017). Three characteristics of the Spanish welfare model are particularly noteworthy – all of them a heritage of the Francoist period: high levels of employment protection for those on permanent contracts; weak social security; and (as a result) a reliance on private forms of (family-based) social security, such as home ownership. Further, during the 1990s and 2000s a creeping neoliberal restructuring and retrenchment of the welfare state took place, especially after the right-wing conservative Partido Popular came to power in 1996 (Haas and Huke, 2015). As a result of these characteristics, public infrastructure in Spain has tended to be underfunded, which has negatively affected its quality and led people to turn to the private sector as an alternative source of welfare provision.

From 2008 onward, the pre-crisis accumulation regime in Spain collapsed due to a real estate crisis, over-accumulation and falling demand in the automotive industry, and credit shortages in the aftermath of the US subprime crisis. Unemployment soared, which led to rising public spending due to automatic stabilisers (e.g. unemployment benefits).

The mortgage repayments of hundreds of thousands of Spanish citizens were thereby put into question. To secure the availability of credit, moreover, the state intervened in the financial sector, especially focusing its efforts on the bank, *Cajas de Ahorro*, which had been largely dependent upon the mortgage market. In order to secure the country's financial sector it was necessary, in 2012, to borrow from the European Financial Stability Facility (EFSF) of the so-called 'Troika', and in turn to sign a *Memorandum of Understanding* which brought with it draconian austerity measures. In addition, as rating agencies and investors started to doubt the solvency of the Spanish state, refinancing costs for public debt rose. The crisis therefore led to a reduced capacity of the Spanish state to provide social welfare (Haas and Huke, 2015).

The Spanish case therefore highlights starkly the pressures placed upon welfare by dynamics of financialized capitalist accumulation and the European system of austerity that was adopted during the so-called 'age of austerity', or what others have referred to as the 'age of permanent strain' (Pavolini *et al.*, 2016: 153). This resulted in what has been termed a 'frontal attack' on welfare (Navarro, 2013: 189). In turn, however, mass movements developed that not only criticized the measures being implemented, but also demanded a progressive transformation of the Spanish welfare system towards a 'society that puts people first'. It is these developments that we chart in this present section.[5] In the Spanish case, moreover, the general characteristics of the so-called 'age of austerity' were especially pronounced, witnessing a more radical attempt to restructure the welfare model than was observed outside of the European periphery (Haas and Huke, 2015).

As a result of the crisis, the Spanish public sector was exposed to a series of cuts and restructuration measures. Already in May 2010, the *Real Decreto-ley* (RDL) 8/2010 cut wages by five per cent and imposed a freeze on public sector wages at that level from 2010 onwards (which created a real wages cut from that point forward). Furthermore, special payments were suspended and the number of holidays was reduced, while hours worked per week were raised. Hiring freezes and the non-substitution of retiring workers resulted in massive job loss, which already in 2013 were estimated to have reached around 175,000 jobs lost in the health and the public sectors (vgl. Diagonal, 2013e; Picó Enseñat, Miguel Ramón, 2013). The increased ease through which collective dismissals could be made (as discussed in Chapter 3) was explicitly extended to the public sector (*RD 1483/2012*) (Rodríguez-Piñero Royo, 2012). Each of these measures, moreover, contributed to a worsening of the wage gap between men and women (Antón and Muñoz de Bustillo, 2013: 33). Also as a result, in part, of the reduction in public service employment, public discontent with the provision of public services increased – albeit with a continuation of the high level of popular support for the professionalism of public employees (La Expansión, 2013).

In addition to this decline in public sector employment, the imposition of austerity measures in the area of public spending became commonplace. Austerity was constitutionalized through the introduction of the requirements of the SGP, adopted as Article 135 of the Spanish constitution, thereby placing a permanent strain on the public sector. Indeed, the Spanish debt rules that were adopted were even more restrictive than the European guidelines upon which they were based, including the prioritization of debt repayments over other forms of state spending. This new Article 135 was implemented into law under the *Ley Orgánica 2/2012*, which codified the maximum debt of state institutions at 60 per cent of GDP, of which 44 per cent was reserved for the central state, 13 per cent for the regional governments, and 3 per cent for local governments (Almendral, 2013; Galera Victoria, 2013; Medina Guerrero, 2012; Ridaura Martínez, María Josefa, 2012). The *Ley 27/2013* also further restricted the scope of local governments to provide social assistance to citizens, as it created the rule that spending would only be permissible if it did not threaten the financial stability of the local municipalities (or otherwise, if it was agreed to by the regional government) (Mellado Ruiz, 2014; Oficina Técnica Presidencia, Economía y Hacienda Zaragoza, 2014).

The austerity measures adopted also affected those of pension age. The statutory retirement age was raised from 65 to 67, remaining only at 65 for those with at least 38.5 insurance years. The insurance years required for receiving a pension without deductions were also raised from 35 to 37 years. In addition, the amount of pensions was no longer calculated on the base of the last 15 years of employment, but on the last 25 years, with a transitional period established until 2027. From 2027 a sustainability factor will be introduced that automatically adjusts the parameters of pensions to the development of life expectancy every five years (Busch *et al.*, 2013: 18). State subsidies that compensated for discontinuous employment histories were also reduced. Furthermore, workers without a permanent residency in Spain could no longer receive minimum pensions. The scale of these reductions was such that it was estimated that it would result in a reduction in individual pensions of 25–30 per cent (Pérez Alonso, 2013: 12–13). Surviving on pensions therefore became even more difficult. This was in a context in which it was already the case in 2010 that 25 per cent of pensioned men and 30 per cent of pensioned women were considered poor (Peinado, 2014: 2). One of the Popular Party (PP) Government's responses to this problem was the further imposition of work, by extending the possibility that pensioners could take up paid work (Pérez Alonso, María Antonia, 2013: 12–13).

Other key areas of the public service were also subjected to major reforms. The health system was restructured and experienced far reaching budget cuts. The RDL 16/2012 made access to healthcare conditional upon social security contributions, whereas in the past it had been universal, even to the extent that migrants without formal permission to be within Spain (so-called 'illegal' migrants) were entitled to access healthcare. As a result of these reforms, a large number of people were due to be excluded from being able to access healthcare, including those working in informal employment, the long-term unemployed, and those who had never contributed to social security by the age of 26. However, after the protests of medical staff and migrant support groups (see below) these reforms were mitigated in part, through the establishment of private insurance possibilities and the partial re-opening of the system for so-called 'illegal' migrants (Gallo and Gené-Badia, 2013: 3; Ruiz-Giménez, 2014).

Additional reforms to health care included the decision made by the regional government in Madrid to systematically privatize the local health centres and hospitals – a decision that was subsequently reversed after mass protests and a court decision noting irregularities in the privatization process (see the next section). Government spending on health care dropped sharply. Co-payments were extended, while medical centres shut down or reduced their opening hours, and staff numbers were reduced (Montoya, 2012: 158). The decline in public funding also resulted in extremely long waiting lists for necessary treatment and a rise in the use of private sector provision as an alternative (San José, 2011: 87–88). In addition, access to the system of allowances for nursing care (*Ley de dependencia*) was restricted (Beteta Martín, 2013: 48–49). At the same time, unemployment and evictions resulted in a rise of depression and anxiety disorder rates (Borrell *et al.*, 2014: 95; Gili *et al.*, 2013).

Unemployment benefits and other social benefits were also reduced from 2010 onwards, with some regions seeing tightened access to minimum wage schemes (Ballester, 2012: 15; Sen Galindo, 2013: 23). This was despite the fact that the Zapatero Government had earlier introduced gradual improvements in support for the long-term unemployed, as part of a (somewhat weak) initial Keynesian reaction to the crisis (Seminari d'Economia Crítica TAIFA, 2010: 70). These reductions in social benefits came at a time when the number of households dependent upon benefits was rising, as was the number of households without any income. The rate of unemployed receiving unemployment benefits fell throughout the crisis, reaching 57.9 per cent in April 2014 (Diagonal, 2013f; Sánchez Medero and Tamboloo García, 2013).

All of this resulted in a sharp fall in public approval rates on the question of how the cuts within the Spanish society were being implemented, especially as health and education were regarded as areas of primary concern for society and a broad majority supported keeping or even extending their public character (FOESSA, 2014: 328–329; 339). In addition, family-based support networks which had organized a degree of social security and redistribution during the pre-crisis period became increasingly unable to provide support for their members, prompting an intensification of everyday inter-personal conflict (for instance, within families) and a decline in levels of life satisfaction (FOESSA, 2014: 55; FOESSA, 2014: 511). Poverty rates also increased, especially among groups already vulnerable prior to the crisis, such as single parents, families with children or migrants (FOESSA, 2014: 70).

As we have seen, therefore, the global economic crisis, and subsequent European/Eurozone crisis had a serious and significant impact upon Spanish society. The structure of Spain's economic model prior to the crisis was such that it was left exposed to a number of damaging trends following the onset of the crisis. This, moreover, was exacerbated by the conditions imposed on the country by virtue of its membership of the Euro, which was in turn consolidated by the adoption of more austere measures still by the PP Government.

It is in this context, therefore, that we need to assess the development of an anti-austerity movement across Spain during this period. The cuts in welfare spawned a variety of protest movements throughout the Spanish state that were mostly regional in character, due to the mostly regional nature of welfare provision in areas such as social security and education (Huke and Tietje, 2014a). The welfare movements were in many cases inspired by the 15-M movement (see Chapter 3) and adopted parts of its repertoire of action, such as radical-democratic, or pre-figurative, assemblies. This allowed a range of groups, and types of participants (including workers, service users and local neighbourhoods) to overcome a number of the divisions that had prevented cooperation in the past (Huke, 2016). These groups could also rely upon the broad level of public support for welfare and especially public health and education that existed across Spanish society, with many viewing these as important advances achieved as part of the process of democratization after Francoism (FOESSA, 2014: 328–9; 339; Pastor Verdú, 2014: 234–5).

An exemplary case in this sense is the *marea blanca* in Madrid, which emerged as a reaction to the regional government's radical plan to privatize the health sector in the city. After the plans became public, employees enclosed themselves in the hospitals (*encierros*) and organized assemblies with a massive participation of the workforce. This represented the birth of the *marea blanca* (Gago, 2013: 1097–8). Regular assemblies took place in every one of the affected hospitals that quickly expanded to include users of health services. As an activist recalls

> In health we health sector workers have always been very quiet, we did not protest against anything. [...] This privatisation decree, which woke us up, [...] has caught many people immobile. And then they surprised themselves and surprised the others: 'And you? What are you doing in the street protesting if you have never been there for anything, right?' [...] Seeing that you are talking to a caretaker and you are the head of service and you are at the same demonstrating because you are for the same things, well, that gave you goose bumps saying 'My god, this is really important'.
> (interview with PATU Salud ativist, 20 March 2014, authors' translation)

As part of the *marea blanca*, workers' interests were reframed as common interests of the population. Part of its effectiveness stemmed from its successful framing of health care as a public good which allowed its assemblies to reach a wide political spectrum and increase their social base beyond affected workers: 'Users of public services [...] converged with the workers themselves. [...] A, let's say, absolutely natural convergence was produced' (interview with CCOO trade unionist, 6 March 2014, authors' translation). Public opinion on welfare issues also made it easier to organize public support than it had been regarding workplace conflicts in private enterprises. As one interviewee put it

> if you have a conflict in the health system, it is a lot easier for you to take it to the neighbourhood so that it defends [...] this health centre against being shut down, right? But the experiences are above all in the industrial sector. To try

to find [...] solidarity movements, this is very important for us to be really effective and to maintain the capacity of confederal intervention. As a whole.

(interview with CCOO trade unionist, 6 March 2014, authors' translation)

The political pressure built up by the numerous protests of the *marea blanca* contributed to the failure of the privatization programme in Madrid. In the end, the privatization was stopped by a court verdict due to irregularities in the process, which in turn resulted in the PP Government of the Madrid region abandoning the project (Huke and Tietje, 2014a; Huke, 2016).

Similar developments can be seen in the case of the so-called *Yo Sí Sanidad Universal* movement. This was a campaign that organized support for so-called 'illegal' migrants after their exclusion from public healthcare following the RDL 16/2012 (Gallo and Gené-Badia, 2013: 3; Ruiz-Giménez, 2014). Shortly after the decree was passed, the doctors association, SEMFYC, issued a call for civil disobedience, sparking more than 2000 doctors to declare that they would continue to grant universal access to healthcare despite any potential legal consequences (Gallo and Gené-Badia, 2013: 3; Legido-Quigley *et al.,* 2013: 2). The call for disobedience was taken up by *Yo Sí Sanidad Universal*, a newly established grassroots organization in which activists from migrant support groups and the radical left organized collectively with administrative and medical workers from the health sector:

We came together around a month after the royal decree was passed [...] and started to collect ideas, to think, to debate, to discuss in an assembly-based form. There was no political organisation or union nor any other organisation behind us [...]. There were indignant people that had been working in other social movements [...] coming together with people from the health sector, professional medics, social workers, administrative staff, that were aware of the problems and also annoyed and pissed off and indignant with what had happened. Between them, we formed what today is *Yo Sí*.

(Interview with *Yo Sí Sanidad Universal* activist, 21 May 2015, authors' translation)

Yo Sí Sanidad Universal organized support groups for so-called 'illegal' migrants but also conducted workshops for health workers to inform them of the necessity of civil disobedience, and to point out loopholes and potential ways to continue treating migrants. In addition, the campaign documented and publicized the exclusion of patients and the consequences of those exclusions (including deaths) (Ruiz-Giménez, 2014). In Madrid, where the movement was the strongest, more than 20 support groups were established. These developments were, moreover, successful to the extent that the PP Government issued a statement declaring that so-called 'illegal' migrants were to be readmitted to health care, albeit continuing to deny them health insurance cards (Huke, 2016: 102).

As we have seen, therefore, attempts to imposed significant welfare retrenchment measures were met with considerable public opposition. In the case of both *marea blanca* and *Yo Sí Sanidad Universal* this led to a considerable downscaling of the reforms pursued by the Government. This resulted from a combination of prefigurative forms of radical action, combined with the attempt to express a collective voice by those members of the public who retained their support for welfare reforms, alongside the refusal-prone inclinations of those working directly within the relevant sectors. As we see next, moreover, similar trends could be witnessed in another of the forms of mobilization that gained prominence during the course of the crisis, the Iai@flautas.

Iai@flautas: 'the appropriate moment to provoke'

Although the 15-M has frequently been portrayed as a youth protest movement, its social base has been multifaceted and covered different age ranges, as the case considered here shows. A group of senior people met in Plaça Catalunya, in Barcelona, during the 15-M occupation of the square and decided to start coordinated protests against corruption and government cuts in public services. As one of the activists puts it

> We are sons and daughters of the 15-M. The 15-M was such an important explosion of freedom that it injected us with energy to do things.
> (interview with Iai@flautas activist, June 2014, authors' translation)

Their name, Iai@flautas, derives from the words 'iaio' or 'iaia' (Catalan for 'grandpa' or 'grandma'), and the derogatory name 'perroflauta' (Spanish for 'crusty') that was used in some circles and particularly within the right-wing media to refer to 15-M activists. Hence, they resignified the terms and subverted the usual connotations of idleness and carelessness. Furthermore, they found a name that is pronounced the same in Catalan and Spanish, but they spell it in a mix of both languages in order to illustrate their inner diversity of origins and background.

The initial idea of Iai@flautas was soon replicated in other cities such as Sabadell, Terrassa, Sevilla, Madrid, Valencia, Castelló de la Plana, Palma de Mallorca, Córdoba, Murcia, Girona, Badalona, Mollet del Vallès, Montcada i Reixac and L'Hospitalet de Llobregat. Each of these nodes has its own local assembly, which is self-organized and autonomous from the others. Occasionally, activists from different assemblies meet in order to share their experiences and knowledge, to plan and perform a joint action, and to socialize in a collective meal. However, rather than a concrete organizational structure, what these grassroots assemblies share is a collective worldview that includes the notions of civil disobedience, pacifism, non-partisanship and defence of what is 'common' (interviews with Iai@flautas activists, June 2014, December 2015). To reinforce their horizontal practices, they have always rejected the idea of having a visible leader, and they deliberately try to rotate certain positions and responsibilities within the movement. As with other anti-austerity movements, the main strategy adopted by Iai@flautas has been that of the occupation.

The first target for their disruptive direct actions – which they call 'travesuras', Spanish for 'shenanigans' – was Banco Santander, the main financial group in Spain and the largest by market value in the Eurozone. In October 2011, a group of Iai@flautas activists attempted to occupy one of their offices in the centre of Barcelona to protest against the abuses of the Spanish banking system, and to challenge the decision of the Spanish Government to bail out the country's banks in a period of acute welfare cuts and austerity. In their second action, they tried to occupy an office of Fitch Ratings, one of the world's biggest international credit rating agencies, to show solidarity with the Greek people and their battle against austerity. These first actions were in a sense incomplete, since they could not occupy the targeted offices and they had to gather and protest outside their premises instead. As one participant explains, it was not until they changed their main tactics that the occupations would become more successful:

> The methods we used, which were learned from the 15-M, were basically to say in the social networks: on such a day, at such a time, we're going to occupy this Banco Santander's office. And we arrived at Banco Santander and there was more police than Iai@flautas! Then we tried to occupy Fitch Ratings and we couldn't either. The third attempt was to occupy a local healthcare centre in Barcelona, the construction of which was finished but which was closed due to the Catalan Government's austerity agenda. The action was planned together with the centre's Works Council, and we summoned everybody in the surrounding area. Once a group of 20 people occupied the centre, they advertised the action and asked for the support of other members of the movement, who were already nearby. They entered and we had some snacks all together. That action was our first success. We had found another system, another way of doing things, which now characterizes us: to use the old methods, the ones we used during our clandestine struggles, to occupy things; and once they are occupied, to use the new technologies and social networks to advertise it.
>
> (interview with Iai@flautas activist, June 2014, authors' translation)

In September 2012, Iai@flautas performed one of their most well-known actions, the first-ever occupation of Barcelona Stock Exchange. A few days before the action, two activists were sent as spotters and realized the building was easily accessible. The committee that organized the action decided that six activists – in street clothes and pretending to be three old married couples – would enter the building and the other Iai@flautas would gather outside, trying to disrupt as much as possible the normal activity of the institution. The action was so successful that the six activists could open the doors from the inside, and up to 150 Iai@flautas were able to peacefully access the Barcelona Stock Exchange while shouting 'Iai@flautas, a rising value'. The action was an attempt to delegitimize what they considered the 'symbol and instrument of the criminal organisation of the 1 per cent', and to protest against the planned bailout that would save banks instead of saving people. They also called for a general strike and for the opening of a constituent process that would build a new legal and political framework from below.[6]

A reduced group of activists were able to meet the deputy director whilst the other Iai@flautas were supposed to finish the action with a march to Plaça Catalunya. Once they left the building, however, they realized they were surrounded by 80 anti-riot police officers and that they were being kept inside a kettle. Despite all police attempts, the activists refused to identify themselves and said they would only do so if they were under arrest. Eventually, some of the activists (the average age being 70 years old) started complaining about their health and their need to take their medication, allowing them finally to break through the police cordon. One of the activists explained the events that followed:

> When that Mosso [member of the Catalan police] said: 'clear the way and let them go', we didn't just leave. I took the megaphone and I said that we won, that we had won against the Catalan autonomic police, that we were victorious, that now they knew who they were messing with. I provoked them, I know, but I understood that was the appropriate moment to provoke them. And there has indeed been a big change in their attitude from then on. Then they said: 'OK, now you go'. And we said: 'No! Now we will block the road and we will march to Plaça Catalunya, and then we will do our assembly in Plaça Catalunya'. They said: 'You can't do this, you didn't get the required permission'. We said: 'No, and we're not going to. Our movement is based on civil disobedience!'
> (interview with Iai@flautas activist, December 2015, authors' translation)

A crucial feature of Iai@flautas was that many of the senior people who initially engaged in the movement had been activists in the past, especially during the anti-Franco resistance struggles and during the early years of the transition to democracy in Spain. As such, one of the pillars of the movement was to recover the historical memory of the anti-Franco struggles, that is, to gather the collective knowledge produced in the clandestine struggles against the dictatorship and to share it with younger generations in order to improve current struggles. This is shown in the slogan 'Anem lluny perquè venim de lluny' ('We are going far because we come from afar') a variation of one of the main 15-M slogans 'we are going slow because we are going far'. In their words

> We realised we shouldn't have abandoned the streets as we did after the '78, when democracy arrived and we said: 'the work has been done, let's move on, let's leave political struggle and do cultural stuff or something else instead.' I think the big mistake of our generation was to leave the streets. And during the 15-M, we bumped into old friends that everyone thought were finished, because they were retired and people believed they weren't useful anymore.
> (interview with Iai@flautas activist, December 2015, authors' translation)

This encounter between old and new struggles can be seen not only in the goals and demands of the movement, but also in their strategies and organization. On the one hand, Iai@flautas' central aims are to stop the privatization of social services and cuts in welfare, or in other words, to defend the civil rights and advances in social justice that were achieved during past struggles. As some activists recall

> These social gains – from the salaries to the way working hours are arranged, social security, public healthcare and education – were achieved with a lot of effort. They are our safety net, they guarantee a good quality of life, and the Government should invest in them instead of cutting welfare benefits.
> (interview with Iai@flautas activist, November 2015, authors' translation)

> Iai@flautas is not a franchise, but an instrument to spread the fight. This is our job; we know we have to explain our collective history to our children and grandchildren. And then, walking all together, we can build a future that is worth living for.
> (interview with Iai@flautas activist, December 2015, authors' translation)

An important element of the strategy adopted by Iai@flautas was the use of so-called 'trust networks', usually employed in clandestine struggles to avoid the police. These, moreover, were combined with more open, horizontallyorganized, assemblies, in an attempt to combine radical notions of democracy with more practical concerns associated with the need to avoid police repression. Hence

> The first occupations didn't go well because we advertised them in social networks. Then we decided that we had to use trust, which is what we used to do back in our days during the dictatorship: from mouth to mouth. The objectives and targets are decided in the assembly, but then only a few people prepare the action. The rest of us trust them and go where the former tell us to go. If the action doesn't go well, we talk about it in the following assembly.
> (interview with Iai@flautas activist, December 2015, authors' translation)

Furthermore, these strategies are complemented by contemporary mechanisms of diffusion that they learned from the 15-M, such as the organization and advertisement of their actions through social networks, or the use of viral videos. In order to increase their impact, Iai@flautas began to issue a manifesto for each of their actions, explaining the reasons that motivated them and their specific demands. This manifesto is published in their website[7] and is publicized through different social networks during the occupation, but never before. Through new technologies and social networks, these senior activists inform the media about their actions and motivations, and try to raise awareness about their campaign amongst the population. As an example of this, during the occupation of the Barcelona Stock Exchange Iai@flautas used a live streaming video platform to broadcast their action, especially after they were kept inside the kettle.[8] They also used the hashtag #LaBolsaolaVida ('your money or your life', 'bolsa' being also the Spanish word for 'stock exchange'), which became a global trending topic on Twitter. As a participant explains

Iai@flautas taught me how to use a computer and a smartphone. We master the social networks! Not all of us, but I think 90 per cent of us have now at least a computer, a Facebook account and an email.
(interview with Iai@flautas activist, December 2015, authors' translation)

A key contribution of the initiative is to politicize, empower, give voice, and reactivate a group of people that, since it is not productive for the capitalist economy and receives state pensions and welfare benefits, is not 'useful' to society anymore. Some of the members were politically active before, some of them were not. How did they achieve it? By being non-violent and very friendly, having collective meals after every action and having spaces of common socialization and leisure such as the choir. These collective experiences contribute to the creation of a sense of belonging for people who felt isolated and useless.

For me, what is most important about Iai@flautas is that people that had stopped being useful to society are useful again. Indeed you were working, but at a certain age you retired. You might have been a member of a trade union, but at a certain age you retired. You might have been a member of a political party, but at a certain age you retired. Everything leads you to think that you're not useful anymore, which is not true of course. But it is linked to the current system, which is a system that discards old people. And what we've achieved is to make these people relevant again from a social and political point of view.
(interview with Iai@flautas activist, June 2014,
authors' translation)

Another characteristic of the Iai@flautas movement is that, in one of the activists' own words, it is not an interest group (interview with Iai@flautas activist, November 2015). Although they perform their own actions, their strategies are not directed towards their own benefits in terms of improving their retirement pensions or their access to public health and social services. Instead, Iai@flautas is conceived as a group of trust and support for other social movements and struggles, and they have collaborated with anti-austerity platforms such as *marea blanca*, Marea de Pensionistes, Stop Pujades, Som Manta, the Platform of People Affected by Mortgages, or the strikes of Panrico's and Movistar's workers, among others. For this reason, their main slogan is 'civil disobedience so that our daughters and granddaughters don't live in worse conditions than we do'. Two of their activists summarize Iai@flautas' main goals as follows:

We are trying to recover what was ours in the past, what is common, what is everyone's. We are against privatisations and the neoliberal policies they are implementing in Catalonia and Spain. [...] Our only goal is to leave our daughters and granddaughters a better life, a better world: ecological, feminist, inclusive. [...] A world that works through assemblies, in which they have the power, in which we all participate through this new way of doing politics we're starting to build.
(interview with Iai@flautas activist, December 2015, authors' translation)

I'm struggling for a future I'll never see, but I don't mind. I'm much more satis-
fied with myself because I'm doing it for my grandchildren, if I ever have them.

(Rosario. Video Iai@flautas: Present i futur,
available online, authors' translation)

Conclusion

We might consider the development of welfare during the European/Eurozone
crisis as something of a double movement. We have seen increased disciplinary
pressures from global markets and European institutions and an attempted de-
politization of budgetary discipline on the one hand; combined with increased
everyday vulnerability and social inequality, a deepening legitimacy crisis of
national and European institutions, but also mass protests that push for a re-politi-
zation, on the other. As the case studies of the UK and Spain have shown, austerity and welfare retrenchment are far from uncontested.

As the capacity or willingness to respond to popular demands through public spending has declined, so likewise trust in politicians, political parties and
political institutions has gone into severe decline. This has prompted a widening
of the division between political elites and populations, exacerbating a problem
of European legitimacy that was already present prior to the crisis (Armingeon
and Guthmann, 2014). The decreasing responsiveness of the state, however, as
our case studies have shown, has coincided with a radicalization of social movements targeting the incidence and the effects of cuts in welfare. As established
channels of interest mediation have proven unable to provide the public with an
opportunity to have an impact upon policy making, those seeking a voice have
sought alternative and innovative channels instead. These drew, moreover, upon
pre-crisis instances of activism and movements, witnessing both the participation
of experienced activists, and repertoires of action developed in earlier struggles
and campaigns (Huke, 2016; Flesher Fominaya, 2015a).

Whilst they drew on activists and experiences from the pre-crisis period, however, the post-2008 anti-austerity movements also represented a qualitative change
in the nature of their activity. They relied more heavily on radical-democratic
and prefigurative mechanisms of decision making, such as assemblies. Within
these mechanisms, first-person politics dominated, with affected people being the
key participants – be they those who objected to workfare or medical staff and
patients who directly organized around their everyday needs and demands. The
movements thereby were able to transform individualized experiences into collective demands. Both horizontality and first-person politics were reinforced by
an active use of social media such as Twitter and Facebook, which also provided
a possibility to quickly distribute demands and calls for action. These new forms
made it possible that the new social movements could bring together previously
fragmented and divided social groups, such as different groups of workers, users
and even local neighbourhoods. As one of our interviewees put it

I think that's one of the key things to come out of the move to social network type organising – in that there is a greater willingness to cooperate. You

wouldn't have seen these groups working together during the 1990s. In part this is due to the fact that it's harder to get big groups of people to organise together than in the past. And also if you compare to events like anti-globalization movement and Reclaim the Streets – then there was much more of a sense that these were campaigns around political ideals and explicitly anti-capitalist. In contrast, the current organisations are much more focused on material issues that are concretely affecting people's everyday lives – like claimant conditionality, workfare, sanctions. [...] There is a greater willingness to cooperate – partly because people sense that they are being directly affected by welfare cuts and that they have no real other way in which to try and improve matters. For that reason they are less concerned about the ideological position of those they are working with and more focused on trying to win campaigns.

(interview with Johnny Void, Welfare Rights Blogger and
Campaigner, 17 June 2016)

Civil disobedience and direct actions such as occupations and *encierros* also complemented more standard forms of action such as demonstrations. The movements thereby point beyond established forms of interest mediation and articulation and towards the re-emergence of a previouslydomesticated 'uncontrollable anomaly of the politics' (Papadopoulos *et al.*, 2008: 108). Relying on high levels of popular support for welfare and public infrastructure, the movements were able to question government discourse – that austerity measures were both unavoidable and that the burden was being shared across the population – and point out their immediate and unequal social effects. To do so, the movements published first-hand reports and everyday experiences of those affected. The contrast between government discourses claiming 'there is no alternative', and the everyday suffering of the populations, further contributed to a loss of legitimacy of both the EU and national governments. This deepened crisis of legitimacy – as we will show in our concluding chapter – has also opened a window of opportunity for both the rise of right-wing populist parties, as well as parties, such as Podemos, representing the demands of social movements.

Anti-austerity movements produced significant obstacles, routinely blocking, opposing, and/or making it difficult to implement in full the austerity reforms proposed by the public authorities. In this sense, we see a continuation of the frustration of neoliberal goals that we highlighted for the period prior to 2008. Two examples of that frustration, which we have pointed out in this chapter, are the difficulties experienced during the implementation of workfare in the UK as well as the failed attempt to privatize public hospitals in Madrid. The ongoing resistance of European society to elite-led attempts to reduce spending has therefore ensured that cost-cutting measures were consistently thwarted, either in part or (on occasion) in full.

In sum, these empirical developments point towards an intensification of 'disciplinary neoliberalism' (Gill, 1998), in which investors and rating agencies closely scrutinize democratically elected governments and – in case of non-compliance – punish them by the sheer power of market forces. Additionally, they show how the fiscal capacity of European states has been further limited by a system of measures that comprise an 'authoritarian crisis constitutionalism' (Bieling, 2015; Oberndorfer, 2015). Austerity and neoliberal competitiveness have become the main governing strategies of those seeking to deal with economic crises throughout Europe. The effect is an 'age of permanent strain' (Pavolini *et al.*, 2016: 153), in which elements of welfare provided at the national or sub-national level faced continuous retrenchment, privatizations and access restrictions. As a consequence, the crisis has produced an increase in 'everyday vulnerability' (Pérez Orozco, 2014). This has therefore consolidated trends towards the hollowing out and perforating of social protection that had already begun across the EU prior to the crisis (Haas and Huke, 2015). In doing so, moreover, it has further reinforced trends towards a 'descent society' (Nachtwey, 2016). The degree of descent, however, differed strongly among different strata of society, increasing inequality and producing further social polarization (Moulaert *et al.*, 2005).

These developments have in turn been met by forms of association between those affected that have produced significant instances of self-determination and mutual aid, achieved through forms of community organizing that have coincided with a 'self-enforcement' of social rights (Macías, 2013; Bader, 2014). Exemplarily, this can be seen in the case of *Yo Sí Sanidad Universal* which not only demanded universal healthcare, but also went on to actively provide it, in the face of legal prohibition. These moments of self-enforcement constitute forms of civil disobedience, which act as a democratizing element within the existing political systems (Huke, 2014; Celikates, 2010: 280).

Regarding political subjectivities, the new social movements were also able to politicize and activate previously disengaged, disaffected and disinterested political (non–)actors, by providing platforms to render everyday experiences and invisible politics visible. As the formal political process became more closed, vocal agents of political representation – that is traditional forms of claims-based welfare actors, such as trade unions – tended to recede or to be reduced to symbolic mobilizations. Prefigurative radicals, in contrast, gained in importance but also changed during the crisis, as traditional 'identitarian' leftist collectives made way for more open, everyday-based movements of those affected themselves.

Finally, both elements of these processes – domination and disruptive agency – have developed in an uneven way across the EU (Lehndorff, 2015). As such, everyday living conditions, social security, political experience and subjectivities have each been marked by social polarization. In political terms, and as we return to in Chapter 7, this can be seen in the turn towards right-wing parties in core countries, such as the AfD in Germany or the FPÖ in Austria, contrasting starkly with the successes of left-wing parties in Southern Europe, such as Syriza in Greece or Podemos in Spain. We turn now to consider similar developments of austerity and anti-austerity in the sphere of education.

Notes

1 The full list is: Greece, Germany, France, Italy, Czech Republic, Cyprus, Hungary, Malta, Poland, Slovakia and the United Kingdom.

2 See Hansard, 20 March 2013: www.publications.parliament.uk/pa/cm201213/cmhansrd/
   cm130320/debtext/130320-0001.htm#13032055000001.
3 For the full list, see: http://keepvolunteeringvoluntary.net/.
4 Parts of this section are based on collaborative work between Nikolai Huke and Tobias
   Haas (Haas and Huke, 2015).
5 Parts of this section are based on collaborative work between Nikolai Huke and Tobias
   Haas (Haas and Huke, 2015).
6 For more details, see http://www.iaioflautas.org/blog/2012/09/21/labolsaolavida-por-un-
   proceso-constituyente-y-un-plan-de-rescate-ciudadano/.
7 See http://www.iaioflautas.org.
8 The video is still available at http://bambuser.com/v/2998272.

5 Defending the commons
Struggles against marketization and austerity in education

In this chapter we trace the development of European integration and the way in which it has been used in an attempt to promote neoliberal marketization in the field of education policy. In doing so, we highlight the accompanying development of episodes of disruption and associated forms of disruptive subjectivity. Critical political economy (CPE), we claim, has tended to view European integration as a means by which the neoliberal agenda has been imposed upon the sphere of education. This includes the more general process of welfare retrenchment and fiscal discipline associated with the EU's approach to the welfare state. But it also includes a more specific focus on an 'employability' agenda that has gained ground in EU-level education policy, as part of the broad innovation-based model of growth that forms part of the European neoliberal project.[1] As such, the marketization of education has been portrayed as part of the attempt to create a 'Schumpeterian National Workfare State' (Jessop, 1993); or to advance 'progressive competitiveness' (Albo, 1994), in which competition is achieved through productivity increases rather than declining wages. As with earlier chapters, we argue that such an account fails to properly address the important ways in which this neoliberal agenda, advanced through European education policy, has been contested and disrupted through the development of different forms of opposition and refusal.

When we come to focus on the European crisis, moreover, we show that the process of welfare retrenchment in the field of education, and the process of marketization in search of 'employability' as part of knowledge-based capitalist strategies, have both become heightened in the context of rising sovereign debt, increased disciplinary pressures and an increasingly unstable accumulation process. This intensification, we argue, has been met by more openly disruptive subjectivities developed on the part of students and education workers, who themselves had already prior to the crisis become both increasingly precarious and had developed (partly 'subterranean') forms of militancy within educational institutions. Similar to that which we have witnessed in the field of welfare, therefore, this has resulted in the development of students as political subjects, able and willing to challenge the imposition of neoliberal discipline across the European Union.

Between marketization, new constitutionalism and oppositional students' movements: public education and European integration

In the following pages, we sketch the historical development of education in the context of European integration. Rather than presenting an all-embracing account, instead we seek to develop a reading of education as a field of conflict, in which we locate the social movements that form the focus of our research, especially highlighting the development of students' movements in both the United Kingdom and Spain during the global and European crises.

Public education during Fordism: expansion, contestation, participation

As public education developed from the late eighteenth century onwards, it increasingly served as a mechanism to maintain discipline, social control and legitimacy in a system controlled by dominant economic and political elites. As Chalari summarizes, public education developed 'in post-revolutionary Europe in the late eighteenth century as instruments of state formation and tools for developing a common national identity within specific geographical borders' (Chalari, 2014: 113). Prior to and even throughout the Fordist period, capitalist demand for a qualified workforce was relatively low, as industry relied largely on de-qualified mass workers (see Chapter 2). As a result, schools and universities were able to maintain a considerable degree of autonomy with regard to the accumulation process. Moral and civic education played an important part in school and university curricula, as the Spanish case highlights, despite it being a non-typical case. Up to the 1960s, Spanish schools and even universities, to an important part controlled by the Catholic Church, served largely as elements of the ideological state apparatus, spreading ruling class ideology and especially that of an extremely conservative form of Catholicism. It was not until economic modernization took place in the 1960s and 1970s, however, that the regime started to expand access to education and reoriented public education, from ideological indoctrination to the provision of employment qualifications (García *et al.*, 2001).

Indeed, processes of economic modernization began, from the 1960s and 1970s onwards, to create pressure upon universities across Europe, moving them to focus more greatly on equipping students with employment qualifications. This combination of rapidly increasing student numbers, and heightened pressure to subordinate education to the demands of the labour market, produced a corresponding frustration amongst those students regarding their expectations of autonomy and creativity (Boltanski and Chiapello, 2007: 170). As a result, the years around 1968 witnessed the mobilization of students across the advanced industrial democracies, and beyond, oftentimes focusing on demands for better quality education, greater personal and individual autonomy, more participation for students in the design of education curriculums, and also frequently including broader demands for peace (especially focused on the Vietnam war) and the registering of objections to the stultifying nature of modern bureaucratic life (Suri, 2003: 166–74).

For instance, in Germany the socialist student body, the *Sozialistischer Deutscher Studentenbund* (SDS) – which had originally been created as a student body of the Social Democratic Party of Germany (SPD), but was expelled by the party in 1961 on the grounds that it had become too radical and was suspected of having communist infiltrators – published a major document, *Hochschule in der Demokratie*, which rallied the movement around the democratization of universities. In 1966, the Free University of Berlin experienced its first student sit-in in response to a proposal to impose time limits on law and medicine studies. This prompted a mass wave of mobilization by students that included mass demonstrations, and sometimes involved violent clashes with the police, especially following the shooting of the SDS's charismatic leader, Rudi Dutschke (Levitt, 1989).

These movements were enabled by the widespread expansion of tertiary education across much of the so-called 'first world', and were driven by a set of grievances underpinned by an analysis of the post-war period which considered (albeit unequally distributed) material wealth to have been achieved at the expense of individual autonomy and the placing of excessive constraints upon the scope for human creativity to flourish (Altbach, 1989).

One of the lasting effects of the '1968' protests was the move by governments, especially in continental Europe, to pass higher education legislation that would create formal channels of student representation allowing students to have co-decision rights in the university (Klemenčič, 2014: 397; 2012). In addition, the pressure created by the heightened proclivity of workers and students to protest throughout the 1960s, combined with a growing view amongst the political elite themselves that a higher skilled workforce would be beneficial, led in most European countries to experiments to increase participation and expand recruitment numbers in higher education. This witnessed, for instance, the creation of the Open University in the UK and similar institutions in France (the University Institutes of Technology, IUTs) and Norway (Norwegian Regional Colleges), the introduction of the Swedish 25/5 Scheme (which made higher education accessible to mature students), the Polish Preferential Point System (which made access easier for students from worker or peasant families), and the faltering attempt to create a university system in Germany which was to be made up of an integrated tier of higher education (*Gesamthochschule*) (Cerych and Sabatier 1986). It also included initiatives for student participation in the governance of universities across much of Western Europe, especially France, Germany, the Netherlands and Sweden (Cerych and Sabatier, 1986; Altbach, 2006).

Following 1968, students continued to play a disruptive role in the politics of a number of European countries. This was especially notable in those countries that had yet to become formal democracies. Thus, in the dictatorships of Southern Europe, student mobilization proved to be an important disruptive factor – most obviously in the case of the 1973 occupation of the Athens Polytechnic, which marked the beginning of the end for the military junta in Greece (Kritidis, 2014: 67). As Kornetis (2013) discusses, whilst the students who participated in the Greek underground movement faced quite different obstacles and opponents to those in much of Western Europe; nevertheless, the so-called '3-Ms' (Marx, Mao and Marcuse) influenced the student movement in much the same way as they did in other countries.

In Portugal, likewise, Accornero (2013) shows how student protests were central to the rebellion that produced the 1974 revolution and downfall of the dictatorship. This had many of the same features of student unrest that were witnessed across the world at the time. A key event was a demonstration against the Vietnam War in 1968 in Lisbon, which prompted the creation of the Student Democratic Left. This represented a move towards Maoism for many within the student movement, and a corresponding move away from the Portuguese Communist Party. The Portuguese student movement also focused on educational reforms, connected to regime change on the grounds that any attempt to reform education would also require a change in the political system. This radical new left development witnessed students rise to become one of the most important sources of rebellion facing the regime, as evinced by the high proportion of political prisoners that were members of the student movement (over 40 per cent of all political prisoners in 1973). As Accornero highlights, the students 'adopted ever more disruptive forms of protest, including lightning demonstrations (*manifestações relâmpago*), often involving the destruction of cars and shop fronts, irruptions in lecture halls and the interruption of classes, and the occupation of university premises' (Accornero, 2013: 1043). In addition, students were instrumental in facilitating military desertions and neighbourhood assemblies. As such, Accornero argues, the student mobilization played a major role in the destabilization of the dictatorship (Accornero, 2013; likewise, the memories of the 1974 Revolution would go on to inform and inspire Portuguese anti-austerity movements during the European crisis, see Baumgarten, 2017).

After the expansion of public education in the 1960s and 1970s, Spain also witnessed a wave of student protests, as Marxist, leftist catholic and other nonconformist ideas gained ground within the universities. A number of new publications and collectives developed that were dedicated to critical theoretical and literary perspectives developing outside of Spain. Further, due to its rigid structures, the Francoist regime was only able to act by repression, which in turn led to an anti-Francoist radicalization of Spanish students (García and Carnicer, 2001: 210–211; López, 2015: 101, 107).

We can also witness similar trends in central and Eastern Europe, oftentimes against the communist regime and its lack of civil liberties (Pinheiro and Antonowicz, 2015: 59). The student movement of 1968 therefore played an important part in the political transformation of eastern Europe. For instance, 1968 witnessed one of the first major uprisings against the communist regime in Poland. In a context of rising anti-semitism, propagated especially by General Mieczyslaw Moczar (who was rumoured to be attempting to position himself to rival First Secretary, Gomulkar), a wave of anti-communist students began to campaign around civil rights and the right to stage a play, *Dziady* (which was considered to be critical of the regime). This student opposition, led by Warsaw University student, Adam Michkin, escalated into a nationwide conflict during March 1968 (Eisler, 1998). These events subsequently prompted the Communist regime to re-organize the student unions that they had created (Antonowicz *et al.*, 2014: 473), although the backlash by the Gomulkar regime was such that it remains unclear the degree to which the events weakened or strengthened his rule. What the events did mark, though, were the beginning of the emergence of genuinely independent opposition to the communist regime (Eisler, 1998: 251). As a result, students represented a key group within the Solidarity movement that by the early 1980s had grown to a size where it could seriously destabilize the regime. Rebellious students associated with the Solidarity movement took part in a 29-day student occupation strike in the early 1980s in opposition to the regime. These students formed a new student organization, the Independent Association of Students (NZS), which was initially legalized by the regime, but was later outlawed following the imposition of martial law in December 1981. By 1986, moreover, the NZS had the support of over half of the student population (although much less of them actually joined the association, due to fear of being associated with an outlawed organization). Between 1988 and 1989 the NZS held a series of strikes in demand of its legalization and registration as a formal student association, representing a significant mobilization that added to the pressure upon the regime ahead of its imminent collapse (Antonowicz *et al.*, 2014: 473–5).

Whilst higher education became an increasingly active site of contestation across Europe during the Fordist period, however, the role of European integration in these developments was minimal. As such, it was not until new measures of fiscal discipline were developed at the European level (starting, as we have seen, with the EMS in 1979, and later on strengthened by the single European market, single currency and Stability and Growth Pact) and the subsequent adoption of strategies of innovation and knowledge-based growth, that the impact of European integration would be felt within the sphere of education.

Public education during the 1980s and 1990s: the new spirit of capitalism and the decreasing fiscal capacity of the state

As Boltanski and Chiapello have highlighted, the critique of alienation developed under Fordism, and the demand for autonomy that emerged within the variety of student movements witnessed during the 1960s, 1970s and 1980s, each began after some time to connect with and shape neoliberal capitalist strategies. This could be seen with the move towards so-called 'innovation-based' and 'knowledge-based' growth strategies, each of which relied upon individual skills rather than de-qualified mass work. The result of these developments, claim Boltanski and Chiapello, was a new spirit of capitalism that strengthened the autonomy of workers, in turn inscribing capitalist discipline into the worker-selves. One of the key aims of this management strategy was to overcome problems of absenteeism, delays, turnover, obstruction, defective work, below-average productivity, strikes and criticisms, protests or temporary stoppages in the workplace, by strengthening the autonomy and self-motivation of workers (Boltanski and Chiapello, 2007: 187). Skills-based accumulation strategies were also embraced by policy makers and capitalist firms throughout Europe, not least in an attempt to overcome the relative competitive advantages of US firms (Mandel, 1968; Jessop, 1993: 23).

This skills-based accumulation strategy has been somewhat contradictory, however, in that it has also been accompanied by a flexibilization of the labour market. On the one hand, therefore, firms increasingly demand higher skilled labour, but on the other hand the increased fluidity of the labour market has dis-incentivized firms from providing that necessary training and instead encouraged them to 'poach' trained workers away from other firms (Albo 1994: 151). This has therefore created a requirement for states to gear labour market and social policy towards improved competitiveness (Jessop, 1993: 9). As such, public education came, from the early 1980s onwards, to be increasingly focused on ensuring that workers would have the skills required by firms that wished to act competitively (Zgaga *et al.*, 2013: 28; Amaral and Neave, 2009: 283). Throughout Europe, a restructuring of public education along the lines of Taylorist managerialism took place, in which the goal of universities has been increasingly steered towards the production of profit, including a heightened focus on ensuring that university graduates acquire the necessary skilled technical knowledge required for their employment within the so-called 'knowledge society'; a process considered by some to be a form of 'academic capitalism' (Bousquet, 2008; Slaughter and Rhoades, 1999).

At the same time as this transition to a skills-based accumulation strategy was occurring, European integration also came increasingly to play a role in both European education policy (albeit with member states retaining considerable control over national education policies), and in facilitating the spread of this skills-based strategy through the educational institutions of Europe. Thus, as Maassen and Musselin highlight, the EU 'has gradually established a policy presence in the area of education, demonstrating a movement from no EC involvement in education policy to the situation at the end of the 1990s where education policy decisions were taken at both the national and EC levels [...]' (Maassen and Musselin, 2009: 5). The most visible manifestation of this trend has been the so-called Bologna Process, which began in 1999 (and which we consider below in more depth). A number of prior developments, however, can also be discerned. One important first step was the Erasmus programme, established in 1987, which aimed in part at strengthening the development of an open European labour market (Corbett, 2009).

This European-wide move towards the adoption of skills-based training at university level has also been accompanied by reforms to the financing of university education. In particular, we see an increased individualization of financing – albeit with significant cross-country variation – and especially the introduction of tuition fees (Tsiligiris, 2012). The financial investment in education and the necessity to repay large amounts of debt, has in turn resulted in a heightened concern amongst students for the financial rewards associated with particular academic courses. Students are therefore increasingly encouraged by the market to pursue skills in sectors where a perceived skill-shortage exists (Feigenbaum and Iqani, 2013: 55). In this sense, we can speak of an individualization of the risk of skill training in the context of neoliberal capitalism, in part associated with the declining fiscal capacity of the state (Saltman, 2014: 42).

The move towards self-financed skills-based training for much of the neoliberal period has, however, also been accompanied by significant and visible forms of opposition, largely from the student bodies across European countries. One early example can be seen in the case of Greece. Thus, a key neoliberal reform to Greek education came in 1990 when the school and university reform bill was introduced by New Democracy (ND) Government. The reforms represented an attempt by the government to impose greater discipline upon universities. This prompted nationwide protest, involving between 60–70 per cent of school and university students, and including occupations of universities and schools across the country. Following the killing of one of the teacher trade union activists – Nikos Teboneras – in Patras, three days of riots ensued and more than 25,000 protesters took part in a demonstration in solidarity with Teboneras and in opposition to the reforms. This was sufficient to halt the reforms, seeing them withdrawn by the Government and seriously undermining the ND Government (Kritdis, 2014: 78). The mobilizations of 1990–1991 also caused a subsequent radicalization of the student movement, feeding into the development of an anarchist social centre movement especially focused around Exarcheia. The students and teachers' unions adopted increasingly militant techniques of resistance, and were also heavily influenced by anarchist, horizontal and direct action principles. This continued to be evident for many years – witnessed, for instance, in the wave of opposition that took place in 2006 following the attempt by the ND Government to introduce a number of reforms to higher education, including the end to university asylum and academic self-administration, and an opening of higher education to market principles, much of which was underpinned by the Bologna Process. This later wave of opposition also included occupations, clashes with the police, civil disobedience and other forms of militant activism, all of which contributed to the successful blocking of nearly all of the Bologna measures (Kritdis, 2014: 80–1).

Similarly, in Hungary in 1995, student mobilizations emerged in response to the so-called Bokros package, which introduced higher education tuition fees. A range of protests erupted that included students from most of Hungary's 70 universities and colleges, and witnessed the staging of street protests throughout the country (Cerami, 2010: 243; MTI Econews, 1995a). In Italy, Italian Socialist Minister of Education, Antonio Ruberti, proposed a number of reforms to the Italian higher education system in 1989 that would decentralize the system and aimed to make it more flexible and adaptable to the demands of wider society. This was fiercely opposed by the student movement, who largely viewed the reforms as the first step in a process of *de facto* privatization. This opposition also combined with a more 'imperceptible' form of dissent on the part of the university professors – who openly supported the reforms, but in practice undertook a form of 'passive resistance', whereby the decentralized authority that was offered to them was not acted upon (Ballarino and Perotti, 353–4).

In France in 1986 the newly elected conservative government led by Chirac (cohabiting with Mitterrand) proposed a series of reforms to the higher education system that would seek to limit access to the university, pass greater control of the running of the higher education system to scientific councils (and away from the universities), reduce the input of students in the running of universities, and ensure that 30 per cent of the seats on the scientific councils would be reserved for people outside the university. These reforms, named Devaquet's law, after the minister responsible for proposing them, witnessed the mass spontaneous mobilization of both students and high school pupils (with the latter forming the majority). The scale of opposition, moreover, which included a series of nationwide mass demonstrations (and sometimes clashes with the police) was such that the law eventually had to be withdrawn and Devaquet resigned (the turning point came when one of the protesters was beaten to death by the police, sparking even further demonstrations) (Fields, 1989: 231–3).

The period prior to the adoption of the Bologna Declaration was therefore one in which attempts at neoliberalization of European education had been limited and faltering – in large part due to the widespread opposition that attempts at reform had faced. This, however, set the stage for a more concerted (European-level) attempt at university reforms, as we shall see, with the Bologna Declaration being at their centre.

Bologna and its limitations: the disrupted path towards managerialism in higher education

> To put it briefly, the mix of attempts to corporatize the higher education system, resistance coming from the old power system, and a chronic lack of resources has steadily turned most universities into knowledge transmission factories where research, critical thinking and debate have become increasingly difficult.
>
> (Terranova, 2015: 4)

CPE scholars have noted the way in which the rise of post-Fordist skill-based strategies of capital accumulation has coincided with an increasingly active role for European institutions in public education. The key pillar of this development was the so-called Bologna Process, which has been viewed within the critical political economy literature as a process through which the pressures and demands of market forces have been gradually but consistently imposed upon European education schemes, especially in the sphere of higher education. This therefore represents a similar iteration of the transition observed in the other spheres of European capitalism that we have covered in this book. That is, we witness a move from the Fordist period (characterized by the 'massification' of higher education, or the 'mass university') to a post-Fordist one (characterized by a far greater focus on teaching students how to be flexible, precarious, available, and geared towards the demands of multinational corporations, or a 'corporate university') (Fernández, 2012: 175). Accompanying Bologna was a discourse that pictured universities and existing institutional frameworks as incapable of meeting 'the fast-growing demand for higher-level skills and competencies, and research-based commercial technologies' (Olsen and Maassen, 2007: 3). In addition, European universities were criticized for lagging behind their US counterparts (Olsen and Maassen, 2007: 14).

The aim of Bologna was therefore to make students more employable and to bring higher education more in line with business needs – evidenced perhaps most visibly by the fact that BusinessEurope (the European business confederation) was a key consultative member throughout the process (Mercille and Murphy, 2015: 5). The Bologna objectives were directly linked to the aim of securing economic gains through the creation of a common education area and the establishment of innovation, entrepreneurship and market orientation as key guidelines for universities (Amaral and Neave, 2009: 289). Higher education in turn became

> increasingly commercialized and privatized [...], indeed, 'capitalist' [...]. Universities have seen their role shift toward providing services, research and labor to the corporate sector [...]. Their funding now comes to a greater extent from private sources, ranging from domestic and international student fees to philanthropic donations, while public funding has been curtailed. Further, higher education workers have become increasingly precarious, monitored and controlled by management.
>
> (Mercille and Murphy, 2015: 3)

The Bologna Process was launched by the Bologna Declaration of 1999 and was initially created as an apparently technical measure to ensure harmonization between education models and systems within (mainly) the EU member states. As de Wit (2006) makes clear, in adopting the Sorbonne Declaration in 1998 (which was the precursor to the Bologna Declaration), the governments of both France and Italy (two of the four signatory countries) were keen to recruit the support of the United Kingdom and Germany (the other two signatories) in their attempt to impose reforms upon their higher education systems, 'something that had previously been blocked by massive protests' (de Wit, 2006: 474). Signing the Bologna Declaration, the member countries also loosened their embrace of the principle of subsidiarity and gave up (to a degree) their opposition to the principle of harmonization (Maassen and Musselin, 2009: 6; Zgaga *et al.*, 2013: 14).

Bologna therefore provided the governments of member states with the possibility of securing and legitimating already sought-after (neoliberal) domestic reforms of national higher education systems (Amaral and Neave, 2009: 293). For instance, in seeking to introduce national reforms to the Italian higher education system, Guido Martinotti[2] explicitly highlighted the importance of the European Union (and the commitments made under the Sorbonne Declaration) in his attempt to drive through the reforms (despite their clearly national origin, as they had been drafted during 1997, prior to the adoption of the Sorbonne Declaration). This was a clear attempt, therefore, to portray national reforms in terms that emphasized the pressure imposed by European integration. In 1999, likewise, a revised series of higher education reforms were adopted by the new D'Alema Government, in accordance with the Bologna Declaration, and in many ways undoing the moves towards university autonomy that had been introduced under earlier (Ruberti) reforms (Ballarino and Perotti, 2012: 355–60).

In 2010, the European Higher Education Area, which was created by the Bologna Process, was formally declared. At the time of writing (January 2017) this consists of 48 signatory states. The Bologna Process is technically voluntary, as it falls outside of the formal competence of the European Union, although as Voegtle *et al.* (2011) show, it has also produced substantial 'convergence effects', especially between the signatory states; on the willingness of member states to participate and adhere to 'monitored coordination', despite the formally voluntary nature of Bologna, see Ravinet, 2008). Since the adoption of the Lisbon Agenda in 2000, moreover, the Bologna Process has combined with the so-called Lisbon criteria to heighten the degree to which it projects a core organizational mission – the fundamental transformation and reform of higher education across the European Union. As Capano and Piattoni put it:

> From the incremental, piecemeal convergence towards a common curricular format and comparable quality assurance schemes at the core of the Bologna Process, to the institutional autonomy and accountability that are the most significant elements introduced by the Lisbon Agenda, higher education reform evolved into an open-ended, and potentially never-ending, process of transformation of what were once well-established higher education systems and traditions.
>
> (Capano and Piattoni, 2011: 585)

This transformation, moreover, is not only organizational, but is also marked by its neoliberal content. Thus, we see a process of 'Lisbonization', especially geared around the move in 2005 to re-launch the Lisbon Agenda, and including a specific attempt to ensure the connection between Bologna and Lisbon. This is perhaps most clearly evident with the publication in 2005 of the Commission document, 'Communication on the mobilization of universities in support of the Lisbon Strategy' (for a discussion of this document, see Capano and Piattoni, 2011: 586). Central to this process was the move towards ensuring that higher education would be put to the service of ensuring the increased and improved competitiveness of the European Union, especially by improving 'human capital'. This therefore puts European integration at the heart of attempts to render higher education subordinate to the requirements of the post-knowledge economy. As de Wit (2006: 462) describes, the combination of Lisbon and Bologna 'are the foundation for a reform agenda that not only requires more transparency and the removal of obstacles for internal labor and student mobility, but also must make education and research more competitive in the context of the global knowledge economy' (see also Keeling, 2006). This was also a part of a broader move by member states to tackle what was widely seen as a recurring problem whereby universities produced knowledge that did not tally with the skills required by the market – in part a trend associated with the legacy of the student-led protests and associated development of universities from 1968 onwards (Capano and Piattoni,

2011: 587). As such, it was due to the signatory governments' 'perception that European universities are not functioning well enough and are not competitive in a global setting, [that] they launched a process of higher education policy harmonization' (Vögtle, 2014: 76).

The transition produced by 'Lisbonisation' (or 'Lisbonised Bologna'), therefore, is one characterized by the move from the 1960s – in which we saw a large expansion of the university sector marked by the dramatic escalation of demands by students and faculty for radical democratic input, and which culminated in the rise of the New Left (most evidently with the events of 1968), through to the 1980s onwards, in which neoliberal reforms have sought to challenge these demands for self-determination amongst university students and faculty as 'the societal relevance of the universities demanded by critical students was turned on its head to become economic relevance to business and industry in the knowledge society' (Lorenz, 2012: 600; on the contribution of Lisbon to a general marketization of European society, see also Levidow, 2002). This was a longer-term process, therefore, whereby governments explicitly sought to improve the degree to which universities supported national economic competitiveness. The underlying rationale underpinning much of the (Lisbonized) Bologna Process can therefore be summed up as follows:

> Europe as a whole, or rather a more integrated Europe, could compete better in the world, it could assert its own particular values and model of society [...] by building a society based on knowledge [...] and can help in this way to achieve better competitiveness, social cohesion and greater well-being for all European countries.
>
> (Matei, 2015: 39)

This process of transformation, moreover, is perhaps best considered an iterative one, with governments as the main proponents of reform, and interests within higher education often representing the main source of resistance and opposition. Indeed, as noted in the previous section, compliance with the Bologna Declaration is entirely voluntary due to its inter-governmental status; yet commitment to abiding by its principles is high amongst most member states. This reflects the fact that in many ways it is designed as an enabling mechanism to be taken up by states seeking to achieve reforms to universities that they have otherwise been prevented from achieving due to domestic resistance (Vögtle, 2014: 10). Thus

> Deeply rooted traditions in higher education, and the entrenched interests that such traditions bred, have fiercely opposed reform, and thus the implementation of reform has been spearheaded by the governments of the countries in question.
>
> (Capano and Piattoni, 2011: 589)

One of the key ways in which the Bologna Process has facilitated these reforms and goals has been through the standardization of degrees across signatory countries, thereby creating a more level playing field between universities, and therefore greater opportunity for market competition, with the goal being to maximize the number of student-customers (Van Damme, 2009). Thus,

> The basic idea and drive behind the Bologna Process is to standardize all of higher education in Europe in terms of interchangeable modules. If successful, Bologna will deterritorialize all higher education in the EU and create one integrated European higher educational market, with the European Credit Transfer System (ECTS) point functioning as the educational equivalent of the euro.
>
> (Lorenz, 2012: 612)

Moreover, the focus on quality control and quality assurance is intrinsically linked to the promotion of managerialism within higher education – as universities become focused on the need to be efficient and well-managed service providers, so student-customers require some means by which the quality of the product can be assured. Bologna has therefore been noted for both the way in which it empowers external institutions which favour a managerial approach to public service provision (such as the European Commission), and to facilitate the day-to-day operation of the market which that managerialism seeks to create and oversee (Vögtle, 2014: 70–4). In addition, the Bologna Process aims to produce neoliberal subjectivity and a neoliberal rationality of governance. That is, it promotes the notion of individual personal responsibility, an independence from the state, entrepreneurialism, and the need to invest in one's own human capital in order that a model European citizen might be produced, one who is 'flexible, autonomous and self-regulating' (Fejes, 2008; for a similar argument, see also Mitchell, 2006; Reinalda, 2008).

One example of these trends can be witnessed in the case of the transformation of higher education in Denmark. Here the University Act adopted in 2003 introduced reforms to the governance of universities that would ensure that they were more centrally controlled by the internal university management, and more clearly subjected to instructions from external societal actors (by which was meant private profit-seeking companies). This was largely driven by the EU, Bologna and the Lisbon Process. The Act, moreover, undid a number of the internal mechanisms of democracy that had been introduced in an earlier set of reforms in 1970 in response to the 1968 student rebellions in the country. As Hansen details,

> Boards with a majority of external members have replaced the university senates, and elected leaders have been replaced by appointed leaders. In the present system, the vice-chancellor is appointed by the board, the pro-vice-chancellors and the deans are appointed by the vice-chancellor, and the heads of department are appointed by the deans. The earlier bottom-up based system has been replaced by a strict, hierarchical, top-down system.
>
> (Hansen, 2011: 236)

In sum, since the Bologna Declaration was signed in 1999, the European Union (or, more accurately, the signatories to the Bologna Declaration) set out to facilitate the national-level imposition of a neoliberal model of higher education upon European society. This consisted of a threefold process of reforms: standardization of the degree qualification (which encouraged competition); accreditation (which provided the stamp of approval on higher education as a sellable commodity); and an efficiency drive that focused predominantly upon the shortening of study times (and therefore reduced costs of production). Each of these three moves, moreover, were accompanied by, and acted to facilitate and encourage, the expansion of the role of a managerial class within the institutions of higher education, who in turn became a key advocate within the sector for advancing each of these developments further.

In response to the adoption of the Bologna Process, however, universities across Europe have witnessed a series of anti-marketization struggles throughout much of the post-1999 period. There have been a range of anti-Bologna protests and anti-reform student protests across Europe.[3]

> In Italy (2005), around school and college reforms; in Spain (2008) around the Bologna Process; in Austria (2011) and Germany (2003), against budget cuts in public education; in Denmark (2005) against reforms prohibiting collective college exams; in Greece (2006) against the new law of higher education; and in France (2007) as a result of the law on the autonomy of universities (Pécresse)
>
> (Pinheiro and Antonowicz, 2015: 60).

In addition, the European Social Forum represented an important opportunity to coordinate struggles, frequently facilitating the tactic of student occupations to protest reforms that were attempted to be introduced in education (Fernández, 2012).

A key flashpoint occurred in Germany and Austria in autumn 2009 when almost every university town in both countries faced large-scale public strikes and protests in opposition to a swathe of reforms being introduced under the Bologna Process. Opposition was especially focused on the move to shorten the period of study, to introduce selection at the MA level, and to introduce tuition fees (Lorenz, 2011: 53). Opposition to the Danish reforms of 2003, mentioned in the previous section, also witnessed 3000 academics sign a statement in 2008 that was handed to the parliament and called for a change to research policy and to the 2003 Act. In addition, the office of the Vice-Chancellor of the University of Copenhagen was occupied for two days in Spring 2009 (Hansen, 2011).

In Italy, attempts to introduce a research assessment exercise that would be similar to that of the REF in the UK were resisted by Italian academics. The scheme, known as the VQR, required academics in 2016 to submit two pieces of work that they had published between 2011 and 2014. This prompted a boycott by a proportion of academics opposing the assessment, in turn resulting in reduced income for those universities in which the boycott rates were highest. Whilst the boycott was unable to prevent the conduct of the assessment, nevertheless as two observers pointed out, the rectors of those universities were increasingly concerned about the impact upon income that the boycott would have. As they put it, 'active academic resistance to research assessment can make university leaders take notice in a way that no amount of grumbling in the common room can' (Baccini and De Nicolao, 2016).

Indeed, alongside these quite visible instances of opposition to managerial reforms other more imperceptible or 'everyday' forms of resistance have also often been observed. As Anderson (2008) highlights, albeit with reference to the case of Australia (where similar developments can be witnessed), academics frequently find opportunities to subvert managerial demands. Methods employed include: making frequent reference to the demands of external professional associations with regard to quality (and which prevent so-called efficiency-saving measures from being workable); 'forgetting' to complete unnecessary tasks they had been allocated; and supplying unimportant data (such as student numbers) which they knew to be inaccurate, but which they could nevertheless plausibly claim to have believed was accurate, in order to, at least ostensibly, comply with management instructions. As a result, Anderson concludes,

> academic resistance to managerialism is a force with which university management must reckon. The intention of managerial practices is routinely subverted by the resistant practices deployed by academics. Those in this study merited Trowler's description of academics as 'clever people', skilled in rebellion and innovation. They were by no means passive recipients of managerial change. Their resistance may be seen as limited insofar as it acts to ameliorate – rather than to overthrow – managerialism, but it is strong in terms of its ideological underpinnings. Moreover, the subterranean, every day, routine forms of resistance employed by academics in this study were effective.
>
> (Anderson, 2008: 267)

It is, therefore, perhaps in the light of the ongoing and various forms of political opposition to Bologna (and the processes of neoliberalization of which it is a part) that we can understand the difficulties that the Bologna Process has faced. Thus, by 2015, and despite the declaration of the European Higher Education Area in 2010, a number of the key goals of Bologna had still not been achieved. In the words of the Head of the Education Department of the Council of Europe

> A number of countries have yet to establish and self-certify their national qualifications frameworks or set up quality assurance agencies that comply with European Standards and Guidelines (Bologna Process, 2012). All but Greece have ratified the Lisbon Recognition Convention, but far from all have implemented the provisions of the Convention in their own legislation and practice. The notion that one should look for how a foreign qualification may be recognized rather than how recognition may be denied has still not been universally absorbed. Almost ten years after the deadline by which Ministers pledged to issue the Diploma Supplement automatically, free of

charge, and in a widely-spoken language, the pledge is still conjugated in the future tense.

(Bergan, 2015: 729)

Thus, whilst Harmsen rightly notes that in much of western Europe[4] there has been a tendency amongst national level education policy actors to seek to close down debates – limiting discussion to that of how to implement HE reforms (rather than whether or not to do so – which in turn has prompted a wave of anti-Bologna protests, as opponents have objected to both the undemocratic and neoliberal nature of the reforms, themselves considered objectionable precisely on the basis that they had been imposed externally by the European Union. As Harmsen argues, this attempt at depoliticization somewhat ironically had the opposite effect to that which was intended: 'The strategic reconstruction of Bologna requirements, intended to restrict debate, could thus be seen to have reaped a predictable whirlwind, prompting a corresponding systemic opposition to the European process itself' (Harmsen, 2015: 793). It is to the interaction of these already-existing pressures for the marketization of European higher education, the role of European integration in promoting this process, its contestation, and the onset of crisis in 2008, that we now turn to consider in the following section.

Education in the European crisis: austerity-driven marketization meets public protest

As we have seen, European integration has created two key sources of pressure upon public education. First, the general pro-retrenchment effect of European integration has resulted in declining public funds being allocated to education provision. Second, European integration (and especially the Bologna Process) has been used as a process through which to advance the marketization of public education (and especially university level education), as part of a broader skills-based accumulation strategy. These pressures, however, have also faced considerable and obstructive opposition, especially from students and faculty within the national education systems. As we shall see in this section, however, the so-called 'age of austerity' that followed the onset of crisis in 2008 has provided an opportunity for governments and education ministries across the European Union to seek to impose further marketization still. Indeed, following the predictions of Lorenz, for whom 'Whatever the problem, the solution proposed [...] is always more management, more efficiency, and more control' (2012: 616), the public sector debt crisis was used in multiple instances across the European Union as a means by which to advocate the further subordination of higher education to the demands of the market. As Holborow argues, employers and the state used 'the recession to implement a double-pronged strategy: to tie higher education more closely to the needs of capital and, also to entrench neoliberal ideology in what is taught and thought and in the way higher education work is done' (Holborow, 2012: 24). De-funding and marketization have therefore become even more strongly interlinked than in previous periods (Saltman, 2014: 44).

For many commentators, however, the experience of the post-2008 crisis period has also been one in which European integration has stalled, particularly in the field of education. One of the consequences of this has been to prompt a shift in values, away from the 'knowledge society' and its development via Bologna, and towards a greater degree of caution and/or policy indecision. As Matei (2015) puts it,

> It is not a secret to anybody that the European integration process is stalled (which may help to explain why Bologna is stalled as well). There is no political vision for a common European future and the public support for European integration has largely vanished. This, in turn, results in a different attitude to the idea of continental efforts, let alone integration or alignments in any area including higher education, and makes the future more uncertain. We are also witnessing at least some corroding of the knowledge society narrative. This results, in turn, in less political support for and commitment to higher education. … reflected in reduced budgets and a different attitude to enrolment ('we need fewer students, not more students').
>
> (Matei, 2015: xxxix–xl)

In addition, the intensification of debt rules due to the European promotion of austerity, in combination with economic crises and increasingly sceptical investors in many European countries, have further limited the possibilities for government spending on education in the post-2008 context. Salaries of staff have been cut and hiring freezes implemented, while workload (the number of lessons taught and the number of pupils or students per class) has increased and contracts have become increasingly precarious. As a result, the quality of public education has deteriorated (Flores and Ferreira, 2016; Huke and Tietje, 2014a; Koulouris *et al.*, 2014). Subsidies for students (such as transport, teaching materials, and school meals) have declined. In addition, the groups most affected by these changes have been those who were already socially excluded, witnessing, for instance, dropout rates increase as a result of the removal of financial assistance programmes and the increased reliance on private sources of finance for education (Fundación Secretariado Gitano, 2013; Glasper, 2016; Mercille and Murphy, 2015: 9–10).

As in other sectors, social inequality within the educational system has also increased, as policies implemented under the rubric of austerity have 'affected disproportionately the poor and more vulnerable segments of the population, which depend to a greater extent on public services' (Mercille and Murphy, 2015: 2). As Greek and Portuguese teachers have reported, poor children have increasingly begun to come to school hungry, without the teaching materials needed and inadequately clothed (Chalari, 2014: 126; Flores and Ferreira, 2016: 410). Stress and tension within the classroom has grown as conflict within families has intensified due to crisis-induced precarity and poverty (Chalari, 2014: 61). Education has increasingly been used by the unemployed or precariously employed in the European periphery as a substitute strategy until finding work, while the potential to find work has decreased (Boura, 2012; Holborow, 2012: 27). One of the results of these trends in Europe's periphery (where they have been more marked) has been increased pressure to emigrate to the European core (see Chapter 4). This context of cuts and social deprivation was also coupled with pressure for further marketization and de-democratization within the education sector, for instance as a result of heightened competitive pressure between educational institutions (Holborow, 2012; Huke and Tietje, 2014a; Flores and Ferreira, 2016: 406).

2009 was also a key moment in the development of the Bologna Process, as it marked both ten years since the initial signing of the Declaration and also a point at which ministers took the opportunity to reflect on progress so far and to set the agenda for future higher education reforms for the decade to come. The document arising from that meeting, *The Bologna Process 2020 – The European Higher Education Area in the new decade*, also explicitly noted 'the consequences of a global financial and economic crisis', and the need for higher education policy to be focused on tackling those consequences (Communiqué of the Conference of European Ministers Responsible for Higher Education, 2009). An additional concern that was noted was the extent to which higher education policies had been 're-nationalized' post-2008 (i.e. decision-making had shifted away from the supranational and towards the national level, as noted by Matei, above). Whilst the ability of signatory states to utilize the machinery of Bologna to impose neoliberal reforms upon European higher education might therefore have declined, the sentiments of Bologna nevertheless remained rife amongst EU member states. That is, the higher education policies that have now been relatively re-nationalized post-2008 have nevertheless witnessed the expression of the same commitment to neoliberal goals.

The post-2008 context has therefore seen a combination of continued commitment to market competition, centralized management of universities, and a managerialist process of quality control. This was clearly reflected in the sentiments expressed in the 2009 *Communiqué* (Communiqué of the Conference of European Ministers Responsible for Higher Education, 2009). At the same time, we also witness a reduced commitment to the justifying logic of investment in R&D and the need to develop human capital, and a related increase in concern for costs, efficiency savings and the attempt to further shift the burden of funding higher education from public to private finance. Further, heightened market competition for the provision of higher education – something which had been (somewhat unevenly, as we have seen) promoted across Europe as a result of the Bologna Process – has been consistently heralded as one of the key factors necessitating the cost- and efficiency-focused reforms that have been attempted across European higher education in the post-2008 context. That is, having created heightened market competition through Bologna, EU states are now citing that market pressure as the reason why universities must be made more competitive into the future.

The means adopted by the European Ministers in their attempt to achieve this declared goal of post-crisis recovery have largely following the same neoliberal course of the pre-2008 period. This includes ensuring that 'all higher education institutions are responsive to the wider needs of society' (Communiqué of the Conference of European Ministers Responsible for Higher Education, 2009), which sounds innocuous, but more substantive passages within the *Communiqué* made it clear that this should more specifically be interpreted as a continuation of the competitiveness agenda, including a commitment to: 'greater compatibility and comparability of the systems of higher education and [...] making it easier for learners to be mobile and for institutions to attract students and scholars from other continents'. In addition, 'employers' were singled out as the only named stakeholder of relevance outside of the HE sector, The *Communiqué* also included a clear continued focus on 'quality assurance'. The agenda set out for the coming decade, moreover, included a strong focus on: 'employability', which 'will allow institutions to be more responsive to employers needs and employers to better understand the educational perspective'; 'the potential of higher education programmes, including those based on applied science, to foster innovation'; and the promotion of higher education as a means by which to be globally competitive. Specifically, on funding, the Ministers declared that 'Greater attention should be paid to seeking new and diversified funding sources and methods' (Communiqué of the Conference of European Ministers Responsible for Higher Education, 2009).

These post-2008 developments were increasingly justified in terms of a lack of public funding available to support alternative approaches, with alternative suggestions typically disparaged as self-indulgent notions of 'public-mindedness', which needed to be replaced by more 'hard-headed' notions of 'value for money' and the importance of shoring up economic growth. In different contexts, this took different forms; but as a general rule it included proposals to increase tuition fees, and an appeal to universities to become more competitive internationally, both in the international market for students and the international market for global research, reputation and innovation.

This agenda was starkly evident, for instance, with the introduction in 2009 of the 'impact' agenda for evaluating research in British universities, which introduced a strong focus on ensuring that research aims at 'fostering global economic performance, and specifically the economic competitiveness of the United Kingdom'.[5] As Holmwood noted at the time of its introduction, this impact agenda contributed to

> the rise of privatelynegotiated user-researcher relationships and the replacement of disciplinary hierarchies by those of government strategic priorities operating through funding agencies (with individual universities increasingly mirroring those hierarchies with their own strategic priorities adapted to the priorities of funding bodies).
>
> (Holmwood, 2011: 14–15)

More 'public-minded' activities, a commitment to which, universities had at least in the past paid lip service to, were increasingly placed under threat by the new competition-focused model of higher education. This included a move away from such notions as quality critical education, the promotion of alternative and civic-oriented learning, and 'blue-sky research' that might not have an immediate economic value (see Lorenz, 2011: 54–9 for a detailed critique).

The consequences of the European crisis – both regarding further austerity and marketization processes – in turn led to a rising discontent within educational communities. Whilst staff saw their working conditions deteriorate and increasingly faced unemployment or precarious conditions, pupils and students as well as parents became more worried about the quality of education and future job prospects (Flores and Ferreira, 2016; Huke and Tietje, 2014a). Further, contradictions were perceived between top-down, retrospective measures to increase quality and innovations imposed by the governments (such as surveys and indicator-based rankings), and austerity programmes that at the same time undermined efforts to achieve quality (Feigenbaum and Iqani, 2013: 48). The social effects of the economic crisis, and the feelings and worries they caused, led to an increased interest in political processes among pupils and a politicization of educational institutions (Chalari, 2014: 127).

It is within this context of heightened competition and declining support for public education, therefore, each either directly or indirectly associated with both earlier processes of European integration (marketization under Bologna, and welfare retrenchment under Europe's austerity regime), that we see the development of a series of education-focused anti-austerity movements. Indeed, protests and movements for public education emerged throughout Europe and played an important part in anti-austerity coalitions, as our subsequent case studies on the United Kingdom and Spain will highlight. Within these struggles, we argue, we see both the defence of public education and also the emergence of fragile (utopian) horizons that point towards education as a common (Terranova, 2015).

UK: the anti-tuition fee movement and beyond

One of the earliest eruptions of contestation over higher education in the United Kingdom during the post-2008 context was that witnessed in opposition to the proposed closure of Middlesex University's philosophy department. On hearing of the University's plans for closure of the department, in April 2010, students engaged in an occupation of the department building. This was, as far as we know, the first use of the occupation method by students in direct response to proposals for austerity during the post-2008 period. It represented in part a continuation of the strategy that had been developed the previous year in opposition to the Government's lack of criticism of Israel during the latter's military conflict with Palestinian armed forces.[6] The Middlesex dispute created considerable attention amongst the student movement, and eventually lead to the wholescale move of the permanent faculty to Kingston University, a move which represented a partial victory for those campaigning. The use of occupations as a means of opposing university spending cuts and restructuring was also subsequently adopted in Sussex the following month, when campaigning students occupied part of the university in opposition to a proposal to reduce the university budget.

These events were only the forerunner, however, for what was to come in November 2010, as part of the NUS protest event in opposition to the government announcement that had been made the previous month, that the cap on undergraduate tuition fees would be tripled (from £3,000 to £9,000) as part of reforms intended to increase funding for the higher education sector and reduce the costs paid for out of the public purse. The demonstration, which was due to take place on 10 November 2010, was planned as a 'standard' demonstration and march through central London, which would include a walk past parliament. However, the title given to the demonstration by the NUS, 'Demo-lition', appeared to have been prescient when what appeared to have been a coordinated detour by the march witnessed protesting students and school children breaking the windows of the Conservative Party Headquarters building, Millbank, and eventually witnessing thousands of protesters gathering outside, with hundreds entering the building, breaking onto the roof of the building, and waving flags of assorted revolutionary identities from the rooftop. The scenes were striking – broadcast through both traditional media and social media – including anarchist flags (amongst others) being waved from the roof of the building, students occupying the building, and a large group of protesters gathering outside the building. These acts of disruption sparked a massive wave of dissent amongst the student community (and oftentimes, as we have seen, spilled over into additional and overlapping cycles of struggle within the broader anti-austerity movement).

This event marked the beginning of the biggest wave of student mobilization in over three decades, forming a major part of the anti-austerity movement witnessed in the United Kingdom, including roughly one-third of all protest events reported during 2010 (Bailey, 2014). Thus, almost immediately after the 10 November demonstration and Millbank protest, students at the University of Manchester staged one of the first occupations of university buildings in an attempt to register dissent at the proposed tuition fee rises. By the end of the month similar occupations had occurred at SOAS, Manchester Metropolitan University, University College London, University of Birmingham, University of Oxford, University of Cambridge, University of Bristol, University of Plymouth, the Warwick Arts Centre at the University of Warwick, the University of Leeds, University of Edinburgh, University of Brighton, Cardiff University, Queens University Belfast, and Nottingham Trent University. Students also staged occupations in, or demonstrations outside of, a number of Liberal Democrat MPs constituency offices. This included an occupation of the office of John Hemming in Birmingham, Jenny Willott in Cardiff, and Simon Hughes (Bermondsey and Old Southwark). It also included a series of subsequent demonstrations that sought to further galvanize the protest momentum that had been witnessed in Millbank, through subsequent demonstrations in Central London, on 24 November 2010, 30 November, and 9 December, each of which witnessed clashes with the police following their inability to contain the student protesters within pre-defined marching routes. The media images associated with each of these events also added further momentum to the student movement, creating a growing sense of escalating public and student opposition to the tuition fees regime.

In terms of putting pressure on the Coalition Government to reverse the proposed tuition fee hike, the small amount of time between the announcement in October 2010, that tuition fees would be nearly tripled, and the adoption of the necessary secondary legislation in parliament in December 2010 to implement the measure, meant that there was little scope for concessions to be introduced. Nevertheless, the pressure upon the Coalition – and especially upon the junior coalition partner, the Liberal Democrats – was such that some kind of compromise needed to be struck. The main concession that the Liberal Democrats negotiated was the agreement that the £21,000 repayment threshold (below which graduates would not begin repaying their loan) would raise annually in line with inflation (McGettigan, 2013: 23); although in 2015 it was announced that this commitment was to be abandoned and instead the threshold would be frozen until at least April 2021 (see Bolton, 2016). A secondary concession was the requirement that universities charging over £6000 in annual fees were required to negotiate an 'access agreement' with OFFA (Office for Fair Access), which would show how some of the revenue from the tuition fees would be used to widen participation, for instance by increasing support for students from lower income backgrounds. These access measures were estimated to cost between 20–30 per cent of the tuition fee revenue that comes from fees over £6,000 (McGettigan, 2013: 31). In addition, it was agreed that any unpaid loans that remain unpaid after 30 years had elapsed would be written off.

In total, therefore, the concessions won were substantial in terms of the degree to which the government was able to increase revenue through the austerity measure. In particular, the setting of the threshold, above which graduates must begin to repay their debt, created a number of unintended consequences which have resulted in significant financial problems for the funding of higher education. The complexity of the funding scheme adopted was such that it proved difficult for the government to calculate the extent to which loans would be repaid, as this depends on inflation and the wages secured by graduates. As a result, the estimate of the amount to be repaid was significantly written down, by around £3 billion, in 2014 (compared with the 2010 estimate) (McGettigan, 2015). This meant that the savings achieved by the reforms were thought to be as little as 5 per cent of the total support that was previously spent by the government per student (Crawford *et al.*, 2014). In addition to the consequences associated with implementation, the Liberal Democrats also suffered a massive loss of electoral support, which most commentators explained directly as a result of the tuition fee issue – with the inconsistency of the tuition fee position of the party (it had committed itself prior to the election to abolishing tuition fees) ensuring that it was tarnished with an image of duplicity and dishonesty; an image that the tuition fee protests worked hard to establish and embed within popular consciousness.

Whilst the anti-tuition fee protests represented a high point in terms of the mobilization of student dissent (albeit one marked by disappointment that the proposed tuition fees hike went ahead despite the widespread opposition), the student movement was also invigorated by the events of November to December 2010. One of the immediate consequences was the continuation of student occupations across the country as a mark of opposition to the marketization of higher education in the United Kingdom. One of the most high-profile examples of this was the creation of what came to be called the 'Free Hetherington' between February and August

2011. This created a space at the University of Glasgow where public meetings could be held to highlight the impact that cuts to university spending and the quasi-privatization of higher education would have. It also enabled the flourishing of a discourse and practice of opposition – including at one point representing the focal point around which opposition to the co-opted nature of the NUS could be mobilized (especially on one notable occasion, when occupants of the Free Hetherington were associated with an attempted 'kettling' of NUS President, Aaron Porter). It also offered a model to students across the country on how a successful and long-lasting occupation could be made to work. One of the more well-known stories surrounded the occasion during the early stage of the occupation when the University management sought to evict the occupation, following which the evictees and their supporters moved to occupy the Senate rooms of the University. This in turn prompted the University management to permit the reoccupation of the Hetherington Building, on the condition that they would vacate the Senate rooms.

Alongside the occurrence of antagonistic anti-fees protest movements, a number of experiments in more participatory, prefigurative, alternatives to state-regulated higher education were observed. For instance, Sealey-Huggins and Pusey describe the experiments in critical and participatory education undertaken by the 'Really Open University' between 2010 and 2012. This included campaigns on campus against fees and cuts, the publication and distribution of a critical newsletter (the *Sausage Factory*), and events which sought to facilitate critical questioning of the role of education and experimentation with alternative forms of education, such as open workshops designed around creative and political education (activist talks, tactical discussions around resistance, discussions of the role of education, film-making, and collaborative learning) (Sealey-Huggins and Pusey, 2013: 90–91). Similar experiments were also conducted by the Social Science Centre in Lincoln.

Whilst the range of visible student protest events dwindled from late 2011 onwards, witnessing only one major national demonstration during that year, organized by NCAFC (on which see more below), in November 2011, a culture of dissent was maintained across the country that enabled protest organizations to be mobilized, often at short notice. For instance, a group of students were able in 2011 to organize a protest event that disrupted a bookshop talk being given by A.C. Grayling, the controversial founder of the New College of the Humanities, which was viewed as a further step towards the privatization of the higher education sector. The protest included the release of a smoke bomb, as a result forcing the talk to be cancelled. After a lull that might in part have been explained by a sense of exhaustion amongst those student activists that had been engaged in campaigns throughout much of 2010 and 2011, 2013 saw a further upturn in mobilization. This included the occupation of Sussex University by students protesting plans to privatize part of the University services, both in February and again in November, and clashing with the authorities trying to prevent the protest. Whilst this protest resulted in the suspension of a number of the university students, the university was subsequently forced to apologize and compensate those students on the grounds that it had wrongly suspended them.

December 2013 also saw a wave of student support for university staff taking part in industrial action as part of the UCU pay dispute. This included occupations in support of the striking staff at a number of universities, including Warwick University, Goldsmiths, University of Exeter, University of Sheffield, University of Birmingham, and the University of Edinburgh. This round of dissent also subsequently developed into a 'cops off campus' movement in response to what was widely perceived to have been heavy-handed policing of one of the London occupations. Academic year 2014–15 saw another round of protests, with 10,000 students attending the NCAFC-organized protest event against tuition fees and paint being thrown at the offices of the NUS in opposition to their refusal to support the demonstration, as well as the march resulting in the occupation of Parliament Square. This round of mobilization also witnessed a further development around the issue of policing student protests, with hundreds of students attending a solidarity protest event at Warwick University following the heavy-handed eviction of students staging an earlier protest inside the University. This in turn witnessed so-called 'yobgate', following an incident where the outgoing Warwick University Vice Chancellor, so-called radical scholar Nigel Thrift, was caught on camera denigrating protesting students for their allegedly 'yob'-like behaviour. The video of the incident was widely shared around the campus through social media and was held by many to be one of his lowest moments, contributing to the growing sense that the University leadership was out of touch with its own student community. Indeed, the role of social media in publicizing both the Warwick evictions, the protest movement that emerged against the actions of the police, and the 'yob'-gate incident, all highlight the growing importance that social media represented for the burgeoning student movement, and the wider protest movement, as it emerged around the context of austerity of anti-austerity under Cameron's Government.

As mentioned, NCAFC (National Campaign Against Fees and Cuts) played an important role in the organization of a number of the protests staged throughout this cycle of dissent. This emerged as an organization challenging the leadership role played by the NUS within the anti-fees campaign, taking a much more strident position in opposition to tuition fees, promoting direct action forms of protest, as well as being critical of the internal democracy of the NUS. Indeed, from the outset NCAFC had focused its attention on campaigning student organizations rather than on student unions. As one of the founding organizers put it, this represented anger at how

> appallingly right-wing and insipid, student unions and the NUS have been historically [...] we were focused on providing unequivocal support for student occupations and we knew in the back of our heads that NUS after the big national demo or after whatever had been in the autumn, would then have a strategy which was crap. And that turned out to be true and we knew that there had to be an organization, there had to be something – even though arguably NCAFC wasn't even an organisation at this point because it didn't have a national committee or anything, it was just a network – but there had

to be something that, after whatever NUS called, kept stuff going, and that was very much the role that we played.

(interview with NCAFC activist, 27 June 2014b)

NCAFC combined being a formal organization with a strategy that was largely based around prefigurative principles of direct action protest and horizontalist decision-making. One of its key disagreements with the NUS was over the latter's opposition to direct action as a strategy.[7] Thus, NCAFC deliberately took up disruptive methods as a means by which to seek voice and influence. As one activist put it,

> I would definitely say that, specifically for student activism, methods which basically disturb the everyday processes of the university, or language which gets press attention, and embarrasses and shames the university, are the ones that work. Because of tuition fees, universities are like big companies now and the fact that they want customers who pay; and also vice chancellors or people who work at the university are not necessarily loyal to the university – they want to get their next big job. And so basically the more you embarrass the university and the more you embarrass specific characters within the university, the worse for them, because they'll get less students and they'll go down the ranking and they'll have lower chances of getting the next job, I guess.

(interview with NCAFC student activist, 27 June, 2014a)

In addition, however, and perhaps somewhat contradictorily, many of the key NCAFC actors also sought to gain election to office within the NUS, evincing the pragmatism with which their commitment to prefigurative action was held. In the words of one activist quoted above, 'We operate as a faction within NUS as well. People are very open about the fact that we're NCAFC inside NUS' (interview with NCAFC activist, 27 June 2014b).

In this sense, NCAFC represented an attempt to gain a more effective voice. In seeking to challenge the resource implications of the tuition fee hike, NCAFC members would be simultaneously committed to direct action, horizontal and fluid decision-making structures, the formal decision-making structures of the NCAFC organization, *and* seek election within the established institutions of the NUS (of which they were highly critical).

The student anti-tuition fee movement was also able to form an effective coalition with other anti-austerity movements. This included support for campaigns run by university staff trade unions.[8] Academic year 2015–16 also witnessed a growing connection between student protest and the growing housing crisis (and associated housing movement) that emerged during 2015. The most visible signs of this were the vibrant rent strikes that emerged during 2015 and 2016 at UCL, as we shall see in the following chapter.

The student movement in the United Kingdom represented one of the most vibrant and ongoing instances of popular opposition to the austerity measures associated with the post-2008 period. Whilst focusing on the anti-tuition fee campaign initially, many members of the student movement would subsequently become key players in a number of the other anti-austerity campaigns witnessed throughout the post-2008 period, and in turn many became active contributors to the campaign to elect Jeremy Corbyn as leader of the Labour Party. This perhaps reflects the pragmatic nature of the demands being developed by the anti-tuition fee movement, especially within NCAFC.[9] In this sense, therefore, those participating in the anti-tuition fee movement were exemplary in the way that they represented a 'pragmatically prefigurative' form of disruptive agency that actively destabilized the austerity rhetoric that would otherwise have prevailed through much of the post-2008 context.

'Public education by everyone for everyone': cuts, marketization and new social movements for public education in Spain

As was the case when we looked at welfare reforms, reforms to Spanish education during the European crisis have exemplified a number of general trends throughout the EU, characterized by a particularly strident austerity-driven process of marketization, but also new and innovative social movements that arose in response (Huke and Tietje, 2014a; Huke, 2016). In the following sections, we trace the implementation and effects of this austerity-driven marketization in Spain. We then go on to show how the changes during the crisis caused increasingly precarious living conditions for both students and staff, but also lead to a politicization and unification of parts of the educational community, which in turn paved the way for a development of horizontal social movements such as *marea verde* movements in different regions. In addition, these movements, as we show, drew on the radical-democratic repertoire of action that emerged within the 15-M movement.

The austerity measures imposed in Spain, in part as a result of the conditions placed on financial support by the Troika, had significant effects on the educational system. State funding of both regions and the central state were slashed. Neoliberal marketization was strengthened and democratic mechanisms within educational institutions were removed. The number of staff employed within universities fell, whilst the precarious nature of working conditions increased for those remaining in employment in the higher education sector (Borrell *et al.*, 2014: 95; Cortese and Masa, 2013: 61; Hernández Armenteros and Pérez García, 2015: 83; Villota and Vázquez-Cupeiro, 2016: 204). One highly illustrative example was that seen in the Madrid region, where teachers were hired on a daily basis to mark exams (elboletin.com, 2013). The Government also introduced legislation to institutionalize worse conditions within the education sphere. For instance, one new law, RDL 14/2012, raised the number of pupils per class and the number of lessons taught per teacher, while extending the waiting period before substitute teachers were hired (Uzuriaga Ruiz, 2013: 34). Universities also increased the amount of lessons taught per person, with negative effects for the quality of teaching and research. Public investments in R&D dropped sharply. As a result, the majority of universities faced financial deficits and a lack of staff (Caballero Klink *et al.*, 2015; Villota and Vázquez-Cupeiro, 2016: 204).

Support mechanisms for pupils and students, such as scholarships, but also including payments for learning material, meals and transport, were all reduced (Cortese and Masa, 2013: 64; El País, 2013a; Fundación Secretariado Gitano, 2013: 27). Competition between educational institutions increased as the *Ley Orgánica 8/2013 para la Mejora de la Calidad Educativa* (LOMCE) introduced new, centralized exams and evaluation mechanisms; and increased the possibility of selection for school places and performance-related funding ((Uzuriaga Ruiz, 2013). Democratic mechanisms were also dismantled within the education system, while the role of directors was strengthened. Subventions to private educational institutions (mainly Catholic), meanwhile, were cut to a lesser degree or exempted from cuts, thereby deepening tendencies of creeping privatization (Bernal Agudo and Lorenzo Lacruz, 2012: 91; Díez Gutiérrez, 2013). University tuition fees also soared in an attempt to compensate for the reduction in public funding (Diagonal, 2013d; Hernández Armenteros and Pérez García, 2015: 93).

High youth unemployment rates also boosted demand for higher education, as education was seen as a possible means of bridging the crisis period, as well as a necessity in order to increase individual employability (Villota and Vázquez-Cupeiro, 2016: 209) Education places were however unable to meet this increase in demand, resulting in professional training courses increasingly rejecting applicants (El País, 2013b). Due to high rates of youth unemployment and increasing rates of precarious employment, education nevertheless became less and less able to serve as a means to guarantee a certain degree of social security. Spanish university graduates also faced a higher risk of poverty than those in other European countries (Público.es, 2013). As a result, young Spaniards found themselves under pressure to emigrate:

> I thought I wouldn't go abroad, I thought I would go for a period and come back but now I am sure that going back is not an option or at least one of the last options … everybody is leaving. Everybody who can afford to leave, who speaks English or has some international experience is just going because they know that there is no way out of this thing … coming from the South to the North, you are moving, you are qualified and you are moving in Northern Europe to do a non-qualified job and that is considered even better than staying in Spain.
>
> (Interview quoted in Boura, 2012: 8)

The proportion of private household spending dedicated to education increased during this period, particularly so for the two poorest quintiles of the population (Sanz-Magallón Rezusta *et al.*, 2014). In many cases, families were increasingly unable to pay for school meals, transport, learning materials, clothing, and out-of-school activities (Fundación Secretariado Gitano, 2013: 28; Martínez, 2013: 3). As such, 'there were a lot of children that have left the school canteen, because the families were unable to pay due to the situation of crisis' (interview with

STES activist, 18 March 2014, authors' translation). Amongst certain disadvantaged groups, school dropout rates increased (while the general dropout rates decreased), in part as a result of individual support programmes being cut due to a lack of funds. In those cases, families – already under strain due to the crisis – had to increase the amount of unpaid labour invested in the education of their children (Beteta Martín, 2013: 50; euobserver.com, 2013; Fundación Secretariado Gitano, 2013: 28). Austerity-driven marketization of the education sector thereby reinforced the social selectivity of the Spanish educational system, as well as increasing pressure upon poorer families (Bernal Agudo and Lorenzo Lacruz, 2012: 93; Díez Gutiérrez, 2013: 77; Hernández Armenteros and Pérez García, 2015: 93). These were, moreover, measures unpopular with the public. Thus, as was the case when we considered the health sector (Chapter 4), the support for cuts in education within the Spanish population was low (FOESSA, 2014). As we shall see, this also contributed to the vibrancy of the education-related movements in the Spanish case.

We might also consider the 15-M movement to be the first education-related protest movement to erupt during the Spanish crisis (see Chapter 3). The broad majority of the participants of the 15-M movement possessed a higher education background (Calvo, 2013: 243); some of whom had gained prior experience through activity in anti-Bologna struggles that had occurred earlier in Spain (on this influence of pre-crisis student movements on anti-austerity movements during the crisis, see Zamponi and Fernández González, 2017). Organizations derived from these struggles, such as *Juventud Sin Futuro*, also played an important role (Huke, 2016: 24). For many participants, 15-M represented a reaction to the disjuncture between the expectation of gaining a middle-class career as a result of attending university, and the reality of a bleak or precarious future:

> To many of us here in Spain, they sold us the motto that […] if you studied, if you made an effort you would achieve a good job and a good salary, a good house – although with a mortgage, but everything would work out, the capitalist dream for the masses would be possible.
>
> (interview with CCOO activist, 17 July 2012, authors' translation)

15-M also shared some of the organizational forms that had been adopted by earlier student movements. Student organizations had previously experimented with methods such as assemblies and first-person politics and in so doing they had gained experiences that they were able to inscribe into 15-M:

> They had assemblies in the university and had come to the conviction that to do something a bit bigger, that resonated within society and that was visible, banners and names of organisations had to disappear […]. Collectives had come together that had understood that they could not go out with […] the acronyms of these collectives if they wanted to do something.
>
> (interview with 15-M activist, 17 July 2012, authors' translation)

While 15-M surged and many students also participated in subsequent struggles, such as those around housing and mortgages (see Chapter 6), participation within student activism in the Spanish universities nevertheless went into a period of decline:

> In the three strikes that were called this term, the level of support has been high, but the participation was extremely low. [...] The student movement is dead, but that doesn't mean that the people do not participate in social centres and neighbourhood assemblies.
>
> (interview with student activist, quoted in Diagonal, 2013a, authors' translation)

In contrast, however, strong social movements emerged within the Spanish school system in a number of Spanish regions. These drew on the repertoire of action and political climate created by 15-M. The movements were also often subsumed under the label, *marea verde*, a name derived from green shirts, with the demand for public schools for everyone, which became a symbol of the protest.

The first eruption of the *marea verde* movement came in 2011 in Madrid, following cuts executed by the regional PP Government prior to the RDL 14/2012 (including increases in the number of hours taught and the dismissal of nearly 3000 substitute teachers). Reacting to these cuts, the major trade unions of the sector organized city-wide assemblies that, in the climate of radical democracy established by 15-M, triggered a process of workplace organizing at the margins of trade unions. Newly established assemblies soon took place on a regular basis in a large number of schools, witnessing the active participation of education sector employees – especially the teaching staff, and a notable, although less intense participation of pupils and parents. As a trade union official of the left education union STES recalls,

> they started to mobilise in a way that was totally horizontal. That is in every institute, every secondary school, and every school, there was a support group for the mobilization. They gathered in zones and neighbourhoods and, well, they organised very important demonstrations, they did strikes that were supported by the parents.
>
> (interview with STES activist, 18 March 2014, authors' translation)

The *marea verde* thereby was 'obviously, in a way, the heir of 15M, right? Emanated a bit that air of popular sovereignty, right? That came out of 15M, right?' (interview with USTEA activist, 13.11.2013, Sevilla, authors' translation). This contrasted with the pre-crisis experience, in which

> the teachers had routinely found their experiencing of working with trade unions to be frustrating; in which the teachers mobilised themselves very little and there was little class consciousness within the teaching staff, and strikes gained little following.
>
> (interview with USTEA activist, 13 November 2013, authors' translation)

Despite (and, in part, because of) the participatory and grassroots' nature of the assemblies, there existed a certain degree of unease in their relationship with the major trade unions. In some cases, the trade unions actively sought to slow down the campaigns and planned actions of the assemblies. This included a plan to stage unlimited strike action three days a week in Madrid, which CCOO, UGT and STEM each significantly watered down, seeking to ensure that the number of strike days would be finite, and also seeking to combine strike days with 'action days' in order to maintain cooperation with the more conservative trade unions, ANPE and C-SIF (Huke and Tietje, 2014a: 537). As a result, the tensions between the new structures of the *marea verde* and the traditional forms of trade unionism became increasingly visible. As one interviewee summed up, the desired form that the relationship between the assemblies and the trade unions should take, from the perspective of the trade unions, was a logic of: 'ok, assemblies, yes. [...]. Assemblies to make proposals and all decisions are taken within the trade union' (interview with STES activist, 18 March 2014, authors' translation).

By the end of 2011 the protests in Madrid and participation in assemblies had gone into decline, without achieving the same level of success as that of the *marea blanca* (see Chapter 5).

> We met with a wall, the community of Madrid. And we have remained there somehow. The mobilisation was helpful on a symbolic level for some things but not to change politics. We had a platform and none of the demands were reached.
>
> (interview with *marea verde* activist, quoted in Diagonal, 9 January 2012)

In the following years, however, in part as a response to the experience of cuts and restructuring triggered by the RDL 14/2012 and the LOMCE, the education movement spread to other regions in Spain. On 22 May 2012, a nationwide general strike in the sector of education took place that for the first time counted on the support not only of all relevant unions in the sector, but also of students' and parents' associations. Indeed, central to the strength of this mobilization was the high number of pupils and students that participated (Huke and Tietje, 2014a).

An additional episode in the development of Spanish education movements was witnessed during the school year 2013–14. This saw the teachers of the Baleares go on strike for three weeks in protest at both spending cuts and the adoption by the regional PP Government of a decree committed to the 'integrated treatment of languages' (TIL). The TIL stated that lessons should be taught in equal share in Catalan, Spanish and English. Prior to this, lessons had been mainly (80 per cent) taught in Catalan. As in Madrid, grassroots assemblies and the horizontal use of social media and mailing lists each played a key part in the mobilizations (Riutort Serra, 2014: 831). Even the strike itself was led by what was referred to as the *assemblea de docents*, which coordinated the different assemblies and was supported (but not run) by the trade unions (López Vizuete, 2013). Further actions included civil disobedience against the TIL, which successfully slowed down its implementation. The Government reacted, however, by taking a number of those responsible for the boycott to court, although this sparked a new wave of protest (Huke and Tietje, 2014a: 538). In addition, in part as a result of the opposition it had experienced as a result of adopting the TIL, the PP regional Government heavily lost the 2015 election, witnessing it being replaced in office by the social democratic PSOE and the left regionalist Platforms *Més per Mallorca* and *Més per Menorca* (and with the support of Podemos and *Gent per Formentera*). Once in office, moreover, this new government withdrew the TIL, which itself had anyway already been suspended by the regional High Court (Huke, 2016).

As we can see, therefore, Spanish education reforms sparked a number of opposition movements, including but also drawing on the experiences gained during the developments of 15-M. One of the most high-profile opposition movements, however, was that witnessed over the so-called '3+2' reforms, as we shall see in the next section.

Opposing austerity-era neoliberalism: students and opposition to the '3+2'

As discussed in the previous section, Spain experienced a wave of student activism during the late 2000s that was driven largely by opposition to the implementation of the Bologna Process in Spain. This was followed, as we have seen, by a decline in student activism in Spanish universities. A turnaround came, however, in 2015 after the Spanish government announced a new reform of higher education through the implementation of Royal Decree 43/2015. Although during the Bologna Process the Spanish government decided to maintain the model of four-year bachelor's degrees and one year master's degrees, the reform introduced in 2015 aimed to reduce the length of bachelor's degrees to three years and to increase the duration of master's degrees to two years in order to achieve a convergence with the university systems of the majority of European countries. This reform – popularly known as the '3+2 Decree' or 'Wert Decree' in reference to the Education Minister, José Ignacio Wert – generated high levels of discontent among university students and student groups, who considered it a covered way of increasing the price of tuition (as postgraduate tuition is more expensive per credit) and thereby increasing the elitism of higher education.

According to research carried out by the Spanish trade union, Comisiones Obreras, in the academic year 2015–2016 the average price of each bachelor's degree credit was €18.33, whereas a qualifying master's degree[10] credit cost €27.23 and a non-qualifying master's degree credit cost €39.12 (CCOO 2016a). As one student activist and member of the Catalan left student union SEPC (Sindicat d'Estudiants dels Països Catalans) points out:

> The thing is that, in the beginning, the main message was the rejection of the 3+2 system. But it is obvious that the problem is not whether Bachelor's degrees last three or four years, we understand that some of the current programmes can be perfectly reduced to three years. The problem is that the new

system devalues Bachelor's degrees and makes Master's degrees compulsory in academic and social terms; they will become essential if you want to be employable. So what we are asking for is, if we are moving towards a double cycle system that requires having both a Bachelor's and a Master's degree, then the Master's have to be affordable, not a privilege for the few. So we are struggling for, on the one hand, a wider offer of public master's degrees, and on the other hand, a reduction in their prices. That way we would guarantee a more equitable access to higher education and prevent it from becoming a form of exclusion. We cannot create a new social filter within the university that creates precarious Bachelor graduates with very low job opportunities, and Master graduates with good contracts and working conditions.

(Interview with student activist, 24 July 2015, authors' translation)

The reform was made in a broader context of increasing precarization and marketization of the Spanish university system. As a result of the austerity programmes implemented by the Spanish and the regional governments, between 2010 and 2015 the budgets of public universities had fallen by more than 13.7 per cent on average, and the per-student spending had been reduced by 15.6 per cent – from €7,860 to €6,638 – between the academic years 2009–10 and 2013–14, although in the same period university fees had increased by 20.3 per cent for bachelor's degrees and by 52.9 per cent for non-qualifying master's degrees on average (CCOO, 2016a; CCOO, 2016b). These government cuts also entailed a rising economic dependence of Spanish public universities on the private sector, exemplified by the establishment of a growing number of endowed professorships that are supported by private corporations such as Telefónica, Repsol, Inditex, Deloitte and a broad range of financial institutions and insurance companies.

Furthermore, similar to the changes implemented in the Spanish school system, within higher education institutions representative organisms were also increasingly disempowered, while the role of Rectors and other executive organisms were reinforced. One of these strengthened organisms is the *Consejo Social [Social Council]*, a collegiate body that comprises representatives of different political forces, trade unions and private companies and that is currently in charge, among other things, of supervising the economic activity of the university and whose role is 'to promote the collaboration of society in financing the university' (Art. 14 of the Ley Orgánica 4/2007, authors' translation). This close relationship between business interests and universities is part of the *Estrategia Universidad 2015* (EU2015), a strategic plan developed by the Ministry of Education after the implementation of the Bologna Process, in order to adapt the Spanish university system to the European Higher Education Area (EHEA). As one student activist put it:

All these reforms are being used to move towards a university-business model, i.e. a model in which private companies finance university and therefore they have more power and voice within this institution. This is one of the pillars of the 3+2 reform, and of the whole *Estrategia Universidad 2015*. So with regard to student representation, the *Claustro* [University Senate] and the other representative institutions where students have a voice are losing importance. And we, as part of the university community, are not being able to participate in the discussion.

(Interview with student activist, 29 July 2015, authors' translation)

The wave of mobilization against the 3+2 reform has therefore to be considered part of a broader cycle of dissent amongst the student community. This is part of both struggles against the austerity programmes implemented by the Spanish state and the regional and local governments; but also resistance to the reform of European higher education that began with the Bologna Process. In this sense, the 15-M and the subsequent anti-austerity movements, as well as the anti-Bologna struggles, each clearly influenced the demands, organizational forms and repertoires of action of the movement against the 3+2 reforms. As one of the activists explains, 'this is a permanent struggle that comes from before Bologna, we feel we are its heirs' (La Directa, 03/12/2015). Moreover, some of the high school students who had participated in movements such as the *marea verde* in the period 2011–2014 were during 2015 enrolling at universities. These highly mobilized students soon engaged in the grassroots faculty and campus assemblies that had been created mainly during the anti-Bologna struggles. In consequence:

> Students who are arriving to university this academic year or who will arrive next year are people who have only known the crisis, and who have only known a certain social agitation, and who have started participating politically earlier in life. So an increasing amount of people that arrive to university nowadays are already politically active. [...] A lot of them were politically socialised during the cycle of mobilisations of the 15M; they gained experience then, and now they are maturing politically.
>
> (interview with student activist, 24 July 2015, authors' translation)

The actions developed after the announcement of the Royal Decree 43/2015 were a mixture between forms of protest used traditionally by the student movement and more prefigurative radical practices. The first event organized by some left student unions and trade unions, with the support of student assemblies, was a combination of a general student strike and marches in multiple Spanish cities against the '3+2 Decree' and the LOMCE, which involved not only university students and personnel but also school students, teachers and parents. Other student strikes and marches were organized throughout 2015 and 2016, and were combined with direct actions, including the occupation of university buildings, the establishment of picket lines and the blockage of highways and public transports near universities.

On the one hand, in March 2015, the *Platform for the 3+2 Referendum* created by the student movement in the Community of Madrid organized a referendum in the public universities of this Autonomous Community to canvas opinion of university students about the implementation of the reform. According to the organizers, more than 31,000 students voted in the referendum, and 97.5 per cent voted against the reform.[11] This self-organized referendum was also subsequently replicated in other Spanish public universities with similar results and with turn-out levels that surpassed those of the majority of official Rector Elections.

On the other hand, the student movement established links with some of the main anti-austerity struggles and movements born after the 15-M, and adopted some of their forms of protest:

> This time we are trying to innovate, to make things in a different way. [...] We have strong connections with *Stop Pujades* [movements against the rais-ing prices in the public transport in Barcelona]. The student movement started a campaign called 'We aren't paying', which protested against the prices of public transport because it is linked to the living conditions of students and our everyday lives. So we refused to pay for using public transport, following this logic of peaceful civic disobedience. [...] We also talked with the PAH about what they are doing with the *Obra Social* campaign. We are planning on occupying housing blocs for students, because a lot of people have to move to a new city to study, and they pay exorbitant rents.
> (interview with student activist, 24 July 2015, authors' translation)

Indeed, the project of occupying a housing bloc for students came to fruition in March 2016, when the *Assemblea Llibertària de la UB-Raval* (a libertarian assem-bly created in one of the campuses of the University of Barcelona), along with the Federation of Anarchist Students and the Anarchist Federation of Catalonia, occupied a building that was the property of Barcelona City Council. The squat, named *La Rea* (acronym for 'Self-Organised Student Hall', in Catalan 'Residència d'Estudiants Autogestionada'), not only represents a way of protesting against the difficult access to decent housing and the dynamics of gentrification and real-estate speculation being developed in the city, but also launched an Occupied Social Centre (the *CSO La Rea*) that organizes free language courses, music and arts workshops, talks, and barter markets among many other free and open activities.

Currently (January 2017), the Royal Decree 43/2015 is not being applied in any public or private Spanish university, since the Conferencia de Rectores de las Universidades Españolas (CRUE, Conference of Rectors of Spanish Universities) agreed to postpone its implementation at least until 2017, when they expect to open a process of negotiation with the Spanish government. In addition, on April 2016, and following a petition from the student movement, the Catalan Parliament also placed a moratorium on it. Whilst this was a welcome development, it was also seen by many student activists as insufficient. As one interviewee put it,

> strategically, stopping the 3+2 Decree is not a goal *per se*. In the end, what the student movement wants is to stop the whole university reform and the neoliberal logic that they are introducing at universities, all these privatisa-tions. [...] What we are really defending is a 100 per cent free university with universal access.
> (interview with student activist, 29 July 2015, authors' translation)

Conclusion

European integration, we have argued in this chapter, has affected education throughout the EU, as a result of both the decreasing fiscal capacity of the state associated with the process of European integration, but also as a result of the active promotion through European integration of the marketization of education, and especially higher education (through the Bologna Process). As we have sought to show, however, these processes have been continuously disrupted, impeded and slowed down as a result of social movements developing within the education system. We have witnessed, therefore, the significant and disruptive effect of student protest movements during the '1968' period, the anti-Bologna students' movements, and opposition to the current forms of anti-austerity and anti-marketization movements in the context of the European crisis. Education, we have therefore shown, has witnessed the long-term survival and sedimentation of activism (sometimes in a 'subterranean' form when visible protests have become less frequent). This is despite the fact that the university sector has witnessed the growth of obstacles to critical research, thinking and debate (Terranova, 2015: 4). In this sense, education-based social movements have taken on something of a rhizomatic form: 'Even when 'nothing seems to be happening', rhizome-networks can be growing, developing, readying themselves for the next opportunity to push through the surface and emerge in unpredictable ways' (Tormey, 2012: 133).

As we have shown, the post-2008 global and European crises have resulted in an intensification of pre-existing pressures to reduce public spending and to subordinate education to the demands of a skills-based and 'employability' accumulation strategy. These developments have in turn clashed with the subjectivities of students and education workers that were already becoming increasingly precarious, militant and oppositional within educational institutions. As a result of these conflicts, students also became a driving force of social movements outside the narrow confines of the educational system, as witnessed in the case of the 15-M and with the role of the UK student movement in a range of anti-austerity campaigns. Further, tensions within the education system have led to a politicization and radicalization of parts of the workforce, in addition to students and pupils. Movements such as 15-M have paved the way for these processes as they provided a novel repertoire of everyday organizing and direct interaction of affected groups that made it possible to partially overcome boundaries between staff, students and parents.

The double movement we identified as a general trend for welfare developments during the European crisis – retrenchment on the one side, increased conflict on the other – can therefore also be found within education. However, the 'hardening' of the state has also resulted in the experience of considerable difficulties in gaining concessions from the state, or in influencing government policy. As a result, the education-based social movements might instead be considered to have contributed to the deepening legitimacy crisis of both national and European institutions, as support for public education has remained high despite cuts and continuous attempts to deepen marketization. This in part has contributed to a growing sense of political instability, which has in turn provided opportunities for both populist party strategies that appear to be taking on the demands of social movements (as seen in the case of Podemos or with the rise of Jeremy Corbyn within the Labour Party), as well as nationalist responses (such as that seen with the result of the Brexit vote).

In general terms, therefore, the developments in education mirror those which we have already seen in the sphere of welfare. In each of our spheres of struggle we see a polarization resulting from the experience of European crisis, between the 'hardening' of the state (Agnoli, 2003) and 'presentist democracy' (Lorey, 2011). This represents an intensification of 'disciplinary neoliberalism' (Gill, 1998), combined with authoritarian crisis constitutionalism (Bieling, 2015; Oberndorfer, 2015), resulting in a decline in the responsiveness of the state to popular demands as the scope for 'strategic selectivity' has narrowed around a set of austerity-based alternatives (Jessop, 1999). As a result, we see an increase in the degree to which the state is a *source* of hardship and suffering, rather than one able or willing to offer relief to those symptoms. For activists, the state increasingly appeared as unwilling to either hear or see the suffering or demands of its citizens, and in this sense appeared to be 'hermetically sealed' (Huke, 2016: 105). Attempts to express a voice or achieve political representation have therefore become increasingly difficult.

The processes of 'community organising' (Bader, 2014), 'pragmatic prefiguration' (Bailey *et al.*, 2016) 'self-enforcement' (Macías, 2013) and 'civil disobedience' (Celikates, 2010: 280) – not only in education, but also in the other spheres – have all, we argue, emerged as a response to these trends. Within these processes of organizing from below, therefore, a new 'presentist' democracy has developed that is opposed to established forms of representative democracy, itself increasingly perceived as dysfunctional. This 'presentist democracy', Lorey argues, 'is the opposite of representative democracy'. As such, this 'new form of democracy that is practised in the moment of the assembly in actively becoming presentist is not a non-political form of living' (Lorey, 2011). As we have seen, in the sphere of education, but also in the broader context of anti-austerity movements, these trends have developed, amplified and overflowed into other alternative struggles. We turn now to consider the sphere of housing, where 'presentist democracy' has similarly connected with the material struggle for shelter.

Notes

1 Witness, for instance, the Lisbon Strategy's focus on the EU as a knowledge-based economy.
2 Martinotti had been commissioned by Minister for Education, Luigi Berlinguer, to draft a series of proposed reforms to the Italian higher education system.
3 Whilst these Bologna/Lisbon-led initiatives for higher education reforms swept across Europe through much of the 2000s, anti-Bologna protests have been perhaps most muted in the UK, in part because the UK had already moved to adopt many of the reforms associated with Bologna/Lisbon (or 'Lisbonized Bologna') without reference to the external pressure generated by the Bologna Declaration. That is, the UK has been at the vanguard of marketisation and Bologna has been the instrument ensuring that

other signatory states keep up with it. In this sense, it is not Bologna that UK-based students are opposed to, but rather the reforms that are being developed at the national level (and subsequently transposed to other parts of Europe).

4   This is less the case in Eastern European accession states, where Bologna has generally experienced much less public opposition, oftentimes due to it being considered preferable to the national alternatives.

5   See: http://www.rcuk.ac.uk/innovation/impacts

6   As one activist put it, 'What was helpful was the leftover of the Palestine occupations over Operation Cast Lead, which was still kind of there. Occupations was a thing that people knew how to do' (interview with NCAFC activist, 27 June 2014b).

7   'If they [the NUS bureaucracy] had any strategy for winning it was a nice peaceful quiet demo, and lobbying Lib Dem MPs. Any direct action, any taking to the streets was not part of their plan. They did not want it to take place' (interview with NCAFC activist, 27 June 2014b).

8   'I think there's something to be said for, this year the student movements have been quite closely connected to the UCU strikes [, witnessing] a closer connection between UCU and student groups, and that has happened all across the country and I think that was a very positive experience for a lot of people who were involved. For a lot of people [...] they are idealists [...] and so it's a very positive experience to get involved in strikes and doing something for people who are working' (interview with Kelly Rogers, anti-tuition fee activist, 30 June 2014).

9   As one activist put it, 'I definitely think that for me 'one-foot-in and one-foot-out' is a very deliberate approach [...] I do view, and we do view, influencing Labour Party policy as a worthwhile activity (interview with NCAFC activist, 27 June 2014b).

10 A qualifying master's degrees is a postgraduate degree that is part of a comprehensive study programme (which includes a bachelor's and a master's degree) and that qualifies students for the exercise of a regulated profession such as engineering, architecture, law or psychology.

11 See https://referendum3mas2.com/

6 Everyday endeavours towards needs-based housing policies

Whilst there is a lack of formal housing policy at the European level, nevertheless European integration played an important part in the development of housing throughout Europe since the 1980s. European integration contributed to the rise of a neoliberal discourse surrounding the need to minimize state intervention, and to withdraw the state from housing market intervention and housing provision. Further, through its more general imposition of limits on public expenditure, and heightening of locational competition, European integration contributed to the declining fiscal capacity of the state, thereby consolidating the downward pressure upon public spending, including in the area of housing. In addition, housing finance was affected by the deregulation of European capital markets. Finally, EMU led to falling interest rates for mortgages in peripheral countries; increasing and both the possibility and the demand for access to privatelyowned housing.

As such, European integration has itself become a site of, and prompt for, the development of both tendencies, that which seeks to consolidate the logic of the market in the provision of housing, and that which seeks the contestation of that pro-market tendency. The crisis of post-2008, therefore, has been characterized by both moves to consolidate domination in the sphere of housing, and acts of disruption that have obstructed and disturbed that consolidation of domination, thereby rendering housing open to contestation and the development of emancipatory movements.

Rent strikes, squatting movements and the 'right to the city': European integration and housing struggles

We can identify three broad stages in the development of housing policy and housing provision across Europe. First, the Fordist period was characterized by an expansion of social housing and the regulation of rental markets. Struggles were primarily directed at securing low rent costs (for instance, through the staging of rent strikes), and increasing the infrastructure of residential areas (for instance, through protests of neighbourhood assemblies, and also through more proactive forms of direct action, such as that seen with the various squatting movements that existed during the period). Second, the post-Fordist period was characterized by the growing importance of mortgage-financed private homeownership (in part facilitated by European liberalization of financial markets) and a corresponding decline in private rental housing and social housing. Struggles during this period took the paradigmatic form of anti-gentrification movements that protested against the crowding out of poorer parts of the population and the lack of access to decent housing in metropolitan areas, but also appeared as riots and other more visible forms of social unrest. Finally, the post-2008 global and then European crises witnessed a breakdown of housing and mortgage markets in many European countries, coinciding with over-indebtedness, evictions and everyday movements for decent housing. Across the different periods, therefore, housing appears as a sphere of continuous struggle around issues of social inequality and marketization.

With regard to political subjectivities, the chapter argues, refusal-prone materialists played an important part throughout the Fordist period. The subsequent extension of mortgages and private ownership during the post-Fordist period, however, led to an individualization and privatization of housing issues, which attempted to de-politicize the housing question. This depoliticization strategy was at least partially successful in transforming subjectivities towards disengaged, disaffected and disinterested political (non-)actors. However, this occurred at the same time as processes of segregation, deprivation and exclusion that (especially in larger cities) provided the ground for social unrest (for instance, as seen with the urban riots in France in 2005 and the United Kingdom in 2011). At the same time, prefigurative radical movements (such as those associated with squatters' movements and anti-gentrification campaigns) developed as part of the disaggregation of Fordist modes of inclusion and enclosure, and continued to question the privatized housing market throughout the post-Fordist period. As with the other spheres discussed previously (work, welfare, and education), the European crisis therefore witnessed an extension, reinvention and pragmatic transformation of prefigurative radical movements, as housing conditions deteriorated and evictions and over-indebtedness became everyday phenomena for important sections of the European population.

Struggles for social housing during the Fordist period

During the nineteenth century and into the first half of the twentieth century, housing shortages, overcrowded dwellings and high rents constituted an existential problem for large sections of the working class. Labour movements reacted by developing strategies to disrupt evictions (for instance, blocking roads, helping the evicted persons to re-enter – and silently re-occupy – their home, or persuading movers to make use of civil disobedience). Rent strikes were also organized around slogans such as, 'First food, then the rent!' These were also accompanied by demands for improving housing conditions. For instance, in Germany, the communist party KPD played an important part in organizing the protests. However, here the success of the protests also relied to a considerable degree on the self-organization of tenant communities, which contributed to the fore-grounding of tenants' interests over the general political strategies of the party. Initially, the rent strikes in Germany profited from a degree of legal uncertainty that eventually came to an end with a court decision in 1933, which established that rent strikes could not be considered strikes and therefore could not claim the same legal guarantees. In the same year, moreover, the new Nazi government prohibited independent collective representations of interests and persecuted workers' organizations, leading to a breakdown of housing struggles (Lengemann, 2015; Templin, 2014).

As with contestation in the workplace, the post-Second World War also period saw the European political elite increasingly turn towards the welfare state, this time in an attempt to pre-empt the possibility of the level of pre-war contention that had surrounded housing prior to the war. This was done largely through a commitment to expanding the provision of social housing and to regulating both the rental and mortgage markets. This attempt to regulate and take responsibility for the sphere of housing, however, was continually problematized by the disruptive impact of European workers making a number of significant demands and obstructing policies in a number of ways through a range of acts of refusal (both perceptible and imperceptible). The Fordist phase of European housing therefore included one or a combination of the following: a commitment by most states to ensure the (improved) provision of adequate housing across society, through the regulation of housing markets, direct provision of public or social housing, and/or the introduction of benefits that would subsidize housing or rental costs for tenants. As such, housing developed a strong dependence on national financial, legal and policy systems (Whitehead, 1998: 17). Housing, argue Ball and Harloe, was 'regarded as a component of the welfare state, although with a large role for the market. In Western Europe (less so in the United States) it was treated as a social asset requiring special management and policy skills, extensive state regulation and subsidy' (Ball and Harloe, 1998: 58). Post-war housing in Europe was therefore considerably decommodified during the post-war period.

Perhaps one of the most important forms of refusal witnessed during this Fordist period was that of tenants routinely and effectively opposing increases in rents, especially in the social housing sector, thereby creating a discrepancy between an underfunded but relatively large social housing sector, and a private rental sector that was unable to expand to meet demand due to its coexistence with a cheaper social housing sector (Emms, 1990: 27–8). In addition, technocratic attempts at urban planning that were pursued by (especially) Keynesian governments, also faced considerable protest during the 1960s and 1970s, not least because they heavily relied on the demolition of housing stock that was considered in need of renewal, focusing on substituting this with new modern housing but in the process destroying both existing neighbourhood structures and low-cost housing (Holm and Kuhn, 2011: 653). To make matters worse, residents were routinely excluded from political discussion regarding the form that these controversial modernizing projects would take. As a result, residents and left-leaning community organizing groups would organize various forms of resistance, as Mayer shows:

> Citizens' groups initially used conventional, pragmatic methods to defend their neighbourhoods and chose co-operative tactics and professional strategies such as 'planning alternatives from below'. However, where they confronted unresponsive technocratic city administrations they would resort to

more unconventional forms of politics, including direct action and street protest. Contested issues included not only infrastructure expansion, but also the cost, quality and participation in its design.

(Mayer, 2000: 132)

Any attempt to push up rents during this period had an additional knock-on effect upon the economy in terms of inflation. Given that wages were already being pushed above productivity rises by effective labour organization from the early 1960s onwards (see Chapter 2), and that these were also creating inflationary pressures, governments found themselves facing further difficulties in seeking to resolve the housing problems that they faced. For instance, in attempting during the 1970s to increase rents in the public housing sector, the British Government faced a number of difficulties. The 1972 Housing Finance Act set out to enable a rapid increase in the rents set for council housing. This proved impossible to implement, however, as the inflation generated by the significant wage pressures of the 1970s was such that any additional rise in the rent paid for council housing would have undermined the Government's own price and incomes policy. As a result, local council rents were also included in the government's price controls, undoing the attempts of the 1972 Act to reduce the disparity between council and private rental markets (Emms, 1990: 27–8).

The 1970s also saw the rise of a vibrant squatting movement in many of the advanced industrial democracies, and especially in Western Europe, a dynamic that was partly connected to the effects and disaggregation of social movements in the context of '1968' (Holm and Kuhn, 2011: 645; Martínez López, 2013: 10; see also Chapter 6). The squatting movement commonly adopted radical values of pre-figuration, horizontal consensus-based decision-making and a confrontational attitude towards political (state) authority (van der Steen *et al.*, 2014: 3; Polanska and Piotrowski, 2015). The social base of the movement was mainly made up of (predominantly male) young people that developed a specific dress, discourse and lifestyle (Holm and Kuhn, 2011: 647). Key to the movements was a subcultural version of 'first person politics' that aimed to involve people directly in decisions affecting their everyday lives, sometimes referred to as 'autonomous' (Martínez López, 2013). These movements were also impregnated with political and existential radicalism that also eventually limited their ability to reach broader social constituencies.[1]

The squatting movement represented a more militant means of voicing opposition to the redevelopment of urban centres, as well as to attempts by the authorities to undertake the demolition of housing and to replace it with offices or high-price housing ('redevelopment by eviction') (Holm and Kuhn, 2011: 646). It also represented an additional way in which to vocalise opposition to the lack of affordable quality housing, and provided a direct alternative form of housing for a politicized section of the population (predominantly urban youth), but also for some marginalized people. It thereby challenged housing shortages, urban speculation, private property rights, and the capitalist production of urban space (Martínez López, 2013: 5). In many cases, the squats were occupied 'in working class and industrial areas where different political groups beside the squatters (tenants, countercultural artists, environmentalists, autonomist and libertarian organizations, etc.) confronted the official urban plans' (Martínez López, 2013: 8). As a result, squatting movements oftentimes received considerable public support, to the extent that evictions would result in substantial political damage for those seeking to enforce them. For instance, the mayor of Frankfurt was moved to reverse earlier eviction notices in the wake of widespread indignation following a series of (violent) evictions (Mayer, 2000: 132–4). As a result, most European cities witnessed the emergence of a new political actor: 'a self-confident urban counter-culture with its own infrastructure of newspapers, self-managed collectives and housing co-operatives, feminist groups, etc., which prepared to intervene in local and broader politics' (Mayer, 2000: 135).

This development of a squatting movement could be seen across European cities. In Amsterdam, for instance, a series of empty buildings across the city (including the Grote Keyser) was squatted in 1978, partly in order to take control of the empty buildings and provide an opportunity for local activists to live relatively autonomously; but also as a form of protest at local housing policy and the housing shortage suffered by the city's inhabitants. This ended with a series of violent clashes with the authorities during 1980, including the use of tanks and riot police in an attempt (oftentimes unsuccessful) to clear squatted buildings throughout the year. As the city council sought to evict the squatted buildings, barricades were built by the squatters (including the barricading of the *Vondelstraat* and barricades which blocked the running of public transport). Solidarity efforts were launched by the city's residents (including a demonstration by 10,000 supporters) and a free radio station (*Vrije Keyser*, the Free Emperor) provided regular sympathetic updates. The squatting movement of Amsterdam also included the creation of something akin to a fortress for the squatting movement in the *Staatsliedenbuurt* neighbourhood between 1980 and 1984, with over 500 squatted spaces and considerable public support that reflected widely held concerns for the housing problems that the city faced (Anderiesen, 1980; Kadir, 2014).

Whilst the Amsterdam squatting movement achieved some superficial concessions granted by the local authority, the unwillingness of the Dutch central government to respond to the demands of the squatters resulted in little movement in the area of housing policy. Nevertheless, the terms of the debate were directly shifted towards concern for the housing policy and shortages in the city, thereby evincing (at least) the ability of the squatting movement to successfully politicize the housing question. Further, this built upon an earlier period of politicization associated with the radical student movement in the city during the late 1960s and early 1970s – much of which was focused on opposition to the demolition of sections of the city deemed in need of renovation for the 'general interest' of the city (rather than the interests of the residents themselves), witnessing the creation of a large number of neighbourhood action groups; which ultimately resulted in the Nieuwmarktbuurt conflict in 1975 over the destruction of houses in order to create the subway (Anderiesen, 1980).

In West Germany, and especially West Berlin, similar trends could be observed. As we have noted, already in the early 1930s Berlin was subjected to widespread strikes over rising rents (Vasudevan, 2011: 293). The initiation of a squatting movement in Berlin during the 1970s, and which peaked during the period 1979–1981, was in large part in opposition to the plans of the West Berlin council to respond to a housing shortage through the demolition of central Berlin housing districts without meaningful consultation of the existing residents. The district of Kreuzberg saw the most advanced expressions of opposition and by 1981 over 160 houses were squatted in Berlin. Whilst some of these were eventually evicted, others went on to receive support from the city government to repair and modernize the buildings (Holm and Kuhn, 2011; Vasudevan, 2011: 288–92). Berlin therefore had a vibrant squatting movement. As Vasudevan (2011: 285) puts it:

> While the squatting movement attracted those who wished to protest about the lack of affordable housing, rampant property speculation and the negative effects of post-war urban redevelopment, it also offered an opportunity for many to quite literally build an alternative habitus where the very practice of squatting became the basis for producing a common spatial field, a field where principles and practices of co-operative living intersected with juggled political commitments, emotional attachments, and the mundane materialisms of domesticity, occupation and renovation.

In both Amsterdam and Berlin the squatting movements were most successful in terms of their ability to prevent the demolition of the historical city centres, prompting urban developers to renovate the cities (van der Steen *et al.*, 2014; Pruijt, 2004; Holm and Khun, 2011). Nonetheless, the movements were also relatively successfully marginalized during the 1980s through a combination of state repression and strategies of selective inclusion. In Berlin:

> by the end of 1984 the squatter movement was finally crushed, or rather, 'pacified'. Only a few legalized houses enjoyed financial support under the 'self-help housing' programme launched in 1982. In spite of everything, spaces for collective and alternative lifestyles remained a marginal phenomenon.
>
> (Holm and Kuhn, 2011: 649)

However, occupations in Berlin flared up again in the early 1990s in the context of the dissolution of the German Democratic Republic, which coincided with a massive loss of police and municipal authority, resulting in around 120 squats that were mainly in the Eastern parts of the city. The new squats, in the words of Holm and Kuhn, were an 'anarchistic, libertarian experiment against everything that was petit-bourgeois, against Nazis' (Holm and Kuhn, 2011: 650). Once again, the state reacted with fierce repression, leading to riots, in which the squatters proved unable to defend their houses against the massively deployed police. As a result, many of the squatters opted for negotiated solutions to temporarily safeguard their houses (Holm and Kuhn, 2011: 651).

In Italy we witness arguably the most developed form of urban movements of the period – and certainly the most well-known – with the post-*Operaist autonomia* movement of 1973–9 which peaked with the so-called '77 Movement. This was the counter-cultural strand of the post-*operaist* movement in Italy, made up of students, squatters, the unemployed and unaffiliated activists. It also included the so-called 'metropolitan Indians' who sought to challenge mainstream society in a humorous way, through their use of costumes that included face paint and head-dresses in an open break with the otherwise serious and conservative nature of the left (Cuninghame, 2007). It was often referred to as 'creative Autonomia', in contrast with Organised Workers Autonomy and armed Autonomia. It also included a network of local free radio stations, with Radio Alice in Bologna as the most prominent, and a series of squatted social centres established by the so-called 'Proletarian Youth Clubs' that sought to create counter-cultural spaces that would provide for social and educational needs. The 77 Movement itself was prompted by a move in 1976 by the Minister of Education, Malfatti, to remove a number of the concessions won by the student movement in 1968. In response, by January 1977 students had occupied universities in Palermo, Naples, Salerno, Rome, Bologna, Cagliari, Sassari, Pisa, Florence, Turin, Milan and Padua. This also witnessed a decisive split with the PCI, which up until that point had been something of an interlocutor between the autonomist movement and the establish-ment. In contrast, the '77 movement saw CGIL general secretary and PCI leader, Luciano Lama, repelled with taunts and stones as he sought to negotiate an end to the occupation of Rome University. In response, the PCI increased its hostility toward autonomia, to the extent that the PCI mayor, Zangheri, expressed his sup-port for the police killing of Francesco Lo Russo during a protest in Bologna, and seeing the PCI eventually also support the criminalization of the entire movement and thousands of its militants. This was a movement of significant scale – on a number of occasions rallying 50,000–100,000 participants to events held in an attempt to avoid state repression. Ultimately, however, the scale of imprisonments unleashed from 1979 onwards was enough to terminate much of the movement (Cuninghame, 2002: 161–93).

A wave of squatting also began in the United Kingdom in 1968. This emerged in part from the New Left protest movement, with background in many of the peace movements, including the Vietnam Solidarity Campaign. In particular, it focused on a housing shortage that London was suffering at the time, witnessing the creation of the London Squatters Campaign in November 1968 and increas-ingly overlapping with the punk and autonomist movements in London during the 1970s. The movement created the Family Squatter Advisory Service (FSAS), which by the end of the 1970s had been reformed as the Advisory Service for Squatters (ASS). By the late 1970s there were estimated to be 50,000 squatters across the United Kingdom, 30,000 of them in London. The strength of the squat-ting movement also resulted in a number of legal and policy responses, especially in the late 1970s. Some of these were repressive – e.g. the Criminal Law Act 1977, which made it considerably easier to evict squatters – whilst others repre-sented significant concessions, made largely as a result of the difficulties faced on the part of the authorities in terms of their ability to prevent squatting – e.g. the Homeless Persons Act 1977, Housing Act 1980, the legalization of five thousand squats in London in 1977, and an amnesty offered by the Greater London Council to the 1850 squats owned by the Council in 1977 (Finchett-Maddock, 2014).

Under the dictatorships in Southern Europe a form of squatting movement also developed, especially at the outskirts of larger cities. This could be seen in the *afthereta* (Greece), *viviendas marginales, barracas* (Spain) and *bairros clandestinos, bairros de lata* (Portugal) – each of which were large settlements squatted on the urban peripheries. These housed predominantly working class or informal-sector migrant workers which tended to spring up as a spontaneous 'solution' to the problem of homelessness and unemployment in contexts of rapid urbanization. In the case of Greece this had its roots in the inter-war period, during which empty buildings were occupied by refugees in the large cities (Leontidou, 2010: 1183–4). This therefore represented a trend whereby mass civil disobedience created the possibility of housing:

> squatting in Greece, Italy, Spain and Portugal was indeed conflictual: a form of massive grassroots movements of civil disobedience. Migrants and workers bought plots where it was illegal to build, according to each country's by-laws, but proceeded to disobey these rules and build shacks overnight. People ignored legislation about city building and thus contested state authority. This was tacitly tolerated by the state as a solution to the housing problem and a buffer against social unrest.
>
> (Leontidou, 2010: 1184)

Over the course of the post-war period these dwellings developed into more permanent fixtures – representing a democratization of public space. In some instances, associations or collectives emerged which were radicalized. For instance, in Madrid the Citizen Movement began to exert pressure upon Franco, demanding democracy, amnesty and political freedom, as well as material rights and grass-roots participation in elected institutions of local governments. Another example was Perama, a collective in Athens where land owned by the church was squatted and was the basis for an anti-eviction movement at the point during which the dictatorship was on the decline (Leontidou, 2010: 1185–6). Whilst these were mainly demolished or evacuated by the authorities during the 1980s and 1990s they nevertheless left a legacy, oftentimes providing inspiration for social centres and urban social movements (Leontidou, 2010). Similar trends could also be observed with the privatization of housing stock in post-communist countries and with the widespread practice of demolishing subsidized housing estates and replacing it with private housing schemes (Aalbers and Christophers, 2016: 29; Muire *et al.*, 2005; Polanska and Piotrowski, 2015). Despite their embeddedness in local contexts, the squatters' movements were characterized by a transnational orientation and regular connections among squatters all over Europe (Martínez López, 2013).

In 1950s Spain, meanwhile, 51 per cent of the population were living in rented flats and houses, while the share of rent reached over 90 per cent in larger cities such as Barcelona or Madrid. The standard of housing was relatively low; in 1960 only 38 per cent of the houses had running water and only 8 per cent a bathroom or shower. After mobility restrictions were lifted in 1959, the subsequent decades witnessed mass migration from rural areas characterized by low wages and precarious living conditions to the rural areas of the industrialized regions. At the same time, many Spaniards left Spain to work abroad – especially in the European 'core'. As a result, slums developed on the peripheries of Spanish cities. These were characterized by strong ties of solidarity and close neighbourhood relations, as in many cases entire villages had migrated to the same urban areas. Within these new suburbs, obstinate subcultures developed that conflicted with Francoist ideology and eluded state control. To re-establish control, however, the regime pursued a rapid expansion of home ownership with the explicit aim of using mortgage and private debt to discipline workers, while disintegrating neighbourhood social networks through privatized housing and the spatial isolation of nuclear families. New suburbs were constructed on the outskirts of rural areas. These, however, were characterized by a lack of infrastructure (especially health, education, and public transport), with these everyday problems prompting the development of protest movements and neighbourhood assemblies, which in turn were connected with demands for democratization as the Francoist regime proved unwilling or unable to provide solutions. Indeed, during the 1970s, the neighbourhood movement became one of the key pillars of the anti-Francoist opposition (Huke, 2017).

Our discussion of forms of disruption in the field of housing during, and in the crisis of, Fordism should not however be limited to only visible forms of protest. It also included everyday forms of disruptive agency, witnessing considerable bouts of disengagement, disaffection and disinterested political (non-)action. For example, throughout the period there was an ongoing problem of rising rent arrears. In part, this was due to the fact that social housing was subject to greater obstacles to eviction than that of private housing. This therefore enabled acts of what we might consider to be imperceptible forms of dissent. Most obviously, rents were simply not paid. For instance, in the United Kingdom rent arrears grew from 3 per cent of the total amount of rent due in the mid-1970s, to 3.9 per cent in 1980 and to 5.8 per cent in 1988, with levels consistently higher in inner London and other large metropolitan areas (Emms, 1990).

In their attempt to deal with this bundle of problems (demands on the social housing stock, squatting, opposition to redevelopment, and rising rent arrears), governments increasingly turned to promote private homeownership as its solution. One element of this was the move to promote state support for the liberalization of housing finance, pursued in part through European integration, in an attempt to ensure that funds were available for the increase in homeownership being promoted. As Schelkle (2012: 63) shows, the creation of the housing bubble was in large part the product of what can be viewed as a form of social policy; or, rather, 'promoting homeownership was social policy by somewhat unusual means.' For instance, in the United Kingdom the highly subsidized 'right-to-buy' policy sought to allow council house tenants to buy their own homes, and to subsequently benefit from a rapid increase in the value of those homes. In France, moreover, 'homeownership for low-income households was promoted through loans at fixed interest rates that were negative in real terms when inflation was high' (2012: 64). This policy was in many instances a direct response to political pressure from workers who were unhappy about, and mobilized in various ways against, existing housing provisions, as we've seen in the previous section. To refer to the French example, the development of a new pro-homeownership loan system was the result of growing discontent at the inequalities and ghettoization caused by poor housing provision in the early/mid 1990s, which itself had prompted 'very public concerns' (Schelkle, 2012: 68).

Housing and neoliberal European integration: mortgage-financed housing and the rise of anti-gentrification protests

With the advance of neoliberal efforts in the 1980s, European integration grew as a factor affecting housing across the member states. Whilst housing policy remained undeveloped at the EU-level and largely a responsibility of national governments, nevertheless the indirect effects of European integration had considerable impact (Matznetter and Stephens, 1998: 5).[2] In the context of the Single European Market and EMU, and in part as a response to the problems associated with the earlier, more politicized, field of housing discussed in the previous section, nation-states across Europe increasingly sought to withdraw from housing market intervention (Kadi and Musterd, 2015: 248; Matznetter and Stephens, 1998: 9). Housing came to be regarded primarily as an economic asset (Ball and Harloe, 1998: 58). This, moreover, was a process that especially affected urban housing as it was here that the field of housing had been most decommodified by the welfare state in the earlier period (Kadi and Musterd, 2015: 248).

Those promoting the re-introduction of market forces into the housing market – itself a process which would later be held responsible for the inflation of the housing bubble in the period leading up to 2008 – sought a number of outcomes. The privatization of housing provision, it was hoped, would ensure that that housing would no longer be considered a government responsibility. Further, the rapid increase in house prices created a political constituency that would support the policy of privatized housing, which in turn became a virtuous/vicious circle whereby increased private housing stock followed on from rising house prices and growing support amongst a growing population of private homeowners. Finally, this process would also lead to the marginalization (and therefore silencing) of those on lower incomes who remained reliant upon public/social housing or who sought to demand improved social housing provision. Each of these trends resulted in rapid increases in homeownership from the early 1980s onwards across much of Europe. While this development in part reflects the rise of neoliberal paradigms within nation states, it also relates to a decreasing fiscal capacity of the state in a context of increased locational competition and limits placed upon government spending as a result of the new European constitutionalism, such as the Maastricht convergence criteria (Stephens, 1998). In addition, the liberalization and integration of European financial markets had a direct impact upon the scope for housing finance. In the European periphery, moreover,

EMU resulted in a decline in interest rates that acted to facilitate the increased accessibility of mortgages and private homeownership for significant parts of the populations (Rodríguez López and López Hernández, 2011). Whilst European integration did not see authority over housing policy significantly move to the supranational level, therefore, it was nevertheless an important indirect mechanism facilitating significant changes to the patterns of homeownership and housing across the EC/EU.

As noted, one of the key ways in which housing finance was affected by European integration was through the deregulation of European capital markets. In particular, the Capital Market Directive 88/361/EEC and the Second Banking Directive 89/646/EEC, adopted in 1988 and 1989, respectively, were central to this process (Matznetter and Stephens, 1998: 9). As a result of European regulations, the LTV[Loan-to-Value]-cap was abolished, resulting in higher LTV-ratios; banks were allowed to grant mortgages (while this had been the exclusive terrain of specialized credit institutions until 1990); and both European and national regulations forced bank restructuring which in turn led to increased competition and therefore the entry of foreign competitors into national mortgage markets (Aalbers, 2009: 399). That said, the penetration of foreign firms into national mortgage markets was relatively low prior to the 2007–8 crisis, although the growth of an (international) secondary market for mortgages (mortgage-backed securities) was such that it tripled in volume in Europe in the first half of the 2000s (Aalbers, 2009: 400–2). Thus, both the direct effect of changed regulations, and the indirect effect of heightened competition (and indeed simply the possibility that competition and mergers might increase – even if foreign firms did not directly enter national markets) were sufficient to see a substantial change in both the culture and practice of lending across Europe.

The construction industry, and especially larger building firms, also witnessed a process of Europeanization, as standards and tendering practices were harmonized by a number of European regulations (such as the Coordination Directive on Government Tendering 1971/1989, the Building Products Directive 1988, and the Supplies Directive 1976/1980) (Priemus, 1998: 79). In addition to these indirect effects, the EU also exerted influence through a number of competition directives which enabled it to instruct national governments to change policies, especially with regard to social housing. Sweden, for instance, reacted by abolishing support for non-profit housing companies and forcing them to act as for-profit providers (Kadi and Musterd, 2015: 248).

Each of these processes contributed to a tentative convergence of European housing markets, as national governments liberalized regulations, outsourced social housing provision and limited subsidies for housing. Governments across Europe sought to offload their responsibility for housing provision and make it an increasingly private responsibility, reducing the stock of public housing, and encouraging private home ownership. This saw the erosion of a number of social protection measures, in a series of moves that were both facilitated by and acted to consolidate heightened social inequality and worsening conditions, especially for those on low incomes (Rolnick, 2013; Christophers, 2013).

The underfunded nature of social housing was such that housing estates increasingly became unpopular places to live, harbouring a combination of poverty, crime, unemployment, hopelessness and individual frustrations, and oftentimes boiling over into visible displays of anger and in some cases rioting. Council housing increasingly came to be associated with higher levels of crime, deprivation, unemployment, poor amenities and marginalization. As a result, families in turn became reluctant to move onto estates, resulting in a rising number of empty dwellings.

The grievances of those tenants who remained on council house estates visibly erupted in the early 1980s, often prompting direct government policy responses. In the United Kingdom the Toxteth riots of 1981 directly prompted the Secretary of State for the Environment, Michael Heseltine, to initiate a major redevelopment of one of the most seriously rundown estates – Cantril Farm. This redevelopment, as with many similar initiatives, consisted largely of attempts to switch ownership away from the local government – via housing associations (with the support of private firms) or, more commonly, through Right-to-Buy sales. Indeed, it was Right-to-Buy which represented the major attempt of the UK Government in the 1980s to reduce its heavy involvement in housing provision – by offering a state-backed means by which to encourage private home ownership (Emms, 1990: 51–8). We see a direct connection, therefore, between the problems created by the perceptible and imperceptible forms of dissent associated with the large volume of social housing in the UK housing sector, and the subsequent move by the Government in the 1980s to stimulate a rapid growth in the private housing market and a corresponding increase in the proportion of the country that relied on private homeownership rather than local government housing.

In Spain, urbanization processes continued throughout the 1980s. Despite the struggles of the neighbourhood movements, rural outskirts remained characterized by social exclusion, lacking infrastructure and unemployment until the second half of the 1980s. Drug abuse – and especially heroin use – spread rapidly, while social ties and neighbourhood assemblies were eroded. The state reacted by criminalizing and securitizing users, and imprisonments due to property crime rose dramatically. The Francoist strategy of privileging home ownership over rent was continued by the democratic governments that reduced both tenants' rights and the availability of social housing. Home ownership, in consequence, became the dominant paradigm of housing in Spain. Cheap credit (in part due to declining interest rates in the context of the EMU), and house prices that consistently rose above inflation, led large parts of the Spanish population to take out mortgages in order to purchase real estate. As a result, household debt and the interest burden upon those households increased. While in 1997 the average price of real estate was 380 per cent of average gross annual revenue of households, this had increased to 760 per cent by 2007. Risks were mainly carried by the debtors, as creditors could rely on the restrictive Spanish mortgages law that do not include the possibility of properties being returned in exchange for a cancellation of debt (*dación en pago*) (Huke, 2017).

The post-Fordist housing policies that emerged across Europe, therefore, included: a generalized move towards increased private ownership (although this began to go in reverse after the crash of 2007), accompanied by a widening gap in terms of affordability between those on low and those on middle incomes (Dewilde and De Decker, 2016); an increase in the loan-to-value ratio for mortgage holders and a rise in the mortgage debt-to-GDP ratio; and increased gentrification and shorter-term tenure, especially in those countries – the United States, the United Kingdom, Netherlands, Spain, Ireland – in which the general transformation of housing into a form of investment was most pronounced (on these national differences, see Fernandez and Aalbers, 2016). More generally, this represented a heightened role for the market in the provision of housing across European society (Ball and Harloe, 1998: 60), as well as a governing strategy that sought to ensure social order (Uitermark *et al.*, 2007). Some of the additional effects of these trends were the increasingly residual nature of social housing provision, in which only the very poorest would qualify for social housing; and a growing trend of homelessness, which moved from being previously marginal to now a major phenomenon (Ball and Harloe, 1998: 58; 62).[3]

Whilst direct government support for owner-occupation (in the form, for instance, of tax relief) went into decline across the EU during the 1990s, these subsidies were in large part replaced by a more privatized form of support for housing provision. This echoes those accounts that highlight a 'privatized' form of Keynesianism that developed prior to the crisis (Crouch, 2008). That is, such accounts highlight the impact that rising house prices had upon the perceived wealth (and therefore willingness to spend) of homeowners (Watson, 2010; Montgomerie and Büdenbender, 2015). As such, it was the liberalization of finance that facilitated increased appetite for home ownership alongside a decline in direct government support for housing, and in part due to a decline in the provision of social housing (on this decline in direct support, see Whitehead, 1998: 24). As Ball and Harloe (1998: 68–9) argue, 'many governments aimed to increase owner-occupation in Western Europe by making social housing more expensive and less available, and through financial liberalization.' This was in large part a direct attempt to deal with the same issues that welfare reform of the same period had been designed to tackle. That is, it fitted with the growing consensus, increasingly held by the political elite, that the welfare state had by the 1970s become bloated and unaffordable and therefore required public service provisions to be offloaded onto the market in order to regain sustainability (Harloe, 1995).

This combination of processes therefore created a virtuous circle: increased availability of finance for housing prompted an increased investment in private homeownership, which in turn led to rising demand for private home ownership (plus decreased public sector support for a declining ('residualized') stock of social housing) and rising house prices, thereby rendering housing as an improved option for financial speculation, thereby further increasing the availability of finance for housing, and so on.

The sharp rise in house prices during the late 1990s and early 2000s was therefore driven by a sharp rise in the availability of financial instruments, with these financial instruments eventually being used to finance what, with the benefit of hindsight, we are able to see was the construction of a huge housing market bubble (Aalbers, 2016). Moreover, this housing bubble acted both to pacify opposition to other public policy trends (such as declining welfare generosity and a reduction in the stock of social housing), amongst those whose housing assets were rising in value, and represented a boost to growth. It also had a clear downside, however, which was a widening inequality between those who were homeowners and those who continued to rely upon social housing provision or renting. Whilst this latter group tended to be predominantly lower income households, moreover, it also exacerbated and consolidated pre-exiting inequalities. The transformation of housing patterns that accompanied the transition from Fordism to post-Fordism, therefore, also mirrored, contributed to, and consolidated the broader trends in inequality associated with the move to post-Fordism. That is, the general process of increased precarity, insecurity and inequality that marked the onset of neoliberalism also occurred in its own particular way in the sphere of housing. This created a widening inequality in wealth, but it also produced an inequality in lifestyles as living patterns became increasingly segregated.

The promotion of homeownership increasingly resulted in a situation whereby 'many slightly better-off residents chose to abandon integrated neighbourhoods (inner city in the US and housing estates in Europe) for the private housing market', creating a pool of lower income households left behind in the less popular residential areas (Nichols and Beaumont, 2004: 122). This, moreover, ensured that those living in unpopular 'residual' public housing were denied access to economic opportunities, stigmatized and thereby further excluded from the economic mainstream (Nichols and Beaumont, 2004; Wacquant, 1996; Wilson, 1996). As Aalbers and Christophers (2016: 26) put it, 'housing serves as a principal crucible for the exacerbation of multiply-constituted social inequality.'

One effect of these housing-related patterns of heightened social inequality was a growing pattern of urban unrest. The negative effects of privatized housing provision and underfunded social housing crystallized in urban areas. Deprivation and social exclusion intensified, which in combination with racism, segregation and excessive police controls provided the grounds for a number of urban riot movements (Arbaci, 2007; Mücke and Rinn, 2016; Sutterlüty, 2014). Homeless people and other marginalized groups organized struggles against efforts to drive them out of city centres, supported at times by church groups and social workers (Mayer, 2000: 144). At the same time these processes of urban exclusion were politicized by vocal agents in groups such as the 'Right to the City' and anti-gentrification movements, which emerged in fragmented ways across Europe during the 1990s and 2000s (Holm and Kuhn, 2011: 655–656; Leontidou, 2010; Mayer, 2000: 140). These new movements in many cases developed at the intersection between tenants' movements, leftist organizations and previous subcultural autonomous squatters' movements that:

> broadened their activities to tenants' rights, offering shelter (when possible), opening up of vacant dwellings for individuals and families in need of housing, providing legal counselling to tenants and getting involved in issues concerning housing politics on the national and local level.
>
> (Polanska and Piotrowski, 2015: 275)

Some sections of the squatting movement were therefore able to move from being a marginalized countercultural movement to one able to play more of a role within broader civil society (Polanska and Piotrowski, 2015: 286).

Likewise, there was a politicization of those 'left behind' in the increasingly residualized social housing stock, who continued to demand improved housing. As Nicholls and Beaumont (2004: 126) document, the actions of the *Alliante voor Sociale Rechtvaardigheid* in the Netherlands brought together anti-poverty campaigning church groups, trade unions and welfare advocacy organizations in a loose coalition with links to a range of relatively autonomous urban associations. Similar networks formed in Athens, oftentimes clashing with an unresponsive public sector that would bolster the development of opposition movements (and which would later come to represent an important source of anti-austerity mobilization following the onset of the European crisis) (Arampatzi and Nicholls, 2012). To an extent, however, these movements were hampered by many of the problems facing other social movements during the pre-2008 period: a growing individualization of housing concerns, and growing divisions between middle-class citizens campaigning on neighbourhood-level quality of life issues, newer poor people's movements, and those adopting a 'autonomous' position (Polanska and Piotrowski, 2015: 278; Mayer, 2000: 138–139).

Developments during the European crisis: over-indebtedness, evictions and everyday movements for decent housing

> Home ownership is inevitably an uncertain venture. It involves long-term repayment profiles which have to tie in with life-cycle earnings, interest rates have to be forecast, and employment stability is vital.
>
> (Ball and Harloe, 1998: 66)

The global crisis and subsequent European crisis both exposed the vulnerability of market-based housing provision and the limits of an inflated housing market. This was in part sustained by the low interest rates generated by EMU, as well as being facilitated by the liberalization of European financial markets. The collapse in house prices was especially noteworthy in Spain, the United Kingdom, Ireland, Denmark and Poland. Faced with this collapse in prices, and in order to mitigate as much as possible the consequences that it would have for the wider global economy, the political elite had the option of choosing between one of two strategies: letting the market decide; or intervening to avoid too detrimental an impact upon those who stood to lose as a result of the housing crash. The response witnessed was something of a combination of these two options. On the one hand, the fear of political opposition and widespread dissent was such that the interests of one of the core social constituencies of neoliberalism – middle-class private homeowners – could not be jettisoned (Ansell, 2014; Genovese *et al.*, 2016). On the other hand, the reliance upon market competition as the mechanism through which to seek to order and discipline European society was also such that the rules of the market could not be discarded altogether. The outcome of this dilemma was something of a compromise between, or combination of, these two contrasting pressures.

Thus, governments responded to the crisis with both ultra-low interest rates as a means to offer a degree of support for house owners and mortgage holders, and enforcement of the market through the overseeing of (or failure to prevent) evictions (especially in the case of Spain). Interest rates were lowered radically, monetary policy was loosened dramatically, and quantitative easing was introduced to produce considerable financial stimulus and bolster demand for key finance-dependent assets. This had a largely beneficial effect upon the housing market. Homeowners with mortgages could continue to repay their mortgages, and house prices recovered in value. This was coordinated, moreover, by central banks, including through the actions of the European Central Bank. In Spain we also witnessed an attempt to further consolidate the liberalized housing market, for instance with the introduction of second citizenships for those purchasing property for more than €160,000. Similar initiatives were also introduced in Latvia, the Czech Republic and Austria (Aalbers and Christophers, 2016: 27).

At the same time, however, public finance for social housing was reduced further still, on the grounds that this was unproductive spending and that in the context of strained public finances and broader austerity measures it was important to reduce budget deficits. Finally, lower-income homeowners, who were unable to maintain mortgage repayments, even in a context of monetary policy geared towards stimulating the housing market, were met by a government and financial industry that sought to ensure that property rights would be upheld. These lower-income households were therefore forced to terminate their mortgages and return their houses to mortgage lenders, oftentimes accruing large debts (or 'negative equity'), and resulting (especially in southern Europe, and particularly Spain) in a wave of evictions. This therefore further contributed to the shift from the public to private sector provision of housing, producing a further residualization of social housing. This further exacerbated inequalities connected with house ownership – between those (predominantly middle-income earners) able to afford mortgage repayments in a low interest rate housing market with recovering house prices, and those (predominantly low-income workers, migrants and the young) reliant upon the rising costs of private renting and/or suffering the consequences of evictions (Aalbers, 2015: 55; Green and Lavery, 2015). As a result, we witness increased problems such as homelessness and a lack of affordable housing (Peck *et al.*, 2013: 1092).

It is in this context that we also witness the development of a growing range of housing movements developing in opposition to these sharpening crisis-era forms of inequality. The crisis, we argue, acted as a catalyst for the dissemination of alternative forms of mobilization and housing-related claims that had been developed by earlier housing movements. As a squatter from Madrid puts it:

> messages we tried to spread throughout the years without any success, such as self-organisation and disobedience, suddenly reached all kinds of people who did not fit the profile of revolutionary militant we were used to.
> (activist quoted in Martínez López and García Bernardos, 2012: 8–9)

The new housing movements that developed during the crisis, moreover, emerged not only as a continuation of previous housing movements, but also at the same time involved a rupture with what had increasingly become 'identitarian' processes of subcultural self-ghettoization. The new housing movements substantially increased their ability to bring together broader groups from the local neighbourhoods, and to collectivize what could easily otherwise have been individualized forms of struggle around housing. Radical left subcultures, discourses and claims were, in the process, subordinated to a more pragmatic, 'needs-based' strategy (Huke, 2016; Martínez López and García Bernardos, 2011). As such, the disruptive subjectivities characterizing these newer housing movements increasingly took the form of the 'pragmatically prefigurative' agents we have also charted in our earlier chapters, as we shall see in the next section (Bailey *et al.*, 2016).

Contesting the residualization of social housing in Britain's 'age of austerity'

Struggles over what was essentially a consolidation of the residualization of social and/or affordable housing in Britain during the post-2008 period can perhaps be divided into two periods – an early period (2010–13) during which the key point of contention was that over housing benefits, and especially the so-called 'bedroom tax', and a later period, from 2014 onwards, during which the recovery in the housing market was such that it began to cost out of the market many on lower incomes. During this latter period prices rose in both the private rental and private ownership markets, at the same time as social housing was in insufficient supply, thereby in turn creating a pool of people without sufficient access to affordable housing. This prompted the emergence, especially from 2014 onwards, and especially in London (where these effects were most stark), of a radical housing movement that sought to question the effect that the Government's free market approach to housing provision was having.

The under-occupancy penalty – or 'Bedroom Tax' as it became known – was proposed at the beginning of the Coalition Government, as part of the 2010 emergency budget. Osborne made the proposal as part of a broader attempt to limit housing benefit spending, stating at the time that:

> spending on housing benefit has risen from £14 billion ten years ago to £21 billion today. That is close to a 50 per cent increase over and above inflation. Costs are completely out of control. We now spend more on housing benefit than we do on the police and on universities combined.
>
> (Hansard, 22 June 2010, Column 173–4)

The reforms announced aimed to reduce spending on housing benefit by £1.8 billion per year, or 7 percent of the total budget – this included the aim of 'limiting social tenants' entitlement to appropriately sized homes.

The proposal was to reduce a proportion of a family's housing benefit for each 'spare room' that they had (14 per cent reduction for one 'spare room', and

25 per cent for two). A spare room was considered any room that went beyond one for every two adults, one for every two same-sex children (or mixed-sex for under-10-year-olds), and one for every child aged 10 or over. Given that the penalty for so-called 'under-occupancy' was a reduction in housing benefit, resulting in the possibility of eviction if rents could not subsequently be paid, the proposal was widely considered to be punitive. This was subsequently compounded by the fact that the definition of an unused room was difficult to pin down, in many cases resulting in penalties for disabled residents who required an additional room in order to be able to house equipment related to their disability, or in some cases to recently bereaved parents, or those with a very small 'spare room' that could not in practical terms be used as a bedroom due to its small size. The initiative was therefore widely perceived to be both punitive but also highly targeted in that it would only hit a small minority of housing benefit claimants who were particularly vulnerable.

Prompted by the punitive and regressive nature of the so-called bedroom tax, considerable public opposition emerged at the time of its proposal, eventually resulting in a 'partial U-turn' that saw foster carers and parents of teenage armed forces personnel exempted from the charge just three weeks before it was due to come into force, which itself resulted in the policy being accused by the Labour opposition of being in 'total chaos' (Butler, 2013). Opposition to the proposal included a wave of protests that took place during early-2013 (i.e. on the eve of its implementation), seeing 2,500 people attend a demonstration in Glasgow, a 1,000-strong demonstration outside Downing Street, and similar events in many other cities across the country (including London, Leeds, Cardiff, Manchester and Birmingham). Protests also continued into 2014, with the Anti-Bedroom Tax and Benefits Justice Federation co-organizing a National Stop the War on Benefits workshop with Disabled People Against Cuts in November 2014. This workshop was also attended by members of the high-profile Focus E15 group, which went on to challenge attempts by private landlords to evict them (as we see in the following section) – in part through militant forms of opposition that included occupations of their homes. The so-called Bedroom Tax also faced criticisms from the UN, on the grounds that it undermined the right to housing.

Campaign groups were set up across the country in an attempt to oppose the Bedroom Tax. Some adopted particularly disruptive tactics that focused on anti-eviction methods that had been learned in earlier campaigns. For instance, one local group, Coventry Against the Bedroom Tax, were able to put in place a practice of adopting anti-eviction blockades if/when residents faced eviction as a result of the net increase in the cost of renting that was created by the reduction of housing benefit due to the Bedroom Tax. In 2015, they were successfully able to prevent the eviction of a resident of Coventry, through a combination of blockading the house in order to prevent the eviction, and the adverse publicity that it created for the housing association seeking to carry out the eviction (interview with Coventry Against the Bedroom Tax activist, 2 October 2015). As one of the organizers of the Coventry-based campaign set out:

One of the things that we said from the start was that if it comes to trying to evict people, as we did in the poll tax, we'll get a big bunch of people to stand in the front garden and see the bailiffs off, because they don't have any legal right to enter ... And we said that if the bailiffs get nasty we'll call the police – because we knew from our experience with the poll tax that that [non-intervention in the attempted eviction] would be their response. ... We were saying to people, 'this is how we're going to stop it; it's all going to be peaceful; we're not going to be threatening anybody or pushing and shoving anybody, but we will physically stop bailiffs taking possession. So we said that from the start; we expected that it would work because we've done it in the poll tax campaign.

(interview with Coventry Against the Bedroom Tax activist, 2 October 2015)

Other groups that were focused on tackling the bedroom tax also built on pre-existing campaigns. For instance, the group, Hands Off Our Homes – Leeds, began as a campaign in 2005 as a group aiming to safeguard council housing under threat as a result of the City Councils' regeneration programme. This earlier programme was effectively a residualization process that involved the selling-off and demolition of council housing. Hands Off Our Homes viewed the Bedroom Tax as another attack on social housing and therefore chose to focus on that as well. As a result, the group was involved in setting up one of the main anti-Bedroom Tax protest demonstrations in Leeds in April 2014, which saw about 1,500 participants. The group also began to provide technical and legal support for individuals who either faced evictions, or who sought to challenge the legal basis for the implementation of the bedroom tax in their individual cases (interview with John Davies, Hands Off Our Homes – Leeds activist, 24 June 2014).

The campaign against the Bedroom Tax also enabled information sharing between those at risk of being penalized by the policy. As the Coventry Against the Bedroom Tax activist put it,

Some people came along to the meeting – they were really, I think, as much as anything they wanted to get the rules of it straight. So, 'are you allowed a bedroom for this?' They weren't sure totally how it worked. So we were able to make that crystal clear. 'What if you're a pensioner?' Actually it doesn't apply to a pensioner. [...] We've got the nitty gritty details that we were able to tell people.

(interview with Coventry Against the Bedroom Tax activist, 2 October 2015)

The controversy that was attached to the Bedroom Tax also prompted concern amongst members of the political elite. Indeed, this was seen by many campaigners as a key achievement of the anti-bedroom tax campaign. As the Hands Off Our Homes activist noted,

We call it the bedroom tax – journalists have said to us, from the BBC, we are not allowed to call it the bedroom tax, we have to call it the spare room subsidy – and so the fact that term, everyone knows it as the 'bedroom tax', and they would never call it the removal of the spare room subsidy, is an achievement in itself, that we made it look like it's unfair.

(interview with John Davies, Hands Off Our
Homes – Leeds activist, 24 June 2014)

A number of Conservative MPs also expressed anxiety about the impact that the bedroom tax was having upon their constituents, thereby creating internal opposition and division within the Conservative Party. Indeed, d'Ancona (2013) notes this caution in his tale of how Ian Duncan Smith was confronted by dual pressures. On the one hand, most Conservative MPs wanted more substantial reductions in public spending, ostensibly in order to reduce the public debt/deficit. But on the other hand, many of those same MPs were also wary of the public backlash that was associated with concrete spending reductions once it became apparent that they would result in severe hardship with sometimes extremely negative outcomes. As d'Ancona puts it:

It was one thing to call for IDS to slash the overall bill. But many Tory MPs were unnerved by (for instance) the new under-occupancy penalty – or 'bedroom tax' – that took effect from April 2013 and filled surgeries with troubled constituencies, fearful that they would have to move house because they had a spare room and could not afford the extra payment. The case of Stephanie Bottrill, a Solihull grandmother, who had committed suicide in May and left a note blaming the bedroom tax, sent a shiver through the ranks of every party.

(d'Ancona, 2013: 334)

Indeed, this vulnerability of the political elite, to reputation damage as a result of the implementation of the Bedroom Tax was seen by the campaigners themselves as a key means by which to challenge the Bedroom Tax. As the Hands Off Our Homes activist that we interviewed outlined, their campaign focused on,

publicity to make people aware of the stupidity or iniquity of the bedroom tax […] it's making sure other people realise what is going on, because the whole point about the bedroom tax is that anybody who is in social housing could fall into trouble if their financial circumstances change or their family size changes; all they need is a child who is 17 to move away from home and they've got a spare bedroom.

(interview with John Davies, Hands Off Our
Homes – Leeds, 24 June 2014).

In addition to problems with public support, the implementation of the bedroom tax also proved problem-prone – with a technical detail found in regulations that had been published nearly twenty years earlier creating an unanticipated loophole that exempted around 5 per cent of benefit recipients who were due to pay the Bedroom Tax – a loophole that could not be ignored once its details went viral on social media. Further, in January 2016 an appeal court ruled that the Bedroom Tax was discriminatory in two cases due to its impact on vulnerable people. Indeed, opposition to the Bedroom Tax was such that even Clare Foges (ex-speech writer for David Cameron) wrote in 2015, after the general election, that '[i]t [the Bedroom Tax] is not working as had been hoped and will remain a fly in the one-nation ointment'. She advised, 'Have a principled *mea culpa* moment and move on' (Chorley, 2015). This came amid claims that '[p]rivately every Conservative minister now admits it is a bad policy' (Hardman, 2015). Indeed, the impact of the campaigning that had surrounded the Bedroom Tax could be seen quite clearly in terms of the opinion polls on the topic, with those supporting the tax declining from 49 per cent to 41 per cent, and those opposing it rising from 38 per cent to 49 per cent between March 2013 and July 2014 (Jordan, 2014).

During the campaigns against the Bedroom Tax, connections were also made with a nascent housing movement that focused especially on the problems of lack of affordable housing in London. This movement was first reported in the national press in October 2014 when the group, Focus E15, staged a disruptive protest against the high-end annual property fair, MIPIM, which saw protesters hurling mud at the conference doors and eventually required the police and organizers to close the gates to the venue. This followed the group's occupation of a vacant council house on the Carpenters estate, on the edge of the Olympic Park in east London, where hundreds of homes had been standing empty since the Olympic Games despite a housing waiting list that ran into the tens of thousands (Wainwright, 2014). This in turn sparked the development of a housing movement that used a combination of a skilled media strategy (including cooperation with comedian and political activist Russell Brand), disruptive tactics that often included occupations of unused housing stock, and public demonstrations. In doing so, it gathered considerable attention and was able to place the affordability of housing clearly on the public agenda (for more on the Focus E15 campaign, see Watt, 2016).

A similar campaign emerged later in 2014 when it was announced that the new owner of the New Era Estate, Westbrook Partners, would sell off the housing estate and in the process, evict the 93 families that were living there. This sparked a major campaign which began with the submission of a petition signed by 292,000 people and which gained the support of the Labour Party opposition and the shadow justice minister and shadow minister for London (and later London Mayor), Sadiq Kahn (Booth, 2014). The campaign around the issue eventually forced a U-turn by the property developers. This was followed in early 2015 by a large demonstration and march focused on London's City Hall and London Mayor, Boris Johnson, in which it was demanded that greater attention be made towards the requirements of the city for affordable social housing. This demonstration was attended by campaigners from both the New Era campaign and the Focus E15 campaign (Towsend and Kelly, 2015). This was followed only a couple of weeks later by an occupation of the Aylesbury Estate, again in an attempt to bring attention to the needs of the city dwellers for affordable housing, and also to highlight the existence of available property that was going unutilized. The turn towards radical forms of refusal, such as occupations and squatting, moreover, represented a visible means by which to express demands and seek to ensure that the housing issue be addressed. As one of the activists involved in the occupation put it, 'What's going on here is effectively social cleansing to make London a nice 'clean' place for the rich ... A group of us wanted to stand in the way of that so we took over some of the flats as an act of solidarity' (quoted in Quinn, 2015).

In March 2015, a fourth estate-based campaign soon opened up when evicted residents of the Sweets Way Estate joined again with Russell Brand to take part in a 'sleepover' protest on the estate. This followed on from a squat and occupation of the estate that had begun the week before, and which also fed into a rally in the city centre that was attended by 2,000 people and which called for more to be done for affordable housing (Taylor, 2015). Another occupation to protest evictions followed in April 2015, with the support of Focus E15 campaigner, Jasmin Stone, this time in opposition to an eviction of a tenant who had had her benefits stopped and therefore went into arrears on her rent (Booth, 2015). The Sweets Way Resists and E15 campaigns subsequently joined forces to disrupt the annual Property Awards later the same month, blocking off the entrance to the event and chanting that 'Social Housing is a human right' (Slawson, 2015). Only three days later another occupation sprang up in opposition to plans to demolish council housing, this time in Barnet Council's Dollis Valley estate, which was earmarked to be turned into luxury homes. The protest took the form of an occupation by the families, residents and supporting housing activists occupying the estate's community nursery. A further demonstration with 3,000 participants took place later the same month, this time in Brixton, witnessing protests against what was viewed as the gentrification of the city. This was shortly afterwards followed by what appeared to be the spreading of the housing movement outside of London, as Manchester saw the emergence of a protest camp outside of Manchester City Hall, organized by a group called Homeless Rights of Justice, attended by 30 homeless campaigners and lasting for around 50 days outside the Hall. Finally, 2015–16 also witnessed the emergence of a growing association between the student protest movement and housing issues, with a vibrant rent strike focused initially on UCL.

The housing crisis has also witnessed the development of a myriad of local campaigns. Anti-gentrification campaigns were coordinated by Southwark Notes, which published an Anti-Gentrification Handbook that offered advice on how to run campaigns.[4] The West Kensington and Gibbs Green neighbourhood association also launched a 'People's Plan' for improvements and redevelopment (rather than demolition, which the property owners were proposing) of the West Kensington and Gibbs Green estates.[5] Lambeth Housing Activists organized a series of demonstrations against the estate agency, Savills, that was seen to be associated with gentrification, leading to the closure of three of the agency's offices.[6] On the 9th of July 2016, Sisters Uncut conducted an occupation of an unused building in the East End of London, demanding better provision of social housing, and making the space open to women, non-binary people and their children. The occupation organized a children's lunch club, a know-your-rights session for those in temporary housing, a film screening and a bike maintenance class.[7] At the same time, Focus E15 occupied a police station in Newham, also demanding better public housing provision. July 2016 additionally saw the campaign group, Butterfields Won't Budge, hand-deliver letters of complaints to their landlord by tenants facing eviction.[8] Another form of everyday resistance could be witnessed in the online social media campaign launched by the organization Generation Rent. The group facilitated and encouraged disgruntled renters to vent their grievances online, posting details of their frustrations and unfair experiences, and sharing them through a #VentYourRent feeds on tumblr and twitter.[9] Other feeds included #RantYourRent.

The use of reputation damage as a strategy for contesting housing developments was also used by those with experiences gained through participation in earlier student movements. As we shall see in the next section, the University College London (UCL) rent strike was in part coordinated by those with experience of anti-tuition fee campaigning. In addition, however, a similar overlap of could be seen in an earlier attempt to challenge moves by UCL to develop and gentrify parts of East London. In one instance, UCL publicized its intention to redevelop the Carpenters Estate in Stratford, London. This would have involved the eviction of 700 residents from social housing, and the demolition of their homes (for a discussion, see Beach, n.d.). In response, student activists used a strategy that we might consider to be one of pre-emptive disruption in order to disincentivize contractors who were bidding to do the construction work. This eventually resulted in UCL cancelling the project, on the grounds that the estimates given by contractors had suggested that it would be too expensive to execute. As one activist explains:

> UCL announced the shortlist for the contractors [...] so we spent a day ringing up every single company on that list, and being like, "hey, you don't know what you're getting yourself into ... you're going to become an absolute pariah if you get yourself involved in this ... and if you do go ahead with it we'll be in front of the bulldozers, you don't want to get yourselves into this. And a couple of months later UCL mysteriously announced – I don't know why – that the estimates returned by all the contractors were a lot higher than they had thought they were going to be, and so the project's been called off. For me, I claim that we defeated that billion-pound plan. We definitely defeated that billion-pound plan by messing with the contractors, and the contractors were like, 'oh, we better raise our estimates for this if this is going to be such a reputational risk'.
>
> (interview with Tom Yongman UCL, Cut the Rent and
> Platform for People Affected by Mortgages (PAH)
> activist, 22 September 2016)

As we have seen, therefore, whilst the post-2008 crisis context has seen a move towards heightened forms of austerity affecting British housing, this has in turn resulted in a range of opposition movements emerging in response (for a broader survey of some of these movements see also Watt and Minton, 2016). As we shall see, this opposition also focused on targeting legislation proposed (and eventually adopted) in 2015–16.

Indeed, one especially controversial response to the post-2008 crisis, was that of the Housing and Planning Act 2016. The proposal for this legislation was introduced in October 2015, and the legislation was passed in May 2016. The background to this legislation was a growing sense of crisis in the provision of housing, especially in London. Rents were rising and in London house prices had returned to a sharp rate of growth following the crash of 2007. As we have seen, housing had begun to become increasingly politicized, with a number of anti-eviction and associated housing protests emerging throughout 2015. The proposed Housing and Planning Bill therefore represented the new Conservative Government's attempt to respond to this problem, in a form consistent with the neoliberal principles that had governed housing policy before the crisis.

The proposed legislation sought to (i) promote homeownership (with the introduction of a new Starter Homes scheme that would subsidize first-time buyers); (ii) further residualize the social housing stock (especially through the extension of the Right to Buy scheme to those in housing association homes); and (iii) increase means-testing (through the introduction of a Pay to Stay scheme and a move to replace lifetime with fixed-term tenancies) (for a detailed overview, see Barnes, 2016).

The response to the Bill saw considerable criticism and opposition. Whilst most of the proposed changes were eventually passed into legislation, a number of concessions were made, and a vibrant opposition movement to the state of housing (especially within London) was galvanized. Much of this opposition was coordinated through the Radical Housing Network, a group that had been created in 2013 in an attempt to bring together the large number of housing rights groups that had emerged across the United Kingdom in the context of increased housing problems, especially for those renting or in social housing.

The Radical Housing Network (RHN) represented an attempt to coordinate the activity of the many different local groups that were contesting what they considered a crisis of housing across London. One of the most visible forms of opposition coordinated by the RHN was a week-long occupation of an empty property in a prime location in Central London, next to Harrods in Knightsbridge, that took place in March 2016. The week-long occupation was used to coordinate protest activity, including a programme of events designed to build opposition to the Housing and Planning Bill. Events included a 'mock eviction' designed to highlight the actions of councillors who systematically ignored residents' demands, an art workshop, a meeting for trade unionists who support housing struggles, a workshop led by Sisters Uncut on the relationship between housing legislation and domestic violence, delivery of over 20,000 copies of the newsletter *Standard Evening* which highlighted London's housing crisis, and a national demonstration against the Housing Bill that was attended by around 1,000 people. In doing so, moreover, the RHN was able to increase popular and political awareness of the Bill as it passed through parliament, and thereby amplify the voice of those seeking to oppose it. In the words of one RHN participant (speaking in a personal capacity),

> From the start of the year [2016] up until March/April time there was this big spike in people campaigning around it, and there was a spike in terms of media coverage of the Bill and politicians being aware of it, because up until that stage the Bill committee knew about it but most other MPs had no idea there was even a Housing Bill going through or any idea of what was in it [...] I think the campaigning made it harder for MPs to say that they knew nothing about it. [...] I think the activism around the Bill pushed it a bit up the public agenda, in terms of media coverage, certainly in papers like the Guardian. [...] I think we made politicians more aware of it.
>
> (interview with Christine Haigh, Radical Housing Network participant, 18 August 2016)

In the wake of public opposition, the government was moved to curtail some of the more draconian aspects of the bill. For instance, in responding to the March 2016 national demonstration, government minister for housing, Brandon Lewis MP, announced the use of a taper system according to which 'Pay to Stay' would take effect. This was contrary to the government's initial plan, which was for an immediate move to market rents upon crossing the earnings threshold (Barnes, 2016). Further, many of the provisions legislated for in the Housing and Planning Act were sufficiently controversial to prompt the government to delay decision making until secondary legislation would be adopted in parliament after the Act was adopted. This led to the 'Kill the Bill' campaign, which had campaigned against the adoption of the Act, now subsequently turn into the 'Axe the Act' campaign, mobilizing against the adoption of secondary legislation and seeking concessions as the remaining parts of the legislation passed through parliament.

UCL rent strikes

The escalation of housing costs in London have also had a considerable effect upon students living in the city. As a result, a combination of both low-quality housing conditions and very high prices prompted students to launch two separate rounds of rent strikes in 2015 and 2016. In doing so, moreover, they were able to draw on a range of experiences that had been achieved as student activists and through the Radical Housing Network.

The first of these strikes began in May 2015 following the failure of the university to respond to complaints about noisy and dusty building work that had been ongoing since November 2014, as well as experiencing rodent infestation and insanitary conditions. The strikes were effective both in gaining media attention, with a series of newspaper reports highlighting the campaign, and eventually resulting in the decision of UCL Complaints Panel to award over £1,000 in compensation to each of the students who had been resident in the housing that was the subject of the complaint (having earlier offered only £132 per student). In one high point of the campaign the UCL management were made to back down from their threat to discipline students by disallowing their academic graduation, as it became clear that this would be both illegal and in breach of the university's student accommodation code (UCL, Cut the Rent, 2015; Gayle, 2015).

The success of this campaign was further built upon in the academic year 2015–16 by a group that named itself UCL, Cut the Rent (UCL-CTR) and also with the support of the Radical Housing Network. Similar to the previous year, this cohort of students found themselves with extremely high rents for remarkably poor accommodation, with the repeated sighting of cockroaches being one of the key grievances of the students. Following the success of the rent strike the previous year, a number of students who had gained experience of student activism through the earlier rent strike, as well as through participation in the tuition fee protest movement of 2010–11, and through association with what was known as the Defend Education UCL protest group (one of a number of local groups with connections to, but separate from, NCAFC), managed to make contact with a number of the resident students who were willing to launch another rent strike (interviews with UCL Cut the Rent activists, August 2016).

The rent strike was launched in January 2016 and lasted until July of that year, following a period of organization by those seeking to respond to the poor conditions of the housing, alongside its excessive price. Indeed, the role of the adverse material conditions in motivating the rent strikers was quite striking. To the extent that those who did and those who did not participate was quite directly related to the condition of the housing that the students faced. As one activist observed:

> There was a weird phenomenon whereby in one half of the building everyone was on rent strike; and in the other half there was barely anybody. [...] It turned out that the conditions were not the same in the two parts of the building. In the other side it was OK, but not in our side.
>
> (interview with Kasandra Tomaszewska, UCL Cut the Rent activist, 18 August 2016)

This, moreover, reflected the relatively non-partisan nature of the rent strike, in that it appealed to students' material grievances rather than to more ideological concerns. This was explicit in the thinking of the rent strike organizers.

> Quite a lot of us were in Def Ed (Defend Education) [...] A lot of people were saying that the student movement has a lot to gain from campaigning about housing because it's one of the most tangible things that people are pissed off about. That's why we had the success that we did and how we got so many people. If you think about mobilising 800 people, that's not easy. People need to be pissed off about something. Those 800 people won't all be political activists. They'll be liberals [...] we had someone who was in Rowing Club, we had people who were maybe Tories, so it was a lot of people, because

people were always talking about rent because the rent has gone up so much. In the last five or six years it's gone up 56 per cent here on average.

(interview with UCL Cut the Rent activist, 18 August 2016)

The strike began with just 150 students pledging to participate in the rent strike. Yet by March this number had risen to 500 students as student support for the campaign grew in a context in which student housing costs were increasingly viewed as unaffordable (UCL, Cut the Rent 2016). From what the UCL-CTR activists could glean from information coming from UCL management, moreover, it appeared that up to 1,000 students were eventually taking part in the rent strike, in part as a result of the large degree of national publicity that the campaign was attracting. What was also remarkable about the strike was that it was held by a group of students with a near universal lack of experience of student activism (the large majority of whom were at university for their first year), and being helped only by a small minority of student activists with previous experience of conducting political campaigns. Indeed, there was a pragmatic connection between those students who were unhappy with their housing conditions and wanted to act, and those students who had experience of campaigning (but were not themselves rent strikers). In the words of two of the activists involved at the time:

Mostly people needed to get to know what to do, so they needed some advice on what to do before they started doing something. [...] People wanted to do something but they didn't know what to do and wanted to ask people. And I was like, 'come on guys we can do it alone', but they were like, 'no we need to ask'.

(interview with Kasandra Tomaszewska, UCL Cut the Rent activist, 18 August 2016)

In some ways it wasn't perfect because it ended up being the more experienced people going in and canvassing people and we would run the meetings because we really wanted this [the strike] to happen, so we'd go in and facilitate the meetings.

(interview with UCL Cut the Rent activist, 18 August 2016)

As with the student tuition fees protest, the experience of UCL Cut the Rent was one in which support from the National Union of Students was minimal, prompting a degree of scepticism and criticism by UCL-CTR activists towards the NUS.

A lot of the Sabbs [sabbatical officers] weren't interested in helping us. [...] They were a bit more interested in appeasing the university rather than acting as a union. We had quite a few of those who just had no interest whatsoever. [...] Also there was so much bureaucracy that didn't really work with our structure. We wanted to get money for a demo – we couldn't get it off the union because in order to do that we had to do a full health and safety report and stewards and all this kind of thing. But some of our demos were called a week in advance, and so it just wouldn't really work that way, so we had to find the money from somewhere else.

(interview with UCL Cut the Rent activist, 18 August 2016)

As noted, one of the strengths of the campaign was its ability to harness media support. Indeed, in the views of the rent strike activists, the publicity that the rent strike received was almost entirely positive. As one activist put it, even newspapers that were routinely hostile to left wing student politics came out in support:

The rent strike didn't really get much bad publicity, which was quite a surprise – that's the thing, everyone agrees that the rent is ridiculous. There was this really funny Tab [student newspaper] article which said something like, 'Even if you're not a loony lefty activist you should still join the rent strike because rent is ridiculous; even if you're more liberal you should still join', and we didn't even ask them to write that, and we were thinking, 'is the Tab on our side!?'

(interview with UCL Cut the Rent activist, 18 August 2016)

The rent strike activists were also able to use the media skills that they had gained in earlier campaigns to their advantage in this campaign. Perhaps one of the high points of this strategy came when Andrew Grainger, director of UCL Estates, was recorded telling students that they should simply accept that 'some people just simply cannot afford to study in London […] and that is the fact of life', a quote which was subsequently reported in the national media, to the chagrin of the UCL management (see, for instance, Ali, 2016a).

The rent strike came to a head when UCL-CTR planned to do a large demonstration timed to coincide with the University Open Day. This was used as a bargaining chip as it had the potential to disrupt the operation of the university at a crucial time for its recruitment process for the following year. The final outcome saw the Cut the Rent group herald a victory, as UCL agreed to make available £350,000 for the academic year 2016/17, to fund accommodation bursaries for those students in most need of financial support, and £500,000 for the following year, as well as agreeing to freeze rent for 2016/17 (UCL, 2016; Ali, 2016b). This offer was made by UCL in an attempt to resolve the dispute and had increased during the negotiations, from a flat refusal to make any offer whatsoever, to £200,000 prior to the planned Open Day demonstration, to £350,000 the day before the demonstration. This increase, moreover, was explicitly acknowledged by the university management to be conditional upon UCL-CTR's ability to call off their demonstration (although an off-campus demonstration did go ahead nevertheless). Indeed, this threat of disruption and reputation damage considerably contributed to the ability of UCL-CTR to enter into meaningful negotiations. As one activist put it,

We sent them an ultimatum kind of thing. […] We were planning to do a big demonstration on campus on the undergraduate open day, which was towards the end of June. So we were planning for that, and telling the management that we planned to seriously disrupt it; essentially shut it down. That spurred a bit more movement in terms of negotiations. We had that hanging over us. We had quite a lot of press as well. The thing was that before the January rent strike started we did all of the little things like petitions, small actions, some marches and sit-ins and things. And so we would call for management to negotiate, but they wouldn't reply to our emails. It was only when the January rent strike launched and loads of national press was interested, and they were contacting UCL for comment, and so all of a sudden they were forced to comment and to acknowledge that it was happening. For a very long time they tried to act as if there was no rent strike. So that meant that they were put into a position where they had to negotiate with us, and so we progressed quite quickly from there.

(interview with UCL Cut the Rent activist, 18 August 2016)

In addition to the narrow goals of the rent strike, the strike activists and those with connections with the RHN also sought to extend the strategy for use in other housing-related campaigns. Indeed, this was in part successful. The UCL rent strike prompted similar actions in 2016 by students based at other universities in London, including Goldsmiths and the University of Roehampton. Further, and largely as a result of the victory at UCL in June 2016, the National Union of Students announced in September 2016 that it would be launching a national policy of rent strikes to tackle rising housing costs for students.

The development of housing struggles therefore continues in the UK context. 2015 saw a number of moves to use occupation strategies in an attempt to bring to the attention of the wider public the issue of over-priced housing and to voice related grievances in an effective manner. The RHN has sought to offer the possibility of coordinating those campaigns. The success of the UCL, Cut the Rent campaign, moreover, has further enabled a dissemination of direct action strategies that appear to have utilized the capacity for disruptive action in an attempt to ensure that housing can be contested in the post-2008 austerity context. Attempts are now being made to 'socialize' these lessons and strategies, for instance through networking and social events that seek to educate others on the use of different methods of disruption. In the words of one activist:

The idea was to demonstrate the rent strike could take place and could be successful. And that's what it's done. So then the question was, 'how can we socialise the lessons of the campaign', and so we came up with the idea of having a rent strike weekender. [...] The aim is to try and socialise the lessons of the rent strike, have a series of workshops with games in, with an introduction in which everybody is given a hypothetical scenario and then split everybody into groups designing a strategy around the issue.

(interview with Ben Beach, former UCL student occupier and activist with the RHN, 23 August 2016)

Housing, everyday precariousness and anti-eviction protests: beyond 'mortgaged lives' in the Spanish context

Housing struggles in Spain witnessed a qualitative and quantitative leap in the context of the European crisis. As we noted above, the background to this development was the crisis of the real-estate led model of accumulation that resulted in over-indebted households, evictions, social exclusion and despair amongst substantial parts of the population, as well as a large stock of empty housing and toxic assets for Spanish financial institutions. Social movements such as the PAH, we argue, were able to politicize these questions and to transform them from problems perceived as ones of individual failure into questions of social justice. To do so, these housing movements developed a sophisticated repertoire of action that was not only able to transform individual despair into collective anger, but also to generate into a social movement that was able to achieve 'little big victories' that – in the cases of those participating in the movements – acted to palliate some of the social effects of the housing crisis.

Spain experienced both the boom and the bust of the European crisis in exaggerated forms, especially in the sphere of housing. Thus, Spain's boom was real-estate led, lasting throughout the 1990s and early 2000s. This was facilitated by cheap (mortgage) credit, low inflation, rising house prices, a lack of housing alternatives (including a small private rental market and only residual social housing) and a perceived situation of employment stability for parts of the middle-classes (Colau and Alemany, 2012; Rodríguez López and López Hernández, 2011). In 2007, this upwards cycle collapsed due to a shortage in credit in the aftermath of the subprime crisis in the USA. At the same time, the car industry suffered cutbacks in production as demand decreased. Mass dismissals, business closures and the destruction of jobs in construction sectors each led to a massive increase in unemployment. In turn, austerity measures were introduced by both the PSOE and subsequent PP governments, and combined with the effect of the economic crisis to produce intensified everyday precarity, witnessing rising poverty rates and an increasing inability of many household to repay their mortgage debt (Haas and Huke, 2015; Navarro and Clua-Losada, 2012).

The effects of this development on housing were threefold. Firstly, hundreds of thousands of households lost their homes due to unrepayable mortgage debt. This wave of evictions subsequently produced a sharp increase in homelessness and housing inequality, rising rates of anxiety disorders and depression, and a number of suicides (Bolivar Munoz *et al.*, 2016; FOESSA, 2014). Secondly, the stock of empty real estate in Spain rose to 3.4 million during the crisis, increasingly concentrated in the hands of financial institutions. Thirdly, the amount of toxic credit held by Spanish banks, and especially the *cajas de ahorro* (which had relied heavily upon the mortgage sector), rose dramatically and led to an increasing instability and unsustainability of parts of the banking sector. In consequence, the *cajas* were restructured and a series of mergers and take-overs took place that significantly increased concentration within the financial sector. To restructure this debt, the Spanish state created a restructuring fund (FROB) and a bad bank

(SAREB), which took over toxic assets – not least real estate property – from over-indebted financial institutions.

The struggles against evictions were also explicitly related to the EU in various ways. The funds used to socialize the debt, especially through the FROB and SAREB, were partly guaranteed by the European Financial Stability Facility (EFSF). As part of this deal, Spain agreed to a Memorandum of Understanding that consented to further austerity measures which worsened the everyday living conditions of the population further still (Álvarez Cuevas, 2014; Charnock *et al.*, 2014: 112; Redondo Ballesteros and Rodríguez Fernández, 2014). In addition, and in more general terms, the authoritarian European system of austerity and its implementation into Spanish law had, as in other spheres of public spending, limited the scope for government spending on housing and thereby reduced the room for manoeuvre of the state in terms of the degree to which it was able to intervene in the social crisis of evictions. Further, DG Ecofin of the European Commission directly intervened against a regional decree in Andalusia that aimed at protecting certain vulnerable groups from being evicted. The decree foresaw the possibility to temporarily dispossess financial institutions, in cases where evictions are connected to a risk of social exclusion or dangers for physical and psychological health. Such a measure, stated the DG Ecofin in its evaluation of the Memorandum of Understanding, would pose a threat to investors in Spanish real estate (Huke, 2013a). In contrast to these developments, the European Court of Justice (ECJ) criticized the Spanish mortgage law for failing to sufficiently protect mortgage holders according to EU 93/13 Directive on consumers' rights and Article 47 of the European Charter of Fundamental Rights. The Spanish government reacted in turn with a number of minor revisions to the legislation, allowing households to claim the existence of an unfair term (Ley 1/2013) and thereby giving both creditors and debtors the opportunity to appeal against the judge's decision on this matter (Royal decreto-ley 11/2014), as well as establishing some protective measures for limited vulnerable groups (Royal Decreto-ley 27/2012, modified by Ley 1/2013 and Royal Decreto-ley 1/2015) (Amnesty International, 2015: 13).

The housing movements that emerged in the context of the Eurozone crisis had their roots in the pre-crisis period. Indeed, activists and organizations with roots in pre-crisis period housing movements played an important part in the creation and development of 15-M (see also, Flesher Fominaya, 2015a). Especially in Madrid, 15-M had a close connection with social centres of the post-autonomous left, such as CSOA Casablanca or Patio Maravillas. These not only housed organizations such as *Juventud Sin Futuro* and a number of working groups of 15-M, but they also played an important part in organizing neighbourhood assemblies. While the 15-M brought new activists to the social centres, the latter provided 15-M with necessary spaces within which it could carry out its activities. As was the case with anti-Bologna struggles feeding into social movements emerging during the European crisis (see Chapter 5), therefore, the experience of activists from housing movements also contributed to the form that 15-M took, oftentimes adopting methods that resembled procedures that had been in previous movements (Huke, 2016: 27; see also Romero Renau and Valera Lozano, 2016).

At a later stage in its development, moreover, 15-M acted as a catalyst for the expansion and regional extension of the housing movement in Spain. As one activist noted, 'There were other housing movements, but [...] it needed a bit, of the 15M, in order to have more' (interview with PAH activist, 14th November 2013 , authors' translation). For 15-M activists, therefore, the housing movements marked a point where:

> this part of 15-M that is academic, intellectual, very 'from the city', had real contact with the popular classes of the residential quarters. [...] There is a space in the centre where social movements are, and the harsh reality of the everyday is in the residential quarters.
>
> (interview with *Intercomisión de Vivienda* activist, 13 November 2013, authors' translation)

Many of the anti-eviction movements had particular regional identities, such as the PAH, housing assemblies of 15-M in Madrid, the housing information and meeting points (PIVE), and the occupied housing blocs in Sevilla (corralas). In addition, the so-called 'neighbourhood movement' was central to facilitating, supporting and expanding anti-eviction movements, especially for the PAH. This built on a long history of defending the right to decent housing, which was begun during the dictatorship, as well as a deep knowledge of the material conditions and social reality of each neighbourhood.

The strategy adopted by the housing movements that emerged during the crisis combined demands for a political voice (for those suffering from evictions) and material concessions (in the form of calls for a change to the mortgage law), with autonomous, prefigurative politics. This combination of methods, moreover, was oftentimes contradictory, pragmatic and at times surprising.

The PAH's organizational structure was based on local grassroots assemblies, where individual experiences with evictions and mortgage debt, as well as ways to counteract these, were shared collectively, and advice on solutions for individual cases was given from all participants:

> In general, the PAH is based on the [...] personal case of every family and every person; that is central. What happens is that then this case is collectivized, and it becomes a problem of all and not only of all but it is also a general problem; well that is the confrontation with the banks and the financial system [...]. Saying that in the end it is, to put it this way, a political problem.
>
> (interview with *Traficantes de Sueños* activist, 19 March 2014; authors' translation)

To allow for collective self-organization – and also due to limited financial funds – the PAH deliberately abstained from providing individuals with housing advice. This related to the way in which those arriving in the PAH were marked by individual feelings of guilt and shame:

> When someone affected comes to the PAH, she comes destroyed, with shame and a feeling of guilt, it is not the profile of a political subject ready to mobilise, to confront a judicial delegation and the police, to stop her eviction
>
> (Macías, 2013: 47)

However, the collective counselling of the PAH and its successes or 'little big victories' in many individual cases – including stopping evictions through acts of civil disobedience, collectively negotiating debt restructuring with the banks, and achieving social rents – were each able to make visible the fact that problems perceived as individual failures were in fact a collective, political problem, but also showed how participation in the PAH resulted in an enhanced capacity to act. In this sense, participation within the PAH was able to transform desperation and disengagement into more effective means of resource-seeking, through the adoption of activity influenced by prefigurative values:

> The platform serves as a life-saver, when you see that you are not the one guilty, you are not the only one. That [...] relieves you a bit of [...] the weight you are carrying on you.' 'There is a negotiation in that bank one day, maybe there are three or four families that have it very badly, that could be on the street in two months and they go there [...] to ask for the *dación en pago*. Then the actions start coming. [...] At the door of the bank. And that gives you power. And then leave the bank. As we leave. With the problem solved. Well, this gives power to anyone.
>
> (interview with PAH activist, 14 November 2013, authors' translation)

An additional important factor contributing to the success of the PAH was the way in which it was able to engender trust between participants. As one activist described:

> I guess working with the PAH gave me a much stronger understanding of the importance of mutual support and care and building spaces of trust and confidence and that emotional, personal support that is necessary for people to be able to take risks together. And that's what the PAH does very well. It's groups of neighbours and groups of people that are supporting one another in a very careful way. [...] It's all about that trust and support and care for one another. And I very much felt that's applicable in so many spaces.
>
> (interview with Tom Youngman, UCL, Cut the Rent and PAH activist, 22 September 2016)

The impact of prefigurative politics upon Spanish housing movements can also be witnessed in the *Obra Social* campaign of the PAH, which occupied housing blocs for evicted families that had no other possibility of housing. Indeed, the prefigurative moment became most visible in the framing of the occupations as an independent assertion of basic social rights (*autotutela de derechos*) (Macías, 2013). This took on a somewhat contradictory and unusual appearance, however, in that it was also combined with more conventional types of lobbying and political activity, displaying the pragmatic way in which prefigurative values were employed by the anti-eviction campaign (on these tensions between conventional and prefigurative, or institutional and autonomous, values, see also Flesher Fominaya, 2015b). The PAH therefore engaged in more symbolic and more traditional forms of campaigning: organizing demonstrations, symbolic occupations of banks, demonstrations in front of politicians and others deemed responsible for the housing crisis (*escraches*), as well as a widely supported petition for a referendum of the Spanish mortgage law that included the demand for a *dación en pago*, for social rents and for stopping evictions of residential property (with retroactive application). While parts of the PAH repertoire were developed in the process of action, other elements included prefigurative experiments developed in the pre-crisis period, including strategies, for community organizing in precarious everyday living situations applied in the Euromayday movement (López *et al.*, 2008; see also Suarez, 2016).

At the margins of the housing movements, people affected by evictions and housing problems developed everyday-based strategies. 'Silent occupations' (*pisos patatada*) spread as people re-occupied the homes they were evicted from or other empty residential property. In some cases, the occupiers were later on able to regularize their situation by signing cheap rental contracts with the banks owning the properties. Both housing movements and silent occupations contributed to a normalization of squatting that lost its previously acquired image of being a strategy only for the autonomous left. owners often reacted by bricking up the windows of empty flats (Huke, 2016: 54–55). We turn, below, to consider in more detail the specific case of the PAH Barcelona.

A nucleus of Spanish anti-eviction protests: the case of the PAH Barcelona

The first major event in the development of Spain's housing movement was the creation of the Platform of People Affected by Mortgages (PAH) in 2009. For many weeks, a small group of activists from V de Vivienda (an organization that had appeared during the 2000s to denounce the housing bubble and the negative impact it was having on the right to housing) met weekly in Barcelona. With the slogan '*No tendrás una casa en la puta vida*' ('You won't have a house in your fucking life'), the group organized marches and rallies in multiple Spanish cities to claim the right to decent housing, and to encourage people struggling to keep up with their mortgage repayments to attend an assembly in order to receive 'collective counselling'. For weeks, no one except the activists attended. One day, however, a man who had reached a point of no return attended the assembly. After assessing his situation, the activists travelled to his home in a residential suburb outside Barcelona and managed to stop his eviction by placing their bodies outside his front door. This use of direct action as a method of refusal was to become the start of the PAH as a real alternative. The man's housing eviction was stopped and the story rapidly spread throughout the country. Subsequent assemblies became increasingly successful in attracting people affected by mortgages.

The three initial goals of the PAH were the *dación en pago* – that is, writing off the debt in exchange for returning mortgaged properties to banks – stopping evictions of residential property, and transforming former mortgaged homes into social rental housing. The PAH also later widened their goals to focus on evictions taking place in the rental market, particularly when the houses from which people are being evicted are owned by large real estates and landowners. These anti-eviction actions each proceeded in the same non-violent but effective manner. On the one hand, PAH activists sought to negotiate with financial institutions and to exhaust all available administrative and legal remedies to guarantee the right to housing. On the other hand, activists gathered in front of homes and blocked access to prevent legal authorities and the police from executing eviction orders. Furthermore, through the *Obra Social* campaign, the PAH has helped evicted families to reoccupy their foreclosed homes, as well as occupying empty housing blocs owned by financial institutions for those that have no other possibility of housing.

> In PAH Barcelona, we started debating whether to initiate the *Obra Social* campaign or not. Some of us had previous experience in the squatting movement, and we knew how difficult it is to manage coexistence and common life. But we saw that it was necessary. So we had to find people who knew how to open a door, how to organise the occupation, how to guarantee the energy and water supply, how to address the whole legal process, etc. But that's one of the greatest things about the PAH: everyone is willing to help.
>
> (interview with PAH Barcelona activist, 18 October 2013, authors' translation)

The movement's composition is enormously heterogeneous. Apart from the initial small group of activists with experience of earlier housing movements, the social base of the PAH includes a broad range of individuals and families affected by foreclosure processes and facing eviction threats. The extent of the impact of unemployment, precariousness and austerity is such that the PAH's social base has been extraordinarily plural, involving people from a multitude of origins, ages, cultures and socioeconomic backgrounds. Many joining the PAH find themselves in a highly critical economic situation. Some are unable to fulfil basic needs and are therefore fighting for their immediate survival. As a result, the movement also experiences high levels of membership turnover and deep differences in the degree to which activists participate in the movement.

In order to overcome some of the problems associated with varying degrees of participation and high turnover, PAH Barcelona developed a complex structure composed of different assemblies, support groups and commissions, through which its everyday activity is organized. Since the PAH is thought of as a dynamic and evolving movement, moreover, its organizational structure varies in time according to its needs. This organic complexity responds to the main goal of the movement, which is to empower its members through the solidarity between affected people, the socialization of experiences, and the creation of spaces of trust and confidence based on the idea of community. In this way, affected individuals and families are not seen as passive subjects in seek of expert assistance, but active subjects who learn from each other's experiences and who are able to transmit their knowledge and abilities to people facing similar situations (Colau and Alemany, 2012). For this reason, the first space to which an affected person arrives is the Welcome Assembly. In this assembly, which meets once a week, old members of the movement answer questions related to mortgages and eviction processes to new members, and give them information about the objectives and functioning of the PAH. In the words of one of the oldest members:

> When you arrive to the PAH for the first time, you go to the assembly and you receive an incredible amount of information. Information is power, this is clear; if you're misinformed, you don't have any power. So you need to understand where you are, what happened to you, that you're not responsible for being in this situation. Only following these steps can you regain power. Step by step. But all this amount of information can be overwhelming, and people need to keep coming to the PAH.
> (interview with PAH Barcelona activist, 31 July 2013, authors' translation)

In addition, the Actions and Support Assembly meets weekly to prepare and inform members about new protest actions and to organize accompanying actions for those who are in the process of negotiating with financial institutions. On the same day as the Actions and Support Assembly meets, there is also a Coordination Assembly, which is more related to the internal organization and everyday functioning of the movement. In addition, a Mutual Help group has been formed. This is a small group in which the most vulnerable people – some of whom have suffered gender violence or have very deteriorated self-esteem – receive psychological aid in order to free them from feelings of guilt and personal failure, fear and hopelessness that paralysed them.

The PAH is also organized in Collective Bargaining groups. These are groups formed by people who have mortgages with the same financial institution. These smaller groups encourage the socialization of knowledge and experiences, and develop negotiating tools to deal with each specific bank or financial institution. The strategies developed by these groups provide affected people with emotional and technical bargaining capabilities, and combine the individual struggles of each specific PAH member with collective negotiations with the bank. The Collective Bargaining groups, together with the accompanying actions, aim to balance the highly unequal power relations between mortgage borrowers and mortgage lenders. As one activist from PAH Barcelona argued:

> one of the key moments for the movement was the creation of the Collective Bargaining groups. I mean, before that we already had this notion of collectivity, there wasn't a change of paradigm in that sense. But it changed our way of functioning because it meant that, through group pressure, we got an

interlocutor from the banks that we would have never got through individual pressure. So, on the one hand, now we can regularly negotiate with banks through a valid interlocutor. And on the other hand, it forces affected people to self-organise, to acquire some sort of collective conscience, although in some cases it's a collective conscience that only includes people who had a mortgage with the same bank. But this forces them to give priority to some cases and to say: "This family is in a worse situation than us, so let's all help them!" This also poses some challenges, such as creating a collective conscience that go beyond these specific groups, but it allowed us to achieve big agreements with the banks that implied general suspensions of evictions and general suspensions of home auctions. And this has never happened before.

(interview with PAH Barcelona activist, 10 October 2013,
authors' translation)

Although each node of the PAH has its own local grassroots assembly, these also periodically meet in what are known as the Catalan PAHs Assembly and the State-wide PAHs Assembly. The aim of these larger meetings is to agree on the general guidelines for the movement, to share experiences and to coordinate wider protest actions. In the interval between these general assemblies, and despite the existence of some thematic commissions with representatives from different local assemblies, each node works autonomously. Each local PAH also tends to develop links with other local socio-political movements and struggles. For instance, PAH Barcelona collaborates with the *Aliança contra la Pobresa Energètica* (Alliance against Energy Poverty), *Iai@flautas*, and recent strikes by the Panrico and Movistar workers.

Hence, the PAH has been struggling to use collective organizing as a means of overcoming isolation and forming a collective identity, that is, to transform a problem that is widely perceived as being a private one, into a collective, political problem. This way, individuals who had previously been overwhelmed with strong feelings of failure, guilt, loneliness and uncertainty can become agents of political transformation. This change in subjectivity has been achieved through the identification of the structural elements from the socio-economic and political system that led to the current housing emergency situation. In this sense, one of PAH's main strengths has been to provide an accurate diagnosis of the real estate and credit bubble that existed in Spain prior to 2007/8, along with an appreciation of the causes of its subsequent burst and the current housing crisis. Together with other movements, such as the 15-M or *Democracia Real Ya*, the PAH has been able to generate an alternative discourse that identifies certain financial and political institutions as those responsible for the crisis, which puts the right to housing (which is recognized in the Article 47 of the Spanish Constitution) at the centre of the political agenda, and proposes different legal and institutional ways to change.

The PAH also uses social networks and mass media to expose abusive banking practices and damage financial institutions' public image. In fact, this has proven to be an effective pressure tool during the negotiating processes with banks. With the slogan '*Este banco engaña, estafa y echa a la gente de su casa*' ('This bank deceives, scams and throws people out of their homes'), the PAH's first campaign consisted of covering bank offices with stickers in order both to draw attention to the rising number of evictions, and to put pressure on financial institutions and damage their public image. Reputation damage has also been targeted at public administrations, with actions such as temporary occupations of social services centres and local housing offices. For this reason, an activist from PAH Barcelona considers that:

> the PAH is the Achilles' heel of some political parties. Because – and this is my own opinion – the PAH is the real opposition; the PAH is acting as the real opposition to the current party in government. The PAH is the one who's made the problem visible. Because they were hiding it, it was like evictions weren't happening in Spain. I think that our green t-shirts [one of the main symbols of the movement] have a lot of power. When you arrive to a bank office wearing a normal outfit, nothing happens. But if they see four green t-shirts, this changes everything. Because we are demolishing their lies. So that's why I think the PAH is making some political parties uncomfortable.
> (interview with PAH Barcelona activist, 31 July 2013, authors' translation)

A final important aspect of the struggle carried out by the PAH is the role of women. Some of the interviewees, and female members of PAH Barcelona in particular, have expressed their view of the movement as a matriarchy because of the immense presence of women and their adoption of formal and informal leading roles (interviews with PAH Barcelona activists, 31 July 2013, 19 June 2014). In this sense, one of the indisputable leadership figures within the PAH has been Ada Colau – the movement's main spokesperson until 2014, and current Mayor of Barcelona – who has tenaciously protested against the violation of the right to housing in Spain, both through the PAH's assemblies and actions, but also in the mass media and in public institutions. Furthermore, women have been leading the majority of negotiations with financial institutions in the context of the Collective Bargaining groups, in adtition to frequently acting as assembly moderators in PAH Barcelona, and actively participating in protest actions, assemblies and commissions.

In addition to conscious efforts to foster the visibility of women in the movement, and to increase opportunities for women to adopt leading roles, there are other factors that can help explain the high level of female involvement in the PAH. A noticeable factor is the effort made to use non-sexist and gender-inclusive language. In addition, a more practical measure through which to facilitate women's participation was the creation of a variety of nursery schools and child care spaces, especially as most of the welfare and social service cuts resulting from the government's austerity programmes have subsequently created additional (unpaid) caring work for women. Furthermore, in the current context of elevated unemployment and job precariousness, and in a society still subject to a highly patriarchal organization of work, the loss of economic capacity has been perceived by many men as a personal failure and an attack on an identity that is largely based on their role as the family's providers. This psychological distress has been disconcerting and paralysing for some men, which has impelled women to take the initiative to seek practical solutions. Thus, the PAH has become a space of political socialization and struggle for working-class women, and also a space for developing social bonds and finding emotional support. An activist, and one of the PAH's founding members, explains:

> I have been an activist before, but I've never seen a social movement where there was so much participation of women. And not only of women, but also immigrants, who participate in the PAH in a similar proportion as compared to native people. The PAH, despite not having a specific discourse on racism and immigration, has been able to bring them together. All of them have joined the PAH more because of our everyday practices than because of our theories or discourses. Theory and discourse only accompany practice, not the other way around. When you generate spaces of empowerment, those who are normally excluded find a way to participate in first person. And it's not only that immigrants and women are present in the movement or have specific functions, but they participate in all levels.
> (interview with PAH Barcelona activist, 19 June 2014, authors' translation)

Conclusion

The move from a Fordist to post-Fordist period of housing policy witnessed the growing indirect influence of European integration. Welfare retrenchment, product deregulation and financial liberalization each contributed to a dual process of residualized social housing and the expansion and inflation of the private housing market. This transformation of European housing was equally accompanied by changing patterns of contestation. Whilst contestation during the Fordist period was largely based around demands to oppose rent rises and in some cases a more subterranean refusal to keep up with rental payments; during the transition to the post-Fordist period we witnessed a rise of squatters' movements throughout the 1970s, 1980s and early 1990s. These questioned individual property rights and claimed housing as a common good. Fierce repression, selective concessions and an increasingly 'identitarian' element to autonomist lifestyles, however, led to a decline and relative isolation of many of these movements. Patterns of residualization in the sphere of social housing also prompted the growth of social inequality, and racist segregation and exclusion within cities, eventually leading to a crystallization of housing problems in certain urban areas. In some cities, riots of excluded groups were witnessed as a result. At the same time, a confluence of tenants' organizations and post-autonomous parts of earlier, more radical housing movements developed and became visible in 'right to the city' movements across the EU.

The European crisis witnessed a re-emergence of the housing question as a key political issue in some countries. Over-indebtedness, evictions and the experience of crisis at the level of everyday led in turn to a rise of everyday movements for decent housing that developed an innovative political repertoire combining acts of civil disobedience, radical democratic assemblies, self-help and collective mobilization. The movements were on a case to case basis (through 'little big victories') able to relieve some of the social problems associated with housing in the context of economic crisis. Furthermore, these movement have put pressure (with varying degrees of success) on national governments to increase support for housing or withdraw cuts affecting housing, as witnessed in the campaign against the 'Bedroom Tax'. With occupations and other strategies, moreover, housing movements have been able to self-enforce and guarantee the protection of rights to housing (albeit in a partial and precarious form), thereby establishing prefigurative structures in which housing was rendered visible as a common good. In their everyday endeavours for needs-based housing policies the movements questioned governing discourses that proclaimed a lack of alternatives, claiming instead that a different approach to housing is possible.

As the case of the PAH illustrates perhaps most explicitly, the rise of what we have termed a form of 'pragmatic prefiguration' can also be seen in the sphere of housing struggles in the crisis-era considered here. In the context of 'everyday vulnerability' (Pérez Orozco, 2014), reinforced trends towards a 'descent society' (Nachtwey, 2016) and increased social polarization (Moulaert *et al.*, 2005), social movements have acted to transform individual suffering into collective demands (Espinar and Abellán, 2012: 147), partially relieving affected people of feelings of guilt and shame. Forms of community organizing, such as the collective counselling of Spanish housing movements, were thereby able to create strong feelings of solidarity and affection that paved the way for new activist subjectivities embracing a commitment to what we term (see also Bailey *et al.*, 2016).

These newly established collectives, however, not only voiced political claims but, where possible, also proceeded towards instances of 'self-enforcement' (Macías, 2013), such as 'silent' or political occupations of houses and flats and the refusal to pay mortgage debt, as well as acts of civil disobedience such as blocking evictions and squatting banks (Celikates, 2010: 280). They were therefore able to improve everyday living conditions through the pursuit and achievement of both 'little big victories' and a political empowerment of their members. Individualized experiences of disengagement, disaffection and disinterest, in contrast, in many cases resulted in frustration, anxiety and depression, prompting some to participate in more active housing movements. The effect of such movements, however, went far beyond individual cases. By showing that different housing policies are possible, and in securing popular support for their claims, many of these actions have undermined the already tarnished legitimacy of both financialized capitalism and the state (Huke, 2016). Indeed, the increasingly non-responsive and hardened institutions of both the state and the European Union have appeared either as aggressors, or as unable to assuage citizens' experience of suffering. It was through their ability to connect concrete everyday demands and struggles with the creation of alternative and radically egalitarian social relations, therefore, that housing movements in the crisis era, or so-called 'age of austerity', were able to develop a pragmatically prefigurative form of disruptive subjectivity and agency.

Notes

1 In combination with fierce repression this led to a decline of the movement in some cities following its initial success (Mayer, 2000). As Holm and Kuhn describe for the case of Berlin, a split emerged in the discussion around the legalisation of squats, between 'non-negotiators' or 'autonomists', and 'negotiators', with the latter accused by the former of giving up the political struggle and resorting to the mere preservation of their own living spaces (Holm and Kuhn, 2011: 647).

2 Indeed, the European Parliament and various NGOs with an interest in housing pushed for a Europeanization of housing policies (e.g. an inclusion of the right to housing in the Community legislation), albeit with little success (Matznetter and Stephens, 1998: 7). Cornerstones of European integration such as the SEA or the Maastricht Treaty avoided any reference to housing (Matznetter and Stephens, 1998: 9).

3 In order to avoid overstating the homogeneity of these trends, we should note that marked differences did persist across Europe with regard to mortgage instruments, the proportion of social housing, and the ownership or legal protection of tenants and mortgage debtors. We might consider this process to be one in which we see a 'layering' of older de-commodified and newer neo-liberal structures' (Kadi and Musterd, 2015: 249; Arbaci, 2007).

4 See https://southwarknotes.wordpress.com/2014/06/13/staying-put-an-anti-gentrification-handbook-for-council-estates-in-london/.

5 See https://westkengibbsgreen.wordpress.com/2016/07/21/residents-launch-peoples-plan-for-improvements-and-new-homes-without-demolition/.

6 https://www.youtube.com/watch?v=Mw3A7KcfN0k.

7 https://eastendsistersuncutoccupy.splashthat.com/; see also: http://www.huffingtonpost.co.uk/entry/sisters-uncut-occupy-council-house-in-hackney-to-fight-gentrification_uk_57838055e4b0935d4b4b2a76?edition=uk.

8 http://www.socialistparty.org.uk/articles/23185.

9 http://londonist.com/2016/04/london-renters-shame-landlords-on-social-media.

7 Trapped between authoritarian constitutionalism, pragmatic prefigurative movements and the 'Brexit'?

Disrupting neoliberal Europe

This book has sought to develop what we term a 'disruption-oriented' critical political economy of European integration. In doing so, we have sought to build upon and extend the insights of what we claim is a more prevalent 'domination-oriented' approach. European integration has oftentimes been presented within the CPE literature as a relatively smooth process in which neoliberal market integration has been imposed and rolled out across Europe, in the interests of both leading fractions of transnational European capital and of an emerging transnational political elite, acting in combination with key segments of the national political elite. Such an account, we claim, has the potential to obscure what are important and ongoing instances of social struggle, contestation, disruption and sometimes 'subterranean' dissent. European integration and its attempt to impose a neoliberal 'solution' should instead be viewed as a fragile, troubled and hard-fought development. The contestation of European integration, we hope to have shown, is part of a broader and ongoing struggle between disruptive workers and the need (but inability) for capitalist authorities to control and contain the actions and demands of those workers.

As we have argued and sought to show, European integration emerged as an important attempt to pacify and deal with the disruptive tendencies of European labour. This, however, has nevertheless prompted new forms of disruption to develop, creating an iterative relationship between European integration as a market-led method of social control, and the ongoing contestation, problematization, adaptation and intensification of that method. In developing this argument, we have done so with reference to what we argue are four key spheres in contemporary European capitalism and in which European integration has played an important role: work, welfare, education and housing. In what follows, we summarize our central argument.

European integration was initiated in the 1950s as part of a broader attempt to consolidate patterns of post-war social order through a combination of scientific management, productivism and Keynesianism. This, however, was subjected to increasingly unmanageable demands, and especially workplace and wage-based demands expressed by militant and/or organized labour. In an attempt to respond to increasingly unmanageable expressions of (especially workplace-based) dissent, from the late-1970s onwards we witnessed the adoption of a market-based governing system commonly referred to as neoliberalism. This neoliberal strategy was also advanced through, and consolidated by, a resurgence of European integration. This began in the late-1970s with the European Monetary System and was accelerated with the adoption of the Single European Act in 1986 and its project to create a single European market. The relaunch of European integration from the mid-1980s onwards, therefore, represented an attempt to deploy the market in attempt to re-stabilize European society, to impose greater market discipline, and to inject a degree of depoliticization into the European workplace.

Rather than simply nullify and neuter contestation and the disruptive capacity of labour, however, the advance of European integration as a neoliberal strategy from the 1980s onwards was both partly hampered by the opposition movements that it encountered, and prompted new forms of opposition to emerge as disruptive subjectivities developed in spheres outside of the workplace. Thus, as we have shown, the imposition of neoliberal reforms within the spheres of welfare, housing and education each brought with them associated movements of resistance despite the disorganization of many of the organized labour movements that had been a strength within the workplace in the pre-neoliberal period.

In addition, this move, from the late-1970s and especially mid-1980s onwards, towards a neoliberal strategy of European integration, brought with it a range of pathologies. Perhaps the most important of these was the creation of a debt-led bubble economy, which as we know subsequently burst in 2007–8, creating a debt crisis and associated 'age of austerity', lower levels of economic growth and subsequently a greater reliance still upon the promotion of market discipline as the means by which to deal with the fallout of that crisis.

The onset of global and more specifically European crises in 2008 and 2010 further exacerbated the tensions that had been present in the European project prior to 2008. As noted, decisions made at the EU-level increasingly resulted in a heightening of the austerity agenda, an additional reliance upon market discipline, and a constitutional consolidation of that pro-market pro-competition agenda.

A central position in the transmission of capitalist discipline in the post-2008 context was played by rating agencies, whose role was widely extended as a result of rising state debt, especially during the Eurozone crisis (Gärtner *et al.*, 2011). The agencies became a key determinant of the budget that governments would need to adhere to in order to meet interest payments, and thus implicitly the amount of revenues which remain to finance all other state expenditures (Altvater, 2011: 278). This increased scrutiny limited the scope for public spending, and represented a narrowing of the structural selectivity of the state (Offe, 2006) and an intensification of 'disciplinary neoliberalism' (Gill, 2000).

This constitutional consolidation of market discipline was further advanced by political authorities at both the national and European levels (including national governments, the European Commission, the European Central Bank, and employers' organizations such as BusinessEurope and the European Round Table of Industrialists). A system of measures was implemented that served to further lock in austerity and neoliberal competitiveness, while decreasing the possibility for democratic processes to influence policy making. Alternative actors were either side-lined or symbolically co-opted (for instance, as was seen with the trade unions in the pact on pensions in Spain). The dominant role of capital in the process of European integration was thereby extended. Measures such as the debt rules of the SGP of the EMU, that prior to the crisis had only limited effects on national governments, became binding in the crisis, especially for countries in need of European financial assistance. The Memoranda of Understanding signed by peripheral countries, the European Financial Stability Facility (EFSF), the European Financial Stabilisation Mechanism (EFSM), the European Stability Mechanism (ESM), the European Semester, the legislative 'Six-Pack' and 'Two-Pack', the agreement on a so-called 'Euro-Plus Pact', and the 'Fiscal Compact' all included different forms of conditionality that furthered the imposition of austerity and neoliberal competitiveness across the European Union. Through a combination of intervention and surveillance, this process of EU-level crisis management thereby forced national governments to pursue pro-cyclical austerity policies that tended to be counterproductive for re-establishing sustained growth. 23 of the 27 member states were subject to the SGP Excessive Deficit Procedure in the period of 2010–15. This was therefore a process of 'crisis constitutionalism' (Bieling, 2015) or 'authoritarian constitutionalism' (Oberndorfer, 2015), with an associated 'hardening' of the state apparatus (Agnoli, 2003).

As a result, Europe experienced a 'hardening' of its institutional political authorities, both at the level of its member states and within the institutions of the European Union (on the latter, see della Porta and Parks, 2016). This in turn sharpened inequalities within the European Union further still, both in terms of income inequality and heightened poverty and precarity, but also in terms of the inequality between the core and periphery of Europe. The effect has been a trend towards 'descent societies' (Nachtwey, 2016) characterized by increased 'social polarisation' (Moulaert *et al.*, 2005) and 'everyday vulnerability' (Pérez Orozco, 2014). For many households, the crisis was connected to an increasingly precarious income situation. In the context of mass dismissals, business closures, unemployment, reduced workers, and trade union rights, an increase in precarious work (especially in the form of more flexible/short-term contracts), declining collective bargaining coverage, and a chronic lack of stable employment, it became difficult to achieve a reasonable and secure standard of living through paid work. At the same time, reductions in social security cuts in pension provision each reduced potential incomes from welfare benefits. As incomes declined, the debt service of many households for mortgages and other forms of credit reached unsustainable heights. Affected households had to adapt their daily routines and life-courses to new, more precarious conditions. Some relied more heavily on private solidarity networks in order to compensate for social security losses.

The crisis thereby placed a strong strain on familial solidarity networks that, especially in the 'Latin rim' welfare models of Southern Europe, had played an important part in guaranteeing a certain degree of social security within the population. In the context of sustained unemployment, precarious working conditions, and falling revenues from social security and benefits, these networks were less and less able to offer protection. As a result standards of living became increasingly brittle for large parts of the population and social conflicts intensified. A decline in household incomes has resulted in limited access to both (mortgage-funded) private home ownership and rented housing. In Spain, for instance, the number of households depending on benefits as well as the number of households without any income have both increased. Poverty rates have increased, especially among groups already vulnerable before the crisis, including single parents, families with children, or migrants. This has led to hundreds of thousands of evictions and a corresponding increase in homelessness and housing inequality.

The decline in the scope for public spending also has had a detrimental effect upon public health and education, including declining funding, reduced staff levels and increasing precarity and workload for those who remained employed within these sectors. In addition, access to education and health has been de-universalized, for instance witnessing the exclusion of illegalized migrants in Spain. This decline in public services has most affected the poorest sections of European society, as these were the group that depended on the services the most. This, at the same time as demand for both education and health has increased.

In such a context, we argue, pre-crisis forms of disruptive agency developed in a number of important ways. Perhaps most importantly, a growing movement that had prior to the crisis developed around the principle and practice of prefiguration, and which was perhaps most closely associated with the 'anti-globalization movement', but which had been largely marginal and subcultural prior to the crisis (Scholl, 2013), was in the crisis context able to connect with those disruptive actors who were increasingly unable to find effective ways in which to express a voice or to demand material improvements in their everyday lives. This therefore prompted the emergence of what we have referred to as the 'pragmatically prefigurative' form of disruptive subjectivity associated with the period of the European crisis (see also, Bailey *et al.*, 2016).

This pragmatically prefigurative subjectivity developed out of moments of 'presentist democracy' (Lorey, 2011), engaged with 'non-standard conflicts' (Schmalz *et al.*, 2015), sometimes exercised acts of civil disobedience (Celikates, 2010: 280), and sought ways to ensure a 'self-enforcement of social rights' (Macías, 2013). This reinvention of disruption has provided strategic points of departure through which to challenge and sometimes overcome the experience of intensified domination. The hardening of the state, the intensification of capitalist discipline and the suffering of populations throughout Europe, each rendered a range of established pre-crisis strategies of disengagement, voice and refusal, either insufficient or inadequate. This is perhaps most evident if we consider the record of formal trade unions during the crisis (Vandaele, 2016). Each of these trends, therefore, have created pressures for the development of a new radicalism from below.

The pragmatically prefigurative disruptive worker displays a number of characteristics:

- disaffection and disconnection towards formal institutions of representation, alongside a practical and instrumental willingness to engage with those

institutions up to the point at which they cease to be useful, with a proclivity to switch towards more autonomous forms of cooperation if and when that looks more likely to facilitate the realization of the goals being pursued;
- a willingness to resort to principles of horizontalism, participation and direct action, either instead of or as part of an engagement with more conventional forms of political and institutional engagement and;
- the use of so-called 'connective action' methods of association more typically associated with radical actors, and/or assisted by those who had developed these skills through alternative radical experiences, as a means to gain access to voice and make demands by those who (pre-2008) had been more willing to accept the lack of voice or a position of material domination, and with this form of association oftentimes being facilitated by social media technology (on which, see especially Bennett and Segerberg 2012).

This new pragmatically prefigurative disruptive subject can be witnessed, we claim, in each of the spheres of European society that we have traced in the foregoing chapters. In the sphere of work, we have seen an increasingly precarious workforce resort to techniques of refusal that have been infused with the ideas, practices and support of prefigurative actors. In the Vestas campaign, there was a clear overlap between workers seeking to refuse their experience of redundancy, and activists who had gained many of their skills from environmental activism. This was put to use in order to challenge the decision of the firm and the government to abandon both the workers and the local community. In the Lindsey Oil Refinery case, we have seen disaffected workers move rapidly to associate outside of formal institutions of representation (trade unions) and challenge an assault on negotiated wages and conditions as well as advancing a voice for 'national workers'. In the case of the Brixton Ritzy workers' living wage campaign we see the use of innovative methods of campaigning by precarious workers, in association with the formal trade union but relying largely upon reputational damage and publicity as the means by which to win the living wage. This disruptive subjectivity is also evident in more recent wage struggles – at the time of writing, for instance, we see the living wage campaign being pursued by the Deliveroo workers, gaining a number of concessions from both the employer (which backed down over the proposed changes to pay) and the state (which insisted that the workers are entitled to the minimum wage), using the tactic of a wildcat strike, largely coordinated and advertised through social media, and facilitated by the independent trade union, IWGB. Likewise, the independent UVW union facilitated the victory of Harrods restaurant employees over the issue of tips being retained by the firm, largely based on a media strategy of reputation damage and vibrant public demonstrations.

In the sphere of welfare, we see the emergence of UK Uncut, making relatively conventional demands around the ending of tax avoidance, in an innovative direct action form, by activists who largely had a background in the radical Camp for Climate Change movement, and displaying a commitment to horizontalism and participation in a somewhat contradictory manner. Likewise, Boycott Workfare was able to see a relatively small group of individuals – some of whom had a radical background – mobilized against the government's workfare policy, using a combination of direct action techniques and publicity-focused actions, largely through social media campaigns, to both give voice to the interests of otherwise marginalized benefit claimants and also to have a significant impact upon the material impact of workfare reforms. In Spain, the cuts in welfare spawned a variety of protest movements throughout the Spanish state. These were often regional in character, and inspired by the 15-M movement, adopting parts of its repertoire of action, including radical-democratic assemblies. Workers' interests were reframed as common interests of the population. This way, they were able to overcome established dividing lines between workers, users and local neighbourhoods. In addition, they were able to rely upon broad support for welfare and especially public health and education within the Spanish population, with many of the members regarding health and education provision as key achievements of democratization after Francoism. *Yo Sí Sanidad Universal* at the same time self-enforced the right to universal healthcare in acts of civil disobedience for excluded parts of the population, such as illegalized migrants. Rather than a smooth process of neoliberal restructuring, therefore, the European crisis witnessed a politicization of welfare reform.

In education in the United Kingdom, we have seen the eruption of a vibrant student movement, in many ways born of a deep-rooted disaffection towards the formal National Union of Students (NUS) and its apparent unwillingness and inability to effectively challenge the introduction of a massive increase in tuition fees. The techniques adopted were typically those of open participation, horizontalism, and direct action; although one of the key facilitating organizations (NCAFC) also adopted a perhaps contradictory position of seeking to gain election to positions within the NUS. That is, in an attempt to gain a more effective voice and in seeking to challenge the resource implications of the tuition fee hike, NCAFC members would be simultaneously committed to direct action, horizontal and fluid decision-making structures, the formal decision-making structures of the NCAFC organization, *and* seek election within the established institutions of the NUS (of which they were highly critical). The student movement, moreover, subsequently went on to provide a number of the sources of inspiration, and key individuals, involved in other anti-austerity protests, including for instance that of UK Uncut, as well as being influential in the subsequent leftward shift of the Labour Party with the election of Jeremy Corbyn.

In Spain, the anti-austerity movement spawned the highly visible 15-M, which itself was influenced by and connected with prior struggles, including the anti-Bologna education movement and earlier housing movements. These movements had already experimented with prefigurative methods, such as assemblies and first-person politics. 15-M, in turn, spawned social movements that would go on to contest the imposition of austerity and marketization in the spheres of education, housing and welfare. This includes the *marea verde*, a name derived from green shirts, with the demand for public schools for everyone. Newly established assemblies met regularly and in a large number of schools, witnessing the active participation of education sector employees, teaching staff, and a notable (although less intense) proportion of pupils and parents. The grassroots structure of these assemblies, moreover, led to a certain unease in terms of their relationship with the major trade unions.

15-M also acted as a catalyst for the expansion and regional extension of anti-eviction movements in Spain. The strategy of these housing movements included a series of actions that combined demands for a political voice (for those suffering from evictions) and material concessions (in the form of calls for a change to the mortgage law) with autonomous, prefigurative politics in a contradictory, pragmatic and somewhat surprising way.[1] The organizational structure was based on local grassroots assemblies, where individual experiences with evictions and mortgage debt, as well as strategies to counteract these, were shared collectively and advice on solutions for individual cases was given from all participants. The collective counselling and its successes or 'little big victories' in many individual cases – such as stopping evictions with civil disobedience, collectively negotiating debt restructurings with the banks, and achieving social rents – were able not only to make visible the fact that problems perceived as individual failures were in fact a collective, political problem; but also showed how participation in housing movements resulted in an enhanced capacity to act, thereby transforming desperation and disengagement into more effective means of resource-seeking activity through the adoption of activity influenced by prefigurative values. In the United Kingdom, we have increasingly seen the adoption of a combination of direct action and horizontalist techniques in an attempt to challenge the residualization of housing – for instance, seeking to challenge the Bedroom Tax, and using occupations and social media campaigns to challenge evictions, as well as targeting the selling off of social housing, and the Housing and Planning Act 2016.

This combination of a newly emergent, pragmatically prefigurative disruptive subjectivity, alongside a hardening and unresponsive European state apparatus, has acted to consolidate the legitimacy crisis faced by the institutions of European integration. Thus, we experience an age of 'permanent strain', with decision-making processes characterized by haste, tension and anxiety across the population, alongside growing public unrest (Pavolini *et al.*, 2016: 153). This can be seen, for instance, in the rise of both formal and informal opposition movements targeting the European Union. It can also be witnessed in terms of the electoral success of Euro-cautious political parties and leaders, such as Podemos and Jeremy Corbyn. It is perhaps most evident, however, with the outcome of the so-called Brexit referendum in June 2016.

The pragmatic nature of these austerity-era movements also perhaps explains the move, by in many cases self-declared 'horizontalists', towards formal institutions of representative democracy which had earlier been dismissed as entirely unrepresentative. Indeed, what Kiersey and Vrasti have described as this 'curious twist in the tale' can arguably be seen with the success of Syriza, Podemos, Ada Colau, and Jeremy Corbyn (Kiersey and Vrasti, 2016: 88). Illustratively, several of our interviewees had experience of anti-tuition fee campaigning, participation in UK Uncut, the Vestas dispute, and campaigning for Jeremy Corbyn, and in some instances, were working in the offices of Momentum (the group created to support Jeremy Corbyn). This combination of approaches and experiences, and the way in which it appealed to some mid-point between prefigurative politics and more institutional types of politics, was also noted by anti-austerity activists adopting this institutional turn. As one activist, with experience in Climate Camp, the anti-tuition fee campaigns, the Vestas protests, UK Uncut, the Radical Housing Network, and Momentum, put it:

> Momentum and the Corbyn thing are partially a meeting point between these two ideas: classic lefty stuff and these post-Climate Camp, post-UK Uncut kind of things, and how they are playing out is not yet clear. [...] There is this moment now where people are meeting. It's interesting. That moment was happening in the Radical Housing Network as well. [...] [Another activist] was getting more and more into this horizontal thing, as people like myself were moving away from this horizontal thing and looking for a more structured thing. There's this kind of meeting point happening in the middle. [...] It makes sense as a lifestyle choice, a prefigurative existence. I quite like living in squats and sharing everything and doing one thing in the morning and doing a different thing in the evening and having a communistic kind of lifestyle. That was fine. But politically I think, you can have a more social democratic form of capitalism; it is achievable. We've had it before. Obviously, those things have their own contradictions. But maybe it's worth pushing through those contradictions, rather than just imagining the utopia.
>
> (interview with activist and Momentum volunteer,
> 23 September 2016)

Other interviewees also expressed their surprise at this institutional turn in the anti-austerity movement, and the way more formal institutions could be used to advance the anti-austerity agenda.

> If you'd told me on all those occasions that literally last week I would be sitting on a press conference panel [...] saying 'we look forward to working with the NUS' as they plug our rent strike, I wouldn't have believed you. Essentially we need to take the position that is most strategically advantageous to us at the time. For ages it was apparent that the NUS offered no effective mode of struggle that was in any way a useful use of time and resources. That composition has now changed and we've got at least an onside NEC, who ultimately hold a lot of the power [...] If you had that logistical infrastructure out of the NUS it would enable a war machine. That would be an interesting change if people figured out how to use it properly.
>
> (interview with Ben Beach, former UCL student
> occupier and activist with the RHN, 23 August 2016)

The constraining dissensus of the pre-crisis period thereby made way for open dissent, whether be in the form of riots of subalterns whose political claims were unheard (Spivak, 2008), social movements such as 15-M voicing 'They don't represent us', or in the form of a right-wing nationalist response. In order to escape popular pressures, moreover, the EU has tended to foreclose its institutional infrastructure further still, thereby compounding the problem.

This legitimacy crisis has also contributed towards the current pressures pointing towards the disintegration of the EU. Racist and right-wing populist parties and movements have been able to profit from reduced employment possibilities and the bleak prospects for the future within so-called 'native' parts of the working class. As the claim of 'British jobs for British workers' shows, in its everyday forms of disruption, labour is not necessarily connected to emancipatory demands, but may also be connected to a reassertion of the nation as the primary locus through which grievances are articulated and envisioned. We have seen the emergence of welfare chauvinism, in which distinctions are drawn between the natives that are perceived to deserve the benefits and the racialized 'others', who are portrayed as undeserving and exploiting the welfare system. Deeply rooted racism, in combination with fears of material deprivation, have contributed to new forms of hostility towards migrants and ethnic minorities. Immigrants have served as a scapegoat and been blamed for reducing working class opportunities in schools, jobs, and housing. The rise of right-wing parties throughout the EU (such as the FN in France, AfD in Germany, PiS in Poland, Fidesz and Jobbik in Hungary, and UKIP in the United Kingdom), as well as the Brexit referendum, have each been strongly influenced by nationalist anti-European sentiments (Werts *et al.*, 2013). For the EU, these processes have produced a trajectory of partial disintegration, as countries have unilaterally restructured national systems of state apparatuses in an authoritarian and nationalist way (for instance, in Hungary and Poland) or suspended European agreements (such as the guarantee for a free movement of persons within the Schengen area). Again, the Brexit vote represents further evidence of this scope for disruption by Britain's disaffected workers (Becker *et al.*, 2016). This is a form of disaffection that has been channelled into xenophobia, nationalism, and a populist conviction that it is migrants, as well as the political mainstream, that represents the cause of the current malaise.

How, then, should we expect European integration to develop and move beyond the present crisis? We consider there to be four potential trajectories. First, Europe might continue with its system of fragile government without consent, including a continuation of technocratic rule and the hardening of the European ensemble of state apparatuses. Second, we might see a reform of the EU, with concessions aimed at re-including excluded sections of the European population into the European project, along the lines of a re-emboldened Social Europe agenda. Third, there exists the possibility that an alternative European socio-economic formation be constructed from below, perhaps by the pragmatically prefigurative disruptive agents that have developed during the crisis era (whether this be supported by new left governments or not). Finally, we might see a disintegration of the European project as a result of rising right-wing populism and authoritarianism. The first of these routes (a continuation of fragile government without consent) appears unsustainable in the long-term as it will remain susceptible to constant legitimation crises and challenges to its authority. The second route (a re-emboldened Social Europe agenda) seems unlikely to come to fruition, due to the deeply enshrined neoliberal tendencies of the EU. The third route, in our view, therefore represents the necessary precondition for preventing the fourth, which is the most dismal of them all.

It is in this sense, therefore, that we must seek the flourishing of those disruptive subjectivities and agents that are able to produce a Europe reconstructed from below. Indeed, one aim, in developing our disruption-oriented critical political economy of European integration, is to contribute towards that end. The left melancholy of a CPE disconnected from social struggle not only risks obscuring the existence of an agency built upon hope, but in a context of instability, everyday suffering and the heightened risk of a nationalist *disintegration* of Europe, is also a luxury we cannot afford.

Note

1 One of the perhaps more surprising developments was the election of Ada Colau, leader of the prefigurative PAH movement, as the Mayor of Barcelona.

References

Aalbers, M. B., 2009, 'The globalization and Europeanization of mortgage markets', *International Journal of Urban and Regional Research*, 33(2): 389–410.

Aalbers, M. B., 2015, 'The Great Moderation, the Great Excess and the global housing crisis', *International Journal of Housing Policy*, 15(1): 43–60.

Aalbers, M. B., 2016, *The Financialization of Housing*, London: Routledge.

Aalbers, M. B. and Christophers, B., 2016, 'Centring housing in political economy', in M. A. Aalbers, *The Financialization of Housing*, London: Routledge.

Abels, G. and Behrens, M., 2005, 'ExpertInneninterviews in der Politikwissenschaft. Geschlechtertheoretische und politikfeldanalytische Reflexion einer Methode', in A. Bogner, B. Littig and W. Menz (eds.), *Das Experteninterview: Theorie, Methode, Anwendung*, Wiesbaden: VS Verlag für Sozialwissenschaften, pp. 173–190.

Abendroth, W., 2008, 'Europäische Integration und demokratische Legitimation', in M. Buckmiller, J. Perels and U. Schöler (eds.), *Gesammelte Schriften: Band 2*, Hannover: Offizin, pp. 205–215.

Accornero, G., 2013, 'Contentious politics and student dissent in the twilight of the Portuguese dictatorship: Analysis of a protest cycle', *Democratization*, 20(6): 1036–1055.

Adamczak, B., 2007, *gestern - morgen: Über die Einsamkeit kommunistischer Gespenster und die Rekonstruktion der Zukunft*, Münster: Unrast.

Adkins, L., 2015, Disobedient workers, the law and the making of unemployment markets. *Sociology,* doi: 10.1177/0038038515598276.

Agnoli, J., 1968, 'Die Transformation der Demokratie', in J. Agnoli and P. Brückner (eds.), *Die Transformation der Demokratie*, Frankfurt/Main: Europäische Verlagsanstalt, pp. 5–87.

Agnoli, J., 2003, 'Die Verhärtung der politischen Form. Das Kapital und die Zukunft des Faschismus Ende der liberaldemokratischen Epoche', in S. Grigat (ed.), *Transformation des Postnazismus: Der Deutsch-österreichische Weg zum Demokratischen Faschismus,* Freiburg: Ça Ira, pp. 17–26.

Albo, G., 1994, '"Competitive austerity" and the impasse of capitalist employment policy', *Socialist Register*, 30: 144–170.

Alesina, A. and Ardagna, S. 2010, Large changes in fiscal policy: Taxes versus spending, in Brown, J. (ed.), *Tax Policy and the Economy*, vol. 24, Cambridge, MA: National Bureau of Economic Research.

Ali, A., 2016a, 'UCL rent strike: Student support in fight against "social cleansing" and soaring accommodation costs increases', *Independent,* 3 March 2016. Available: http://www.independent.co.uk/student/news/ucl-rent-strike-student-support-in-figh-against-social-cleansing-and-soaring-accommodation-costs-a6907181.html.

Ali, A., 2016b, 'UCL rent strike: Students "declare victory" as 5-month long dispute is resolved', *Independent*, 5 July 2016. Available: http://www.independent.co.uk/student/student-life/accommodation/ucl-rent-strike-resolved-student-accommodation-in-london-a7120421.html.

Almendral, V. R., 2013, 'The Spanish legal framework for curbing the public debt and the deficit', *European Constitutional Law Review*, 9(2): 189–204.

Altbach, P. G., 1989, 'Perspectives on student political activism', *Comparative Education*, 25(1): 97–110.

Altbach, P. G., 2006, 'Student politics: Activism and culture', in J. J. F. Forest and P. G. Altbach (eds.), *International Handbook of Higher Education*, Dordrecht: Springer, pp. 329–346.

Altvater, E., 2011, 'From subprime farce to Greek Tragedy: The crisis dynamics of financially driven capitalism', in L. Panitch, G. Albo and V. Chibber (eds.), *Socialist Register 2012. The Crisis and the Left*, Pontypool: Merlin Press, pp. 271–287.

Álvarez Cuevas, A., 2014, *Efecto de la burbuja inmobiliaria en la Banca Española: SAREB*. Available: https://buleria.unileon.es/xmlui/bitstream/handle/10612/3715/09806495p_GADE_julio14.pdf?sequence=1.

Amaral, A. and Neave, G., 2009, 'On Bologna, weasels and creeping competence', in A. Amaral, G. Neave, C. Musselin and P. Maassen (eds.), *European Integration and the Governance of Higher Education and Research*, Dordrecht: Springer Netherlands, pp. 282–299.

Amnesty International, 2015, *Evicted rights: right to housing and mortgage evictions in Spain*. Available: https://doc.es.amnesty.org/cgi-bin/ai/BRSCGI.exe/EUR4170015-27160%20Evicted%20Rights?CMD=VEROBJ&MLKOB=34293751010.

Ancelovici, M., 2011, 'In search of lost radicalism. The hot autumn of 2010 and the transformation of labor contention in France', *French Politics, Culture & Society*, 29(3): 121–140.

Ancelovici, M., 2015, 'Crisis and contention in Europe: A political process account of anti-austerity protests', in H.-J. Trenz, C. Ruzza and V. Guiraudon (eds.), *Europe's Prolonged Crisis*, London: Palgrave Macmillan, pp. 189–209.

Anderiesen, G., 1980, 'Tanks in the streets: The growing conflict over housing in Amsterdam,' *International Journal of Urban and Regional Research*, 5: 83–95.

Anderson, G., 2008, 'Mapping academic resistance in the managerial university', *Organization*, 15(2): 251–270.

Ansell, B., 2014, 'The political economy of ownership: Housing markets and the welfare state', *American Political Science Review*, 108(2): 383–402.

Antón, J.-I. and Muñoz de Bustillo, R., 2013, *Public-private sector wage differentials in Spain. An updated picture in the midst of the great recession*. Available: http://mpra.ub.uni-muenchen.de/48986/.

Antonowicz, D., Pinheiro, R. and Smużewska, M., 2014, 'The changing role of students' representation in Poland: An historical appraisal', *Studies in Higher Education,* 39(3): 470–484.

Apeldoorn, B. v., 2002, *Transnational Capitalism and the Struggle over European Integration*, London and New York: Routledge.

Apeldoorn, B. v., 2004, 'Theorizing the transnational: A historical materialist approach', *Journal of International Relations and Development*, 7(2): 142–176.

Apeldoorn, B., 2006, 'The transnational political economy of European integration: The future of socio-economic governance in the enlarged union', in R. Stubbs and G. R. D. Underhill (eds.), *Political Economy and the Changing Global Order* (third edition), Oxford: Oxford University Press, pp. 306–16.

Apeldoorn, B., 2009, 'The contradictions of "embedded neoliberalism" and Europe's multi-level legitimacy crisis: The European project and its limits', in B. van Apeldoorn, J. Drahokoupil and L. Horn (eds.), *Contradictions and Limits of Neoliberal European Governance: From Lisbon to Lisbon*, Basingstoke: Palgrave Macmillan, pp. 21–43.

Apeldoorn, B. and Hager, S. B., 2010, 'The social purpose of new governance: Lisbon and the limits to legitimacy', *Journal of International Relations and Development*, 13: 209–238.

Apeldoorn, B., Overbeek, H. and Ryner, M., 2003, 'Theories of European integration: A critique', in A. W. Cafruny and M. Ryner (eds.), *A Ruined Fortress?: Neoliberal Hegemony and Transformation in Europe*, Lanham: Rowman & Littlefield Publishers, pp. 17–45.

Apeldoorn, B., Drahokoupil, J. and Horn, L. (eds.), 2009, *Contradictions and Limits of Neoliberal European Governance: From Lisbon to Lisbon*, Basingstoke: Palgrave Macmillan.

Arampatzi, A. and Nicholls, W. J., 2012, 'The urban roots of anti-neoliberal social movements: The case of Athens, Greece', *Environment and Planning A*, 44(11): 2591–2610.

Arbaci, S., 2007, 'Ethnic segregation, housing systems and welfare regimes in Europe', *European Journal of Housing Policy*, 7(4): 401–433.

Arditi, B., 2012, *Insurgencies don't have a plan – they are the plan. the politics of vanishing mediators of the indignados in 2011*. Available: http://bjsonline.org/wp-content/uploads/2011/12/Arditi_Insurgencies_2011_JOMEC.pdf.

Armingeon, K. and Guthmann, K., 2014, 'Democracy in crisis? The declining support for national democracy in European countries, 2007–2011', *European Journal of Political Research*, 53: 423–442.

Armstrong, K.A. and Bulmer, S.J., 1998, *The Governance of the Single European Market*, Manchester: Manchester University Press.

Aznar, J.M., 2012, *Memorias I*, Barcelona: Planeta.

Baccini, A. and De Nicolau, G., 2016, 'Academics in Italy have boycotted assessment. What has it achieved?', *Times Higher Education*, 21 April 2016. Available: https://www.timeshighereducation.com/comment/academics-in-taly-have-boycotted-assessment-what-has-it-achieved-alberto-baccini-university-of-siena-giuseppe-de-nicolao-university-of-pavia.

Bader, P., 2014, *Fruits of organizing*. Available: http://www.zeitschrift-luxemburg.de/fruits-of-organizing/.

Bailey, D. J., 2009, *The Political Economy of European Social Democracy: A Critical Realist Approach*, London: Routledge.

Bailey, D. J., 2010, 'The European rescue, recommodification, and/or reterritorialization of the (becoming-capitalist) state? Marx, Deleuze, Guattari, and the European Union', *Journal of International Relations and Development*, 13(4): 325–353.

Bailey, D. J., 2014, 'Contending the crisis: What role for extra-parliamentary British politics?', *British Politics*, 9(1): 68–92.

Bailey, D. J., 2015, 'Resistance is futile? The impact of disruptive protest in the "silver age of permanent austerity"', *Socio-Economic Review*, 13(1): 5–32.

Bailey, D. J., 2016, 'Hard Evidence: This is the age of dissent – and there's much more to come', *The Conversation*, 11 January 2016. Available: https://theconversation.com/hard-evidence-this-is-the-age-of-dissent-and-theres-much-more-to-come-52871.

Bailey, D. J., 2017, 'Obstacles to 'Social Europe', in P. Kennett and N. Lendvai (eds.), *Handbook of European Social Policy*, London: Edward Elgar.

Bailey, D. J. and Shibata, S., 2014, 'Varieties of contestation: The comparative and critical political economy of "excessive" demand', *Capital and Class*, 38(1): 239–251.

Bailey, D. J. and Shibata, S., 2017, 'Austerity and anti-austerity: The political economy of refusal in "low resistance" models of capitalism', *British Journal of Political Science*, 44(2) :460–475.

Bailey, D. J., Clua-Losada, M., Huke, N. and Ribera, O., 2016, 'Challenging the age of austerity: Disruptive agency after the global economic crisis', *Comparative European Politics*, 20(5): 725–751.

Balchin, P., 1996, *Housing Policy in Europe*, London: Routledge.

Ball, J., 2012, 'Government's work experience: What are the schemes, and do they work?', *The Guardian*, 22 February 2012. Available: http://www.theguardian.com/global/reality-check-with-polly-curtis/2012/feb/22/unemployment-work-programme-welfare.

Ball, M. and Harloe, M., 1998, 'Uncertainty in European housing markets', in M. Kleinman, W. Matznetter and M. Stephens (eds.), *European Integration and Housing Policy*, London and New York: Routledge, pp. 57–74.

Ballarino, G. and Perotti, L., 2012, 'The Bologna Process in Italy', *European Journal of Education*, 47(3): 348–363.

Ballester, R., 2012, *Los programas de garantía de rentas en España: La renta mínima de inserción catalana y sus componentes de inserción laboral*. Available: http://www.pucp.edu.pe/departamento/economia/images/documentos/DDD333.pdf.

Banks, R. F., 1969, 'The reform of British industrial relations: The Donovan Report and the Labour Government's policy proposals', *Relations industrielles/Industrial Relations*, 24(2): 333–382.

Barnard, C., 2009, '"British jobs for British workers": The Lindsey Oil Refinery Dispute and the future of local labour clauses in an integrated EU market', *Industrial Law Journal*, 38(3): 245–277.

Barnes, S., 2016, 'The Housing and Planning Act', *Inside Housing*, 19 May 2016. Available: http://www.insidehousing.co.uk/the-housing-and-planning-act/7015275.article.

Baumgarten, B., 2017, 'The children of the Carnation Revolution? Connections between Portugal's anti-austerity movement and the revolutionary period 1974/1975', *Social Movement Studies*, 16(1): 51–63.

Bayat, A., 2010, *Life as Politics: How Ordinary People Change the Middle East*, Amsterdam: Amsterdam University Press.

Beach, B., n.d., 'Debt and dispossession: Is the contemporary university an agent of gentrification?', MA dissertation. Available: https://www.academia.edu/3084945/Debt_and_Dispossession_Is_the_Contemporary_University_an_Agent_of_Gentrification.

Beattie, J., 2013, 'Local councils "exploiting" Back to Work Scheme to fill roles left empty due to coalition cuts', *Mirror*, 28 December 2013. Available: http://www.mirror.co.uk/money/jobs/local-councils-exploiting-back-work-2965041.

Becker, J., Jäger, J. and Weissenbacher, R., 2015, 'Uneven and dependent development in Europe. The crisis and its implications', in J. Jäger and E. Springler (eds.), *Asymmetric Crisis in Europe and Possible Futures: Critical Political Economy and Post-Keynesian Perspectives*, London: Routledge, pp. 81–97.

Becker, S. O., Fetzer, T. and Novy, D., 2016, 'Who voted for Brexit? A comprehensive district-level analysis', Working Paper No. 305, Centre for Competitive Advantage in the Global Economy, Department of Economics, University of Warwick.

Beckmann, M., 2006, 'Marxistische Europaforschung', in H.-J. Bieling and M. Lerch (eds.), *Theorien der europäischen Integration*, Wiesbaden: VS, Verlag für Sozialwiss., pp. 117–144.

Beckmann, M., Deppe, F. and Heinrich, M., 2006, 'In schlechter Verfassung? Ursachen und Konsequenzen der EU-Verfassungskrise', *PROKLA*, 36(3): 307–324.

Bedford, K. and Rai, S., 2010, 'Feminists theorize international political economy', *Signs*, 36(1): 1–18.

Belina, B. and Schipper, S., 2009, *Die neoliberale Stadt in der Krise?* Available: http://www.zeitschrift-marxistische-erneuerung.de/article/465.die-neoliberale-stadt-in-der-krise.html.

Bellofiore, R., 2013, 'Two or three things I know about her': Europe in the global crisis and heterodox economics', *Cambridge Journal of Economics*, 37(3): 497–512.

Bengtsson, E., 2015, 'Wage restraint in Scandinavia: During the postwar period or the neoliberal age?', *European Review of Economic History*, 19: 359–381.

Benítez, I. and Rosetti, H., 2016, *Panrico: La vaga més llarga*, Barcelona: Edicions del 1979.

Bennett, W. L. and Segerberg, A., 2011, 'Digital media and the personalization of collective action', *Information, Communication and Society*, 14(6): 770–799.

Bennett, W. L. and Segerberg, A., 2012, 'The logic of connective action: Digital media and the personalization of contentious politics', *Information, Communication and Society*, 15(5): 739–768.

Benz, T. A., 2014, 'At the intersection of urban sociology and criminology: Fear of crime and the postindustrial city', *Sociology Compass*, 8(1): 10–19.

Benz, M. and Schwenken, H., 2005, 'Jenseits von Autonomie und Kontrolle: Migration als eigensinnige praxis', *PROKLA*, 35(3): 363–378.

Bergan, S., 2015, 'The EHEA at the cross-roads. The Bologna Process and the future of higher education [Overview Paper]', in A. Curaj, L. Matei, R. Pricopie, J. Salmi and P. Scott (eds.), *The European Higher Education Area: Between Critical Reflections and Future Policies*, London: Springer, pp. 727–742.

Bernal Agudo, J. L. and Lorenzo Lacruz, J., 2012, 'La privatización de la educación pública: Una tendencia en España', *Profesorado*, 16(3): 81–109.

Berta, G., 1998, *Conflitto industriale e struttura d'impresa alla FIAT*, Bologna: Il Mulino.

Beteta Martín, Y., 2013, 'La feminización de la crisis financiera global: La regresión del estado de bienestar en España y su impacto en las políticas de igualdad y de erradicación de la violencia contra las mujeres. Nuevos retos', *Asparkía*, 24: 36–52.

Bibow, J., 2006, 'Europe's quest for monetary stability', *International Journal of Political Economy*, 35(1), pp. 24–43.

Bieler, A., 2015, 'Social Europe and the Eurozone crisis: The importance of the balance of class power in society', in A. Crespy and G. Menz (eds.), *Social Policy and the Eurocrisis: Quo Vadis Social Europe*, Basingstoke: Palgrave Macmillan, pp. 24–44.

Bieler, A. and Morton, A. D. (eds.), 2001, *Social Forces in the Making of the New Europe: The Restructuring of European Social Relations in the Global Political Economy*, Basingstoke: Palgrave.

Bieler, A. and Morton, A. D., 2004, 'A critical theory route to hegemony, world order and historical change. Neo-Gramscian perspectives in international relations', *Capital & Class*, 28(1): 85–113.

Bieler, A. and Erne, R., 2014, *Transnational solidarity? The european working class in the Eurozone crisis*. Available: http://researchrepository.ucd.ie/handle/10197/6062.

Bieling, H.-J., 2015, 'Uneven development and "European crisis constitutionalism", or the reasons for and conditions of a "passive revolution in trouble"', in J. Jäger and E. Springler (eds.), *Asymmetric Crisis in Europe and Possible Futures: Critical Political Economy and Post-Keynesian Perspectives*, London: Routledge, pp. 98–113.

Bieling, H.-J. and Buhr, D., 2015, 'Auswertung: Welten der Krise in vergleichender Perspektive', in H.-J. Bieling and D. Buhr (eds.), *Europäische Welten in der Krise:*

Arbeitsbeziehungen und Wohlfahrtsstaaten im Vergleich, Frankfurt am Main: Campus-Verl., pp. 327–52.

Bieling, H.-J. and Deppe, F., 1996, 'Gramscianismus in der internationalen politischen Ökonomie', *Das Argument*, 38(217): 729–740.

Bieling, H.-J. and Steinhilber, J., 2000, 'Hegemonic projects in the process of European integration', in H.-J. Bieling, J. Steinhilber and F. Deppe (eds.), *Dimensions of a Critical Theory of European Integration*, Marburg: FEG am Institut für Politikwissenschaft des Fachbereichs Gesellschaftswissenschaften und Philosophie der Philipps-Universität Marburg, pp. 33–58.

Bieling, H.-J. and Lux, J., 2014, 'Crisis-induced social conflicts in the European Union – trade union perspectives: The emergence of "crisis corporatism" or the failure of corporatist arrangements?', *Global Labour Journal*, 5(3): 153–175.

Bieling, H.-J., Steinhilber, J. and Deppe, F. (eds.), 2000, *Dimensions of a Critical Theory of European Integration*, Marburg: FEG am Institut für Politikwissenschaft des Fachbereichs Gesellschaftswissenschaften und Philosophie der Philipps-Universität Marburg.

Bilous, A., 1998, 'Some minimum social benefits given pre-Christmas boost', *EurWork*, 27 December 1998. Available: http://www.eurofound.europa.eu/observatories/eurwork/articles/some-minimum-social-benefits-given-pre-christmas-boost.

Blyth, M., 2002, *Great Transformations: Economic Ideas and Institutional Change in the Twentieth Century*, Cambridge: Cambridge University Press.

Bohle, D., 2006a, 'Neogramscianismus', in H.-J. Bieling and M. Lerch (eds.), *Theorien der Europäischen Integration*, Wiesbaden: VS, Verlag für Sozialwiss., pp. 197–221.

Bohle, D., 2006b, 'Neoliberal hegemony, transnational capital and the terms of the EU's eastward expansion', *Capital & Class*, 30(1): 57–86.

Böhm, S., Dinerstein, A. C. and Spicer, A., 2010, '(Im)possibilities of autonomy: Social movements in and beyond capital, the state and development', *Social Movement Studies,* 9(1): 17–32.

Bolívar Muñoz, J., Bernal Solano, M., Mateo Rodríguez, I., Daponte Codina, A., Escudero Espinosa, C., Sánchez Cantalejo, C., González Usera, I., Robles Ortega, H., Mata Martín, J. L., Fernández Santaella, M. C. and Vila Castellar, J., 2016, 'The health of adults undergoing an eviction process', *Gaceta sanitaria / S.E.S.P.A.S*, 30(1): 4–10.

Bologna, S., 2009, 'Der Operaismus: Eine Innenansicht. Von der Massenarbeit zur selbständigen Arbeit', in M. van der Linden, K.-H. Roth and M. Henninger (eds.), *Über Marx hinaus: Arbeitsgeschichte und Arbeitsbegriff in der Konfrontation mit den Globalen Arbeitsverhältnissen des 21. Jahrhunderts*, Berlin: Assoziation A, pp. 155–81.

Boltanski, L. and Chiapello, E., 2007, *The New Spirit of Capitalism*, London: Verso.

Bolton, P., 2016, 'Student loan statistics', *House of Commons Library* Number 1079, 20 January 2016. Available: http://www.parliament.uk/briefing-papers/sn01079.pdf.

Bonefeld, W., 2001, 'European Monetary Union: Ideology and class', in W. Bonefeld (ed.), *The Politics of Europe: Monetary Union and Class*, Basingstoke: Palgrave, pp. 64–106.

Bonefeld, W., 2002, 'European integration: The market, the political and class', *Capital and Class*, 77, pp. 117–142.

Bonoli, G., 1997, 'Pension politics in France: Patterns of co-operation and conflict in two recent reforms', *West European Politics*, 20(4): 111–124.

Booth, R., 2014, 'Pressure rises on Westbrook Partners to scrap New Era estate evictions plan', *The Guardian*, 1 December 2014. Available: http://www.theguardian.com/uk-news/2014/dec/01/new-era-estate-hoxton-westbrook-protest-labour-shameful.

Booth, R., 2015, 'Focus E15 housing activist arrested on suspicion of squatting', *The Guardian*, 15 April 2015.

Borosch, N., Kuhlmann, J. and Blum, S., 2016, 'Opening up opportunities and risks? Retrenchment, activation and targeting as main trends of recent welfare state reforms across Europe', in K. Schubert, P. de Villota and J. Kuhlmann (eds.), *Challenges to European Welfare Systems*, Cham: Springer, pp. 769–792.

Borrell, C., Rodríguez-Sanz, M., Bartoll, X., Malmusi, D. and Novoa, A. M., 2014, 'El sufrimiento de la población en la crisis económica del estado Español', *Salud Colectiva*, 10(1): 95–98.

Boura, S., 2012, *Who Are the Victims of the Crisis? The social impact of the crisis on youth unemployed university graduates from Greece and Spain in a European comparative analysis*. Available: http://papers.ssrn.com/sol3/papers.cfm?abstract_id=2210366.

Bousquet, M., 2008, *How the University Works: Higher Education and the Low-Wage Nation*, New York: New York University Press.

Boycott Workfare, 2011a, 'Success! Workfare conference cancelled due to protest', *Boycott Workfare*, 7 June 2011. Available: http://www.boycottworkfare.org/?p=53.

Boycott Workfare, 2011b, 'Protect your data from workfare providers', *Boycott Workfare*, 25 July 2011. Available: http://www.boycottworkfare.org/?p=101.

Boycott Workfare, 2012a, 'Temporary suspension of sanction activity on 3 of the 5 government workfare schemes', *Boycott Workfare*, 21 April 2012. Available: http://bworkfare.mayfirst.org/?p=912.

Boycott Workfare, 2012b, 'UK-wide day of action against workfare – Saturday 3rd March', *Boycott Workfare*, 8 February 2012. Available: http://www.boycottworkfare.org/?p=359.

Boycott Workfare, 2012c, 'An amazing day of action against workfare', *Boycott Workfare*, 3 March 2012. Available: http://www.boycottworkfare.org/?p=799.

Boycott Workfare, 2012d, 'Universal jobmatch: Do not sign!', *Boycott Workfare*, 20 November 2012. Available: http://www.boycottworkfare.org/?p=1766.

Boycott Workfare, 2013a, 'In 2012 you helped stem workfare. In 2013 let's win more!', *Boycott Workfare*, 2 January 2013. Available: http://www.boycottworkfare.org/?p=1934.

Boycott Workfare, 2013b, 'Workfare a quick update', *Boycott Workfare*, 15 February 2013. Available: http://www.boycottworkfare.org/?p=2035.

Boycott Workfare, 2013c, 'Sue Ryder Rolling Online Picket', *Boycott Workfare*, 25 February 2013. Available: http://www.boycottworkfare.org/?p=2121.

Boycott Workfare, 2013d, 'More success as Sue Ryder announces withdrawal from workfare!', *Boycott Workfare*, 26 February 2013. Available: http://www.boycottworkfare.org/?p=2142.

Boycott Workfare, 2013e, 'Three protesters infiltrate conference to disrupt Hoban's speech', *Boycott Workfare*, 17 May 2013. Available: http://www.boycottworkfare.org/?p=2518.

Boycott Workfare, 2013f, 'Government abandons new workfare scheme', *Boycott Workfare*, 1 June 2013. Available: http://bworkfare.mayfirst.org/?p=2593.

Boycott Workfare, 2013g, 'Take action on the charities creating hunger and homelessness', *Boycott Workfare*, 11 July 2013. Available: http://www.boycottworkfare.org/?p=2776.

Boycott Workfare, 2013h, 'Brisfest and workfare', *Boycott Workfare*, 25 September 2013. Available: http://www.boycottworkfare.org/?p=3001.

Boycott Workfare, 2013i, 'UK councils use half a million hours of workfare', *Boycott Workfare*, 28 December 2013. Available: http://www.boycottworkfare.org/?p=3107.

Boycott Workfare, 2014a, '2014: Two weeks in and already winning!', *Boycott Workfare*, 12 January 2014. Available: http://www.boycottworkfare.org/?p=3260.

Boycott Workfare, 2014b, 'Osborne's flagship sinking as voluntary sector rejects role in scheme', *Boycott Workfare*, 28 April 2014. Available: http://www.boycottworkfare.org/?p=3543.

Boycott Workfare, 2014c, 'The list of shame: Court tells DWP to reveal workfare users', *Boycott Workfare*, 23 July 2014. Available: http://www.boycottworkfare.org/?p=3680.

Boycott Workfare, 2014d, 'Big thanks to all who took part: Week of action gets results!', *Boycott Workfare*, 18 October 2014. Available: http://www.boycottworkfare.org/?p=3891.

Boycott Workfare, 2014e, 'It's working against workfare: Bulky Bob's and LAMH pull out of Community Work Placements scheme', *Boycott Workfare*, 26 November 2014. Available: http://www.boycottworkfare.org/?p=3924.

Boycott Workfare, 2015, 'Mandatory Work Activity and Community Work Placements to go! But what's coming next?', *Boycott Workfare*, 29 November 2015. Available: http://www.boycottworkfare.org/?p=4535.

Boycott Workfare, 2016a, 'Mustard Tree: from workfare exploiter to workfare refuser', *Boycott Workfare*, 19 January 2016. Available: http://www.boycottworkfare.org/?p=4556.

Boycott Workfare, 2016b, 'Another win: 4-year legal battle finally reveals workfare exploiters!', *Boycott Workfare*, 31 July 2016. Available: http://www.boycottworkfare.org/?p=6675

Brixton Blog, 2014a, 'Ritzy workers campaign for the London Living Wage', 20 January 2014. Available: http://www.brixtonblog.com/ritzy-workers-fight-london-living-wage/19452.

Brixton Blog, 2014b, 'Brixton Ritzy Cinema workers to vote over industrial action in fight for the Living Wage', 10 March 2014. Available: http://www.brixtonblog.com/brixton-ritzy-cinema-workers-vote-industrial-action-fight-living-wage/20966.

Brixton Blog, 2014c, 'Ritzy cinema closed today due to strike by staff who want to be paid London Living Wage', 11 April 2014. Available: http://www.brixtonblog.com/ritzy-cinema-closed-tpday-due-to-strike-by-staff-over-london-living-wage/21772.

Brixton Blog, 2014d, 'In Pictures: Ritzy Cinema staff strike in London Living Wage row', 11 April 2014. Available: http://www.brixtonblog.com/in-pictures-ritzy-cinema-staff-strike-in-london-living-wage-row/21792.

Brixton Blog, 2014e, 'Ritzy Pay Row: Staff to strike on Saturday after Picturehouse London Living Wage talks collapse', 4 June 2014. Available: http://www.brixtonblog.com/ritzy-pay-row-staff-to-strike-on-saturday-after-picturehouse-london-living-wage-talks-collapse/23015.

Brixton Blog, 2014f, 'Ritzy staff reject pay deal', 27 August 2014. Available: http://www.brixtonblog.com/ritzy-staff-reject-pay-deal/24286.

Brixton Blog, 2014g, 'Picturehouse plan redundancies at the Ritzy', 25 October 2014. Available: http://www.brixtonblog.com/picturehouse-announce-brutal-redundancies-at-the-ritzy/25552.

Brotherstone, T., 1992, 'Does Red Clydeside really matter any more?', in R. Duncan and A. McIvor (eds.), *Militant Workers: Labour and Class Conflict on the Clyde 1900–1950 Essays in Honour of Harry McShane, 1891–1988*, Edinburgh: John Donald Publishers, pp. 52–80.

Brown, W., 1999, 'Resisting Left Melancholy', *Boundary 2*, 26(3): 19–27.

Bruff, I., 2010, 'Germany's Agenda 2010 reforms: Passive revolution at the crossroads' *Capital and Class*, 34(3): 409–28.

Bruff, I. 2014, 'The rise of authoritarian neoliberalism', *Rethinking Marxism*, 26(1): 113–129.

Bruni, F., 2003, 'Strike against proposal to raise retirement age paralyzes Italy', *New York Times*, 25 October 2003.

Buchanan, B., 2017, 'The way we live now: Financialization and securitization', *Research in International Business and Finance*, 39: 657–1008.

Buch-Hansen, H. and Wigger, A., 2012, 'The ascendancy of neoliberal competition regulation in the European Community', in P. Nousios, H. Overbeek and A. Tsolakis (eds.), *Globalisation and European Integration: Critical Approaches to Regional Order and International Relations*, London and New York: Routledge, pp. 112–129.

Buckel, S. and Oberndorfer, L., 2009, 'Die lange Inkubationszeit des Wettbewerbs der Rechtsordnungen – Eine Genealogie der Rechtsfälle Viking/Laval/Rüffert/Luxemburg aus der Perspektive einer Materialistischen Europarechtstheorie', in A. Fischer-Lescano, F. Rödl and C. U. Schmid (eds.), *Europäische Gesellschaftsverfassung: Zur Konstitutionalisierung Sozialer Demokratie in Europa*, Baden-Baden: Nomos, pp. 277–296.

Burgmann, V., 2013, 'The Multitude and the Many-Headed Hydra: Autonomist Marxist theory and labor history', *International Labor and Working-Class History*, 3(1): 170–90.

Burnham, P., 2014, 'Depoliticisation: Economic crisis and political management', *Policy and Politics*, 42(2): 189–206.

Busch, K., Hermann, C., Hinrichs, K. and Schulten, T., 2013. *Euro Crisis, Austerity Policy and the European Social Model: How Crisis Policies in Southern Europe Threaten the EU's Social Dimension*. Available: http://library.fes.de/pdf-files/id/ipa/09656.pdf.

Buti, M., 2009, 'Foreword', in European Commission (ed.), *Economic Crisis in Europe: Causes, Consequences and Responses*, Luxembourg: Office for Official Publications of the European Communities.

Buti, M., 2011, 'Editorial', in European Commission (ed.), *European Economic Forecast – Autumn 2011*, Luxembourg: Office for Official Publications of the European Communities.

Butler, J. 2011, *Bodies in Alliance and the Politics of the Street*. Available: http://eipcp.net/transversal/1011/butler/en/print.

Butler, P., 2013, 'Bedroom tax "in chaos" after Iain Duncan Smith announces exemptions', *The Guardian*, 12 March 2013. Available: http://www.theguardian.com/society/2013/mar/12/bedroom-tax-iain-duncan-smith.

Butler, S., 2017, 'Harrods demonstrators block doorways during tips protest at store', *The Guardian*, 7 January 2017.

Caballero Klink, R., Cano, J. M., Torralbo Rodríguez, M. and Ortega, J. G., 2015, *La transformación de la universidad a la luz de las ultimas reformas*. Available: http://revistaselectronicas.ujaen.es/index.php/rej/article/view/2767/2253.

Cafruny, A. W., 2015, 'The European crisis and the rise of German power', in J. Jäger and E. Springler (eds.), *Asymetric Crisis in Europe and Possible Futures: Critical Political Economy and Post-Keynesian Perspectives*, London: Routledge, pp. 61–73.

Cafruny, A. W. and Ryner, M. (eds.), 2003, *A Ruined Fortress?: Neoliberal Hegemony and Transformation in Europe*, Lanham: Rowman & Littlefield Publishers.

Cafruny, A. W. and Ryner, J. M., 2007, *Europe at Bay: In the Shadow of US Hegemony*, Boulder: Lynne Rienner Publishers.

Cafruny, A. W. and Ryner, M., 2012, 'The global financial crisis and the European Union: The irrelevance of integration theory and the pertinence of critical political economy', in P. Nousios, H. Overbeek and A. Tsolakis (eds.), *Globalisation and European Integration: Critical Approaches to Regional Order and International Relations*, London: Routledge, pp. 32–50.

Calvo, Á., 2010, *Historia de Telefónica: 1924–1975. Primeras Décadas: Tecnología, Economía y Política*, Madrid: Ariel and Fundación Telefónica.

Calvo, K., 2013, 'Fighting for a voice: the Spanish 15-M/Indignados movement', in C. Flesher Fominaya and L. Cox (eds.), *Understanding European Movements: New Social Movements, Global Justice Struggles, Anti-austerity Protest*, London: Routledge, pp. 236–253.

Campos Lima, M. d. P. and Artiles, A. M., 2011, 'Crisis and trade union challenges in Portugal and Spain: Between general strikes and social pacts', *Transfer: European Review of Labour and Research*, 17(3): 387–402.

Candeias, M. and Völpel, E., 2014, *Plätze sichern!: ReOrganisation der Linken in der Krise: Zur Lernfähigkeit des Mosaiks in den USA, Spanien und Griechenland*, Hamburg: VSA.

Capano, G. and Piattoni, S., 2011, From Bologna to Lisbon: The political uses of the Lisbon 'script' in European higher education policy, *Journal of European Public Policy*, 18(4): 584–606

Carew, A., 1987, *Labour Under the Marshall Plan: The Politics of Productivity and the Marketing of Management Science*, Detroit: Wayne State University Press.

Carrasco Carpio, C., 2016, 'Immigration and Economic Crisis: An Analysis of the Impact in Spain, 2007–2013', *Critical Sociology*, doi: 10.1177/0896920515624746.

Castoriadis, C., 1980, *Sozialismus oder Barbarei: Analysen und Aufrufe zur Kulturrevolutionären Veränderung*, Berlin: Wagenbach.

Cattaneo, C. and Tudela, E., 2014, 'iEL Carrer Es Nostre! The Autonomous Movement in Barcelona, 1980–2012', in B. van der Steen, A. Katzeff and L. Van Hoogenhuijze (eds.), *The City is Ours: Squatting and Autonomous Movements in Europe from the 1970s to the Present*, Oakland, CA: PM Press, pp. 95–129.

Celikates, R., 2010, 'Ziviler Ungehorsam und Radikale Demokratie Konstituierende vs. Konstituierte Macht?', in T. Bedorf and K. Röttgers (eds.), *Das Politische und die Politik*, Berlin: Suhrkamp, pp. 274–300.

Cerami, A., 2010, 'The Politics of Social Security Reforms in the Czech Republic, Hungary, Poland and Slovakia', in B. Palier (ed.), *A Long Goodbye to Bismarck? The Politics of Welfare Reforms in Continental Europe*, Amsterdam: Amsterdam University Press, pp. 233–253.

Cerych, L. and Sabatier, P., 1986, *Great Expectations and Mixed Performance: The Implementation of Higher Education Reforms in Europe*, Trentham: Trentham Books.

Chalari, M., 2014, 'Greek national identity and the Greek education system in the age of austerity: How do teachers experience and understand the current situation?', 教育資料集刊, 61: 107–152.

Charnock, G., Purcell, T. and Ribera-Fumaz, R., 2014, *The Limits to Capital in Spain: Crisis and Revolt in the European South*, Basingstoke: Palgrave Macmillan.

Charnock, G., Purcell, T. F. and Ribera-Fumaz, R., 2015, 'The limits to capital in Spain: The roots of the "New Normal"', *Critique*, 43(2): 173–188.

Chen, R., Milesi-Ferretti, G. M., Tressel, T., 2013, 'External Imbalances in the Eurozone', *Economic Policy*, 28(73), pp. 101–142.

Chorley, M., 2015, 'How the Tories can shed their nasty image, by Cameron's speechwriter who wants to axe the bedroom tax and ban knighthoods for tax dodgers', *Mail Online*, 9 June 2015. Available: http://www.dailymail.co.uk/news/article-3116682/How-Tories-shed-nasty-image-Cameron-s-speechwriter-wants-axe-bedroom-tax-ban-knighthoods-tax-dodgers.html.

Christophers, B., 2013, 'A monstrous hybrid: The political economy of housing in early twenty-first century Sweden', *New Political Economy*, 18(6): 885–911.

Clifton, J., Comin, F. and Diaz Fuentes, D., 2006, 'Privatizing public enterprises in the European Union 1960–2002: Ideological, pragmatic, inevitable?', *Journal of European Public Policy*, 13(5): 736–756.

Clua-Losada, M., 2010. 'Solidarity, global restructuring and deregulation: The Liverpool Dockers' Dispute 1995–1998'. PhD thesis, University of York.

Clua-Losada, M., 2015, 'Tracing the competitiveness discourse in Spain: Social dumping in disguise?' In Bernaciak, M. (ed.), *Social Dumping: Political Catchphrase or Threat to Labour Standards?*, London: Routledge, Routledge Advances in European Politics.

Clua-Losada, M. and Horn, L., 2015, 'Labour and the Crisis in Europe', in J. Jäger and E. Springler (eds.), *Asymmetric Crisis in Europe and Possible Futures: Critical Political Economy and Post-Keynesian Perspectives*, London: Routledge, pp. 208–23.

Clua-Losada, M. and Ribera-Almandoz, O., 2017, 'Authoritarian neoliberalism and the disciplining of labour' In Tansel, C. B. (ed.), *States of Discipline. Authoritarian Neoliberalism and the Crises of Capitalism*, Lanham: Rowman & Littlefield International.

Cocks, P., 1980, 'Towards a Marxist theory of European integration', *International Organization*, 34(1): 1–40.

Cohen, S., 2006, *Ramparts of Resistance: Why Workers Lost Their Power and How to Get It Back*, London: Pluto Press.

Colau, A. and Alemany, A., 2012, *Vidas hipotecadas: De la burbuja inmobiliaria al derecho a la vivienda*, Barcelona: Cuadrilátero de libros.

Commission of the European Communities (CEC), 1988, *European Economy 36: Creation of a European Financial Area: Liberalization of Capital Movements and Financial Integration in the Community*. Available: http://ec.europa.eu/economy_finance/publications/publication7416_en.pdf.

Commission of the European Communities (CEC), 1999, *1999 Annual Report: The EU Economy at the Arrival of the Euro: Promoting Growth, Employment and Stabilty*, Brussels: CEC. Available: http://ec.europa.eu/economy_finance/publications/publication8067_en.pdf.

Commission of the European Communities (CEC), 2005, *Communication from the Commission to the Council and the European Parliament: Public finances in EMU – 2005*. Available: http://ec.europa.eu/economy_finance/publications/publication7816_en.pdf.

Communiqué of the Conference of European Ministers Responsible for Higher Education, 2009, 'The Bologna Process 2020 – The European higher education area in the new decade', Communiqué of the Conference of European Ministers Responsible for Higher Education, Leuven and Louvain-la-Neuve, 28–29 April 2009. Available: http://www.ond.vlaanderen.be/hogeronderwijs/bologna/conference/documents/leuven_louvain-la-neuve_communiqu%C3%A9_april_2009.pdf.

Corbett, A., 2009, 'Process, persistence and pragmatism: Reconstructing the creation of the European University Institute and the Erasmus Programme, 1955–1989', in A. Amaral, G. Neave, C. Musselin and P. Maassen (eds.), *European Integration and the Governance of Higher Education and Research*, Dordrecht: Springer Netherlands, pp. 59–80.

Cortese, F. and Masa, O., 2013, 'La Marea Verde o la salida democrática a la doble crisis de la educación', *El Viejo Topo*, 306–307: 61–65.

Cowell, A., 1996, 'Austerity plan for workers is approved in Germany', *New York Times*, 29 June 1996.

Cowles, M. G., 1995, 'Setting the agenda for a new Europe: The ERT and EC 1992', *Journal of Common Market Studies*, 33(4): 501–526.

Cox, R. W., 1981, 'Social Forces, States and World Orders: Beyond International Relations Theory', *Millennium*, 10(2): 126–155.

Cox, R. W., 1998, 'Soziale Kräfte, Staaten und Weltordnungen: Jenseits der Theorie Internationaler Beziehungen', in FEG (ed.), *Weltordnung und Hegemonie: Grundlagen der 'Internationalen politischen Ökonomie'*, Marburg: FEG, pp. 28–68.

Crawford, C., Crawford, R, and Jin, W., 2014, 'Estimating the public cost of student loans', IFS Report R94. Available: http://www.ifs.org.uk/comms/r94.pdf.

Crespy, A., 2016, *Welfare Markets in Europe: The Democratic Challenge of European Integration*, London: Macmillan Press.

Crouch, C., 1978, 'Preface', in C. Crouch and A. Pizzorno (eds.), *The Resurgence of Class Conflict in Western Europe Since 1968: Volume 2 Comparative Analyses*, London: Macmillan Press, pp. 9–12.

Crouch, C., 1993, *Industrial Relations and European State Traditions*, Oxford: Clarendon Press.

Crouch, C., 2008, 'What Will Follow the Demise of Privatised Keynesianism?', *The Political Quarterly*, 79(4): 476–487.

Cruces, J., Álvarez, I., Trillo, F. and Leonardi, S., 2015, 'Impact of the euro crisis on wages and collective bargaining in southern Europe – a comparison of Italy, Portugal and Spain', in G. van Gyes and T. Schulten (eds.), *Wage Bargaining under the New European Economic Governance: Alternative Strategies for Inclusive Growth*, Brussels: European Trade Union Institute ETUI, pp. 93–138.

Cuninghame, P.G., 2002, *'Autonomia:* A Movement of Refusal – Social Movements and Social Conflict in Italy in the 1970s'. Unpublished PhD thesis, Middlesex University.

Cuinghame, P. G., 2007, '"A Laughter That Will Bury You All": Irony as Protest and Language as Struggle in the Italian 1977 Movement', *International Review of Social History*, 12(1): 153–168.

d'Ancona, M., 2013, *In It Together: The Inside Story of the Coalition Government*, London: Penguin.

Daniel, C., 1998, 'Widespread protests by unemployed people: towards a new form of social movement?', *EurWork*. Available: http://www.eurofound.europa.eu/observatories/eurwork/articles/widespread-protests-by-unemployed-people-towards-a-new-form-of-social-movement.

Darlington, R., 2008, *Syndicalism and the Transition to Communism: An International Comparative Analysis*, Aldershot: Ashgate.

Davis, M., 2009, *Comrade or Brother? A History of the British Labour Movement* (second edition), London: Pluto Press.

de la Dehesa, G., 2006, *Europe at the Crossroads: Will the EU Ever Be Able to Compete with the United States as an Economic Power?*, New York: McGraw-Hill.

de Wit, H., 2006, 'European Integration in Higher Education: The Bologna Process Towards a European Higher Education Area', in J. J. F. Forest and P. G. Altbach (eds.), *International Handbook of Higher Education*, Dordrecht: Springer, pp. 461–482.

Dean, J., 2012, 'Occupy Wall Street: after the anarchist moment', in L. Panitch, G. Albo and V. Chibber (eds.), *Socialist register 2013. The question of strategy*, Pontypool: Merlin Press, pp. 52–62.

Della Porta, D. and Parks, L., 2016, 'Social movements, the European crisis, and EU political opportunities', *Comparative European Politics*, 1–18.

Demirović, A., 2012, *Mut zum Ungehorsam. Eröffnung.* Available: http://www.youtube. com/watch?feature=player_embedded&v=JEqYy8CyJ8o.

Deppe, F. (ed.), 1976, *Arbeiterbewegung und westeuropäische Integration*, Köln: Pahl-Rugenstein.

Deppe, F., 1993, 'Von der 'Europhorie' zur Erosion – Anmerkungen zur Post-Maastricht-Krise der EG', in F. Deppe and M. Felder (eds.), *Zur Post-Maastricht-Krise der Europäischen Gemeinschaft (EG)*, Marburg, pp. 7–62.

Deppe, F., 2001, 'Zur Post-Maastricht-Krise der Europäischen Union', in R. Kirt (ed.), *Die Europäische Union und ihre Krisen*, Baden-Baden: Nomos, pp. 205–216.

Deppe, F., 2008, 'Krise der Demokratie – auf dem Weg zu einem autoritären Kapitalismus?', in F. Deppe, H. Schmitthenner and H.-J. Urban (eds.), *Notstand der Demokratie: Auf dem Weg in einen autoritären Kapitalismus?*, Hamburg: VSA, pp. 10–45.

Dewilde, C. and De Decker, P., 2016, 'Changing Inequalities in Housing Outcomes across Western Europe', *Housing, Theory and Society*, 33(2): 121–61.

Di Paola, P., 2009, 'Biennio Rosso, 1919–1920', in I. Ness (ed.), *The International Encyclopedia of Revolution and Protest: 1500 to the Present*, Oxford: Blackwell Publishing, pp. 384–387.

Diagonal, 2013a, '¿Pero cómo se hace eso de "unir todas las mareas"?', *Diagonal*, 5 February 2013.

Diagonal, 2013b, 'Cuenta atrás para el primer gran pulso entre la PAH y el banco malo', *Diagonal*, 15 October 2013.

Diagonal, 2013c, 'Estrasburgo aplaza el desalojo del bloque del banco malo en Salt', *Diagonal*, 16 October 2013.

Diagonal, 2013d, 'La universidad en Madrid sube un 65% en dos años', *Diagonal*, 13 August 2013.

Diagonal, 2013e, 'Salarios congelados para lo público en los Presupuestos de 2014', *Diagonal*, 17 October 2013.

Diagonal, 2013f, 'Se expande la pobreza, crece el apoyo mutuo', *Diagonal*, 29 October.

Díez Gutiérrez, E. J., 2013, 'La gran involución educativa', *Papeles de Relaciones Ecosociales y Cambio Global*, 123: 73–84.

Dinerstein, A. C., 2014a, *The Politics of Autonomy in Latin America: The Art of Organising Hope*, Basingstoke: Palgrave.

Dinerstein, A. C., 2014b, 'Too bad for the facts: Confronting value with hope (Notes on the Argentine Uprising of 2001), *South Atlantic Quarterly*, 113(2): 367–78.

Dokko, J., Doyle, B. M., Kiley, M. T., Kim, J., Sherlund, S., Sim, J. and Van Den Heuvel, S., 2011, 'Monetary policy and the global housing bubble', *Economic Policy*, 26(66): 237–287.

Dokos, T., Poli, E., Rosselli, C., i Lecha, E.S. and Tocci, N., 2013, *Eurocriticism: The Eurozone Crisis and Anti-Establishment Groups in Southern Europe.* Available: http:// www.eliamep.gr/wp-content/uploads/2013/09/iai.pdf.

Dörre, K., 2011, 'Funktionswandel der Gewerkschaften. Von der intermediären zur fraktalen Organisation', in T. Haipeter and K. Dörre (eds.), *Gewerkschaftliche Modernisierung*,Wiesbaden: VS Verlag für Sozialwissenschaften / Springer Fachmedien Wiesbaden GmbH, Wiesbaden, pp. 267–301.

Drainville, A. C., 1994, *International Political Economy in the Age of Open Marxism.* Available: http://www.fss.ulaval.ca/cms/upload/soc/fichiers/drainville__marxisme.pdf.

Dribbusch, H., 2011, 'Organisieren am Konflikt: Zum Verhältnis von Streik und Mitgliederentwicklung', in T. Haipeter and K. Dörre (eds.), *Gewerkschaftliche*

Modernisierung, Wiesbaden: VS Verlag für Sozialwissenschaften/Springer Fachmedien Wiesbaden GmbH, Wiesbaden, pp. 231–263.

Dubois, P., 1978, 'New Forms of Industrial Conflict', in C. Crouch and A. Pizzorno (eds.), *The Resurgence of Class Conflict in Western Europe Since 1968: Volume 2 Comparative Analyses*, London: Macmillan Press, pp. 1–34.

Dudman, J., 2015, 'Public service staff face four more years of pay pain', *The Guardian*, 8 July 2015. Available: https://www.theguardian.com/public-leaders-network/2015/jul/08/pay-cap-public-servants-budget-2015.

Dukelow, F., 2016, '"Pushing against an open door": Reinforcing the neo-liberal policy paradigm in Ireland and the impact of EU intrusion', in C. de La Porte and E. Heins (eds.), *The Sovereign Debt Crisis, the EU and Welfare State Reform*, London: Palgrave Macmillan UK, pp. 69–93.

Dullien, S. and Guerot, U., 2012, 'The long shadow of ordoliberalism: Germany's approach to the Euro crisis', European Council on Foreign Relations, Policy Brief. Available: http://www.ecfr.eu/page/-/ECFR49_GERMANY_BRIEF_AW.pdf.

Durand, C. and Keucheyan, R., 2015, 'Financial hegemony and the unachieved European state', *Competition and Change*, 19(2): 129–144.

DWP (Department for Work and Pensions), 2012, 'Employment Minister makes statement on A4e', DWP Press Release, 15 May 2012. Available: https://www.gov.uk/government/news/employment-minister-makes-statement-on-a4e.

Dyer-Witheford, N., 1999, *Cyber-Marx: Cycles and Circuits of Struggle in High-Technology Capitalism*, Chicago, IL: University of Illinois Press.

Egan, M. P., 2015, *Single Markets: Economic Integration in Europe and the United States*, Oxford: Oxford University Press.

Eichengreen, B., 1995, 'The European payments union: An efficient mechanism for rebuilding Europe's trade?', in B. Eichengreen (ed.), *Europe's Post-War Recovery*, Cambridge: Cambridge University Press.

Eichengreen, B., 2007, *The European Economy Since 1945: Coordinated Capitalism and Beyond*, Princeton, NJ: Princeton University Press.

Eisler, J., 1998, 'March 1968 in Poland', in C. Fink, P. Gassert and D. Junker (eds.), *1968: The World Transformed*, Cambridge: Cambridge University Press, pp. 237–252.

El País, 2013a, '1,1 millones de alumnos pierden en un solo curso las ayudas de libros | Sociedad | EL PAÍS', *El País*, 9 November 2013.

El País, 2013b, 'La Formación Profesional es incapaz de asumir la avalancha de estudiantes', *El País*, 9 November 2013.

elboletin.com, 2013, 'Los sindicatos piden a los profesores madrileños que lleven a los tribunales sus contratos por días', *elboletin.com*, 11 September 2013.

Elia, P. and Stone, D., 2016, 'The low paid workers taking on big business to fight for better conditions', *Politics.co.uk*, 8 August 2016. Available: http://www.politics.co.uk/comment-analysis/2016/08/08/low-paid-workers-fight-for-better-conditions.

Elsner, W. and Haeckel, E. (eds.), 1973, *Kritik der Jungen Linken an Europa*, Bonn: Europa-Union Verlag.

Emms, P., 1990, *Social Housing: A European Dilemma?*, Bristol: School for Advanced Urban Studies.

Erne, R., 2015, 'European Economic Governance. Auf dem Weg zu einer erzwungenen Integration nationaler Arbeitsbeziehungen?', in S. Pernicka (ed.), *Horizontale Europäisierung im Feld der Arbeitsbeziehungen*, Wiesbaden: Springer VS, pp. 183–200.

Espinar, R. and Abellán, J., 2012, '"Lo llaman democracia y no lo es". Eine demokratie-theoretische Annäherung an die Bewegung des 15. Mai', *PROKLA*, 42(1): 135–149.

Esping-Andersen, G., 1990) *The Three Worlds of Welfare Capitalism*, Princeton, NJ: Princeton University Press.

Esposito, C., 1995, 'Influencing aid recipients: Marshall Plan lessons for contemporary aid donors', in B. Eichengreen (ed.), *Europe's Post-war Recovery*, Cambridge: Cambridge University Press.

Esser, J., Görg, C. and Hirsch, J., 1994, 'Von den "Krisen der Regulation" zum "radikalen Reformismus"', in J. Esser, C. Görg and J. Hirsch (eds.), *Politik, Institutionen und Staat: Zur Kritik der Regulationstheorie*, Hamburg: VSA-Verlag, pp. 213–235.

euobserver.com, 2013, 'EU Bailouts: Misery for Old people, Children, Single Mothers', *euobserver.com*, 14 February 2013.

European Commission, 2010, *European Economic Forecast – Autumn 2010*, Luxembourg: Office for Official Publications of the European Communities.

European Commission, 2011, *European Economic Forecast – Autumn 2011*, Luxembourg: Office for Official Publications of the European Communities.

European Commission, 2012, *European Economic Forecast – Autumn 2011*, Luxembourg: Office for Official Publications of the European Communities.

European Commission, 2016, *European Economic Forecast – Winter 2016*, Luxembourg: Office for Official Publications of the European Communities.

European Council, 2011, 'Conclusions of the European Council, 24/25 March 2011', EUCO, 10 January 2011. Available: http://www.consilium.europa.eu/uedocs/cms_data/docs/pressdata/en/ec/120296.pdf.

Ezrow, L. and Hellwig, T., 2014, 'Responding to voters or responding to markets? Political parties and public opinion in an era of globalization', *International Studies Quarterly*, 58: 816–827.

Featherstone, D., 2015, 'Thinking the crisis politically: Lineages of resistance to neo-liberalism and the politics of the present conjuncture', *Space and Polity*, 19(1): 12–30.

Federici, S., 2004, *Caliban and the Witch*, New York: Autonomedia.

Federici, S., 2012, *Revolution at Point Zero: Housework, Reproduction, and Feminist Struggle*, Oakland, CA: PM Press.

Feigenbaum, A. and Iqani, M., 2013, 'Quality after the cuts? Higher education practitioners' accounts of systemic challenges to teaching quality in times of "austerity"', *Journal of Further and Higher Education*, 39(1): 46–66.

Fejes, A., 2008, 'European citizens under construction: The Bologna process analysed from a governmentality perspective', *Educational Philosophy and Theory*, 40(4): 515–530.

Fernández, J., 2012, 'The new wave of student mobilizations in Europe explained as a Fordist-Postfordist transition', in B. Tejerina and I. Perugorria (eds.), *From Social to Political: New Forms of Mobilization and Democratization*. Conference proceedings, 9–10 February 2012, University of the Basque Country, Bilbao, Spain.

Fernandez, R. and Aalbers, M. B., 2016, 'Financialization and housing: Between globalization and varieties of capitalism', *Competition and Change*, 20(2), 71–88.

Fernández Rodriguez, C. J., Ibáñez Rojo, R. and Martinez Lucio, M., 2016, 'Austerity and collective bargaining in Spain: The political and dysfunctional nature of neoliberal deregulation', *European Journal of Industrial Relations* (Online first): 1–14.

Ferrera, M., 2009, 'The JCMS annual lecture. National welfare states and European integration: In search of a "virtuous nesting"', *JCMS: Journal of Common Market Studies*, 47(2): 219–233.

Fields, A. B., 1989, 'France', in P. G. Altbach (ed.), *Student Political Activism: An International Reference Handbook*, New York: Greenwood Press, pp. 223–236.

Finchett-Maddock, L., 2014, 'Squatting in London: Squatters' rights and legal movment(s)', in B. van der Steen, A. Katzeff and L. Van Hoogenhuijze (eds.), *The City is Ours: Squatting and Autonomous Movements in Europe from the 1970s to the Present*, Oakland, CA: PM Press, pp. 207–231.

Flassbeck, H. and Lapavitsas, C., 2015, *Against the Troika: Crisis and Austerity in the Eurozone*, London: Verso.

Flesher Fominaya, C., 2015a, 'Debunking spontaneity: Spain's 15-M/Indignados as autonomous movement', *Social Movement Studies*, 14(2): 142–163.

Flesher Fominaya, C. 2015b, 'Redefining the crisis/redefining democracy: Mobilising for the right to housing in Spain's PAH movement,' *South European Society and Politics*, 20(4): 465–485.

Flick, U., 2011, *Qualitative Sozialforschung: Eine Einführung*, Reinbek bei Hamburg: Rowohlt-Taschenbuch-Verl.

Flora, P. (ed.), 1987, *Growth to Limits: The Western European Welfare States Since World War II*, Berlin: de Gruyter.

Flores, M. A. and Ferreira, F. I., 2016, 'Education and child poverty in times of austerity in Portugal: Implications for teachers and teacher education', *Journal of Education for Teaching*, 42(4): 404–416.

FOESSA, 2014, *VII Informe Sobre Exclusión y Desarrollo Social en España*, Madrid: Fundación FOESSA; Cáritas Española Editores.

Fraser, N., 2013, *The Fortunes of Feminism: From State-Managed Capitalism to Neoliberal Crisis*, London: Verso.

Fraser, A., 2015, *Urban Legends: Gang Identity in the Post-Industrial City*, Oxford: Oxford University Press.

Fundación Secretariado Gitano, 2013, *El Impacto de la Crisis y las Medidas de Austeridad en la Situación de la Comunidad Gitana en España*. Available: http://www.gitanos.org/upload/09/50/el_impacto_de_la_crisis_en_la_comunidad_gitana.pdf.

Gärtner, M., Griesbach, B. and Jung, F., 2011, 'PIGS or Lambs? The European Sovereign Debt Crisis and the Role of Rating Agencies', *International Advances in Economic Research,* 17(3): 288–299.

Gago, A., 2013, *Los sindicatos mayoritarios españoles, CCOO y UGT, ante la crisis económica: ¿declive o revitalización?* Available: http://revistes.ub.edu/index.php/ACS/article/download/6359/8115.

Galera Victoria, A., 2013, 'La Ley Orgánica de estabilidad presupuestaria y sostenibilidad financiera. La exigencia de estabilidad presupuestaria del sector público', *Revista de Derecho Político*, (86): 255–80.

Gall, G., 1995, 'The emergence of a rank and file movement: The Comitati di Base in the Italian Workers' Movement', *Capital and Class*, 19(1): 9–20.

Gall, G., 2011, 'Contemporary workplace occupations in Britain', *Employee Relations*, 33(6): 607–623.

Gall, G., 2012, 'Quiescence continued? Recent strike activity in nine Western European economies', *Economic and Industrial Democracy*, 34(4): 667–691.

Gallo, P. and Gené-Badia, J., 2013, 'Cuts drive health system reforms in Spain', *Health Policy*, 113(1–2): 1–7.

Gayle, D., 2015, 'University College London students withhold rent over building works; UCL offers £132 in compensation to students at Hawkridge House and Campbell House, amid protests that building work has prevented them from studying', *The Guardian*, 11 June 2015.

Geary, D., 1981, *European Labour Protest 1848–1939*, London: Croom Helm.

Georgi, F. and Kannankulam, J., 2012, Das Staatsprojekt Europa in der Krise. Available: http://rosalux-europa.info/userfiles/file/Staatsprojekt-Europa-Okt-2012.pdf.

Genovese, F., Schneider, G. and Wassmann, P., 2016, 'The Eurotower strikes back. crises, adjustments, and Europes austerity protests', *Comparative Political Studies*, 49(7): 939–967.

Georgel, J., 1972, *El Franquismo. Historia y Balance 1939–1969*, Ruedo Ibérico: Paris.

Gibson-Graham, J. K., 2006, *A Postcapitalist Politics*, Minneapolis, MN: University of Minnesota Press.

Gili, M., Roca, M., Basu, S., McKee, M. and Stuckler, D., 2013, 'The mental health risks of economic crisis in Spain: evidence from primary care centres, 2006 and 2010', *The European Journal of Public Health*, 23(1): 103–108.

Gill, S., 1992, *The Emerging World Order and European Change: The Political Economy of European Union*. Available: http://socialistregister.com/index.php/srv/article/view/5613/2511.

Gill, S., 1997, 'An emu or an ostrich? EMU and neo-liberal globalisation; limits and alternatives', in P. Minkkinen and H. Patomäki (eds.), *The Politics of Economic and Monetary Union*, Helsinki: UPI, pp. 205–229.

Gill, S., 1998, 'European governance and new constitutionalism: Economic and Monetary Union and alternatives to disciplinary Neoliberalism in Europe', *New Political Economy*, 3(1): 5–26.

Gill, S., 2000, 'Theoretische Grundlagen einer neo-gramscianischen Analyse der europäischen Integration', in H.-J. Bieling and J. Steinhilber (eds.), *Die Konfiguration Europas: Dimensionen einer kritischen Integrationstheorie*, Münster: Westfälisches Dampfboot, pp. 23–50.

Gill, S., 2001, 'Constitutionalising capital: EMU and disciplinary neo-liberalism', in A. Bieler and A.D. Morton (eds.), *Social Forces in the Making of the New Europe: The Restructuring of European Social Relations in the Global Political Economy*, Basingstoke: Palgrave, pp. 47–69.

Gill, S., 2002, 'Constitutionalizing Inequality and the Clash of Globalizations', *International Studies Review*, 4(2): 47–65.

Gill, S., 2003, 'A neo-Gramscian approach to European integration', in A.W. Cafruny and M. Ryner (eds.), *A Ruined Fortress? Neoliberal Hegemony and Transformation in Europe*, Oxford: Rowman and Littlefield, pp. 47–70.

Gill, S. and Cutler, A. C., 2014, 'New constitutionalism and world order: General introduction', in S. Gill and A.C. Cutler (eds.), *New Constitutionalism and World Order*, Cambridge: Cambridge University Press, pp. 1–22.

Glasgow Labour History Workshop, 1992, 'Roots of Red Clydeside: The Labour Unrest in West Scotland, 1910–14', in R. Duncan and A. McIvor (eds.), *Militant Workers: Labour and Class Conflict on the Clyde 1900–1950 (Essays in Honour of Harry McShane, 1891–1988)*, Edinburgh: John Donald Publishers, pp. 81–105.

Glasper, A., 2016, 'Funding nurse education in a climate of austerity', *British Journal of Nursing*, 25(1): 64–65.

Glyn, A., 2006, *Capitalism Unleashed: Finance, Globalization and Welfare*, Oxford: Oxford University Press.

Glyn A. and Sutcliffe, B., 1972, *British Capitalism, Workers and the Profits Squeeze*, Harmondsworth: Penguin.

Goldhammer, A., 2013, 'Interests and collective action'. In Cole, A., Meunier, S. and Tiberj, V. (eds.), *Developments in French Politics 5*, Basingstoke: Palgrave, pp. 136–152.

Gracia García, J., Ruiz Carnicer, Miguel Angel, 2001, *La España de Franco, 1939–1975*, Madrid: Editorial Síntesis.

Graeber, D., 2009, *Direct Action: An Ethnography*, London: AK Press.

Green, J & Lavery, S, 2015, 'The regressive recovery: distribution, inequality and state power in Britain's post-crisis political economy'. *New Political Economy*, 20: 894–923.

Guajardo, J., Leigh, D. and Pescatori, A., 2011, 'Expansionary austerity: New international evidence', IMF Working Paper WP/11/158.

Guillén, A., 2010, 'Defrosting the Spanish Welfare State: The Weight of Conservative Components', in B. Palier (ed.), *A Long Goodbye to Bismarck? The Politics of Welfare Reforms in Continental Europe*, Amsterdam: Amsterdam University Press, pp. 183–206.

Gumbrell-McCormick, R. and Hyman, R., 2013, *Trade Unions in Western Europe: Hard Times, Hard Choices*, Oxford: Oxford University Press.

Gumbrell-McCormick, R. and Hyman, R., 2015, *International Trade Union Solidarity and the Impact of the Crisis*. Available: http://www.sieps.se/sites/default/files/2015_1epa%20eng%20A4%20korr7.pdf.

Haas, T. and Huke, N., 2015, 'Spanien – "Sie wollen mit allem Schluss machen"'; in H.-J. Bieling, D. Buhr (eds.), *Europäische Welten in der Krise: Arbeitsbeziehungen und Wohlfahrtsstaaten im Vergleich*. Frankfurt am Main: Campus-Verl., pp. 165–190.

Hansen, H. F., 2011, 'University reforms in Denmark and the challenges for political science', *European Political Science*, 10(2): 235–247.

Hardman, I., 2015, 'David Cameron wants to 'detoxify' the Tories. Shame about their slapdash policymaking, then', *Independent,* 19 May 2015. Available: http://www.independent.co.uk/voices/comment/cameron-wants-to-detoxify-the-tories-shame-about-their-slapdash-policymaking-then-10261862.html.

Hardt, M. and Negri, A., 1994, *Labor of Dionysus: A Critique of the State-Form*, Minneapolis, MN: University of Minnesota Press.

Hardt, M. and Negri, A., 2000, *Empire*, Cambridge, MA: Harvard University Press.

Hardt, M. and Negri, A., 2005, *Multitude: War and Democracy in the Age of Empire*, London: Penguin.

Hardt, M. and Negri, A., 2011, *Commonwealth*, Cambridge, MA: Belknap Press of Harvard University Press.

Harloe, M., 1995, *The People's Home? Social Rented Housing in Europe and America*, London: Blackwell.

Harmsen, R., 2015, 'Future scenarios for the European higher education area: Exploring the possibilities of "experimentalist governance"', in A. Curaj, L. Matei, R. Pricopie, J. Salmi and P. Scott (eds.), *The European Higher Education Area: Between Critical Reflections and Future Policies*, London: Springer, pp. 785–803.

Harvey, D., 2005, *A Brief History of Neoliberalism*, Oxford, Oxford University Press.

Hatton, T. and Boyer, G., 2005, 'Unemployment and the UK labour market before, during and after the golden age', *European Review of Economic History*, 9: 35–60.

Hay, C., 2000, 'Contemporary capitalism, globalization, regionalization and the persistence of national variation', *Review of International Studies*, 26: 509–531.

Hayes, G., 2017, 'Regimes of austerity', *Social Movement Studies*, 16(1): 21–35.

Heinrich, M., 2015, 'EU governance in crisis: A cultural political economy perspective on European crisis management 2007–2014', *Comparative European Politics*, 13(6): 682–706.

Heins, E. and La Porte, C. de, 2016, 'Depleted European social models following the crisis: Towards a brighter future?', in C. de La Porte and E. Heins (eds.), *The Sovereign Debt Crisis, the EU and Welfare State Reform*, London: Palgrave Macmillan UK, pp. 207–221.

Hernández Armenteros, J. and Pérez García, J. A., 2015, 'La financiación universitaria como instrumento dinamizador de cambio en la universidad pública española', *CIAN*, 18(1): 79–96.

High Level Group chaired by Wim Kok (HLG), 2004, *Facing the Challenge: The Lisbon Strategy for Growth and Employment: Report from the High Level Group Chaired by Wim Kok, November 2004*, Luxembourg: Office for Official Publications of the European Communities. Available: https://ec.europa.eu/research/evaluations/pdf/ archive/fp6-evidence-base/evaluation_studies_and_reports/evaluation_studies_and_ reports_2004/the_lisbon_strategy_for_growth_and_employment__report_from_the_ high_level_group.pdf.

Hinrichs, K., 2003, 'The politics of pension reform in Germany', Paper prepared for the Conference Pension Reform in Europe: Shared problems, sharing solutions?', London School of Economics, Hellenic Observatory / The European Institute, London, 5 December 2003. Available: http://www.lse.ac.uk/europeanInstitute/research/ hellenicObservatory/pdf/pensions_conference/Hinrichs.pdf.

Hinrichs, K., 2010, 'A social insurance state withers away. Welfare state reforms in Germany – Or: Attempts to turn around in a cul-de-sac', in B. Palier (ed.), *A Long Goodbye to Bismarck? The Politics of Welfare Reforms in Continental Europe*, Amsterdam: Amsterdam University Press, pp. 45–72.

Hobsbawm, E., 1993, *Revolutionaries*, London: Abacus.

Hobson, J. M. and Seabrooke, L., 2007, 'Everyday IPE: Revealing everyday forms of change in the world economy', in J. M. Hobson and L. Seabrooke (eds.), *Everyday Politics of the World Economy*, Cambridge: Cambridge University Press, pp. 1–24.

Hodson, D., 2016, 'Eurozone governance: From the Greek drama of 2015 to the five Presidents' Report', *Journal of Common Market Studies*, 54(S1): 150–166.

Hofmann, J., 2015, 'Grenzüberschreitende gewerkschaftliche Antworten auf die Krise', in S. Pernicka (ed.), *Horizontale Europäisierung im Feld der Arbeitsbeziehungen*, Wiesbaden: Springer VS, pp. 201–228.

Hogan, M. J., 1987, *The Marshall Plan: America, Britain, and the Reconstruction of Western Europe, 1947–1952*, Cambridge, Cambridge University Press.

Holborow, M., 2012, 'Austerity, capitalism and the restructuring of Irish higher education', *Irish Marxist Review*, 1(2): 24–36.

Holland E. W., 2011, *Nomad Citizenship: Free Market Communism and the Slow-Motion General Strike*, Minneapolis, MN: University of Minnesota Press.

Holloway, J., 2010, *Crack Capitalism*, London and New York: Pluto Press.

Holloway, J. and Picciotto, S., 1980, 'Capital, the state and European integration', *Research in Political Economy*, 3: 123–154.

Holm, A. and Kuhn, A., 2011, 'Squatting and urban renewal. The interaction of squatter movements and strategies of urban restructuring in Berlin', *International Journal of Urban and Regional Research*, 35(3): 644–658.

Holman, O. and van der Pijl, K., 1996, 'The capitalist class in the European Union', in G. A. Kourvetaris and A. Moschonas (eds.), *The Impact of European integration: Political, Sociological, and Economic Changes*, Westport, CT: Praeger, pp. 55–74.

Holman, O. and van der Pijl, K., 2003, 'Structure and process in transnational European business', in A. W. Cafruny and M. Ryner (eds.), *A Ruined Fortress?: Neoliberal Hegemony and Transformation in Europe*, Lanham: Rowman and Littlefield Publishers, pp. 71–93.

Holmwood, J., 2011, 'Viewpoint – The impact of "impact" on UK social science', *Methodological Innovations online*, 6(1): 13–7.

Holton, B., 1976. *British Syndicalism: 1900–1914: Myths and Realities*, London: Pluto Press.

Hooghe, L. and Marks, G., 2009, 'A postfunctionalist theory of European integration: From permissive consensus to constraining dissensus', *British Journal of Political Science*, 39(1): 1–23.

Horkheimer, M., 1937 [1982]) 'Traditional and critical theory', in M. Horkheimer, *Critical Theory: Selected Essays*, translated by Matthew J. O'Connell *et al.*, New York: Continuum, pp. 188–243.

Huber, E. and Stephens, J. D., 2001, *Development and Crisis of the Welfare State: Parties and Policies in Global Markets*, Chicago, IL: University of Chicago Press.

Huke, N., 2013a, 'Anreize für die Fortsetzung des Schuldendienstes. Die Europäische Kommission greift im Namen der Finanzstabilität im Konflikt um Zwangsräumung in Spanien ein', *analyse & kritik*, 14 August 2013.

Huke, N., 2013b, 'Autoritäre Austeritätspolitik in der Euro-Krise als Herausforderung für Gewerkschaften und soziale Bewegungen: Das Fallbeispiel Spanien', in W. Friedrich, C. H. Schwarz and S. Voigt (eds.), *Gewerkschaften im Demokratischen Prozess*, Düsseldorf: Hans-Böckler-Stiftung, pp. 155–176.

Huke, N., 2014, 'Die Kriminellen sind auf der anderen Seite'. Zur Normalisierung von Ungehorsam in den spanischen Krisenprotesten', in F. Burschel, A. Kahrs and L. Steinert (eds.), *Ungehorsam! Disobedience!: Theorie & Praxis kollektiver Regelverstöße*, Münster, Westf: edition assemblage, pp. 85–100.

Huke, N., 2016, *Krisenproteste in Spanien: Zwischen Selbstorganisation und Überfall auf die Institutionen*, Münster: edition assemblage.

Huke, N., 2017, *'Sie repräsentieren uns nicht.' Soziale Bewegungen und Krisen der Demokratie in Spanien'*. Münster: Westfälisches Dampfboot.

Huke, N. and Schlemermeyer, J., 2012, 'Warum so staatstragend?', *PROKLA*, 42(3): 455–465.

Huke, N. and Syrovatka, F., 2014, *Kein Comeback in Sicht: Eine Antwort auf Hans-Jürgen Urbans Thesen zur Rolle der deutschen Gewerkschaften in der Krise*. Available: http://www.labournet.de/politik/gw/krise08gew/kein-comeback-in-sicht-eine-antwort-auf-hans-jurgen-urbans-thesen-zur-rolle-der-deutschen-gewerkschaften-in-der-krise/.

Huke, N. and Tietje, O., 2014a, 'Gewerkschaftliche Erneuerung in der Eurokrise. Neue Organisationsformen der spanischen Gewerkschaften während des Protestzyklus ab 2011', *PROKLA*, 44(4): 531–548.

Huke, N. and Tietje, O., 2014b, 'Zwischen Kooperation und Konfrontation. Machtressourcen und Strategien der spanischen Gewerkschaften CCOO und UGT in der Eurokrise', *Industrielle Beziehungen*, 21(4): 371–389.

Huke, N., Clua-Losada, M. and Bailey, D. J., 2015, 'Disrupting the European Crisis: A critical political economy of contestation, subversion and escape', *New Political Economy*, 20(5): 725–751.

Hyman, R., 1979, 'The politics of a workplace trade unionism: Recent tendencies and some problems for theory', *Capital and Class*, 3(2): 54–67.

iaioflautas, 2016, *Somos hijas del 15M*. Available: http://www.iaioflautas.org/blog/2016/06/21/somos-hijas-del-15m/.

Ince, A., Featherstone, D., Cumbers, A., MacKinnon, D. and Strauss, K., 2015, 'British jobs for British workers? Negotiating work, nation, and globalisation through the Lindsey Oil Refinery disputes', *Antipode*, 47(1): 139–157.

Jabko, N., 2006, *Playing the Market: A Political Strategy for Uniting Europe, 1985–2005*, Ithaca, NY: Cornell University Press.

Jackson, A. Y. and Mazzei, L. A., 2012, *Thinking with Theory in Qualitative Research: Viewing Data across Multiple Perspectives*, London: Routledge.

Jäger, J. and Springler, E., 2015a, 'Debating the future of Europe: Critical political economy and post-Keynesian perspectives', in J. Jäger and E. Springler (eds.), *Asymmetric Crisis in Europe and Possible Futures: Critical Political Economy and Post-Keynesian Perspectives*, London: Routledge, pp. 1–14.

Jäger, J. and Springler, E. (eds.), 2015b, *Asymmetric Crisis in Europe and Possible Futures: Critical Political Economy and Post-Keynesian Perspectives*, London: Routledge.

Jessop, B., 1993, 'Towards a Schumpeterian workfare state? Preliminary remarks on post-Fordist political economy', *Studies in Political Economy*, 40: 7–39.

Jessop, B., 1999, 'The strategic selectivity of the state: Reflections on a theme of Poulantzas', *Journal of the Hellenic Diaspora*, 25(1–2): 41–77.

Jessop, B., 2007, *State Power: A Strategic-relational Approach*, Cambridge: Polity.

Jessop, B., 2015, 'Neoliberalism, finance-dominated accumulation and enduring austerity: a cultural political economy perspective', in K. Farnsworth and Z. Irving (eds.), *Social Policy in Times of Austerity: Global Economic Crisis and the New Politics of Welfare*, Bristol: Policy Press, pp. 87–112

Jessoula, M. and Alti, T., 2010, 'Italy: An uncompleted departure from Bismarck', in B. Palier (ed.), *A Long Goodbye to Bismarck? The Politics of Welfare Reforms in Continental Europe*, Amsterdam: Amsterdam University Press, pp. 157–81.

Jordà, Ò. and Taylor, A. M., 2016, 'The time for austerity: Estimating the average treatment effect of fiscal policy'. *Econ J*, 126: 219–55.

Jordan, W., 2014, '"Bedroom tax" as divisive as ever', *YouGov.UK*, 18 July 2014. Available: https://yougov.co.uk/news/2014/07/18/bedroom-tax-divisive-ever/.

Kadi, J. and Musterd, S., 2015, 'Housing for the poor in a neo-liberalising just city: Still affordable, but increasingly inaccessible', *Tijdschrift voor economische en sociale geografie*, 106(3): 246–262.

Kadir, N., 2014, 'Myth and reality in the Amsterdam squatters' movement, 1975–2012', in B. van der Steen, A. Katzeff and L. Van Hoogenhuijze (eds.), *The City is Ours: Squatting and Autonomous Movements in Europe from the 1970s to the Present*, Oakland, CA: PM Press, pp. 21–61.

Kahmann, M., 2015, 'When the strike encounters the *sans papiers* movement: the discovery of a workers' repertoire of actions for irregular migrant protest in France', *Transfer: European Review of Labour and Research* 21(4): 413–428.

Kaindl, C., 2013, 'Neoliberalismus und Rechtsextremismus im Wandel', in P. Bathke and A. Hoffstadt (eds.), *Die neuen Rechten in Europa: Zwischen Neoliberalismus und Rassismus*, Köln: Papyrossa, pp. 20–30.

Karanikolos, M., Mladovsky, P., Cylus, J., Thomson, S., Basu, S., Stuckler, D., Mackenbach, J. P. and McKee, M., 2013, 'Financial crisis, austerity, and health in Europe', *The Lancet*, 381(9874): 1323–1331.

Karger, H., 2014, 'The bitter pill: Austerity, debt, and the attack on Europe's welfare states', *Journal of Sociology & Social Welfare*, 41(2): 33–53.

Katsiaficas, G., 2006, *The Subversion of Politics: European Autonomous Social Movements and the Decolonization of Everyday Life*, Oakland, CA: AK Press.

Kaufman, R. R., 2007, 'Market reform and social protection: Lessons from the Czech Republic, Hungary, and Poland', *East European Politics and Societies*, 21(1): 111–125.

Kautsky, K., 1911, 'Krieg und Frieden: Betrachtungen zur Maifeier', *Die Neue Zeit*, 29(2): 97–107.

Keeling, R., 2006, 'The Bologna process and the Lisbon research agenda: The European Commission's expanding role in higher education discourse', *European Journal of Education*, 41(2): 203–223.

Kelly, J., 2015, 'Conflict. Trends and forms of collective action', *Employee Relations*, 37(6): 720–732.

Kemeny, J., 1995, *From Public Housing to the Social Market: Rental Policy Strategies in Comparative Perspective*, London: Routledge.

Kern, A., Marien, S. and Hooghe, M., 2015, 'Economic crisis and levels of political participation in Europe, 2002–2010): The role of resources and grievances', *West European Politics*, 38(3): 465–490.

Keskinen, S., Norocel, O. C. and Jorgensen, M. B., 2016, 'The politics and policies of welfare chauvinism under the economic crisis', *Critical Social Policy*, 36(3): 1–9.

Keune, M., 2015, 'The effects of the EU's assault on collective bargaining: Less governance capacity and more inequality', *Transfer: European Review of Labour and Research*, 21(4): 477–483.

Kiersey, N. and Vrasti, W., 2016, 'A convergent genealogy? Space, time and the promise of horizontal politics today', *Capital and Class*, 40(1): 75–94.

Kipping, M., 1997, 'Consultancies, institutions and the diffusion of Taylorism in Britain, Germany and France, 1920s to 1950s', *Business History*, 39(4): 67–83.

Kirchlechner, B., 1978, 'New Demands or the Demands of New Groups? Three Case Studies', in C. Crouch and A. Pizzorno (eds.), *The Resurgence of Class Conflict in Western Europe Since 1968: Volume 2 Comparative Analyses*, London: Macmillan Press, pp. 161–176.

Klemenčič, M., 2012, 'The changing conceptions of student participation in HE governance in the EHEA', in A. Curaj, P. Scott, L. Vlasceanu and L. Wilson (eds.), *European Higher Education at the Crossroads: Between the Bologna Process and National Reforms*, Heidelberg: Springer, pp. 631–653.

Klemenčič, M., 2014, 'Student power in a global perspective and contemporary trends in student organising', *Studies in Higher Education*, 39(3): 396–411.

Köhler, H.-D. and Calleja Jiménez, J. P., 2013, *Die Gewerkschaften in Spanien: Organisation, Rahmenbedingungen, Herausforderungen*. Available: http://library.fes.de/pdf-files/id/10133.pdf.

Köhler, H.-D. and Calleja Jiménez, J. P., 2014, 'Spanien: Massenmobilisierungen gegen das Austeritätsdiktat', *WSI Mitteilungen*, 67(5): 369–377.

Komp, K., Starke, P., van Hooren, F., Schneckenburger, E., Simonsen, H., Heuer, S. and Rahn, E., 2013, *In the Wake of the Economic Crisis. Social Change and Welfare State Reforms*. Available: http://www.soc.umu.se/digitalAssets/132/132147_3_2013_komp_mfl-1.pdf.

Konzelmann, S. J., 2014, 'The political economics of austerity', *Cambridge Journal of Economics*, 38(4): 701–741.

Kornetis, K., 2013, *Children of the Dictatorship: Student Resistance, Cultural Politics, and the 'Long 1960s' in Greece*, New York: Berghahn.

Koulouris, A., Moniarou-Papaconstantinou, V. and Kyriaki-Manessi, D., 2014, 'Austerity measures in Greece and their impact on higher education', *Procedia – Social and Behavioral Sciences*, 147: 518–526.

Kritidis, G., 2014, 'The rise and crisis of the anarchist and libertarian movment in Grece, 1973–2012', in B. van der Steen, A. Katzeff and L. Van Hoogenhuijze (eds.), *The City is Ours: Squatting and Autonomous Movements in Europe from the 1970s to the Present*, Oakland, CA: PM Press, pp. 63–93.

Krzeslo, D., 1998, 'Unemployed people demonstrate against tougher sanctions and benefit cuts', EurWork. Available: http://www.eurofound.europa.eu/observatories/eurwork/articles/unemployed-people-demonstrate-against-tougher-sanctions-and-benefit-cuts.

Kuhlmann, J., Schubert, K. and Villota, P. de, 2016, 'Recent developments of European welfare systems: Multiple challenges and diverse reactions', in K. Schubert, P. de Villota and J. Kuhlmann (eds.), *Challenges to European Welfare Systems*, Cham: Springer, pp. 1–10.

Kuhn, G., 2014, 'Syndicalism in Sweden: A hundred years of the SAC', in I. Ness (ed.), *New Forms of Worker Organization: The Syndicalist and Autonomist Restoration of Class Struggle Unionism*, Oakland, CA: PM Press, pp. 168–183.

Kus, B., 2013, 'Consumption and redistributive politics: The effect of credit and China', *International Journal of Comparative Sociology*, 54(3): 187–204.

La Expansión, 2013, 'CCOO denuncia que el Gobierno "degrada conscientemente los servicios públicos"', *La Expansión*, 21 August 2013.

La Porte, C. de and Heins, E., 2016a, 'A new era of European integration? Governance of labour market and social policy since the sovereign debt crisis', in C. de La Porte and E. Heins (eds.), *The Sovereign Debt Crisis, the EU and Welfare State Reform*, London: Palgrave Macmillan, pp. 15–41.

La Porte, C. de and Heins, E., 2016b, 'Introduction: Is the European Union more involved in welfare state reform following the sovereign debt crisis?', in C. de La Porte and E. Heins (eds.), *The Sovereign Debt Crisis, the EU and Welfare State Reform*, London: Palgrave Macmillan, pp. 1–13.

Ladi, S. and Graziano, P. R., 2014, '"Fast-forward" Europeanization: Welfare state reform in light of the Eurozone crisis', in R. Coman, T. Kostera and L. Tomini (eds.), *Europeanization and European Integration: From Incremental to Structural Change*, Basingstoke: Palgrave Macmillan, pp. 108–126.

Lapavitsas, C., Kaltenbrunner, A., Labrinidis, G., Lindo, D., Meadway, J., Michell, J., Painceira, J. P., Pires, E., Powell, J., Stenfors, A., Teles, N. and Vatikiotis, L., 2012, *Crisis in the Eurozone*, London: Verso.

Lebowitz, M. A., 2003, *Beyond Capital: Marx's Political Economy of the Working Class*, Basingstoke: Palgrave Macmillan.

Legido-Quigley, H., Otero, L., Parra, D. L., Alvarez-Dardet, C., Martin-Moreno, J. M. and McKee, M., 2013, 'Will austerity cuts dismantle the Spanish healthcare system?', *BMJ*, 346: 1–5.

Lehndorff, S., 2015, 'Europe's divisive integration – an overview', in S. Lehndorff (ed.), *Divisive Integration: The Triumph of Failed Ideas in Europe, Revisited*, Brussels: ETUI, European Trade Union Institute, pp. 7–38.

Leibfried, S., 1993, 'Towards a European welfare state?', in C. Jones (ed.), *New Perspectives on the Welfare State in Europe*, London and New York: Routledge, pp. 120–143.

Leibfried, S., 2000, 'National welfare states, European integration and globalization: A perspective for the next century', *Social Policy and Administration*, 34(1): 44–63.

Lengemann, S., 2015, 'Erst das Essen, dann die Miete!' Protest und Selbsthilfe in Berliner Arbeitervierteln während der Großen Depression 1931 bis 1933', *Jahrbuch für Forschungen zur Geschichte der Arbeiterbewegung*, 14(3): 46–62.

Lenin, W. I., 1915, *Über die Losung der Vereinigten Staaten von Europa*. Available: http://www.vulture-bookz.de/marx/archive/volltext/Lenin_1915~Ueber_die_Losung_der_Vereinigten_Staaten_von_Eur.html.

Leontidou, L., 2010, 'Urban social movements in 'weak' civil societies. The right to the city and cosmopolitan activism in southern Europe', *Urban Studies*, 47(6): 1179–1203.

Levidow, L., 2002, 'Marketizing higher education: neoliberal strategies and counter-strategies', in K. Robins and F. Webster (eds.), *The Virtual University? Knowledge, Markets and Management*, Oxford: Oxford University Press, pp. 227–48.

Levitt, C., 1989, 'Federal Republic of Germany', in P.G. Altbach (ed.), *Student Political Activism: An International Reference Handbook*, New York: Greenwood Press, pp. 209–21.

Levy, C., 1999, *Gramsci and the Anarchists*, Oxford: Berg.

Lewis, P., Gabbatt, A., Taylor, M. and Jeffery, S., 2010, 'UK Uncut protesters spied upon by undercover police', *The Guardian*, 3 December 2010. Available: http://www.theguardian.com/uk/2010/dec/03/uk-uncut-protests-undercover-police.

Leys, C., 2013, 'The British ruling class', in L. Panitch, G. Albo and V. Chibber (eds.), *Socialist Register 2014: Registering class*, Pontypool: Merlin Press, pp. 108–137.

Liao, T. F., 2010, 'Visual symbolism, collective memory, and social protest: A study of the 2009 London G20 protest', *Social Alternatives*, 29(4): 37–43.

Lindemann, A. S., 1974, *The 'Red Years': European Socialism Versus Bolshevism, 1919–1921*, Berkeley: University of California Press.

Lindsey Strike Committee, n.d., 'Victory for Construction Workers!!'. Available: http://afed.noflag.org.uk/wp-content/uploads/2009/07/lindsey_support_reply_letter.pdf.

Linebaugh, P. and Rediker, M., 2000, *The Many-Headed Hydra: Sailors, Slaves, Commoners, and the Hidden History of the Revolutionary Atlantic*, Boston: Beacon Press.

López, S., Martínez, X. and Toret, J., 2008: 'Las oficinas de derechos sociales: Experiencias de organización y enunciación política en el tiempo de la precariedad'. Available: http://eipcp.net/transversal/0508/lopezetal/es/print.

López Vizuete, M., 2013, *La Asamblea de Docentes de Illes Balears nos enseña el camino*. Available: http://www.rebelion.org/noticia.php?id=174821.

Lorenz, C., 2011, 'Riddles of neoliberal university-reform: The student protests of 2009 as Bologna's "Stress Test"', in C. Krijnen, C. Lorenz and J. Umlauf (eds.), *Wahrheit oder Gewinn? Über die Ökonomisierung von Universität und Wissenschaft*, Würzburg: Königshausen & Neumann Verlag, pp. 53–67.

Lorenz, C., 2012, 'If you're so smart, why are you under surveillance? Universities, neoliberalism, and new public management', *Critical Inquiry*, 38(3): 599–629.

Lorey, I., 2011, *Non-representationist, Presentist Democracy*. Available: http://eipcp.net/transversal/1011/lorey/en.

Luebbert, G. M., 1987, 'Social foundations of political order in interwar Europe', *World Politics*, 39(4): 449–78.

Lumley, R., 1990, *States of Emergency: Cultures of Revolt in Italy from 1968 to 1978*, London, Verso.

Luque Balbona, D. and González Begega, S., 2015, 'Austerity and welfare reform in south-western Europe: A farewell to corporatism in Italy, Spain and Portugal?', *EJSS*, 17(2): 271–292.

Luxemburg, R., 1911, *Friedensutopien*. Available: http://www.marxists.org/deutsch/archiv/luxemburg/1911/05/utopien.htm.

Maassen, P. and Musselin, C., 2009, 'European integration and the Europeanisation of higher education', in A. Amaral, G. Neave, C. Musselin and P. Maassen (eds.), *European Integration and the Governance of Higher Education and Research*, Dordrecht: Springer Netherlands, pp. 3–14.

Macías C., 2013, 'Del empoderamiento a la autotutela de derechos: El caso de la PAH', *El Viejo Topo*, 306/307, 45–8.

Maier, C. S., 1987, *In Search of Stability: Explorations in Historical Political Economy* Cambridge: Cambridge University Press.

Malik, S., 2011, 'Fortnum and Mason protesters convicted of aggravated trespass', *The Guardian*, 17 November 2011. Available: https://www.theguardian.com/uk/2011/nov/17/fortnum-mason-protesters-convicted-trespass.

Malik, S. 2014a, 'DWP orders man to work without pay for company that let him go', *The Guardian*, 3 November 2014.

Malik, S., 2014b, 'UK councils found to benefit from half a million hours of unpaid labour', *The Guardian*, 3 January 2014. Available: http://www.theguardian.com/politics/2014/jan/02/councils-benefit-half-a-million-hours-unpaid-labour-foi-request.

Mandel, E., 1968, *Die EWG und die Konkurrenz Europa – Amerika*, Frankfurt/Main: Europäische Verl.-Anst.

Manicastri, S., 2014, '*Operaismo* Revisited: Italy's state-capitalist assault on workers and the rise of COBAs', in I. Ness (ed.), *New Forms of Worker Organization: The Syndicalist and Autonomist Restoration of Class-Struggle Unionism*, Oakland, CA: PM Press, pp. 20–38.

Marien, S., Hooghe, M., and Quintelier, E., 2010, 'Inequalities in non-institutionalised forms of political participation: A multi-level analysis of 25 countries', *Political Studies*, 58(1): 187–213.

Martínez López, M. A., 2013, 'The squatters' movement in Europe. A durable struggle for social autonomy in urban politics', *Antipode*, 45(4): 866–887.

Martínez López, M. A. and García Bernardos, Á., 2011, *Ocupar las plazas, liberar los edificios*. Available: http://www.miguelangelmartinez.net/IMG/pdf/articulo_ACME_8000_v1_doc.pdf.

Martínez López, M. A. and García Bernardos, Á., 2012, *The Occupation of Squares and the Squatting of Buildings: Lessons from the Convergence of Two Social Movements*. Available: http://www.miguelangelmartinez.net/IMG/pdf/articulo_Bilbao_v4_book_doc.pdf.

Martínez, R., 2013, 'Políticas de infancia: Crisis y austeridad', *En la calle*, 25: 2–4.

Marx, K., 1867 [1976], *Capital: A Critique of Political Economy: Volume One*, London: Penguin.

Mason, R. and Perraudin, F., 2015, 'Unemployed young people will be sent to work boot camp, says minister', *The Guardian*, 17 August 2015. Available: http://www.theguardian.com/society/2015/aug/17/unemployed-young-people-work-boot-camp-tory-minister.

Matei, L., 2015, 'Introduction', in A. Curaj, L. Matei, R. Pricopie, J. Salmi and P. Scott (eds.), *The European Higher Education Area: Between Critical Reflections and Future Policies*, London: Springer, pp. 35–43.

Martínez Lucio, M., 2011, 'From action to communication?', *Employee Relations*, 33(6): 654–669.

Mates, L. H., 2016, *The Great Labour Unrest: Rank-and-File Movements and Political Change in the Durham Coalfield*, Manchester: Manchester University Press.

Matznetter, W. and Stephens, M., 1998, 'Introduction: From comparative housing research to European housing research', in M. Kleinman, W. Matznetter and M. Stephens (eds.), *European Integration and Housing Policy*, London: Routledge, pp. 1–15.

Mayer, M., 2000, 'Social movments in European cities: Transition from the 1970s to the 1990s', in A. Bagnasco and P. Le Galès (eds.), *Cities in Contemporary Europe*, Cambridge: Cambridge University Press, pp. 131–152.

McGettigan, A., 2013, *The Great University Gamble: Money, Markets and the Future of Higher Education*, London: Pluto Press.

McGettigan, A., 2015, 'Cash Today: Who profits from student loans?', *London Review of Books*, 37(5): 24–28.

McKenzie, L., 2015, *Getting By: Estates, Class and Culture in Austerity Britain*, Bristol: Policy Press.

McNamara, K., 1998, *The Currency of Ideas: Monetary Politics in the European Union*, Ithaca, NY: Cornell University Press.

Medina Guerrero, M., 2012, 'La reforma del artículo 135 CE', *Teoría y Realidad Constitucional*, 29: 131–164.

Mellado Ruiz, L., 2014, 'Consecuencias derivadas de la supresión del principio de mayor proximidad', *La Ley*, 500: 1–9.

Mercille, J. and Murphy, E., 2015, 'The neoliberalization of Irish higher education under Austerity', *Critical Sociology*, 43(3), pp. 371–387.

Merkens, A., 2004, 'Erziehung und Bildung im Denken Antonio Gramscis. Eckpunkte einer intellektuellen und politischen Praxis', in A. Merkens (ed.), *Gramsci-Reader. Erziehung und Bildung*, Hamburg: Argument-Verl., pp. 15–46.

Meuser, M. and Nagel, U., 1991, 'ExpertInneninterviews – vielfach erprobt, wenig bedacht: ein Beitrag zur qualitativen Methodendiskussion', in D. Garz and K. Kraimer (eds.), *Qualitativ-empirische Sozialforschung: Konzepte, Methoden, Analysen*, Opladen: Westdt. Verl., pp. 441–471.

Meyer, J. W., Ramirez, F. O. and Nuhoğlu Soysa, Y., 1992, 'World expansion of mass education, 1870–1980', *Sociology of Education*, 65(2): 128–149.

Milward, A., 1992, *European Rescue of the Nation State*, London: Routledge.

Mitchell, K., 2006, 'Neoliberal governmentality in the European Union: Education, training, and technologies of citizenship', *Environment and Planning D: Society and Space*, 24: 389–407.

Montgomerie, J. and Büdenbender, M., 2015, Round the houses: Homeownership and failures of asset-based welfare in the United Kingdom, *New Political Economy*, 20(3): 386–405.

Montoya, N., 2012, 'Es scheint, als ob mit dem Streik eine vereinte Bewegung enstanden ist', in A. Gallas, J. Nowak and F. Wilde (eds.), *Politische Streiks im Europa der Krise*, Hamburg: VSA, pp. 156–164.

Morell, M. F., 2012, 'The Free Culture and 15M Movements in Spain: Composition, Social Networks and Synergies', *Social Movement Studies*, 11(3–4): 386–92.

Moulaert, F., Rodriguez, A. and Swyngedouw, E. (eds.), 2005, *The Globalized City: Economic restructuring and Social Polarization in European Cities*, Oxford: Oxford University Press.

MTI Econews, 1995a, 'Students protest against new tuition fees', *MTI Econews*, 22 March 1995.

MTI Econews, 1995b, 'Teachers stage demonstration in Budapest', *MTI Econews*, 30 March 1995.

MTI Econews, 1995c, 'May 1 Teachers' demonstration attracts 10,000', *MTI Econews*, 2 May 1995.

Mücke, J. and Rinn, M., 2016, 'Keine Riots in Deutschland? Die Ereignisse in Hamburg-Altona im Sommer 2013', *Sub\urban*, 4(1): 111–130.

Mudde, C., 2004, 'The Populist Zeitgeist', *Government and Opposition*, 39(4): 542–563.

Mullis, D., Belina, B., Petzold, T., Pohl, L. and Schipper, S., 2016, 'Social protest and its policing in the 'heart of the European crisis regime'. The case of Blockupy in Frankfurt, Germany', *Political Geography*, 55: 50–9.

Murie, A., I. Tosiccs, M.B. Aalbers, R. Sendi and B. Černič Mali, 2005, 'Privatisation and after', in R. Van Kempen, K. Dekker, S. Hall and I. Tosics, (eds.), *Restructuring Large Housing Estates in European Cities*, Bristol: Policy Press, pp. 85–103.

Nachtwey, O., 2016, *Die Abstiegsgesellschaft: Über das Aufbegehren in der regressiven Moderne*, Berlin: Suhrkamp.

Navarro, V. and Clua-Losada (eds.), 2012, *El impacto de la crisis en las familias y en la infancia*, Barcelona: Editorial Ariel.

Navarro, V., 2013, 'The social crisis of the Eurozone. The case of Spain', *International Journal of Health Services*, 43(2): 189–192.

Navarro, V. (ed.), 2004, *El estado de bienestar en España*, Madrid: Tecnos.

Nedergaard, P. and Snaith, H., 2015, '"As I drifted on a river I could not control": The unintended ordoliberal consequences of the Eurozone crisis', *Journal of Common Market Studies*, 53(5): 1094–1109.

Negri, A., 1972, *Zyklus und Krise bei Marx*, Berlin: Merve.

Negri, A., 1973, 'Krise des Plan-Staats, Kommunismus und revolutionäre Organisation', in A. Negri (ed.), *Krise des Plan-Staats, Kommunismus und revolutionäre Organisation*, Berlin: Merve, pp. 7–54.

Negri, A., 1977, *Massenautonomie gegen historischen Kompromiss*, München: Trikont-Verlag.

Negri, A., 1996, 'Twenty theses on Marx: Interpretation of the class situation today', in S. Makdisi, C. Casarino and R. E. Karl (eds.), *Marxism beyond Marxism*, New York: Routledge, pp. 149–180.

Negri, A., 2009, 'Twenty Theses on Marx: Interpretation of the Class Situation Today', in S. Makdisi, C. Casarino and R.E. Karl (eds.), *Marxism Beyond Marxism*, New York: Routledge, pp. 149–180.

Negt, O. and Kluge, A., 1993, *Geschichte und Eigensinn*, Frankfurt am Main: Suhrkamp.

Neville, S. and Treanor, J., 2012, 'Starbucks to pay £20m in tax over next two years after customer revolt', *The Guardian*, 6 December 2012. Available: https://www. theguardian.com/business/2012/dec/06/starbucks-to-pay-10m-corporation-tax.

Nichols, W. J. and Beaumont, J. R., 2004, 'The Urbanisation of Justice Movements? Possibilities and Constraints for the City as a Space of Contentious Struggle', *Space and Polity*, 8(2): 119–135.

Nousios, P., Overbeek, H. and Tsolakis, A., 2012a, 'Globalisation and European integration: The nature of the beast', in P. Nousios, H. Overbeek and A. Tsolakis (eds.), *Globalisation and European Integration: Critical Approaches to Regional Order and International Relations*, London: Routledge, pp. 3–31.

Nousios, P., Overbeek, H. and Tsolakis, A. (eds.), 2012b, *Globalisation and European Integration: Critical Approaches to Regional Order and International Relations*, London: Routledge.

Nowak, J. and Gallas, A., 2014, 'Mass strikes against austerity in western Europe – A strategic assessment', *Global Labour Journal*, 5(3): 306–321.

O'Hagan, M., 2011, 'The Fortnum & Mason protest verdict: A farcical injustice', *The Guardian*, 17 November 2011. Available: https://www.theguardian.com/commentisfree/2011/nov/17/fortnum-mason-verdict-uk-uncut-protesters.

Oberndorfer, L., 2015, 'From new constitutionalism to authoritarian constitutionalism: New Economic Governance and the state of European democracy', in J. Jäger and E. Springler (eds.), *Asymmetric Crisis in Europe and Possible Futures: Critical Political Economy and Post-Keynesian Perspectives*, London: Routledge, pp. 186–207.

Occupy London, 2011, Economics Statement, 6 December 2011. Available: http://occupylondon.org.uk/about/statements/statement-on-economy/.

Offe, C., 2000, *The democratic welfare state: A European regime under the strain of European integration*. Available: http://www.ssoar.info/ssoar/handle/document/24658.

Offe, C., 2006, *Strukturprobleme des kapitalistischen Staates: Aufsätze zur Politischen Soziologie*, Frankfurt/Main, New York: Campus.

Oficina Técnica Presidencia, Economía y Hacienda Zaragoza, 2014, *Evaluación de la afectación de la Ley 27/2013, de racionalización y sostenibilidad de la Administración Local, a los servicios prestados por el Ayuntamiento de Zaragoza*. Available: http://zaragozaprensadotcom1.files.wordpress.com/2014/01/evaluacic3b3n-lrsal-a-servicios-ayto-zaragoza-ok-24-01-2014.pdf.

Olsen, J. P. and Maassen, P., 2007, 'European debates on the knowledge institution: The modernization of the university at the European level', in P. Maassen and J. P. Olsen (eds.), *University Dynamics and European Integration*, Berlin: Springer, pp. 3–22.

Overbeek, H., 2004, 'Transnational class formation and concepts of control: towards a genealogy of the Amsterdam Project in international political economy', *Journal of International Relations and Development*, 7(2): 113–141.

Overbeek, H. (ed.), 1993, *Restructuring Hegemony in the Global Political Economy: The Rise of Transnational Neo-liberalism in the 1980s*, London: Routledge.

Palier, B., 2010, 'The dualizations of the French welfare state', in B. Palier (ed.), *A Long Goodbye to Bismarck? The Politics of Welfare Reforms in Continental Europe*, Amsterdam: Amsterdam University Press, pp. 73–100.

Palley, T. I., 2013, 'Europe's crisis without end: The consequences of neoliberalism', *Contributions to Political Economy*, 32: 29–50.

Papadopoulos, D., Stephenson, N. and Tsianos, V., 2008, *Escape Routes: Control and Subversion in the Twenty-first Century*, London: Pluto Press.

Papadopoulos, T. and Roumpakis, A., 2015, 'Democracy, austerity and crisis: Southern Europe and the decline of the European social model', in S. Romano and G. Punziano (eds.), *The European Social Model Adrift: Europe, Social Cohesion and the Economic Crisis*, Farnham: Ashgate, pp. 189–212.

Pare, P. P. and Felson, R., 2014, 'Income inequality, poverty and crime across nations', *The British Journal of Sociology*, 65(3): 434–458.

Pasquinelli, M., 2014, 'To anticipate and accelerate: Italian Operaismo and reading Marx's notion of the organic composition of capitalism', *Rethinking Marxism*, 26(2): 178–192.

Past Tense, 2009, 'Report and reflections on the UK Ford-Visteon dispute 2009: A post-Fordist struggle'. Available: https://libcom.org/history/report-reflections-uk-ford-visteon-dispute-2009-post-fordist-struggle.

Pastor Verdú, J., 2014, *El 15 M, las mareas y su relación con la política sistémica: El caso de Madrid*. Available: http://dialnet.unirioja.es/servlet/articulo?codigo=4978512&orden=0&info=link.

Paulsen, R., 2014, *Empty Labor: Idleness and Workplace Resistance*, Cambridge: Cambridge University Press.

Paulsen, R., 2015, 'Non-work at work: Resistance or what?', *Organization*, 22(3): 351–367.

Pavolini, E., León, M., Guillén, A. M. and Ascoli, U., 2016, 'From austerity to permanent strain? The European Union and Welfare State Reform in Italy and Spain', in C. de La Porte and E. Heins (eds.), *The Sovereign Debt Crisis, the EU and Welfare State Reform*, London: Palgrave Macmillan, pp. 131–157.

Peck, J., Theodore, N. and Brenner, N., 2013, 'Neoliberal urbanism redux?', *International Journal of Urban and Regional Research*, 37(3): 1091–1099.

Peinado, P., 2014, 'A dynamic gender analysis of Spain's pension reforms of 2011', *Feminist Economics*, 20(3): 163–190.

Pelling, H., 1966, *A History of British Trade Unionism*, London: Palgrave Macmillan.

Peräkylä, A., 1994, 'Analyzing text and talk', in N. K. Denzin and Y. S. Lincoln (eds.), *Handbook of Qualitative Research*, Thousand Oaks, CA: Sage Publications, pp. 351–374.

Pérez Alonso, M. A., 2013, 'La Pensión de Jubilación en España tras las recientes reformas (Ley 27/2011 y RDL 5/2013)', *Revista Internacional y Comparada de RELACIONES LABORALES Y DERECHO DEL EMPLEO*, 1(3): 1–16.

Pérez Orozco, A., 2014, *Subversión feminista de la economía: Aportes para un debate sobre el conflicto capital-vida*, Madrid: Traficantes de sueños.

Pettis, M., 2013, *The Great Rebalancing: Trade, Conflict, and the Perilous Road Ahead for the World Economy*, Princeton, NJ: Princeton University Press.

Phillips, L., 2009, 'European wind lobby distances itself from UK turbine factory occupation', *euobserver.com*, 24 July 2009. Available: https://euobserver.com/environment/28493.

Phillips, L., 2011, "New system of European governance' demands deeper austerity', *euobserver.com*, 9 June.

Pichelmann, K., 2002, 'Wage discipline in EMU. A feature of the early years. Only?', in Buti, M. and A. Sapir (eds.), *EMU and Economic Policy in Europe: The Challenge of the Early Years*, Cheltenham, Edward Elgar, pp. 281–299.

Picó Enseñat, Miguel Ramón, 2013, '¿Qué fue de las «Pagas Extraordinarias» de los Funcionarios Públicos con la crisis?', *Revista de Derecho*, 13: 333–356.

Pierson, P., 1994, *Dismantling the Welfare State? Reagan, Thatcher, and the Politics of Retrenchment*, Cambridge: Cambridge University Press.

Pinheiro, R. and Antonowicz, D., 2015, '"I am tired of reading history. Now I want to make it!" The rise and fall of the university campus as a space for social rebellion', in M. Klemenčič, S. Bergan and R. Primožič (eds.), *Student Engagement in Europe: Society, Higher Education and Student Governance*, Strasbourg: Council of Europe Publishing, pp. 51–66.

Piven, F. F. and Cloward, R., 1977, *Poor People's Movements: Why They Succeed, How They Fail*, New York: Vintage Books.

Pizzolato, N., 2004, 'Workers and revolutionaries at the twilight of Fordism: The breakdown of industrial relations in the automobile plants of Detroit and Turin, 1967–1973', *Labor History*, 45(4): 419–443.

Polanska, D. V. and Piotrowski, G., 2015, 'The transformative power of cooperation between social movements: Squatting and tenants' movements in Poland', *City*, 19(2–3): 274–296.

Polanyi, K., 2005, *The Great Transformation: The Political and Economic Origins of Our Time*, Princeton, NJ: Recording for the Blind & Dyslexic.

Poulantzas, N., 2002, *Staatstheorie: Politischer Überbau, Ideologie, autoritärer Etatismus*, Hamburg: VSA.

Press Association, 2013, 'UK Uncut forces closure of HSBC branches in tax protest', *The Guardian*, 20 July 2013. Available: https://www.theguardian.com/uk-news/2013/jul/20/uk-uncut-closure-hsbc-tax.

Press Association, 2014, 'New Help to Work programme comes into force for long-term unemployed' *The Guardian*, 28 April 2014. Available: http://www.theguardian.com/society/2014/apr/28/help-to-work-programme-long-term-unemployed.

Priemus, H., 1998, 'The impact of European integration on the construction industry', in M. Kleinman, W. Matznetter and M. Stephens (eds.), *European Integration and Housing Policy*, London and New York: Routledge, pp. 75–91.

Pruijt, H., 2004, 'The impact of citizens' protest on city planning in Amsterdam', in L. Deben, W. Salet and M. T. van Thoor (eds.), *Cultural Heritage and the Future of the Historic Inner City of Amsterdam*, Amsterdam: Amsterdam University Press, pp. 228–244.

Przeworski, A., 2008, 'Conquered or granted? A history of suffrage extensions', *British Journal of Political Science*, 39: 291–321.

Público.es, 2013, 'España tiene el porcentaje más alto de universitarios en riesgo de pobreza de la Unión Europea', *Público.es*, 17 July 2013.

Quinn, B., 2015, 'Six arrested as police help in evictions from London estate', *The Guardian*, 18 February 2015.

Ravinet, P., 2008, 'From voluntary participation to monitored coordination: Why European countries feel increasingly bound by their commitment to the Bologna process', *European Journal of Education*, 43(3): 353–367.

Redondo Ballesteros, D. and Rodríguez Fernández, J. M., 2014, 'Crisis en las entidades de crédito españolas: Un estudio mediante análisis discriminante', *Estudios de Economía Aplicada*, 32(2): 617–644.

Rees, J., Whitworth, A. and Carter, E., 2014, 'Support for all in the UK work programme? Differential payments, same old problem', *Social Policy and Administration*, 48(2): 221–239.

Reinalda, B., 2008, 'The Bologna process and its achievements in Europe 1999–2007', *Journal of Political Science Education*, 4(4): 463–476.

Relations industrielles/Industrial Relations, 1968, Report of the Royal Commission on Trade Unions and Employers Association (Donovan), *Relations Industrielles / Industrial Relations*, 23(4): 686–698.

Rhodes, M., 1995, '"Subversive liberalism": Market integration, globalization and the European welfare state', *Journal of European Public Policy*, 2(3): 384–406.

Ribeiro, A. T., 2016, 'Recent trends in collective bargaining in Europe', *E-Journal of International and Comparative LABOUR STUDIES*, 5(1): 1–21.

Richter, E., 2015, 'Demokratische Gestaltungsmacht und europäische Integration. Die potentiale demokratischer Einflussnahme auf die politische Ordnung der Europäischen Union', in N. Abbas, A. Förster and E. Richter (eds.), *Supranationalität und Demokratie*, Wiesbaden: Springer Fachmedien Wiesbaden, pp. 207–235.

Ridaura Martínez, María Josefa, 2012, 'La reforma del artículo 135 de la constitución española: ¿Pueden los mercados quebrar el consenso constitucional?', *Teoría y Realidad Constitucional*, 29: 237–60.

Riutort Serra, B., 2014, *La movilización de la educación en las Illes Balears*. Available: http://revistes.ub.edu/index.php/ACS/article/viewFile/10374/13164.

Roca Martínez, B. and Díaz Parra, I., 2013, *De la tierra a los supermercados: El SAT como ejemplo de particularismo militante y renovación sindical*. Available: http://revistes. ub.edu/index.php/ACS/article/viewFile/6348/8103.

Roca, B. and Diaz-Parra, I., 2016, 'Blurring the borders between old and new social movements. The M15 movement and the radical unions in Spain', *Mediterranean Politics*, 22(2): 1–20.

Rodríguez López, E., 2015, *Por qué fracasó la democracia en España: La Transición y el régimen del '78*, Madrid: Traficantes de sueños; Fundación de los Comunes.

Rodríguez López, E. and López Hernández, I., 2011, 'Del auge al colapso. El modelo financiero-immobilario de la economía española, 1995–2010)', *Revista de Economía Crítica*, (12): 39–63.

Rodríguez Martínez, E., 2012, 'La complejidad de los derechos de ciudanía en el fordismo y el postfordismo', *Revista Republicana*, 12: 239–266.

Rodríguez-Piñero Royo, M., 2012, *El despido colectivo en el sector público*. Available: http://grupo.us.es/sej322/biblioteca/reforma2012/despidoAAPP-MRP.pdf.

Rodríguez-Ruiz, Ó., 2015, 'Unions' response to corporate restructuring in Telefónica: Locked into collective bargaining?', *Employee Relations*, 37(1): 83–101.

Rohrschneider, R. and Whitefield, S., 2016, 'Responding to growing European Union-skepticism? The stances of political parties toward European integration in Western and Eastern Europe following the financial crisis', *European Union Politics*, 17(1): 138–161.

Rolnick, R., 2013, 'Late neoliberalism: The financialization of homeownership and housing rights', *International Journal of Urban and Regional Research*, 37(3): 1058–1066.

Romero Renau, L.d. and Valera Lozano, A., 2016, 'From NIMBYsm to the 15M: A Decade of Urban Conflicts in Barcelona and Valencia', *Territory, Politics, Governance*, 4(3): 375–395.

Roos, J. E., 2016, 'Why Not Default?: The Structural Power of Finance in Sovereign Debt Crises'. EUI PhD thesis, Florence.

Roos, J. E. and Oikonomakis, L., 2013, 'We are everywhere! The autonomous roots of the real democracy movement', paper delivered at 7th annual ECPR general conference: 'Comparative Perspectives on the New Politics of Dissent' Democracy of the Squares: Visions and Practices of Democracy from Egypt to the US, Sciences Po Bordeaux, September 4–7, 2013. Available: https://www.academia.edu/4342422/The_Autonomous_Roots_of_the_Real_Democracy_Movement.

Roper, B.S., 2013, *The History of Democracy: A Marxist interpretation*, London: Pluto.

Rosenberg, C., 1987, *1919: Britain on the Brink of Revolution*, London: Bookmarks.

Rüddenklau, E., 1982, *Gesellschaftliche Arbeit oder Arbeit und Interaktion?: Zum Stellenwert des Arbeitsbegriffes bei Habermas, Marx und Hegel*, Frankfurt am Main, Bern: Lang.

Ruiz-Giménez, J. L., 2014, 'Experiencia de la lucha socio sanitaria en España: YOSI Sanidad Universal y Marea Blanca', *Rescoldos*, 31: 28–40.

Rürup, B., 2002, 'The German pension system: Status quo and reform options', in M. Fedlstein and H. Siebert (eds.), *Social Security Pension Reform in Europe*, Chicago, IL: University of Chicago Press.

Ryner, J. M., 2014, 'The European Monetary Union: An unfolding disaster?', in N. P. Petropoulos and G. O. Tsobanoglou (eds.), *The Debt Crisis in the Eurozone: Social Impacts*, Newcastle upon Tyne: Cambridge Scholars, pp. 14–22.

Ryner, J. M., 2015, 'Europe's ordoliberal iron cage: critical political economy, the euro area crisis and its management', *Journal of European Public Policy*, 22(2): 275–294.

Ryner, M. and Cafruny, A., 2016, *The European Union and Global Capitalism: Origins, Developments, Crisis*, Basingstoke: Macmillan.

Sacchi, S., 2016, 'Conditionality by other means: European Union involvement in Italy's structural reforms in the sovereign debt crisis', in C. de La Porte and E. Heins (eds.), *The Sovereign Debt Crisis, the EU and Welfare State Reform*, London: Palgrave Macmillan, pp. 159–179.

Saltman, K. J., 2014, 'The austerity school: Grit, character, and the privatization of public education', *symploke*, 22(1–2): 41–57.

San José, C., 2011, 'Pacto del euro, déficit y recortes sanitarios', *Apuntes Ciudadanos*, 1: 75–88.

Sánchez Medero, G. and Tamboloo García, R., 2013, 'Política y derechos sociales en tiempos de crisis en España', *BARATARIA*, 15: 239–253.

Sandbeck, S. and Schneider, E., 2014, 'From the sovereign debt crisis to authoritarian statism: Contradictions of the European state project', *New Political Economy*, 19(6): 847–871.

Sandholtz, W. and Zysman, J., 1989, '1992: Recasting the European bargain', *World Politics*, 42(1): 95–128.

Sanz-Magallón Rezusta, G., Izquierdo Llanes, G. and Curto González, T., 2014, 'El gasto de las familias madrileñas en enseñanza privada tras la crisis económica de 2008', *Revista de Educación*, 364: 222–49.

Sauer, B., 2003, 'Den Staat ver/handeln. Zum Zusammenhang von Staat, Demokratie und Herrschaft', in A. Demirović (ed.), *Modelle Kritischer Gesellschaftstheorie: Traditionen und Perspektiven der Kritischen Theorie*, Stuttgart: Metzler, pp. 152–175.

Scharpf, F. W., 1996, 'Negative and Positive Integration in the Political Economy of European Welfare States', in G. Marks, F. W. Scharpf, P. C. Schmitter and W. Streeck (eds.), *Governance in the European Union*, London: SAGE, pp. 15–39.

Scharpf, F. W., 2000, 'Economic changes, vulnerabilities, and institutional capabilities', in F. W. Scharpf and V. A. Schmidt (eds.), *Divers Responses to Common Challenges*, Oxford: Oxford University Press, pp. 21–124.

Scharpf, F., 2010, 'The asymmetry of European integration, or why the EU cannot be a "social market economy"', *Socio-Economic Review*, 8(2): 211–250.

Scharpf, F., 2013, 'Monetary union, fiscal crisis and the disabling of democratic accountability', in A. Schäfer and W. Streeck (eds.), *Politics in the Age of Austerity*, Cambridge, Polity, pp. 108–42.

Scharpf, F. W., 1999, *Governing in Europe: Effective and Democratic?*, Oxford: Oxford University Press.

Schelkle, W., 2012, 'A crisis of what? Mortgage credit markets and the social policy of promoting homeownership in the United States and in Europe', *Politics and Society*, 40(1): 59–80.

Schmalz, S., Liebig, S. and Thiel, M., 2015, 'Zur Zersplitterung des sozialen Konflikts in Westeuropa: Eine Typologie nichtnormierter Kämpfe um Arbeit', *Arbeits- und Industriesoziologische Studien*, 8(2): 49–66.

Schmidt, I., 2013, 'Legitimationsprobleme des Euro-Kapitalismus. Krise, soziale Frage und politische Alternativen', in S. Friedrich and P. Schreiner (eds.), *Nation – Ausgrenzung – Krise: Kritische Perspektiven auf Europa*, Münster: edition assemblage, pp. 30–42.

Schofer, E. and Meyer, J. W., 2005, 'The worldwide expansion of higher education in the twentieth century', *American Sociological Review*, 70(6): 898–920.

Scholl, C., 2013, *Two Sides of a Barricade: (Dis)order and Summit Protest in Europe*, New York: SUNY Press.

Schulten, T., 2014, *Troika attackiert Tarifsysteme*. Available: http://www.boeckler.de/impuls_2014_02_5.pdf.

Sciolino, E., 2003, 'Huge strike by public workers paralyzes France', *New York Times*, 14 May 2003.

Scott, J. C., 1990, *Domination and the Arts of Resistance: Hidden Transcripts*, New Haven, CT: Yale University Press.

Screpanti, E., 1987, 'Long cycles in strike activity: An empirical investigation', *British Journal of Industrial Relations*, 25(1): 99–124.

Sealey-Huggins, L. and Pusey, A., 2013, 'Neoliberalism and depoliticisation in the Academy: Understanding the "new student rebellions"', *Graduate Journal of Social Science*, 10(3): 80–99.

Seminari d'Economia Crítica TAIFA, 2010) *La crisis en el estado español: El rescate de los poderosos*. Available: http://informes.seminaritaifa.org/pdf/Informe_07_ES.pdf.

Sen Galindo, M., 2013, *La prestación por desempleo de nivel contributivo: Evolución historica*. Available: http://cerro.cpd.uva.es/bitstream/10324/3086/1/TFG-B.148.pdf.

Shalev, M., 1978, 'Lies, damned lies, and strike statistics: The measurement of trends in industrial conflict', in C. Crouch and A. Pizzorno (eds.), *The Resurgence of Class Conflict in Western Europe since 1968: Volume 1*, London: Macmillan, pp. 1–19.

Shepherd, J., 2011, 'NUS President says non-violent tactics of UK Uncut should be model for students', *The Guardian*, 9 August 2011. Available: https://www.theguardian.com/education/2011/aug/09/nus-president-student-protests.

Shields, S., Bruff, I. and Macartney, H., 2011, 'Conclusion: IPE *and* the international political economy? IPE *or* the international political economy?', in S. Shields, I. Bruff and H. Macartney (eds.), *Critical International Political Economy: Dialogue, Debate and Dissensus*, Basingstoke: Palgrave, pp. 169–172.

Shukaitis, S., 2007, 'Plan 9 from the capitalist workplace: Insurgency, originary accumulation, rupture', *Situations: A Project of the Radical Imagination*, 2(2): 95–116.

Sirianni, C. J., 1980, 'Workers' control in the era of World War I: A comparative analysis of the European experience', *Theory and Society*, 9(1): 29–88.

Slaughter, S. and Rhoades, G., 1999, *Academic Capitalism: Politics, Policies and the Entrepreneurial University*, Baltimore, MD: Johns Hopkins University Press.

Slawson, N., 2015, 'Social housing and anti-gentrification campaigners disrupt Property Awards', *The Guardian*, 21 April 2015.

Smith Tuhiwai, L., 2012, *Decolonizing Methodologies: Research and Indigenous Peoples*, London: Zed Books.

Smith, C. S., 2003, 'French strikes against cuts in pensions jams traffic', *New York Times*, 11 June 2003.

Smith, M. P., 2005, *States of Liberalization: Redefining the Public Sector in Integrated Europe*, New York: State University of New York Press.

Soskice, D., 1978, 'Strike waves and wage explosions, 1968–1970: An economic interpretation' in C. Crouch and A. Pizzorno (eds.), *The Resurgence of Class Conflict in Western Europe Since 1968: Volume 2 Comparative Analyses*, London: Macmillan Press, pp. 221–246.

Sott, S., 2016, *Exklusion und Desartikulation: Afrokolumbianische, Indigene und Gewerkschaftliche Positionen im Kolumbianischen Transitional Justice Prozess*. Unveröffentlichtes manuskript.

Souliotis, N. and Alexandri, G., 2016, 'From embedded to uncompromising neoliberalism: Competitiveness policies and European Union interscalar relations in the case of Greece', *European Urban and Regional Studies*, 24(3): 227–240.

Spivak, G. C., 2008, 'Can the subaltern speak?', in H. Steyerl, A. Joskowicz and S. Nowotny (eds.), *Can the Subaltern Speak?: Postkolonialität und subalterne Artikulation*, Wien: Turia + Kant, pp. 17–118.

Stanley, L., 2014, '"We're reaping what we sowed": Everyday crisis narratives and acquiescence to the age of austerity', *New Political Economy*, 19(6): 895–917.

Stanley, L., 2016, 'Governing austerity in the United Kingdom: Anticipatory fiscal consolidation as a variety of austerity governance', *Economy and Society*, 45(3–4): 303–324.

Stark, J., 2001, 'Genesis of a pact', in A. Brunila, M. Buti and D. Franco (eds.), *The Stability and Growth Pact: The Architecture of Fiscal Policy in EMU*, Basingstoke: Palgrave, pp. 77–105.

Steger, M. B. and Wilson, E. K., 2012, 'Anti-globalization or alter-globalization? Mapping the political ideology of the global justice movement', *International Studies Quarterly*, 56(3): 439–454.

Stephens, M., 1998, 'Fiscal restraint and housing policies under economic and monetary union', in M. Kleinman, W. Matznetter and M. Stephens (eds.), *European Integration and Housing Policy*, London: Routledge, pp. 93–109.

Stockhammer, E., 2012, 'The Euro crisis, European neoliberalism and the need for a European welfare state', *Soundings*, 50: 121–130.

Stockhammer, E. and Köhler, K., 2015, 'Linking a post-Keynesian approach to critical political economy: Debt-driven growth, export-driven growth and the crisis in Europe', in J. Jäger and E. Springler (eds.), *Asymmetric Crisis in Europe and Possible Futures: Critical Political Economy and Post-Keynesian Perspectives*, London: Routledge, pp. 34–49.

Strange, G., 2002, 'Globalisation, regionalism and labour interests in the new international political economy', *New Political Economy*, 7(3): 343–365.

Streeck, W., 1996, 'Neo-voluntarism: A new European social policy regime?', in G. Marks, F. W. Scharpf, P. C. Schmitter and W. Streeck (eds.), *Governance in the European Union*, London: SAGE, pp. 64–94.

Street, T., 2015, 'UK Uncut: direct action against austerity', in N. Manning (ed.), *Political (Dis)Engagement: The Changing Nature of the 'Political'*, Bristol: Policy Press.

Suarez, M., 2016, 'The Subprime Middle-Class. Precarious Labour, Mortgage Default, and Activism among Ecuadorian Migrants in Barcelona'. PhD thesis, Goldsmith, University of London.

Suri, J., 2003, *Power and Protest: Global Revolution and the Rise of Détente*, Cambridge, MA: Harvard University Press.

Sutterlüty, F., 2014, 'The hidden morale of the 2005 French and 2011 English riots', *Thesis Eleven*, 121(1): 38–56.

Syal, R., 2013, 'UK Uncut loses legal challenge over Goldman Sachs tax deal with HMRC', *The Guardian*, 16 May 2013. Available: https://www.theguardian.com/uk/2013/may/16/uk-uncut-goldman-sachs-tax-deal-hmrc.

Tagliabue, J., 2003, 'Protest Strike in France Interrupts Travel', *New York Times*, 4 April 2003.

Tarrow, S., 2010, 'The strategy of paired comparison: Toward a theory of practice', *Comparative Political Studies*, 43(2): 230–259.

Taylor, D., 2015, 'Sleepover protest led by Russell Brand draws 150 to Sweets Way estate', *The Guardian*, 19 March 2015.

Telefónica, 1994, *Annual Report*, Madrid: Telefónica.

Telefónica, 2014, *Annual Report*, Madrid: Telefónica.

Templin, D., 2014, 'Erst das Essen, dann die Miete. Zwangsräumungen und Mieterproteste charakterisierten auch die städtischen Konflikte am Ende der Weimarer Republik', *analyse & kritik*, 16 September 2014.

Terranova, T., 2015, 'Introduction to Eurocrisis, Neoliberalism and the Common', *Theory, Culture & Society*, 32(7–8): 5–23.

Theodoropoulou, S., 2015, 'National social and labour market policy reforms in the shadow of EU bail-out conditionality: The cases of Greece and Portugal', *Comparative European Politics*, 13(1): 29–55.

Thimann, C., 2015, 'The microeconomic dimensions of the Eurozone crisis and why European politics cannot solve them', *Journal of Economic Perspectives*, 29(3): 141–64.

Tiratsoo, N. and Tomlinson, J., 1993, *Industrial Efficiency and State Intervention: Labour, 1939–1951*, London: Routledge.

Tobin, L. and Spanier, G., 2014, 'Ritzy cinema in U-turn on job cuts: bosses back down in row over London Living Wage', *Evening Standard*, 30 October 2014. Available: http://www.standard.co.uk/news/london/ritzy-cinema-in-u-turn-on-job-cuts-bosses-back-down-in-row-over-london-living-wage-9827867.html.

Tormey, S., 2012, 'Occupy Wall Street: From representation to post-representation', *Journal of Critical Globalisation Studies*, 5: 132–137.

Townsend, M. and Kelly, L., 2015, 'Thousands gather in London to protest against lack of affordable housing', *The Guardian*, 31 January 2015.

Tremlett, G., 2001, 'Shanty town pricks Spain's conscience', *The Guardian*, 28 July 2001. Available: https://www.theguardian.com/world/2001/jul/28/gilestremlett.

Tridico, P., 2012, 'Financial crisis and global imbalances: Its labour market origins and the aftermath', *Cambridge Journal of Economics*, 36: 17–42.

Trotzki, L., 1923, *Vereinigte Staaten von Europa*. Available: http://www.marxists.org/deutsch/archiv/trotzki/1923/06/vse.htm.

Tsianos, V. and Hess, S., 2010) 'Ethnographische Grenzregimeanalyse', in S. Hess and B. Kasparek (eds.), *Grenzregime: Diskurse, Praktiken, Institutionen in Europa*, Berlin: Assoziation A, pp. 243–64.

Tsiligiris, V., 2012, *Higher education in times of austerity and high unemployment: The role of financial markets*. Available: http://www.academia.edu/2049983/Higher_education_in_times_of_austerity_and_high_unemployment_the_role_of_financial_markets.

Tyler, I., 2013, *Revolting Subjects: Social Abjection and Resistance in Neoliberal Britain*, London: Zed Books.

Ubico, A., 2016, '"La revolución en los sindicatos es llegar a esa masa de trabajadores sin representación": Entrevistamos a Luis y Javier, delegados del Comité de Empresa de Cotronic (Movistar) en Zaragoza', *La Izquierda Diario*, 9 April 2016. Available: http://www.laizquierdadiario.com/spip.php?page=movil-nota&id_article=36239.

UCL, 2016, 'UCL, UCLU and UCL Cut the Rent agreement'. Available: https://www.ucl.ac.uk/news/news-articles/0616/240616-ucl-uclu-ctr.

UCL, Cut the Rent, 2015, 'Victory for UCL rent strike, Campbell House students win nearly £100,000 compensation!', Press Release. Available: https://www.facebook.com/uclcuttherent/photos/pcb.447649945419329/447649872086003.

UCL, Cut the Rent, 2016, 'OVER 500 STUDENTS PLEDGE TO JOIN UCL', Press Release. Available: https://www.facebook.com/uclcuttherent/posts/487411581443165:0.

Uitermark, J., Duyvendak, J. W. and Kleinhans, R., 2007, 'Gentrification as a governmental strategy: Social control and social cohesion in Hoogvliet, Rotterdam', *Environment and Planning A*, 39(1): 125–141.

Umney, C., Greer, I., Onaran, Ö. and Symon, G., 2015, *The state and class discipline: European labour market policy after the financial crisis*. Available: http://gala.gre.ac.uk/14120/1/GPERC33_Umney_etalF.pdf.

Unite, 2014, 'Visteon workers successfully conclude their pensions campaign', press release, 10 June 2014. Available: www.unitetheunion.org/news/workers-successfully-conclude-their-pensions-campaign.

Uzuriaga Ruiz, L., 2013, 'Movilización y cambio social en el sistema educativo español'. Abschlussarbeit, Universidad de la Rioja, La Rioja.

Van Damme, D., 2009, 'The search for transparency: Convergence and diversity in the Bologna Process', in F. A. van Vught (ed.), *Mapping the Higher Education Landscape*, Dordrecht: Springer.

van der Pijl, K., 1989, 'Ruling classes, hegemony, and the state system: Theoretical and historical considerations', *International Journal of Political Economy*, 19(3): 7–35.

van der Pijl, K. and Yurchenko, Y., 2014, 'Neoliberal entrenchment of north Atlantic capital: From corporate self-regulation to state capture', *New Political Economy,* 20(4): 1–23.

van der Pijl, K., Holman, O. and Raviv, O., 2011, 'The resurgence of German capital in Europe: EU integration and the restructuring of Atlantic networks of interlocking directorates after 1991', *Review of International Political Economy*, 18(3): 384–408.

van der Steen, B., Katzeff, A. and van Hoogenhuijze, L., 2014, 'Introduction: Squatting and autonomous action in Europe, 1980–2012', in B. van der Steen, A. Katzeff and L. Van Hoogenhuijze (eds.), *The City is Ours: Squatting and Autonomous Movements in Europe from the 1970s to the Present*, Oakland, CA: PM Press, pp. 1–20.

van Kersbergen, K., Vis, B. and Hemerijck, A., 2014, 'The Great Recession and welfare state reform: Is retrenchment really the only game left in town?', *Social Policy & Administration*, 48(7): 883–904.

Vandaele, K., 2014, 'Ende des Abwärtstrends? Zur Entwicklung des Streikvolumens in Westeuropa seit Beginn der Weltwirtschaftskrise', *WSI Mitteilungen*, 5: 345–352.

Vandaele, K., 2016, 'Interpreting strike activity in western Europe in the past 20 years: The labour repertoire under pressure', *Transfer*, 22(3): 277–294.

Vasudevan, A., 2011, Dramaturgies of dissent: The spatial politics of squatting in Berlin, 1968–, *Social & Cultural Geography*, 12(3): 283–303.

Vega García, R., 2013, *España: la última gran huelga de mineros*. Available: http://revistes.ub.edu/index.php/ACS/article/view/6347/8102.

Villota, P. de and Vázquez-Cupeiro, S., 2016, 'The restructuring of the Spanish welfare state: one step forward, two steps back?', in K. Schubert, P. d. Villota and J. Kuhlmann (eds.), *Challenges to European Welfare Systems*, Cham: Springer, pp. 197–221.

Voegtle, E. M., Knill, C. and Dobbins, M., 2011, 'To what extent does transnational communication drive cross-national policy convergence? The impact of the Bologna-process on domestic higher education policies', *Higher Education*, 61(1): 77–94.

Vögtle, E. M. and Martens, K., 2014, 'The Bologna Process as a template for transnational policy coordination', *Policy Studies*, 35(3): 246–63.

Vögtle, E. M., 2014, *Higher Education Policy Convergence and the Bologna Process: A Cross-National Study*, Basingstoke: Palgrave.

Vonyó, T., 2008, 'Post-war reconstruction and the Golden Age of economic growth', *European Review of Economic History*, 12: 221–241.

Wacquant, L., 1996, 'Red belt, black belt: Racial division, class inequality and the state in the French urban periphery and the American ghetto', in E. Mingione (ed.), *Urban Poverty and the Underclass: A Reader*, Cambridge MA: Blackwell, pp. 234–274.

Wahl, A., 2014, *European Labor: Political and Ideological Crisis in an Increasingly More Authoritarian European Union*. Available: http://monthlyreview.org/2014/01/01/european-labor/.

Wainwright, O., 2014, 'Protests disrupt propery fair in London', *The Guardian*, 15 October 2014. Available: http://www.theguardian.com/society/2014/oct/15/protests-mipim-property-fair-london.

Walker, P., 2012, 'Wheelchair users block Oxford Circus to protest at disability cuts', *The Guardian*, 29 January 2012. Available: https://www.theguardian.com/society/2012/jan/29/wheelchair-users-block-oxford-circus.

Watson, M., 2010, 'House price Keynesianism and the contradictions of the modern investor subject', *Housing Studies*, 25(3): 413–426.

Watt, N., Wintour, P. and Malik, S., 2012, 'Government U-turn on work scheme', *The Guardian*, 29 February 2012. Available: http://www.theguardian.com/politics/2012/feb/29/government-work-experience-scheme-uturn.

Watt, P., 2016, 'A nomdic war machine in the metropolis: En/countering London's 21st-century housing crisis with Focus E15', *City*, 20(2): 297–320.

Watt, P. and Minton, A., 2016, 'London's housing crisis and its activisms', *City*, 20(2): 204–221.

Waylen, G., 2006, 'You still don't understand: why troubled engagements continue between feminists and (critical) IPE', *Review of International Studies*, 32(1): 145–164.

Weatherburn, M. R., 2014, 'Scientific Management at Work: the Bedaux System, Management Consulting, and Worker Efficiency in British Industry, 1914–48'. PhD thesis, Imperial College London. Available: https://spiral.imperial.ac.uk/handle/10044/1/25296.

Werts, H., Scheepers, P. and Lubbers, M., 2013, 'Euro-scepticism and radical right-wing voting in Europe, 2002–2008: Social cleavages, socio-political attitudes and contextual characteristics determining voting for the radical right', *European Union Politics*, 14(2): 183–205.

Whitehead, C., 1998, 'Are housing finance systems converging within the European Union?', in M. Kleinman, W. Matznetter and M. Stephens (eds.), *European Integration and Housing Policy*, London: Routledge, pp. 17–29.

Whitston, K., 1995, 'Scientific Management Practice in Britain: A History'. PhD thesis, Warwick University.

Wigger, A., 2015, 'Enhancing "competitiveness" in response to the European crisis: A wrong and dangerous obsession', in: J. Jäger and E. Springler (eds.), *Asymmetric Crisis in Europe and Possible Futures: Critical Political Economy and Post-Keynesian Perspectives*, London: Routledge, pp. 114–130.

Wilks, S., 2010, 'Competition Policy: Towards an Economic Constitution?', in H. Wallace, M. A. Pollack and A. R. Young (eds.), *Policy-Making in the European Union*, Oxford, Oxford University Press, pp. 133–155.

Wilson, W., 1996, *When Work Disappears: The World of the New Urban Poor*, New York: Vintage Books.

Wood, J. D. G., 2016, 'The effects of the distribution of mortgage credit on the wage share: Varieties of residential capitalism compared', *Comparative European Politics*, doi: 10.1057/s41295-016-0006-5.

Worth, O., 2011, 'Reclaiming Critical IPE from the 'British' School', in S. Shields, I. Bruff and H. Macartney (eds.), *Critical International Political Economy: Dialogue, Debate and Dissensus*, Basingstoke: Palgrave, pp. 117–131.

Worth, O., 2013, *Resistance in the Age of Austerity: Nationalism, the Failure of the Left and the Return of God*, London: Zed Books.

Wright, S., 2002, *Storming Heaven: Class Composition and Struggle in Italian Autonomist Marxism*, London: Pluto.

Wright, S., 2008, 'Mapping pathways within Italian autonomist Marxism: A preliminary survey', *Historical Materialism*, 16(4): 111–140.

Young, A. R., 2010, 'The single market: Deregulation, reregulation, and integration', in H. Wallace, M. A. Pollack and A. R. Young (eds.), *Policy-Making in the European Union*, Oxford, Oxford University Press, pp. 107–132.

Young, B., 2014, 'The role of German Ordoliberalism in the Euro crisis', in N.P. Petropoulos and G. O. Tsobanoglou (eds.), *The Debt Crisis in the Eurozone: Social Impacts*, Newcastle upon Tyne: Cambridge Scholars, pp. 2–13.

Zageimeyer, S., 1998, 'Nationwide protests as unemployment reaches new record high', *EurWork*. Available: http://www.eurofound.europa.eu/observatories/eurwork/articles/labour-market/nationwide-protests-as-unemployment-reaches-new-record-high.

Zamponi, L. and Fernández González, J., 2017, 'Dissenting youth: How student and youth struggles helped shape anti-austerity mobilisations in Southern Europe', *Social Movement Studies*, 16(1): 64–81.

Zgaga, P., Teichler, U. and Brennan, J., 2013, 'Introduction: Challenges for European higher education: "Global" and "national", "Europe" and "sub-Europes"', in P. Zgaga, U. Teichler and J. Brennan (eds.), *The Globalisation Challenge for European Higher*

Education: Convergence and Diversity, Centres and Peripheries, Frankfurt am Main: Peter Lang Edition, pp. 11–30.

Ziltener, P., 1999, *Strukturwandel der Europäischen Integration*, Münster: Westfälisches Dampfboot.

Ziltener, P., 2004, 'The economic effects of the European Single Market Project: Projections, simulations – and the reality', *Review of International Political Economy*, 11(5): 953–979.

Zukas, A., 2009, 'German revolution, 1918–1923', in I. Ness (ed.), *The International Encyclopedia of Revolution and Protest: 1500 to the Present*, Oxford: Blackwell Publishing, pp. 1358–1366.

Index

For Product Safety Concerns and Information please contact our EU
representative GPSR@taylorandfrancis.com
Taylor & Francis Verlag GmbH, Kaufingerstraße 24, 80331 München, Germany

www.ingramcontent.com/pod-product-compliance
Ingram Content Group UK Ltd.
Pitfield, Milton Keynes, MK11 3LW, UK
UKHW021013180425
457613UK00020B/920

* 9 7 8 0 3 6 7 8 7 2 3 8 0 *